JERSEY GOLD

JERSEY GOLD

The Newark Overland Company's Trek to California, 1849

Margaret Casterline Bowen
and
Gwendolyn Joslin Hiles

University of Oklahoma Press : Norman

Publication of this book is made possible through the generosity of Edith Kinney Gaylord.

Library of Congress Cataloging-in-Publication Data

Names: Bowen, Margaret Casterline, 1954– author. | Hiles, Gwendolyn Joslin, 1944– author.
Title: Jersey Gold : the Newark Overland Company's Trek to California, 1849 / Margaret Casterline Bowen and Gwendolyn Joslin Hiles.
Description: Norman : University of Oklahoma Press, 2017. | Includes bibliographical references and index.
Identifiers: LCCN 2016037669 | ISBN 978-0-8061-5714-6 (hardcover : alk. paper)
Subjects: LCSH: Overland journeys to the Pacific. | Newark Overland Company—History. | California—Gold discoveries. | Pioneers—West (U.S.) | Pioneers—California.
Classification: LCC F593 .B7425 2017 | DDC 978/.02—dc23
LC record available at https://lccn.loc.gov/2016037669

1 2 3 4 5 6 7 8 9 10

To our fathers,
William Hale Casterline and Reuben Graves "R.G." Joslin,
the link to our adventurous ancestors
who sparked this journey

Contents

CONTENTS

Part III. After 1849

Appendixes

Illustrations

⌒

FIGURES

ILLUSTRATIONS

MAPS

Preface

⌒

"He crossed rivers on horseback," was one of the few things Margaret Bowen knew about her Casterline ancestry, along with speculation that the family had gained and lost large sums of money. It meant nothing until she found the December 1900 obituary of her great-great-grandfather Benjamin Casterline and learned that he was an original forty-niner who had returned from California with a comfortable fortune. The exciting discovery led to a determined search for more information.

Gwen Hiles, on the other hand, had always known that her ancestor had participated in the 1849 gold rush. Her great-great-grandfather William T. Lewis founded the town of Lewis Center, Ohio, and local history books included information about his life. A growing interest in genealogy motivated her to delve further into her Lewis line. Finding his name on a list of three dozen men who traveled overland together in 1849 piqued her curiosity. At least three names on the list appeared to be relatives. She wanted to know more about these men and their quest for gold.

Unknown to one another and living several states apart, the two authors were independently building inventories of gold rush research until early 2008. A fortuitous online encounter united the pair when Bowen found the name Benjamin Casterline on a website identifying the members of the Newark Overland Company from a *New York Herald* article dated March 5, 1849. Along with Casterline's name was that of William T. Lewis, the only name followed by an email address. Bowen and Hiles were in touch within hours, and unbeknownst to them at the time, a fascinating project was launched.

Combining resources, the two learned they had each discovered the published journal of company member Charles G. Gray, which was transcribed and annotated by historian Thomas D. Clark as *Off at Sunrise* (Huntington Library 1976), and each had also collected journals by Alexander Cartwright, Robert Bond, and Cyrus Currier. Beyond the common ground, they had made significant progress on different fronts. Together they theorized that if two descendants of this unique group of men had connected, there must be more. What came next transformed the genealogy pastime into a legitimate historical research effort.

"Gwen, there's an article in the paper about the gold rush," announced Gary Hiles one Sunday morning in November 2008 as he handed the arts section of the *Columbus Dispatch* to his wife.

Bowen had been on the trail of a man from Pennsylvania who was believed to be in possession of the original journal of his forty-niner ancestor. Yet the trail had run cold, very cold, until that November morning. The *Columbus Dispatch* article detailed not just a trail journal but letters, sketches, and paintings by Charles B. Gillespie, a nineteenth-century Renaissance man whose great-grandson had come forward to publicize his family's rich collection. It was the mother lode of unpublished gold rush material, it was from a Newark Overland Company member, and it was located just a two-hour drive from the Ohio residence of Hiles.

Within the month, another descendant item was tracked and located through a University of Texas professor, who produced a letter written before the group had reached St. Louis. Then came not one but five letters from the Currier family and another handful from a Meeker descendant.

The discussions about writing this book started early and grew more certain with each new discovery that helped bring the gold rush experience of this group to life. Findings about the activities of the men after the historic 1849 journey revealed remarkable associations that linked them to the Hawaiian royal family, Andersonville Prison, James W. Marshall, Peter Lassen, the Confederate States Army, Eadweard Muygridge, Henry Clay, the Baseball Hall of Fame, John Sutter, the Comstock Lode, Leland Stanford, and more. As the collection of data mushroomed, another aspect emerged that convinced the authors to tell this story. The personalities and human nature detected in the firsthand material told a tale that included heartbreak, scandal, wealth, suffering, and lasting legacies. The information was compelling, and the manuscript began to come together, aided by a database of several thousand entries that could be sorted chronologically and by subject.

EDITORIAL NOTES

Decisions regarding style were made early in the development of the manuscript. Painstaking research was conducted to insure terminology was appropriate to the time period and that background descriptions were accurate. Current geographical names that were not known in 1849 would be used to aid the reader and avoid unnecessary confusion as to where the men were on the Overland Trails; however, slight variations of recognizable place names would be retained. Quotations of primary source material would be verbatim except where lack of punctuation, capitalization, or gross misspelling would impede the reader's understanding. The voices, language, and observations of the firsthand accounts would be presented as they were recorded, without judgment and commentary.

ACKNOWLEDGMENTS

No project of this magnitude can be accomplished without the assistance of many generous individuals. The authors would first like to acknowledge the contributions provided to them from family collections of several fellow descendants who were located through both genealogical research and uncanny luck. Richard Rogers of Bowling Green, Ohio, became a friend and a great supporter of the project. He opened his extensive collection of trail journals, letters, and sketches of the overland journey and days in the mining region, written and drawn by his ancestor Charles B. Gillespie. Scott Ritchie of Austin, Texas, provided a letter from Augustus Baldwin to his wife during the early part of the 1849 journey as well as a photo of Baldwin with his family in Hibernia, Florida. Cyrus Currier's descendants, including Dr. Ewen Currier McEwen and Nancy Currier Dorian, shared fascinating letters written between Cyrus and Nancy Currier during his absence in California—letters that expressed many details and a deep love between the couple. Margaret Riddle shared a set of letters from the Meeker family, again with rich details of the early days in California including the female perspective. Another Meeker relation, Captain Dick Collins, of Fallon, Nevada, offered research assistance, as well as a venture into the desolate Black Rock Desert of northwestern Nevada where the Newark Overland Company met with fatal disaster. (A Google Earth tour was chosen instead.) Alexander J. Cartwright IV was contacted by phone and spent almost two hours sharing information of his ancestor, Baseball Hall of Fame member Alexander J. Cartwright Jr. The great-great-grandson of Joseph Freeman, Jerome Marshall, was unaware of his ancestor's gold rush participation (and took some convincing) but was able to share Civil War military records. Like Marshall and *Jersey Gold* author Bowen, Fred Kellogg was also unaware of his ancestor's historic journey to California and his prominence in Newark, New Jersey. Kellogg is the great-great-great-grandson of the iconic Newark Overland Company leader, John S. Darcy. The authors are grateful to all the descendants they met through this project, including those not directly mentioned here.

The research journey took the authors across the country from New Jersey (New Jersey State Archives, Newark Public Library, and Rutgers University) to California (San Francisco Public Library, Society of California Pioneers, Huntington Library, and Mechanics' Institute). Other research sites included the University of Kentucky, which houses the papers of Thomas D. Clark, and Salt Lake City, where the company camped for five days in 1849. Driving trips along the historic trails netted hands-on awareness of the terrain and climate with stops at the National Trails Museum (Independence, Missouri), Scotts Bluff National Monument (Nebraska), Fort Laramie National Historic Site (Wyoming), the desolate City of Rocks National Reserve (Idaho), and many other trail landmarks along the Platte, Sweetwater, and Little Sandy Rivers (Wyoming). Visits were made to Parks Bar on the Yuba River that afforded a walk on the very riverbank where the Newark men mined for gold, and to the American River and the Marshall Gold Discovery State Park (California). During these travels many individual staff members and volunteers at institutions and historic sites generously assisted the authors in digging for puzzle pieces that eventually fit together to flesh out this story. Though they are too many to name, the authors thank them for their contributions. Also appreciated is the assistance provided during countless hours spent at the Library of Congress, DAR Library, and National

Archives, and the numerous inter-library loans provided by the Delaware County Library (Ohio).

Similarly, thanks go to individuals at historical societies and libraries who were contacted by phone or email and gave selfless hours to uncover tidbits of information that confirmed speculation or gave clarity to vague details. Jennifer Bryan of the Siskiyou Historical Society (Shasta County, California) became as relentless at the authors in her pursuit of one company member. It is believed that John Hunt, General Darcy's servant, may have settled in the area and married a local Native American woman. The evidence was very compelling but in the end not conclusive enough to include in the manuscript.

Images throughout the work came from institutions and private collections. The authors are appreciative of all who provided assistance to this effort, with particular thanks to Rick Stewart for generously contributing eight items from the Rees-Jones Collection.

The authors' research led to the acquaintance of several people who share the passion for overland trails and gold rush history, both professionally and privately, who provided encouragement and pointed the authors in important directions. John Ireland, through his *California Bound* website containing the list of the Newark men who traveled with General Darcy, was the conduit for the two authors coming together. His invaluable material can now be found online at SFgenealogy.com. Publisher Robert A. Clark learned of the project three to four years into the research. His support provided much-needed confirmation that the authors' material and approach would be a contribution to the genre and well worth developing. Geography professor Richard L. Rieck kindly shared his overland trail journal transcriptions and knowledge gleaned from years of trail research. The Huntington Library provided access to the Gray Journal through contact with Peter Blodgett. Michael Landon of the LDS Family History Center contributed one of the "Eureka" moments when he provided Hiles with the list of names enumerated by Mormon clerks when the gold seekers traveled through Salt Lake City—a concise handwritten roster of the Newark Overland Company. Thanks to all for their invaluable time and guidance. The authors are also grateful for all of the assistance from the University of Oklahoma Press.

And finally, a salute to Dr. Thomas D. Clark who started the ball rolling in 1964 with his curiosity in the journal of Charles G. Gray.

Prologue

There would be very few people at the funeral.

On St. Nicholas Avenue, as all over the city, dry leaves rustled in corners wherever buildings, stairwells, and retaining walls intersected at protective angles. Winter winds had begun to appear in recent weeks, causing the spent foliage to levitate, twirl, and swirl before touching down in another sheltered city corner.

The heels of pedestrians clipping the brick and concrete sidewalks accelerated in response to the playful gusts. Women's long black skirts were occasionally caught and lifted naughtily above and about the ankles while heads shielded in scarves, bowlers, and brimmed caps momentarily turned against the oncoming current. This was normal December weather in New York City, with premature darkness accompanied by frosty temperatures and graying skies. With Christmas in seven days, the shopping bustle and pedestrian traffic would continue undeterred. Likewise, the weather would not keep anyone from attending a funeral.

On that wintery day, newsboys hailed their dailies to those passing by, though nothing more than the mundane chew of local and world events appeared scattered about the pages. The press was following every move of recently elected Woodrow Wilson, with the *New York Times* reporting his daily agenda. One reporter could not resist mentioning that baseball legend Ty Cobb had called on the president-elect at his Princeton residence.[1]

There was certainly no news to compare with the story that had shocked the world eight months earlier. After the agony of Belfast and Southampton, there was no place more devastated than New York City, where the *Titanic* had failed to reach port as scheduled.

Devotees of daily news may have missed an obituary that April morning and subsequently missed a funeral as the frenzied reports of the *Titanic's* demise consumed their attention. However, no such front-page drama prevailed on December 18, 1912. Any regular reader of the newspaper would have browsed past the headlines and seen the three paragraphs announcing the passing of Caleb Dudley Boylston at his daughter's residence on St. Nicholas Avenue.[2]

Abby Wood Smith expected the funeral of her father to draw only ten, maybe twenty fellow grievers. The reason was quite simple. At ninety-one years of age, Boylston had outlived his contemporaries. The men with whom he had associated in the craft of masonry and the business of building structures throughout the metropolitan sprawl were long deceased. Perhaps an aging widow would stop by to pay her respects. Perhaps an apprentice or junior builder who found Boylston a valuable mentor may have an hour or two to mourn with the family. But there would be few.

Not only had Boylston outlived his contemporaries, but sadly, he had also endured the pain of losing four of his six children. Two surviving daughters would share in the duty of burying their father, and together would escort their mother to the Evergreen Cemetery across the Hudson River in New Jersey.[3]

Beyond family and friends, Boylston had also outlived the group of men with whom he shared a page of history. Sixty-three years before his death they had journeyed west, participating in the single most significant year of US western expansion, when men and ever so few spirited women had converged on the riverbeds of central California.

The year was 1849. Boylston was a young, single man living near Elizabethtown, New Jersey, when news of the gold discovery swept the country. People from all segments of the population were catching the excitement of gold fever and rushing to California for the opportunity to strike it rich. Boylston wanted in. So did his acquaintance Joseph T. Doty, also from Elizabethtown.

The two men made arrangements to join a company from neighboring Newark, organizing under the leadership of Dr. John Stevens Darcy.

Most groups from New York and New Jersey were forming stock companies and outfitting ships for passage to California, but Darcy, a well-respected physician, opted for an overland route following the emigrant trails out of the Missouri frontier town of Independence. Those desiring to travel under his guidance were welcome to join his loosely organized group of prominent citizens and young men, each providing his own way. Boylston and Doty signed on as a team and agreed to share a wagon, stock animals, provisions, and the arduous work involved in such travel. Joseph Doty would never see California. Caleb Boylston would make it his home for ten years.

The destinies of Boylston, Doty, and the others with whom they departed Newark's Market Street train station on the afternoon of March 1, 1849, were vastly unimaginable on that chilly day as they stepped off the planked platform and onto the iron rail passenger car. For those who reached California, it was the *ultimate* adventure of a lifetime, and they would eventually become known as "forty-niners."

Caleb Boylston was the last surviving member of the Newark Overland Company.

PART I

Before 1849

John Stevens Darcy, circa 1847. Copies of this engraving, considered a "spirited like-ness," went on sale in Newark bookstores a month after Darcy's departure for Cali-fornia. Cost: 25 cents. Courtesy of the collection of the New Jersey Historical Society, Newark, New Jersey.

Chapter 1

Headliners of 1848

Dr. John Stevens Darcy, an ardent Democrat, went to the polls on November 7, 1848, to cast his vote for the party's presidential nominee, Lewis Cass. Several weeks later he would watch the opposing Whigs parade through the streets of Newark, publicly celebrating the election of Gen. Zachary Taylor.

Col. John R. Crockett could not have been in a better mood. As president of "The Grand Celebration in Honor of the Election of Taylor and Fillmore," he had the honor of leading the torchlight procession through the city center. The title of grand marshal suited him well. A man of deep pride in his country, he had served as Newark's chief fire engineer before opening a leather and cloth mercantile business. During the two weeks after Taylor was elected the twelfth president of the United States, Crockett and his organizing committee planned an elaborate patriotic program for the citizens of Newark, intending to stir memories of the nation's independence.[1] Crockett and most of the organizers were sons and grandsons of Revolutionary War military men and owned their patriotism from firsthand accounts of their ancestors.

Snow had already fallen in Newark, which prompted the committee to plan for inclement conditions. But the weather proved more than satisfactory for the late November celebration—it would remain almost balmy until darkness descended. The event afforded a long-awaited release of frustration for the men of Newark who for years had rallied for Whig Party causes but rarely had reason for festivity.[2] The election of war veteran Gen. Zachary Taylor fifteen days earlier had generated outpourings of political triumph across the Union. Years of Jacksonian democracy were finally being put to rest.

Taylor had become a national hero after leading US forces to victory in the recent Mexican-American War, securing the vast expanse of Texas for the United States. But his leadership background was strictly military and his experience in politics slim, having only casually associated with the Whig Party when standard-bearers had encouraged him to run for office. Taylor's narrow win over Lewis Cass stunned the Democratic Party, especially following the term of popular James K. Polk. As promised during his presidency, Polk had declined to run for a second term, leaving the Democrats divided. Cass, their nominee from Michigan, was a firm believer in states' rights, as evidenced in his 1847 letter espousing that "Congress has no right to say that there shall be slavery in New York or that there shall be no slavery in Georgia, nor is there any other human power but the people of those States, respectively, which can change the relations existing therein."[3] But many Democrats felt this view indirectly supported the Southern position and prompted former Democratic president Martin Van Buren to run on the ticket of the breakaway Free Soil Party, whose political stand mandated the prohibition of slavery in all new US territories, making them truly *free soil.* Van Buren's third-party candidacy pulled just enough votes from Cass to allow a victory for Taylor, who was both a Southerner and, ironically, a slaveholder.[4]

The celebratory events of November 22, 1848, were set in motion at 5:00 P.M. with 163 guns fired from the hill just above the courthouse, symbolizing the number of electoral votes Taylor received. The residual smoke settled like fog in the street below, gradually thinning to haze. Some thirty minutes later, Washington Hall, Newark's Whig headquarters and the designated gathering point for parade participants, opened to the public.[5] Shortly after 6:00 P.M., signal rockets were launched from the Military Common announcing the imminent start of the pageantry. Grand Marshal Crockett and six military aides, all on horseback, began the march up Broad Street. There was no holding back Crockett's swaggering excitement.

Behind the military contingent, citizens followed closely, some also on horseback, others in the comfort of carriages. The horns of the Newark

Brass Band sent patriotic songs down side streets and separated the parade leaders from the assemblages of Rough and Ready Clubs proudly displaying their insignias and banners, a few bringing their own musical accompaniment. Bloomfield, Belleville, and Jersey City were among those represented. Blazing tar barrels mounted on wheels followed a number of the delegations, while others shot off hissing, crackling Roman candles that showered sparks dangerously close to wide-eyed spectators.[6]

Up Broad Street, around the town square, across Washington, and back down Broad Street, the parade filled Newark with an exuberance seldom experienced in the chill of a late autumn evening. Citizens on foot filed in, all coming to a brief stop at the Military Common, where a display of fireworks sent Chinese Grandiflora and Flying Salamanders above the barren trees, briefly interrupting the darkness with bursts of brilliance and causing young ones to cover their ears. The night was fiery, festive, and on patriotic overload.

Before returning to Washington Hall, the procession wound around the neighborhood streets, where residents had been requested to light their houses to greet Crockett and his entourage. Some windows glowed in red, blue, and green where colored transparencies had been placed over panes.[7] Not all homes were decorated, possibly indicating opposition to the Whigs. One such residence might have been that of Democrat John S. Darcy, who, despite opposing Taylor, shared a similar patriotic heritage with the parade organizers.

A few streets over, James Adolphus "Dolph" Pennington might have similarly refrained from lighting his home. Pennington was alderman of Newark's Fifth Ward and stood with Darcy in supporting the Democratic Party. The Penningtons were a founding family of Newark and claimed a rich legacy of service to state and local politics. New Jersey governor William Sanford Pennington had entered office in 1813, the year his grandson Dolph was born. The governor had been a captain in the Continental army, putting the Penningtons into the elite class of both founders and patriots. More recently, another William Pennington, Dolph's uncle, had completed six years as the state's governor, succeeding his father in the office. Powerful and popular, Uncle William was a Whig, making Dolph the odd man out in family politics.

By nine o'clock Colonel Crockett and his aides returned to Broad Street for the final countermarch to Washington Hall, where supporters would revel in speeches and congratulatory exchange for a few more hours. As the parade ended, a crowd of participants spilled into the Whig headquarters, gas- and candle-lit homes along the route went dark one by one, and the streets of Newark returned to normal sleepiness.[8]

A Newark paper dedicated a full page to coverage of the extravaganza, asserting, "The triumph of Whig principles, and the consummation of patriotic effort zealously put forth for the public good, in the election of Taylor and Fillmore, was fitly and heartily celebrated in this never fail-ing old Whig city." There was little mention of any disapproval during the two-and-a-half-hour procession. The article simply characterized the insults and negative shouts from the crowd as voiced by "some worthless fellows of the opposition," and only shared this information in the last paragraph.[9] It is no wonder the overall report was favorable. Like many of the parade organizers, *Newark Daily Advertiser* proprietor and editor William Burnet Kinney descended from a prominent local family and, likewise, he was a solid member of the Whig Party.[10]

The presidential election dominated the pages of Kinney's news-paper until late summer, when another topic captured readers' attention. Reports proclaiming the discovery of gold, said to be unlimited in the rivers of the recently annexed US territory of Alta California, surfaced in East Coast media. The papers published letters from the territory that described the mass abandonment of shops, ships, crops, and even local newspaper offices across California, as workers thronged to the gold-fields. These reports, however, were so unbelievable that they bordered on rogue journalism. Were men actually abandoning their livelihoods for the chance of striking it rich? Was there really gold gleaming from river-beds, and was it really so easily picked up and claimed by the finder? The author of one such article recognized that his story might be met with skepticism by saying that it contained "facts stronger than fiction." But he affirmed that "a gold fever arises—strikes everyone, and drives every-one from his home. . . . The forge stops, the boards remain unplained, houses are closed, dinners uncooked, the sick recover, the plaintiff leaves his case untried, the defendant is gone, the Alcalde is going . . . all bound to the American Fork and Feather River branches, of the Sacramento. Rivers whose banks and bottoms are filled with pure gold."[11]

While the news was beginning to reach the stateside papers in Sep-tember, the actual gold discovery had taken place in January. Even Cali-fornia papers had taken two months to report that gold had been found far inland near the headwaters of the American River. A paragraph in the *Californian* on March 15, 1848, understated the event in matter-of-fact words: "Gold Mine Found—In the newly made raceway of the Saw Mill recently erected by Captain Sutter, on the American Fork, gold has been found in considerable quantities. One person brought thirty dollars worth to New Helvetia, gathered there in a short time. California, no doubt, is rich in mineral wealth; great chances here for scientific capitalists. Gold has been found in almost every part of the country."[12]

The report gave no credit to the man who made the discovery and no date was referenced to mark the event. James W. Marshall had developed a business relationship with landowner John A. Sutter in late 1847. He had agreed to take a small crew upstream some thirty miles from Sutter's headquarters at New Helvetia (Sutter's Fort, Sacramento) to locate an appropriate place for a sawmill and then oversee the site preparation and construction of the facility. By Christmas heavy rains, typical of the winter months in central California, had commenced, interrupting the project. The dreary conditions threatened all-out desertion by the laborers, most of them Mormon men who had remained in the territory after volunteering for the military exercise that claimed California from Mexico. They were eager to rejoin their brethren in the valley of the Great Salt Lake, where Brigham Young had led his followers the previous summer. The wretched weather gave the men plenty of reasons to quit Sutter's employ and begin their eastbound pilgrimage.

Marshall was able to retain the workers into January. On the nineteenth day of the month, according to Marshall's initial recollection, he spied a gleaming object in the waters just below the mill. Skeptical that he had found gold, Marshall returned to the fort, where he and Sutter consulted the *Encyclopedia Americana* and used a variety of geologic tests to evaluate the samples.[13] Marshall and Sutter determined to keep their findings to themselves until the mill was finished, but the workers who were aware of the discovery needed no tests to confirm what they had seen. The news found its way to San Francisco within weeks. "Scientific capitalists," as predicted by the *Californian,* were soon on their way to central California. No one could have imagined just how many there would be, all captivated by the prospect of instant wealth.

The initial response to the discovery at Sutter's Mill was a local gold rush involving those with proximity to California. Many of them were US soldiers and sailors assigned to the annexed territory. So severe was the desertion rate by April 1848 that Lt. William T. Sherman, second in command of the territory, offered the substantial reward of $30 for anyone who could "arrest and deliver to the commanding officer of any Military Post in California, the person of a deserter from the army of the United States."[14]

News of the gold rush crept across the Pacific on whaling ships sailing from San Francisco destined for Honolulu in the Sandwich Islands. Soon the Pacific kingdom was in crisis over the exodus of its labor force that was rushing to the American River. Trade ships running the coast to Mexico and Peru carried the excitement to Central and South American ports, which would soon experience a similar loss of workers. Mormons finally able to conclude their contractual service with Sutter made their way to Great Salt Lake City in the spring, further spreading the word of California's newfound wealth.

By the first of September 1848 normal business in California was turned upside down, yet New Yorkers, Washingtonians, and Kentuckians, along with most Americans, were oblivious to the frantic digging that was taking place on the far western side of the continent. John S. Darcy and John R. Crockett were busy in Newark with their respective professions and actively supporting their opposing political candidates. Like the majority of the US population, they were clueless about the activity underway in California riverbeds. Their ignorance would end in mid-September.

The arrival of Lt. E. Fitzgerald Beale in Washington, DC, after a trip at record-setting speed from California, began to shift the perception of California's gold from laughable hogwash to probable truth. The initial report by Beale was published in the *Washington Union* on September 20, and within days was copied by newspapers across the country. Beale not only brought his own observations of the dramatic transformation taking place in California, he also delivered an official letter from US naval agent Thomas O. Larkin, stationed in the territorial capital of Monterey. Both accounts confirmed the vast quantities of gold coming from California rivers. The story was picked up by the *Newark Daily Advertiser,* and the first genuine inkling of the richness of California's placers was clarified to readers. Darcy, Crockett, Pennington, and a host of their prominent colleagues now realized that the highly implausible reports of a modern-day El Dorado might be true.

Private letters written from San Francisco around the same time added further confirmation. "The demand for all sorts of merchandize," one person wrote, "was so great that the cargoes of 16 vessels from our Atlantic cities were sold at once."[15] Newark and many other eastern ports began to see an increase in maritime traffic bound for California. While some vessels were chartered by the government to transport troops, others went "not to hunt gold, but to supply those who do with something more indispensable—the means of life."[16] The Beale report roused curiosity and excited entrepreneurs, but it did not ignite the stateside frenzy for gold.

Over the next two months much of the nation's energy remained directed at choosing a successor to James K. Polk, the man responsible for obtaining from Mexico the newest US territory and all its wealth. Newark's focus was no different. Election coverage and day-to-day events took precedence over news of California gold. On October 23, a hurricane ravaging Savannah captured the headlines. The following day, it was the arrival of the circus in Newark, led "by a huge Elephant and six Camels, glittering in spangled harnesses."[17]

On a more ominous note, bulletins from boards of health around the country released warnings of an impending cholera epidemic. Reports of the disease moving west from Russia to London had been confirmed, and with immigration on the rise, there was widespread concern about the dreaded killer breaking out in American disembarkation ports.[18] Still, especially in William B. Kinney's paper, news about Whig candidate Zachary Taylor consumed the columns.

In November, while John R. Crockett and other Whig leaders throughout the country were conducting postelection celebrations, another assessment was about to arrive from Monterey. Lieutenant Beale's news had turned heads, but the official report by California governor Col. Richard B. Mason in late November dispelled any remaining doubts about gold in his territory. "It is reported with truth and reason . . . that Colonel Mason of the army, commanding our forces in California, has sent an official account of the extraordinary gold and quicksilver mines of California," newspapers announced. Previous reports were now undeniably confirmed.[19]

Mason's lengthy discourse described the conditions in California as a new reality. As military governor, he had visited Sutter's Fort in June and with his top aide, Lieutenant Sherman, spent the next month compiling both scientific data and personal observations. The report, mostly written by Sherman, identified James Marshall as the finder of the first gold nuggets at Sutter's Mill. Details about the mining process, wages, prices of goods, and the relationship with local Indians dominated the writing. Finally Mason insightfully recommended that a mint be established in San Francisco before "many millions of dollars . . . pass yearly to other countries to enrich their merchants and capitalists."[20]

Governor Mason expressed particular concern about the status of the military, as the current pay could not sustain any soldier since inflation had driven prices to astronomic levels. A correspondent covering the Mason report put it in clear terms: "Who, indeed, can expect that men will voluntarily stay for $7 a month, when they see every loafer around them making from 20 to 30 dollars a day?"[21]

The latest information brought from California to Washington prompted President Polk to address Congress on December 5, 1848, when he made it official: gold had been discovered in California. The remaining weeks of 1848 witnessed a dramatic mobilization of men in towns and villages across the Union, struck by gold fever and making plans to capitalize. Like everywhere else, Newark was seduced by the news, and its citizens hurriedly made plans to participate. Within days of Polk's message, consigners placed classified ads for their services in the *Newark Daily Advertiser*, ads directed specifically at those about to depart for the West Coast. Likewise, ads offering shares in stock companies outfitting for California popped up overnight and seemed to double in number every few days.

There were even plenty of opportunities for those with no intention of ever setting foot in California. Another paper reported that in New York "a wealthy gentleman has taken a novel method at securing a share in the California gold. He effects insurance on the lives of those seized with the California fever, expecting that enough of them will die to make it a profitable operation."[22]

A more optimistic enterprise opened its doors at 134 Market Street in Newark, where Harris and Gore established the California News Depot for the purpose of receiving and distributing reports from the mining region.[23]

Products useful for traveling and gold digging, along with items thought to be in short supply in California hit the market with similar

Whimsical 1849 interpretation of gold rush fever by Nathaniel Currier, a cousin of Newark Overland Company member Cyrus Currier. Nathaniel Currier, *Grand Patent India-Rubber Air Line Railway to California*, 1849. Hand-colored lithograph, 14 x 21.13 in. Courtesy of the collection of the Oakland Museum of California (A68.90.2).

immediateness. An industrious Trenton man hastily produced one dozen frame houses to be shipped to San Francisco.[24] Another man had the idea of sending products certain to sell like wildfire—dice, spirits, and playing cards. Merchants also filled their shops with India rubber goods such as those used by Col. John C. Fremont on his western topographical expeditions. One article claimed that an India rubber boat could be converted into a makeshift eight-by-eleven-foot shelter.[25] There was no shortage of ideas and marketing ploys.

While the stateside population was mobilizing for the goldfields, California was recoiling from its frenzied spring and summer of gold mania. By October 1848 seasonal rains had again commenced. As the flow in the riverbeds increased, the flow of gold seekers nearly halted altogether. The waters were too high for digging and the weather too abusive for prolonged outdoor labor. Genuine ague replaced the gold fever state of mind, and dire sickness overcame many mining camps. Cholera, typhus, and dysentery epidemics broke out and began to claim lives as furiously as those lives had claimed gold.

There was other trouble brewing in California resulting from the chaotic events of 1848. Territorial governor Mason continued to face challenges resulting from a runaway society. Wives and children had been abandoned across the territory when men of all occupations had suddenly made gold mining their profession. Desertion rates for the military had continued unchecked over the summer, leaving fledging towns and villages unprotected and lawless. Alarmed and concerned for public safety, Mason issued a proclamation warning of consequences to anyone hindering the military's effort to end desertion and reinstate civil order. The decree was issued from Monterey in both English and Spanish in order to reach the majority of his multilingual constituency.

As a career military man, Colonel Mason was also bothered by the freewheeling pillage of California's gold. He reminded citizens that they "enjoyed the high privilege of digging gold on Government land without charge and without hindrance."[26] Despite the pleas, there was simply nothing he could do to stop the madness.

The growing lawlessness was but one of Mason's urgent concerns. Economic disaster was equally foreboding. Ships had begun to pile up in San Francisco Bay, where there was no workforce to unload the cargo and not enough manpower to collect tariffs and duties when the ships were finally discharged. Merchants implored Mason to postpone the collection of the fees as the delays were stifling commercial enterprises.[27] A week after his proclamation on desertion, Mason was compelled to respond to the merchants' requests and defended his position that duties be obtained before goods and wares were released to the markets.[28] It was another headache not of Mason's making.

Many of those caught in the firestorm of the initial gold craze understood Mason's concerns. They had immigrated to California not for gold but for the territory's rich agricultural prospects and the opportunity to establish trade in a burgeoning society. One individual wrote from Monterey, "We are gathering the elements of a great and influential community—if we are not ruined by this gold excitement."[29] Another's words were more prophetic: "Where, and how, all this is to end, is beyond my comprehension. Sufficient for me is the knowledge of the day. That the '*Placer*,' of California, will bring into the country thousands and thousands of emigrants, is clear."[30]

Governor Mason spent most of the summer of 1848 drafting orders, sending letters, and posting proclamations that were futile attempts to contain the unraveling society and economy. His letter to Washington had been meant to awaken federal lawmakers to the desperate situation in the most recent US territorial acquisition. He emphasized his recommendation that a mint be established to stop the drainage of gold to other countries. It certainly was not his intent to provide the spark for worldwide gold fever. But his letter did just that. The chaos that Mason tried so valiantly to contain and others so helplessly observed throughout 1848 was a mere fraction of what was headed their way in 1849.

The race for California was about to explode into a global phenomenon, and John S. Darcy, one of Newark's most celebrated and distinguished citizens, was preparing to join the exodus.

Chapter 2

Doctor, General, President

Twenty-five years before the world went crazy over California gold, John Stevens Darcy was a highly regarded physician in Morris County, New Jersey. He had followed his father, also named John Darcy, into the medical profession, the senior Darcy having learned his skills as a surgeon's mate during the American Revolution. Like his father, John S. Darcy also distinguished himself militarily, first as a commanding officer during the War of 1812 and then earning the rank of brigadier general in the Morris Brigade a decade later. On September 22, 1824, the younger Darcy enjoyed the honor of receiving French general Marquis de Lafayette on behalf of New Jersey as part of a delegation of elected officials and high-ranking officers.[1]

News had spread over the summer of 1824 that Lafayette was returning to the United States for a much-anticipated reunion with the nation he had helped to liberate. He was designated the "Nation's Guest," and the clamoring to be included in the tour agenda rang in cities throughout the former colonies. Newark, flaunting New Jersey's contributions to the American Revolution, had scored a date on the calendar. General Darcy was among the distinguished men of New Jersey selected to greet Lafayette and accompany him to the city's Military Common, where two thousand troops of the state militia would be presented in the Frenchman's honor.[2]

Under spitting skies, the New Jersey contingent welcomed Lafayette from New York and proceeded to Newark, where a jubilant and excited public pressed into the streets. The reviewing stand prepared for Lafayette was adorned with an elaborate arch under which he passed to observe the parade of the militiamen. General Darcy, representing Morris County, stood on the platform with Lafayette and directed his Jersey troops as part of the afternoon celebration. Upon their introduction and hearing the name Darcy, the Frenchman recalled and inquired about a surgeon's mate with whom he had served during the revolution some forty-five years earlier. Lafayette was so delighted to learn that General Darcy was, in fact, the son of his former acquaintance that he embraced him cordially.[3]

The elder John Darcy, who had passed away two years earlier, had begun his career in medicine at just seventeen years of age after he mustered into the Continental army. He was assigned to the Fifth Battalion, known as the Jersey Line, one of the units under direct leadership of General George Washington.[4] At the completion of his military commitment, Dr. Darcy received bounty land grants in Ohio, a reward for his continuous loyalty.[5] After independence was won, he returned to Morris County and began a career in medicine. He remained active as a military leader, commanding a brigade of the New Jersey militia that was recalled to service in 1812. He never left New Jersey, providing surgical services for his community of Hanover until his death on February 13, 1822. His Ohio land would eventually transfer to his children.[6]

John S. Darcy's maternal side had equally impressive ties to the nation's fight for independence. His mother was Phebe Johnes, the granddaughter of Rev. Timothy Johnes, eminent pastor of the First Presbyterian Church of Morristown, from whom General Washington sought spiritual solace while headquartering there in 1777.[7] It was Phebe Johnes's aunt Theodosia Ford who permitted the grand white estate of her late husband to serve as the headquarters for Washington and his officers over the winter of 1779–80.[8] And it was in Morristown that General Lafayette united with Washington, bringing much-needed French reinforcements.

John and Phebe Darcy had seven children. The oldest, John Stevens Darcy, was born in 1788 and would eventually be compared to his mother in mild and caring temperament and to his father in professional ability.[9]

In 1831, seven years after the celebration of Lafayette's visit, one topic dominated the statehouses of New York, New Jersey, and other populous states—railroads. Established railroad companies were demanding more state funding to expand their profitable networks, but not everyone agreed with the demands. Local businessmen saw monopolies developing and countered with proposals of their own for new, competing businesses. Lobbying for funds was vigorous. Everyone was aware that the building of transportation infrastructures not only facilitated the movement of people and commodities, it made men fortunes.

The efforts of a group from Essex County, New Jersey, were rewarded with a charter for a new rail system specifically stating that Newark was to be a central depot. Funding was set at $775,000. First on the list of the eighteen named commissioners of the new company was John S. Darcy. By a unanimous vote on June 4, 1832, the doctor and general from Morris County was named president of the New Jersey Railroad.[10] Darcy had acquired a third distinguished title.

The first board meeting of the New Jersey Railroad and Transportation Company was held at the Eagle Tavern on Broad Street in downtown Newark.[11] Darcy must have recognized the difficulties of overseeing the construction of a railroad from Morris County. Hanover was a fine place to raise a family and run an established medical practice, but it was too peripheral and distant from Newark for him to manage the new railroad. By that summer he was making plans to move, along with his wife of twenty-one years, Eliza Gray Darcy, and their family. Eliza had been born and raised in Morris County, the daughter of Jacob Gray, a longtime resident who had recently died. The couple's son, Henry, and daughters, Josephine and Caroline, were almost grown, the youngest being in her mid teens, when the family moved to Newark and took up residence at 265 Broad Street.[12]

The move would soon prove as advantageous for Newark as it was for Darcy himself. Just after his arrival in the summer of 1832, an outbreak of Asiatic cholera devastated the city. Immigration from Europe had steadily increased, and with it came the introduction of rapidly transmitted diseases. Cholera thrived in crowded, unsanitary quarters characteristic of less affluent communities. It also moved quickly along waterways such as the Morris Canal that had been recently completed through central Newark by a heavily immigrant labor force. So widespread was the sickness and so fearful were the citizens of its lethal potential that public celebration of the nation's independence in 1832 (for the first time called the "Fourth of July") was canceled save the ringing of church bells and the firing of guns at sunrise.[13]

The superior personal qualities of John S. Darcy soon became familiar to his new community in Newark. He was a man of tremendous stature, carrying 230 pounds on his six-foot-two frame, yet there was nothing imposing about him. Citizens would learn firsthand that this general and railroad magnate was an individual of rare compassion. As the cholera epidemic ravaged Newark and other towns of Essex County, Darcy tirelessly treated the sick with no regard to their social status, religion, or financial ability to reward his efforts. He did not refrain from making house calls to the impoverished neighborhoods of immigrant laborers, and he often refused to accept payment for his services, frequently contributing his own money for medicine and other luxuries to treat the poor.[14] In little time Darcy secured a favorable reputation across Newark's diverse populace, and he became one of the city's most respected and beloved citizens.

The next year, 1833, the same year the Whig Party was established in opposition to the policies of President Andrew Jackson, Newark hosted the Honorable Henry Clay. The Kentucky senator was a colossal figure on the American political scene, having previously gained the public eye while serving as Speaker of the House of Representatives. Clay collaborated with former president John Adams in bringing the Whigs to prominence in a very short time. Despite his opposing political views, Darcy was chosen as Newark's representative to welcome Clay to the city and to announce that its citizens were presenting the statesman with a superb carriage crafted by local artisans. With a price tag of around $900, the gift was expensive, and Clay was said to have been humbled upon receiving it.[15]

In January 1834 Darcy was nominated by President Jackson to become the US marshal for New Jersey. It was more than an honorary title and required his military leadership. He secured the arrest of pirates along the Jersey shore at Barnegat Bay, successfully ending a smuggling operation.[16] He would serve two consecutive terms as US marshal, the second one under President Martin Van Buren.

Success continued to surround Darcy. The first segment of the New Jersey Railroad was completed in just two years, which was regarded as an astonishing triumph. The maiden excursion took place on September 1, 1834, aboard the *Washington,* a passenger car described as "a splendid and beautiful specimen of workmanship, containing three apartments besides seats on top."[17]

Carriage presented to statesman Henry Clay in Newark, 1833, by John S. Darcy. The carriage is still on display today at Ashland, Clay's historic Kentucky home. Courtesy of Ashland, The Henry Clay Estate, Lexington, Kentucky.

Life did not slow down for the General as he progressed into his fifties. He had previously been elected to a term in the New Jersey legislature, and while he was repeatedly approached to run again for public office, he declined, only permitting himself to serve as a delegate at state and national conventions of the Democratic Party.

Still, Darcy devoted time to causes he deemed essential to the promotion of a free and benevolent society. He joined the African Colonization Society (ACS) and worked with the organization to promote the return of emancipated slaves to the settlement of Liberia on the West African coast. At the time, many believed this effort would extend enlightenment and Christianity to Africa and provide free persons of color an escape from the discrimination certain to prevent their advancement in the United States. ACS members assisted Liberians in developing educational, farming, and business enterprises, with New Jersey members lending financial support and expertise in the field of mineral resources. Darcy would be a longtime member of the organization, serving for a period as vice president of the state chapter.[18]

A lesser man could not have kept up with Darcy's many endeavors. His fortitude carried him at full strength until the age of sixty, when his vigorous constitution began to deteriorate. Throughout 1848 he struggled with a severe throat infection and a weakened intestinal condition caused by drinking lead-tainted water, but his professional services remained in high demand. Darcy's expertise as a surgeon prompted many competent physicians to defer to him in cases of the most severe afflictions.

On the night of December 4, 1848, just as President Polk prepared to announce the discovery of gold in California, a local doctor was tending to a Morris County woman who was suffering from a strangulated hernia. Feeling unable to proceed with surgery, he sent for Dr. Darcy. Very early the next morning Darcy was at the woman's bedside preparing her for surgical repair of the hernia and then performing the operation successfully.[19] The patient recovered, but the stress of such late night and early morning house calls and delicate operations had exhausted Darcy. He became his own patient and prescribed a leave of absence to remedy his condition, setting his sights on an overland journey to California.

Few men in Newark were as highly regarded. Few men were as easily recognized. When John S. Darcy announced his planned departure from the city after seventeen years, many wept.

Chapter 3

From Freeport, Pennsylvania

The West intrigued General Darcy as it did many men of the era. His brother Edward had emigrated in the mid-1830s to western Illinois, where he also practiced medical skills learned from his patriot father.[1] Edward Darcy was part of a migration of New Jersey families who followed the National Road into the wilderness of lands bordering the Great Lakes. Newark, Ohio, and Jerseyville, Illinois, were named in recognition of their founders' home origins.

For decades men had been inclined to move west. There was some magnetism, some lure of the wide open spaces inhabited by fur traders and Indians that drew men to its realm, much of it stemming from glorified tales of frontiersmen and dramatic landscapes rendered by artists. Paintings were vital in promoting the West as a land of romance and adventure. These depictions allowed dreamers of all ages to contemplate the reckless freedom of mountain men, imagine encounters with mysterious Native people, and almost feel the earth thundering from the stampede of a buffalo herd during an exhilarating chase. But not one of them could have envisioned the vastness of the landscape so minimally captured with oils and brush.

While most only imagined, some were driven to action, to leave their warm homesteads and full dinner tables, their secure livelihoods and government. Some fled to see for themselves what lay in the wild western half of the continental expanse.

Pennsylvanian Charles B. Gillespie seized the opportunity to experience the frontier by joining a caravan that set out in 1841 for New Mexico, the disputed territory west of the nation of Texas. Gillespie's band of eight, including "seasoned Mexican half-breeds and other American greenhorns," worked their way from Independence, Missouri, toward the settlement of Santa Fe as part of a large wagon caravan.[2] Whenever a spare moment materialized, due to resting animals or waiting for scouts to return, Gillespie took out a sketchbook and captured images of the untamed foreign land.

Gillespie was evidence that young men from broad backgrounds were drawn to the West, not just European immigrants seeking cheap land or men of prominence speculating in real estate. He was Irish Catholic and hailed from Freeport, Pennsylvania, a town northeast of Pittsburgh. Gillespie's immigrant father, Neal, and uncles John and Peter Duffy were early pioneers in western Pennsylvania. Neal Gillespie had served his adopted country as a lieutenant in the War of 1812.[3] A decade later, with a young, growing family, he ran a lively tavern that was patronized by the Irish workforce building the nearby Pennsylvania Canal, one of many transportation projects under construction in the 1820s.[4] His son Charles began his schooling at the nearby Butler Academy and continued his education by studying law. However, Charles B. Gillespie had a passion for drawing and painting, not torts and writs. In addition to being a gifted artist, he was a prolific and talented writer, gung ho about exploring the unknown far from home and bringing those experiences to life with his creative talents.[5]

Gillespie was twenty when he joined the party destined to traverse the prairie, desert, and Rocky Mountain topography of the Southwest, yet to be fully mapped by military expeditions. He later wrote about an evening when he scrambled atop a rise in the sand-hill landscape not far from his camp. On the horizon he could see bluffs cast in purple and outlined from behind with the fiery glow of the sinking sun. There was still enough daylight to see what lay just beyond a mile of sage and scrub: the ruins of an ancient village predating the Spanish influx and any hint of Christianized civilization. Gillespie had been anxious for a chance to visit the ruins nestled at the base of the distant range since scouts had ridden back to camp telling of their existence. He noted that the panorama "filled all the expectations I had formed from the descriptions received from the hunters and trappers who accompanied the caravans."[6]

Gillespie descended the crest and negotiated his way to the ancient site. With the sun descending, the old walls sent stretched shadows over once-lively streets. The solitude was consuming as Gillespie studied the cracked and crumbling structures, dusty and gray. "For many minutes," he wrote, "I stood overpowered by the thoughts which such a scene was calculated to produce." He likened the silence to that of a tomb. He headed first to the largest of the ruins that he believed to be a temple and was surprised to find it mostly intact. While the roof was partially collapsed, a door fastened by massive wooden hinges still served the entryway. A few other structures appeared to have survived in near entirety.[7]

The spiritual experience in the ruins was short-lived for Gillespie. He was snapped out of his mesmerized thoughts by the sudden barking of a dog. Pivoting swiftly toward the noise, he was even more startled to see not just a dog but also a woman standing on "an old tottling platform" leading to one of the structures. Her dress and manners conveyed Mexican peasantry. Behind the woman, just inside a portal, stood a blanketed man, his face mostly hidden by a slouched hat. The woman motioned to Gillespie, apparently welcoming him to her makeshift home. Gillespie stepped forward to oblige her hospitality but stopped short when he remembered he carried no weapon. Still, they managed cordial communication. She brought forward a plate of warm tortillas, which he accepted only after her repeated insistence. He excused himself by the lateness of the hour expecting to return when he could "spend the entire succeeding day exploring and sketching every thing worthy of note."[8]

Upon returning to the caravan, Gillespie shared the experience at a campfire gathering, expressing his awe at the sights of the crumbling village and its humble occupants. His companions could only shake their heads at his curiosity with piles of dirt and stone, calling such artistic pursuits "lady-like amusement" and a waste of good paper.[9]

The caravan eventually pressed on for the provincial capital of Santa Fe, still days away, where it would resupply and continue onward to the Chihuahua, Mexico, region. Along the way Gillespie sold some of his many portraits and sketches to fund his travels.[10] In this manner he managed to support his transient lifestyle for two years, meandering throughout the isolated northern frontier of Mexico and encountering many more opportunities that brought forth his sketchbook. Some of the artwork, including images of Pikes Peak and the Pecos Ruins, where he encountered the mysterious couple and their barking dog, would remain in the Gillespie family collection.

Gillespie returned to Pennsylvania from his foreign travels before James K. Polk was elected to the presidency in November 1844. Polk's election would impact the course of western expansion with the political infighting attached to the process of annexing and granting statehood to Texas and California. Some of the region explored by Gillespie on his two-year trek would become US territory under Polk.

Gillespie's travels may have inspired him to pursue a profession in art, having seen the grand vistas of the frontier. With no interest in practicing law, his expected career path, he chose to develop his artistic talent and set to work amid the galleries of the local fine arts community in Pittsburgh, where he advertised his portrait studio in the local business directory.[11] In addition to painting, he made his living as a journalist, publishing accounts of his western travels in noted literary magazines.

During these years in Pittsburgh, artist Rembrandt Lockwood may have come to Gillespie's attention. Lockwood, a man of profound religious faith like Gillespie, had recently returned from Munich where the study of European art had inspired him to create his own interpretation of *The Last Judgment*. In 1847 Lockwood was working on prototypes of his planned masterpiece at a studio in Newark, New Jersey. His painting depicting heavenly figures glowing above a darkened earth would tower *twenty-seven feet high* on its completion.[12]

In early 1848, Charles B. Gillespie again became restless to wander. He ventured to Harrisburg, Pennsylvania, where he visited the statehouse before heading to the East Coast.[13]

Six months later Gillespie found himself being bumped and jostled while witnessing extravagant Fourth of July events on the crowded streets of New York City, a celebration that far exceeded any he had ever seen in his small Pennsylvania hometown.[14] By December 1848 his friends and family would be writing to him care of the Newark, New Jersey, post office.[15]

PART II

1849

Chapter 4

Organization and Chaos

Eight weeks after Zachary Taylor was elected president, 1849 commenced amid the excitement of gold fever. The president-elect had spent December in New Orleans preparing to resign his military commission and begin the preinaugural journey to Washington. Just before Christmas, his daughter Mary Elizabeth married his personal secretary, Lt. Col. William Wallace Bliss. It was a union far more acceptable than the elopement of his older daughter Sarah to future Confederate president Jefferson Davis.

Gen. Persifer F. Smith, recently appointed territorial governor of California, had also been in New Orleans in December 1848 en route to his new post by way of Panama.[1] He was replacing Richard B. Mason, considered by the *Californian* to be an excellent and worthy governor, who had put remarkable effort into stabilizing the territory in the turbulent wake of James Marshall's creek-bed discovery. Persifer Smith and Zachary Taylor were two of the US Army's highest-ranking generals, and they would soon correspond with one another regarding California's quest for statehood.[2] The matter would not be accomplished during either man's tenure.

Once inaugurated, Taylor would preside over thirty states comprising a nation that was aggressively expanding westward while holding its East Coast doors open to a flood of European immigrants. A *Newark Daily Advertiser* reporter detailed the nation's demographics and predicted the next phase of its growth. Using the federal census numbers beginning in 1790, he calculated a steady population increase of 3 percent and projected that the 1850 count would reach twenty-three million, impressive but still only one-tenth that of Europe. For the long term he estimated, "eighty years from this time the number of inhabitants in our happy land will be *two hundred and forty* million." He failed to calculate civil war, world war, and epidemic. The reporter concluded that "one of the probable events will be this: the spreading of our population over the whole continent, to the very apex of Cape Horn."[3]

While the article may have been insightful, the only population change exciting interest in January 1849 involved California.

Articles about gold had appeared daily in William B. Kinney's newspaper since December 5, when the dispatch of California governor Mason was reported by President Polk in an address to Congress and subsequently published across the county. The confirmation of gold, fortified with Mason's personal observations, stirred the US population like never before.

Enthusiasm for gold rapidly escalated to mania, with daily reports of the hysteria. One story described a young girl from Massachusetts who was discovered on board a ship bound for California disguised as a man, neatly dressed in a sailor's monkey jacket and carrying a newly purchased pistol.[4] Another paper told of a young man earning a healthy salary in a commission house who abruptly quit his job, married his lady friend, and sailed for California all in the same day.[5] For those who set their sights on California, the grand prize of instant wealth was only a continent away, across a rock-crested, sun-dried land inhabited by what some considered "savage" populations. Going was not the question. Getting there was.

The earliest wave of gold seekers opted for passage aboard ships that sailed halfway around the Western Hemisphere, transitioning from the Atlantic to the Pacific at Cape Horn and arriving in San Francisco after a long, monotonous voyage of five to eight months. The route required swinging far out into the Atlantic Ocean toward Africa before turning south and hugging the South American coastline.[6] Stormy seas were frequent on the open ocean, especially when crossing the equator. Executing the turn around Cape Horn was extremely treacherous, with many ships blown backward for days before catching the northbound currents. Many a ship went down trying.

A shorter option involved sailing to Chagres, Panama, across the warm waters of the Gulf of Mexico, traversing the scant bridge of land known as an isthmus, and taking a second ship up the coast to San Francisco. This route was significantly faster, but it was easier said than done. Despite the efforts of ticket agents to convince potential passengers of the safety of crossing the isthmus and the availability of ships on the Pacific side, suspicion ran deep about what happened to travelers after arriving in Panama. In reality, crossing the rugged terrain was at best precarious, and many contracted cholera or one of several insect-borne tropical diseases in the jungle. California governor Persifer Smith found the roads nearly impassible and advised against the route. "The resources of the Isthmus are entirely unequal to the business now thronging to it," he stated in a letter of January 7, 1849.[7] Compounding matters was the lack of ships available on the Pacific side for transport to San Francisco. In Panama City the backlog of passengers, many of them sick, steadily grew throughout January 1849. Smith had expected to depart for San Francisco immediately upon arrival, but remained stranded for weeks until eventually calling for whaling ships to assist in relieving the swelling congestion.[8]

The third option for reaching California was to follow the emigrant trails across 2,500 miles of prairie, desert, and mountain topography that lay between the "jumping-off points" along the Missouri River and the gold placer region of central California. It was the romantic option, with prospects of buffalo hunting, spectacular scenery, and encounters with Native tribes. A downside was the necessity of waiting for spring, when snowmelt would give way to the green pastures vital for the sustenance of mule and ox teams.

The idea of postponing travel until May was unfathomable to many gold seekers. Shipping offices in New York, Boston, and New Orleans had become jammed with prospective miners who would do anything to get on board a steamer or bark bound for California. When the *Falcon* departed New Orleans with Governor Persifer Smith aboard, its manifest contained "over 200 passengers," with "every berth on board . . . secured long before her day of sailing." Many "willingly paid their passage for the mere privilege of being permitted to *go on board*."[9]

On January 3, 1849, the *Ocean Bird* left New York with a full manifest of gold seekers, one of the earliest sold-out sailings following the verification of California's gold.[10] In contrast, just three weeks prior, the *Oregon* had sailed from New York loaded with cargo but with only three passengers destined for San Francisco.[11] Days after the *Ocean Bird's* departure, the schooner *Acton* sailed, having been recently purchased by a joint stock company and fully owned by the passengers aboard. Companies were forming in many towns with the similar objective of purchasing a private vessel and forming cooperative, socialistic agreements.[12]

The New Brunswick and California Mining and Trading Company, out of Middlesex County, New Jersey, was one such stock company that advertised for patrons as early as January 5, 1849. Its offering called for investors at $600 per share, with the intention of funding the purchase of a ship and cargo. By January 10 the company was completely sold out, and one week later they procured the bark *Isabel*, elected company officers, and set February 1 as their sailing date. They would take provisions for two years, to be allocated among the thirty proposed shareholders. The *Isabel* would sail around Cape Horn, resupply at Pacific ports, pass through the Golden Gate, and proceed up the Sacramento River. Upon arrival the vessel would remain docked on the Sacramento waterfront, housing the company's stores and serving as the organization headquarters.[13] It was one of the better plans.

Another option for reaching the gold region was detailed in a *Newark Daily Advertiser* article announcing the California Overland Association. For a much cheaper price per share of $92.25, the company would provide passage from New York to Veracruz, Mexico. From there the members would cross Mexico by land, traveling northwest toward California as a cooperative group, smartly outfitted with sixty days' provisions, basic medical supplies, horses and tack, passport fees, mosquito nets, and a variety of clothing. A proposed side trip to a Mexican gold mine was planned "where the Company would have an opportunity of seeing the method employed at those mines for obtaining and cleansing the precious ore, which might be of great benefit to the members in their mining operations in California." [14]

Once the company reached Mexico's Pacific Coast, two options were mapped for the final leg to San Francisco. In the first, chartered vessels could be obtained at San Blas or Mazatlan for sailing to Monterey, the entry port and territorial capital of California. The second option was a route by land though ninety villages including San Los Angelos (now Los

Ad for the bark *Griffon* as it appeared in the *Newark Daily Advertiser* on January 30, 1849. On board the ship when it sailed in mid-March was John B. Overton, who had expected to depart overland with Darcy. Overton may have been offered passage as a "substitute" shareholder.

Angeles). The overall plan was high on innovation but naïve when it came to topography. A membership of three hundred persons was proposed, with a departure date of January 20. Anyone interested in booking travel with the California Overland Association or obtaining further information was directed to Caleb P. Crockett, a Newark leather merchant and brother of dedicated Whig supporter Col. John R. Crockett.[15]

The number of ads for California outfitters grew daily. One that must have raised eyebrows came from a New York widow named Eliza Farnham, whose husband had perished in California in 1848 while pursuing business opportunities. He had fallen ill, and no doctors or nurses had been available, as medical care, like everything else, had vanished to the goldfields. Eliza Farnham, middle-aged and wealthy, placed ads to recruit "a company of unmarried women, not under twenty-five years of age, who can bring undoubted testimonials as to character, education, &c."

to join her in an expedition to California.[16] Her objective was to set up a hospital to ensure that care for the sick and suffering would be available, and thus prevent others from the unfortunate fate of her husband. It was one of the more bizarre plans.

Booking passage via either the Cape Horn or Isthmus of Panama route was a pricey venture. For those not joining a chartered stock company, individual fares to Chagres, Panama, could be obtained for fees ranging from $50 for steerage to $150 for upper cabins, but that only covered transportation to Panama. Rates for the longer voyage around Cape Horn could run as high as $300.[17]

Regardless of the prices, demand for passage was fierce, and shipping agents were thriving with the spiking business. Ships described by their age and tonnage and with such attributes as "fast sailing" and "copper fastened" were advertised to entice passengers.[18] Never mind how many of these ships had been pulled from wreckage and spruced up only enough to bob in the harbor for the short length of time it took collect fares from desperate gold seekers. The *New York Herald* warned those who were contemplating the Cape Horn route that there were all "classes of vessels up for passengers some of which are unworthy and unsafe." Others were deemed "hardly fit to venture out sight of land, even in the most favorable weather."[19]

Such warnings about rickety ships, combined with the news that California's governor was stuck in Panama, began to raise doubts about the oceangoing options for reaching California. News reports also increased about the susceptibility of travelers to tropical diseases rampant in the murky jungle crossing of Panama. Yet agents pressed on with convincing advertisements. J. Howard and Sons, representatives for the *Crescent City*, running from New York to Chagres, advised that there was "very little, if any, detention at that Port. The facilities for crossing the Isthmus have been increased." To overcome reports of sickness in Panama, one advertiser claimed: "An experienced Physician accompanies the vessel."[20] Never mind that a doctor was just as likely to spend most of the voyage as drunk as the average passenger.

Doubts about sea travel persisted for some, and for others, sailing halfway around a hemisphere was never an option in the first place. In early January 1849, the fourth edition of Edwin Bryant's *What I Saw In California* was published and reviewed in Newark papers. It was a 480-page revision of his best-selling guidebook for crossing the country by way of the Oregon and California Trails. The updated version was released, no doubt, to capitalize on the gold fever, as it contained little new information except for a handy appendix with information on routes and mines. The reviewer for the *Newark Daily Advertiser* called it a must-have for the "Midas-minked multitude" and predicted that it would continue to sell well "while the California epidemic prevails."[21] The publication energized those wary of ocean ventures and galvanized the alternative for overland travel. The downside remained: waiting for an April or May departure date.

Bryant's latest edition may have been the final impetus for John S. Darcy to set his sights on California. The doctor, wearied from the demands of his medical practice, was about to turn sixty-one. His declining health concerned him, and the prospect of venturing into the romantic western landscape seemed the appropriate remedy. The idea of seeing the country, of seeing the land familiar to his brother and other associates who had previously gone west, propelled him to choose the overland route. For someone accustomed to being in charge, planning a terrestrial expedition was the only choice. Bryant's creepy chapter about the ill-fated Donner Party did little to dissuade anyone, let alone General Darcy, who began to organize the Newark Overland Company.

One of those certain to join Darcy was twenty-two-year-old Henry Ashfield Jobes. He was the oldest son of John Jobes, who worked as a brakeman on the New Jersey Railroad.[22] This connection likely provided Ash with employment in the office of John S. Darcy, who had seen him as a young man of great promise and graciously taken him under his wing. The relationship was one of mutual affection. Ash Jobes's dedication to Darcy during his severe illness the previous year had been pivotal to the doctor's recovery.[23] For that service, Darcy was profoundly moved and grateful.

The opportunity to travel with the highly respected Darcy attracted numerous prominent Newarkers. Among them was Whig rallier Col. John R. Crockett, who had chosen not to join the expedition of his brothers, Caleb P. and David B. Crockett, but decided instead to meet them in San Francisco.

Alderman Dolph Pennington was also on the Newark Overland membership list. Pennington and Darcy, both devoted Democrats, were the only two members of the company planning to take along young black boys as personal servants. Darcy's aide was identified by his full name, John Hunt, whenever the company members were enumerated. Newspapers were less respectful in describing him as Darcy's "colored servant boy John."[24] Hunt was most likely sixteen or seventeen years old, while Pennington's young assistant was no more than eleven.

From Newark's East Ward came Maj. Stephen Harris Meeker, son of Obadiah Meeker and grandson of the Revolutionary War patriot and one-time British prisoner-of-war Capt. Obadiah Meeker Sr.[25] Prominent in the community and easily recognized by his flashing red hair, S. H. Meeker was a secretary of the local Whig Party. He had married Caroline Griffen, a well-to-do woman from Rye, New York, who possessed the type of striking beauty that could catch the eye of any dashing officer.[26] Despite their social standing, life had thrown stones in the couple's path. In 1844 Major Meeker sustained significant financial losses from a fire in his Newark umbrella factory.[27] A few years later the Meekers suffered a greater loss and inconsolable grief when oldest son John Griffen Meeker died at age five and a half, putting the marriage under more stress. While Darcy saw the planned overland journey as a way to replenish his body, Meeker may have seen it as a way to restore his spirit. He signed on with Darcy's company, leaving behind his wife and two surviving children. Caroline Meeker would bear no more children fathered by the well-regarded Major Meeker.

Like Meeker and Crockett, William Donaldson Kinney was both a prominent Whig and a descendant of a patriot. He went by the name W. Donaldson Kinney to distinguish himself from his cousin, *Newark Daily Advertiser* publisher William Burnet Kinney.[28] Their common ancestor was Sir Thomas Kinney, an English mineralogist who had found wealth in the iron industry of Morris County and, prior to the revolution, had been knighted and appointed high sheriff by the Crown. Despite these honors, Thomas Kinney had made New Jersey his permanent home and renounced all allegiance to Britain when independence was declared.[29] W. Donaldson Kinney's father, Abraham, like Darcy, was one of the original eighteen stock subscribers of the New Jersey Railroad Company.[30]

The fraternity of Ancient Free and Accepted Masons was another commonality linking some of the men of the Newark Overland Company. Darcy had held the position of grand master of the state of New Jersey and brought the St. John's Lodge into high standing during his leadership.[31] W. D. Kinney was a Royal Arch Mason and was instrumental in expanding the organization by founding new charters.[32] In all, one-quarter of the men planning to travel with Darcy were members of local Masonic lodges.

Lewis Broadwell Baldwin, son of well-known gunmaker Aaron Baldwin, was a member of Newark's Eureka Lodge No. 39. Lewis, who went by the nickname Gun, was also a gunsmith. He would find the difficult overland crossing placid compared to the dire conditions of imprisonment he would endure more than a decade later.[33]

Along with these prominent men was a younger contingent needed for their brawn, subordination, and certainly their youthful spirit. Like Ash Jobes, Benjamin Casterline was also twenty-two years of age and one of the younger members. Benjamin was the son of Mulford Casterline, a Newark grocer whose store was a few doors from the office of John S. Darcy.[34] Mulford Casterline served on the city council from the Fifth Ward along with Dolph Pennington and gunsmith Aaron Baldwin, all active members of the Democratic Party.[35] Going west was part of the pioneering spirit rooted in the Casterline heritage. Benjamin's maternal grandparents had relocated to Ohio in the early 1830s, settling in Licking County not far from the county seat of Newark. Benjamin was a newlywed of some four months at the time of his decision to join Darcy. His young bride, Ann Eliza, would remain behind at the residence of her father-in-law.[36]

Another young bride would also be left behind. The departure date of March 1 was closing in when Ash Jobes proposed to Catherine Gallagher. Father Patrick Moran, who had served for seventeen years as the patriarch of Newark's Catholic community, would marry the couple at his St. John's parish on February 13.[37] Catherine Gallagher had been born in Ireland and came to Newark with her family about the time Father Moran had taken over as priest at St. John's. She had grown up in the city's Irish Catholic community.[38]

Swelling immigration from Ireland, Germany, and elsewhere in Europe generated unease and controversy in a young country that was still honoring its living patriot heroes and reveling in its independence. Not everyone embraced the foreigners, and the Irish Catholics were the least welcome. Many Americans saw Catholics' allegiance as being to Rome and the pope rather than to the United States. Opportunities for the Irish were limited to hard labor and low wages, and many were employed to build the Morris Canal. Newark, like most American cities, accepted the newcomers but only in separate neighborhoods.[39] These lines of division were ones that had been ignored by Dr. Darcy, however, when his medical services were needed.

Ash Jobes was not Catholic, and before he could marry Catherine he had to be rightfully accepted into the church. On January 16, 1849, he was baptized by Father Moran, with Catherine's father serving as his sponsor, clearing the way for the pending nuptials.[40] The sacred vows of matrimony between Ash and Catherine took place on a wintry day four weeks later.[41] Ash Jobes and his bride would have sixteen days together.

As Darcy's overland company developed, the New Brunswick and California Mining and Trading Company departed under the leadership of another physician, Augustus Taylor, a Rutgers graduate who was also the mayor of New Brunswick. Shares in the company had been extended from thirty to forty-five, and the cost had escalated by an additional $100 per person required as a loan to the company. Fortunately, most of the men could afford the venture and saw the price increase as added investment. Cheered by an enthusiastic crowd, the group left the port of New York aboard the *Isabel* just before noon on the morning of February 7, 1849, towed by the steamboat *United States*.[42]

Meanwhile, Darcy's company began drawing interest from outside of Newark. Caleb Boylston and Joseph T. Doty from nearby Elizabethtown signed on, as did others from neighboring communities. Word of Darcy's organization also began to spread beyond New Jersey.

Chapter 5

Outsiders

The cordage from hundreds of world-traveled vessels was dense along the wharves of New York City, stretching several miles. For every ten sailing ships with tall masts and complicated rigging there was one steamer with stacks huffing clouds of hot white vapor. As many as eighty tugs tirelessly worked to control the traffic of larger ships maneuvering through the occasional whitecaps of the February water. Ice was rare in New York Harbor because of the saltwater from the nearby ocean mixing with the freshwater of the converging rivers.[1]

The waterway was home for Benjamin Franklin Woolsey, known to friends and family as Frank.[2] The Woolsey family ran the ferry operations that transported patrons from New York City across the brackish waters to the coordinating New Jersey railroads, canals, and planked roads. It was entirely a family business, with Frank serving as ferryboat captain, his brother Charles as superintendent, and their father, William, as ferry master.[3] Originally from Ulster, New York, the family managed the operation from Jersey City on the shore opposite the busy New York waterfront.[4]

In late February 1849, Frank Woolsey set out for the heart of New York City's center for trade and shipping, crossing the very familiar channel he regularly navigated. At Manhattan's lower end he reached the US Custom House. Constructed six years earlier, it looked very much like the Parthenon with its revived Greek-style architecture and eight tall columns. Its stairs spanned the width of the building, and the entire structure—stairs, columns, and walls—was composed of white marble, both for aesthetic reasons and for the fire-protection quality so valued for a hall of records.[5] There, at Nassau and Wall Streets, Woolsey met friends Thomas W. Seely and Robert Van Rensselaer Schuyler. Tom Seely, a native of Orange, New York, was also a ship captain.

The three proceeded to the office of customhouse broker John C. Niebuhr. There, Woolsey and Seely began the process of obtaining US passports, each subscribing a statement vowing his name, age, place of birth, and status as a US citizen. Schuyler served as witness for both Woolsey and Seely by swearing statements that he was acquainted with said individuals and could attest to the word of each man. Along with the sworn affidavits, a physical description was recorded. Woolsey, at thirty-six, had a dark complexion, hazel eyes, and hair that was dark but graying. In contrast, Seely, at age thirty, was blond with blue eyes and at five foot six was noticeably shorter than Woolsey. All documents were notarized by John C. Niebuhr.[6]

Passport applications had increased in recent weeks. The day before Woolsey and Seely filled out the documentation, their acquaintance Alexander J. Cartwright was in the same office completing the same required paperwork. Cartwright had brought along Fraley Niebuhr, a customhouse clerk, to serve as his character witness.[7] Cartwright was the son of a sea captain and, like Woolsey and Seely, associated with the shipping industry.[8] Like Fraley Niebuhr, he was employed as clerk.

Cartwright, not quite thirty years old, was married with two small children. He was a busy man outside of his employment and family life, volunteering as a fireman for an urban center that was never quiet.[9] New York City firemen, the best in the world, were considered heroic for answering alarms in a city where fast-moving flames endangered congested neighborhoods and crowded commercial districts. Busy as he was, Cartwright also found time for recreation. In yards adjacent to fire stations, he and fellow firemen and clerks would hit balls with bats and run around a circuit of bases. They called their game baseball. The men developed the pastime into a competitive team sport through the efforts of Cartwright, who is credited with ideas for formulating a rulebook and the layout of the baseball diamond. Alex Cartwright and Fraley Niebuhr were both original members of a team called the Knickerbocker Club.

Cartwright would soon leave his wife, children, and the game of base-ball behind in New York to join Frank Woolsey and Tom Seely on a jour-ney to the irresistible gold region in California. As men of the sea, their initial plans were likely to travel by ship around Cape Horn or by way of the Isthmus of Panama. If they had already committed to the overland route, they would not have had to leave US territory and would have had no reason to acquire passports.

For sixty years the US Department of State had been issuing passports, though it would not have sole authority for the assignment until 1856. Passports were not required for foreign travel except during periods of wartime, but instead were used to identify the holder as a citizen of the United States. However, Mexican minister Luis de la Rosa had confirmed as recently as February 10, 1849, that the documentation was required for anyone traveling onto the soil of his country. He also warned that some Mexican states might require a license for travelers carrying weapons and might be opposed to emigrants traveling in large numbers.[10] These regu-lations were prompted by the recent hostilities between Mexico and the United States over the annexation of Texas and California. Gen. Zachary Taylor's entry into Mexico with an armed military force and subsequent victory were all too fresh for the defeated nation not to respond with suspicion and regulation.

Woolsey, Seely, and Cartwright obtained their passports with little more effort than signing documents, but such was not the case for all Americans. Only a few months after the California-bound trio received their official papers, a man from Pennsylvania applied for a passport with the intention of traveling to Europe. His request was denied, and the incident set forth a firestorm of editorials across the county, with particu-lar outrage voiced by the newspapers of Boston. Despite having plenty of witnesses attesting to his character, the man's passport was refused by Secretary of State John M. Clayton, who had been appointed to the posi-tion months earlier by president-elect Zachary Taylor.[11]

Secretary Clayton responded to the criticism by clarifying that a pass-port was "a certificate that the bearer thereof is a citizen of the United States."[12] And the Pennsylvania man, though born in and under the alle-giance of the United States, was not a citizen. He was a free man of color, considered a subject entitled to liberties of his resident state but not to US citizenship. Clayton's response to the criticism was to claim strict compliance to the law. Unfortunately for the naïve secretary, previous administrations had granted passports to free men of color, complicating matters and threatening Clayton's reputation. The *Boston Daily Atlas,* while respectful to Clayton, urged him to "revise his decision, and grant a passport, and then henceforth colored citizens will receive the same privileges as whites."[13]

The Clayton incident was emblematic of the public debate taking place across the United States in churches such as St. John's and public meeting places such as the Newark City Hotel. Slavery was beginning to divide the citizens of the United States like no other issue since the American revolution had separated patriots and loyalists, and the acquisition of new states throughout the 1840s was fueling the debate. On one hand, some believed that each state had the superior authority to decide its own laws. They feared the power of a central federal government to impose unjust control as the British had done to the colonies decades earlier. On the other hand, and equally as passionate, were liberal-thinking communities that savored civil rights for all men. It was a complicated situation, growing more divisive with each editorial, election, and issuance of statehood.

Woolsey, Seely, and Cartwright would abandon thoughts of traveling to California by a sea route. Instead, they opted to cross the country with John S. Darcy by way of the Oregon and California Trails. Like Boylston and Doty, they agreed to travel as a team.[14]

Cartwright may have learned of General Darcy's pending plans through baseball. His Knickerbocker Club was one of a dozen such teams representing firehouses in New York City, and with playing fields at a premium, the teams frequently ventured across the river to New Jersey, in particular to Hoboken, where in 1845 Elysian Field hosted the first ever game of organized baseball.

Cartwright participated in the historic game and may have made the acquaintance of any number of the Newark men at this and subsequent events. Col. John R. Crockett, as chief fire engineer in Newark, may have fostered a relationship with New York firemen. Dolph Pennington, an avid supporter of early sporting clubs in Newark, was known to play cricket, a game that was rising in popularity at the same time as baseball and played on the same fields. S. H. Meeker is also believed to have been involved with athletic events during these years. Both Pennington and Meeker are noted in Cartwright's overland journal in a way that suggests a previous association.

If not through baseball, word of the Newark Overland Company may have reached the shipping district of New York through Charles G. Gray, a twenty-eight-year-old clerk who signed on and agreed to serve as the organization's secretary. Gray was single and living in his parents' Manhattan home when the opportunity for California presented itself. Slight in build, he was a most unlikely candidate for overland travel. As a native New Yorker, born and raised in the city, he had neither military service in his background nor any real outdoor experience. Quite the contrary, Gray was a student of classic literature, and reading consumed his free time. He readily recited the works of Shakespeare, Sir Walter Scott, and John Milton. Rather than dreaming of romantic western adventures, Gray looked to the refined culture of Europe and fancied himself a composer of fine prose. His passion for fine arts may have been inspired by his older brother, Henry Peters Gray. Hens, as he was known to family, had studied painting in Florence and with genuine talent had established himself as a successful commercial artist among the upper echelon of New York society.[15]

While Charles Gray had no special association to the city of Newark, he was very connected to New Jersey, specifically Morris County. His father, George, was the son of Jacob Gray and the brother of Eliza Gray Darcy, making Charles the nephew of John S. Darcy, whom he respectfully addressed as "General" rather than "Uncle."[16] Aunt Eliza may have been influential in recruiting young Gray into her husband's company. Likewise, she may have encouraged her youngest brother, Andrew J. Gray, to join her husband's ranks.

As the members of Darcy's company prepared for travel, they made casual arrangements with each other by forming tentative partnerships. Charles and Andrew Gray would travel out of the same wagon, combining resources and sharing duties. Their cooperative "mess" would be joined by the sometimes boisterous Col. John R. Crockett.[17]

The Gray-Crockett team was trouble from the start. Crockett was intense in celebrating his patriotic heritage. While Charles Gray's paternal line hailed from the revolutionary hotbed of Morris County, his maternal side represented the opposite extreme. A resident of Hempstead,

Charles Gedney Gray, the Newark Overland Company secretary, bore a striking resemblance to his older brother, the artist Henry Peters Gray. Circa 1880. Courtesy of the Huntington Library, Art Collections and Botanical Gardens (HM 16520).

New York, Gray's great-grandfather Harry Peters had served as a Queens County addresser to Lord Howe and when war broke out had become a captain in the king's service. Harry Peters was a loyalist. Following the British surrender at Yorktown, he was arrested for "adhering to the enemies of the State of New York" and was subsequently required to provide justification for his actions in order to prevent confiscation of his property. Unlike many loyalists, however, Peters neither fled the country nor lost his property. In fact, he made an amazing comeback, achieving election to the New York Assembly by 1794 and financial success in his Greenwich Village business.[18] Most likely, Crockett never knew these details about Charles Gray's great-grandfather. Nevertheless, the two had nothing in common. Nothing.

Weeks before the departure, Charles Gray planned ahead by forwarding a trunk of supplies to San Francisco on the *Orbit*, a sailing vessel owned by a company in Columbia, New York. He expected to retrieve his property in California and start his life with a nest egg of wares, comforts, and goods that might not be obtainable from West Coast merchants.[19] Gray also began collecting the necessary items to properly outfit himself for overland travel, likely over-packing by filling a haversack and two additional bags with clothing. Included with his wardrobe was a men's ornamental breast pin, a clear indication of Gray's ignorance about overland travel attire. Another curious article that found its way into his baggage was a thimble.[20]

In the days prior to departure Gray purchased materials sufficient to fulfill his intention of maintaining a day-to-day log of his life on the trail. He carefully packed two leather-bound journals and writing tools.

Another team of men making final travel plans with Darcy's company was from the Lewis family: William T. Lewis, James Lewis Jr., Thomas Payne Fowler, and Job Denman. William Lewis had recently returned to Newark from Delaware County, Ohio, where he and his wife, Sarah, had made their home for the past seven years. Sarah had given birth to their fourth daughter before returning to New Jersey.

Thomas Fowler was Sarah's younger brother and at eighteen was one of the youngest members of the Newark Overland Company. James Lewis Jr. would be one of the oldest at age fifty-five, second only to John S. Darcy himself. James and William Lewis were first cousins. The Darcy and Lewis families were connected like many of the property owners of early Jersey settlements and, with roots in Morris County, had been acquainted for years. The Denmans, with roots in Springfield, New Jersey, were related to the Lewises through Job's mother.

The Lewis unit, like other teams, prepared to join Darcy by financing their pending journey and arranging for the welfare of their families during the long absence. Sarah and her four daughters would remain at her family's home in Newark with her two younger brothers and their mother, Catherine Fowler. James Lewis's wife would be cared for by her grown children, while unmarried Job Denman would leave his widowed mother at home caring for his assortment of siblings.

As the men contemplated the list of supplies to carry with them, Sarah Lewis had her own priorities for her husband's provisions. Knowing the potential for injury or worse from the hardships he would encounter on the trail, and being aware that the journey would take him into areas inhabited by sometimes hostile Natives, she feared for his survival. Sarah asked William to take one specific item with him. He obliged, and she carefully prepared and packed a crisp, white formal shirt among his belongings. Her intentions were righteous even if somewhat morbid. Should the unthinkable happen, she would find peace of mind in knowing her husband would go to his grave looking like a distinguished gentleman.[21]

Far from New Jersey, where comforts were modern and plentiful, the privations of life in the frontier were commonplace to William T. Lewis. In 1837 he had ventured into the West for about a year, where he was a driver for the Ohio Stagecoach Company between Columbus and Sandusky. After returning to New Jersey with a herd of cattle for the East Coast market, he remained for a time before going back to Ohio in 1841, this time with his wife and two daughters with whom he made a home in a refurbished two-room log cabin. His frontier experience and skill as a horseman made him a valuable asset to Darcy's organization. But Ohio was far from the Rocky Mountains, conceivable to easterners only through the grand landscapes painted and sketched by a handful of venturesome artists.

Charles B. Gillespie, the Pennsylvanian who found himself in Newark, New Jersey, in January 1849, six years after a stint in the Southwest, was swept up in the enthusiasm of those outfitting for California. He felt a pang to return to the romantic West, where he could again taste buffalo meat, gallop over sage-scented prairies, and breathe the oxygen-depleted air high above sea level. His experience would be an asset to any overland company.

While on the surface Gillespie and Darcy were remarkably different, both were natural leaders and shared a common reason for embarking on a cross-country adventure. Like Darcy, Gillespie had been suffering from a nagging illness and believed the journey would help restore his health to a vigorous state. For Gillespie, it was chills and fever that had periodically incapacitated him over recent years.[22]

Gillespie became one of the unlikely members of the Newark Overland Company and would once again take his sketchbook and art supplies to capture scenes of western landscapes. In just eighteen months he would meet one of most noted men of gold rush fame. The wayward mill carpenter who had plucked the first nugget from a diverted waterway would share the tale of his troubled life with Gillespie and agree to sit for a portrait sketched by the traveling artist from Freeport, Pennsylvania.

Chapter 6

Farewell

Distinguished guests began arriving just before five o'clock. Carriages delivered the prominent men of Newark to the City Hotel from points north and south along the expansive corridor of Broad Street. The brick-front building, constructed a decade earlier at the corner of William Street, was veiled with three-story columns that supported deep balconies. It had become Newark's de facto meeting place for grand celebrations and political displays in the absence of a formal city hall.

Ninety-three guests attended the complimentary dinner given in honor of John S. Darcy on February 19, 1849.[1] Friends and associates, all holding high-standing positions in business and government across the city and state, had hastily arranged the affair as a farewell gala for their esteemed colleague. Among the guests were brethren of the medical community, fellow officers of transportation corporations, officials of the judiciary, and state and local politicians—many of them, like Darcy, also veterans of military service.

The event's impressive turnout reflected the admiration these prominent men felt for Darcy. Presiding over the Monday evening program was former governor William Pennington, assisted by incumbent Newark mayor James Miller. Both were members of the Whig Party, as were many of the invitees. In fact, one of the first statements by Pennington in his opening remarks alluded to the gathering as one of private friendship, not of partisan politics. He went on to praise Darcy for his ability to put friendship and personal associations over politics and emphasized that no one did it better. Pennington made note of Darcy's public respect for men who held opposing views, pointing to Darcy's genuine grief upon the deaths of presidents Harrison and Adams and remembering Darcy's gracious public greeting some sixteen years earlier for the Statesman of Ashland, the Honorable Henry Clay.

Incumbent New Jersey governor Daniel Haines was unable to make the journey from Trenton, but sent a letter to be read aloud. Haines reiterated the sentiments expressed by almost everyone who rose throughout the evening to speak. Such praise described Darcy as a citizen of exalted character—high-minded, public-spirited—in essence, a generous gentleman. The expressions of adulation seemed endless and were received with vigorous applause and hearty toasts. A spontaneous standing ovation ensued, with men waving handkerchiefs as a full nine cheers were shouted across the hall.

Toasts were also made to "our country," president-elect Zachary Taylor, and Governor Haines. A soloist performed "Our Flag," furthering the patriotic overtone, and a musical rendition of "A Soldier's Life" followed statements praising Darcy's distinguished service as major general of the Second Division, New Jersey Militia.

After the initial round of praise, toasts, and cheers, Darcy rose from his seat to address his friends and colleagues. He towered over most of the guests, but despite his rugged appearance, his voice was weak, the result of a severe throat infection from which he was still recovering. Silence befell the cavernous hall, with some of those in the distant corners straining to hear his words. He spoke purely from the heart as though each man were his brother. So emotional were his words that the *Newark Daily Advertiser* chose not to quote him, fearing that to do so would invade his privacy. Darcy reflected that, while he was not a native of Newark, having moved to the city seventeen years earlier, he was grateful that his acceptance in the community had been so warm and genuine. He assured everyone that his medical practice would be left in the experienced hands of his partners and went on to explain that he was nearly exhausted from his labors and had prescribed for himself a period of rest and relaxation, selecting California as the destination to fulfill the remedy. While potential business opportunities waited at the other end, it was the journey itself he most anticipated, believing the experience

John S. Darcy, circa 1855, was sixty-one years old and in ill health when he led the Newark Overland Company to California. He lived nearly thirteen years after returning home in January 1851. Courtesy of the collection of the New Jersey Historical Society, Newark, New Jersey.

would entirely restore his health. Finally he announced to the crowd that he fully expected to return to Newark within a year and once again be among them. This statement transformed the room from one of utter silence to one of electrified emotion, melting much of the sadness that had shadowed the evening.

Lighter moments began to prevail as subsequent speakers reminisced with humorous anecdotes. A judge told how a *"lady . . . a very pretty one"* from Newark had requested a writ of ne exeat to prevent Darcy from leaving town. Unfortunately, he replied to her, such a writ was only valid for someone leaving the country. The woman retorted that no court action would be necessary in the future, as the United States would soon extend over the entire globe. In another reference to Darcy's ability to win the favor of women, a speaker remarked that Darcy had learned well one of the first lessons of medicine, telling the audience that if you "ingratiate the ladies . . . the men and all the children would soon follow."

Perhaps the warmest words of friendship came from former chief justice Joseph Hornblower, with whom Darcy had shared a long association. While the two traded friendly jibes throughout the evening, Hornblower's speech was so emotional and his words so personal that they, too, were not shared by the paper.

Finally Judge Hewson stood and offered the most poignant comments. He emphasized that while speakers had expressed anguish and sorrow over Darcy's pending departure, their feelings could not compare to those who would miss him most, the poor and suffering of Newark who were about to lose their greatest advocate. He commented how Darcy had extended his medical services to those of all classes. "I know cases," he related, "where not only his professional services were rendered to the poor, but his oft-emptied purse was made to minister to their every other want." Hewson concluded by suggesting that California was driving a good bargain: "Though she yields us her treasure, she receives from us those we prize higher than GOLD."

The ceremony closed with a boisterous and heartfelt outpouring of "Auld Lang Syne." Guests departed around ten o'clock as elegant carriages disappeared into darkened neighborhoods.

One distinguished invitee who was unable to attend the farewell gala was Richard S. Field, whose cousin Robert F. Stockton was the Navy commodore who had taken charge at Monterey, California, in 1847 and whose military leadership had helped secure the annexation of Alta California for the United States.

A week before the expected departure, there was no formal membership roster of those planning the overland trip with Darcy, just some thirty-five or more men who had tentatively signed on to accompany him to the diggings in California. Preferring to direct a group loyal to his leadership, Darcy required no commitment until the majority reached Missouri, where an organizational meeting would be arranged. Most would depart by train on Thursday, March 1, 1849. A few would leave in advance, and others would catch up in the weeks following.

While the majority of the men were from Newark, there were three from New York City and one each from Ohio and Pennsylvania. Most were financially secure. Their ages ranged from teens to sixties. At least twelve were Freemasons. Two were black. Two were Catholic.

Their occupations included teamster, grocer, jeweler (in fact, four were jewelers), leather manufacturer, bookbinder, hardware dealer, mason, accountant, servant, fireman, ship captain, politician, farmer, umbrella maker, and gunsmith. In addition there were Darcy and Gillespie's combined endeavors of doctor, railroad builder, general, artist, lawyer, and journalist.

Fewer than half of the men were married. All but four of those married had children. Two would learn of their wives' pregnancies while away from home. Two were grandfathers. And two, Charles B. Gillespie and Andrew J. Gray, had twin sisters.

By late February, the following men were among the tentative members of General Darcy's company.[2] On arrival in California, the roster would be significantly different.

Baldwin, Augustus
Baldwin, Lewis Broadwell, "Gun"
Bond, Robert
Boylston, Caleb Dudley
Canfield, Moses, "Moss"
Cartwright, Alexander Joy, Jr.
Casterline, Benjamin
Crockett, John R., Colonel
Darcy, John S., General, Doctor
Denman, Joseph, "Job"
Doty, Joseph Tobias
Emery, William
Emery, William, Jr., "David"
Fowler, Thomas
Gillespie, Charles B.

Gray, Andrew J.
Gray, Charles Gedney
Hicks, Charles
Hunt, John, Servant of Dr. Darcy
Jobes, Henry Ashfield, "Ash"
Johnson, Henry L.
Joralemon, Abraham, "Abram"
Kinney, William Donaldson, "Donaldson" or "W. D."
Lewis, James, Jr.
Lewis, William T.
Martin, George W.
Martin, Joseph H.
Meeker, Stephen Harris, "Harry" or "S. H.," Major
Overton, Isaac O.
Overton, John Brewster, Captain
Pennington, James Adolphus, "Dolph," Alderman
Richards, John
Rowe, John, Servant of J. A. Pennington
Sayre, George Davis
Seely, Thomas W., Captain
Woolsey, Benjamin Franklin, "Frank," Captain
Young, Thomas

Chapter 7

February 21, 1849

At Newark's Market Street depot a few men stood on the platform to offer advice and wish Godspeed to Augustus Baldwin. He was leaving in advance of the main contingent of the Darcy party and would rendezvous with the group in St. Louis. Boarding the train with him was John W. Shaff, who had not yet committed to the Newark Overland Company but would make a final decision once en route.[1]

The train carrying Baldwin and Shaff slowly pulled away from the station, destined for Philadelphia, six hours away. From there another train carried them an additional seven hours to Baltimore, where they arrived at midnight, having covered the distance at an average speed of fifteen miles per hour. The late arrival left Baldwin too exhausted to write to his wife, Mary, as he had promised, but he managed to send a brief letter in the morning.

The final segment of train travel was a day's journey to Cumberland, Maryland, the most western point a steam locomotive would transport them on their way to California. In Cumberland the two men would transfer to stagecoach for travel to the Ohio River at Wheeling, Virginia (now West Virginia). The route would take them across the Allegheny Mountains and a treacherous ridge covered with ice known as Laurel Hill.

The train and stage schedules were coordinated tightly enough to prevent long layovers and keep passengers moving. In Philadelphia that meant just enough time for Baldwin and Shaff to disembark and consume some oysters. Upon arriving in Cumberland, the Jerseymen exited the passenger car and headed for the stage depot. On the way they stopped for tea and witnessed unusual excitement buzzing about the town center. They soon learned that Cumberland was the next appointed stop for Gen. Zachary Taylor, the president-elect, who was expected at any time. He was making his way to Washington after relinquishing his military commission in New Orleans just weeks earlier. Traveling north, he had encountered congratulatory crowds at stops across the South before eventually turning east and following the Ohio River to Wheeling. Going against the tide of men rushing to California, Taylor was forced, like everyone else, to take the only option to get from the river vessels of the Ohio to the closest available train in Cumberland. He crossed the icy Alleghenies by stagecoach.[2]

Newspapers across the country were tracking Taylor's eastbound movement and anticipating his inauguration. His arrival in Cumberland put the president-elect one day away from Washington, and speculation about his cabinet appointments was beginning to flurry. Coinciding with Taylor's visit to western Maryland, telegraph wires dispatched news that he was about to meet with the man he planned to name secretary of state, Delaware senator John M. Clayton.[3]

Passengers on the stage carrying Baldwin and Shaff implored the driver to delay departure in order that they might catch sight of the next US president. A thirty-minute wait was granted, but Old Zach's appearance could not be coordinated with the strict stage schedule. Baldwin and Shaff encountered neither Taylor nor Clayton. By the time Taylor greeted the public before his overnight stay in Cumberland, the New Jersey men were headed for the five-mile-long descent of Laurel Hill, the westernmost ridge of the Alleghenies.

Their route was part of the Cumberland Road and provided magnificent vistas of the western Pennsylvania landscape. Behind them stretched parallel ridgelines and narrow valleys repeating into the horizon, while the west-facing panorama swept downhill to Wheeling and the Monongahela Valley. In springtime views from the pinnacle of Laurel Hill were beautiful, with white flowering dogwoods sprinkled among the budding timber that swept across the valleys below, broken only by the occasional homestead of cleared land. April air was usually alive with scents of deep pine, particularly at the summit.

Family man Augustus Baldwin returned to New Jersey after reaching Missouri, perhaps because his wife, Mary, was pregnant with a daughter who would be born in August 1849. Baldwin is seated (*in light jacket, second from right*) next to Mary (*far right*) on the porch of his son-in-law Frederic Fleming's family home in Hibernia, Florida, circa 1898. Courtesy of the Marian Wilkin Fleming Collection.

Not so was the view of the landscape in the grasp of winter. The contrast could not have been more profound. One author reminisced about his winter crossing of the Allegheny Mountains: "The wind blew fresh from the northeast, from whose penetrating power our clothes seemed to afford no protection."[4] Even Horace Greeley, who urged young men to go west, which many did by way of this notorious stagecoach route, would find it impossible to sleep during the difficult journey. The only relief from the cold was the warmth of sardined bodies fortunate enough to have a seat inside the vehicle.[5] Woe to the passenger riding atop the coach.

And so, on a bitter cold day near the end of February 1849, Augustus Baldwin and John W. Shaff found themselves shivering inside a stagecoach with six other men as they began the descent of Laurel Hill. Sleep was impossible. So tiresome was the stage ride that Baldwin felt "like a

Stewed Monkey in the morning," he wrote to Mary. The five-mile plunge down Laurel Hill would generate enough adrenaline to guarantee wakefulness for another forty miles.

After months of snow falling, melting, freezing, and being packed by the constant traffic of the passenger and mail coaches, the road was a sheet of ice. The metal-rimmed wheels could not defend against such conditions, and the terrified travelers held tight as the stage slipped and slid to the bottom of Laurel Hill. The coach pitched to within a foot of tumbling off the mountainside. More than once, Baldwin was ready to spring from his frigid seat in fear that he would "turn somersets down a precipice from one to two hundred feet and lodge in the tops of the trees." Forget the gold nuggets he envisioned in his pockets. "For all of California," he confided in his letter to Mary, "you could not get me to try it again."

There would be no more mountains to cross until they reached the Rockies, which would scale Laurel Hill to exactly that, a hill.

Wheeling, nestled on the steep banks of the Ohio River, was the terminus of the Cumberland stage. Baldwin and Shaff arrived at 4:00 A.M. on Saturday, February 24, after thirty-five hours crammed inside a jolting coach that moved at a miserable ten miles per hour. Finally sleep was possible for both men, but it lasted less than five hours. Baldwin awoke to violent shaking at the hands of Newark acquaintance George D. Sayre.

Sayre, another Darcy recruit who had set out ahead of the core group, had arrived in Wheeling prior to Baldwin and Shaff. Having learned that the next riverboat bound for Cincinnati would depart at nine that morning, he woke his friends, eager for them to join him. Equally eager to continue with Sayre, they skipped breakfast and made their way to the steam-powered vessel and the westward-flowing river.

Chapter 8

March 1, 1849

A considerable number of Newark's industrial workforce took leave of their occupations early on the afternoon of Thursday, March 1, 1849. They left their machine shops, cobbler benches, peddler carts, and other locations of labor to make their way to the residence of John S. Darcy. Still others converged on the Market Street train station adjacent to Newark's central commercial corridor.[1] Friends of Darcy gathered with them for the same purpose: bidding farewell to their esteemed associate.

It was widespread knowledge that the eminent physician, better known as the General, was about to depart the city on an expedition that would separate him from the community for more than a year. The laborers had heavy hearts as they stood outside his home and alongside the tracks waiting to greet the man who had provided them with unyielding support and compassion for almost two decades.

A train of the New Jersey Railroad was on its way from New York, outfitted with an extra passenger car for Darcy and his party. They were embarking on the same route taken eight days earlier by Augustus Baldwin and John W. Shaff, who had made their way by train to Philadelphia, then Baltimore, and finally Cumberland. From there Darcy's group would take a slightly different route, proceeding from Cumberland across the mountains to Pittsburgh, where they would hold the first meeting to discuss the organization of the Newark Overland Company. Their train was due to depart Newark around one o'clock to begin the ninety-mile leg to Philadelphia.[2]

Crockett, Pennington, Kinney, and Meeker, all prominent and recognizable Newarkers, were scheduled for the early afternoon departure. Woolsey, Seely, and Cartwright, from the New York and New Jersey marine-transit industry, were also in Newark preparing to board the private train. Darcy's brother-in-law Andrew J. Gray and nephew Charles G. Gray were meeting at the Market Street depot along with the Lewis family and the Boylston-Doty team. Charles B. Gillespie was again looking forward to an extended trip across the country and was excited about the stop in Pittsburgh, a stone's throw from his Freeport Township home. Somewhere in Newark two newlywed couples filled with both apprehension and dreams were saying their good-byes.

From Lyon's Farm, a community located between Elizabethtown and Newark, Robert Bond made his way to join the group. He was a profoundly religious man whose father had recently helped organize the Elizabeth Avenue Presbyterian Church in Newark. Robert Bond was the grandson of Elihu Bond, a Revolutionary War veteran who lived until 1839 and was known to tell about the anxieties, alarms, and dangers of the Revolutionary era, thus instilling patriotism in the younger generations.[3] Like several other men traveling with Darcy, Bond carried a journal in which he planned to log the day-to-day events of the extraordinary adventure that was about to begin. A notably quiet man, Bond was thirty years old and single, and he would travel in the mess of Maj. S. H. Meeker.[4]

Two jewelers from Newark were also part of the contingent meeting at the Market Street station. The shop of Henry L. Johnson had been severely damaged by fire a few weeks before Christmas, causing $5,000 in losses, including handcrafted watches, clocks, and other valuable items.[5] The prospect of a windfall in gold, a commodity particularly important for his devastated business, may have precipitated Johnson's decision to join Darcy. His financial crisis would persist for his family during his absence in California. For jeweler Moses Canfield, it would be surmised later, the incentive for traveling to California was not only gold but also escaping an unhappy marriage.[6]

When General Darcy finally emerged from his residence, he was "besieged by his fellow-citizens, all eager to grasp him by the hand and bid him farewell ere starting on his journey for California," the *Newark*

Morning Eagle reported. It was a humbling moment that would be repeated by the growing throng of townspeople waiting at the train depot, where Darcy was again "hailed with cheers to which he responded in an off hand manner, but with considerable emotion."[7]

Darcy promised the crowd that he "would transmit correct information in regard to the territory," knowing that many would be eager to hear his wisdom about opportunities in California. His judgment was revered, and the correspondence would be enthusiastically awaited. "The General concluded by shaking hands with all who could get near him, and on the arrival of the train from New York took his departure amid cheers, and the frequent exclamations of God Bless you Doctor, Let me hear from you soon General, &c. &c. The whole scene was an exciting one, and made manifest the strong hold the General has upon the affections of his fellow citizens."[8]

The first hours of the company's journey were filled with exuberant camaraderie as the train moved toward the Pennsylvania border. The ride had some rough moments when baggage shifted, but was otherwise uneventful. That evening the party arrived in Philadelphia, where they remained overnight before continuing on to Baltimore in the morning. Bond began his journal with a simple notation: "Robert Bond, Direct to William S. Bond or Mr. D. Price, Newark, New Jersey," presumably adding this should something unexpected befall him. On the hundred-mile trip to Baltimore his comments were brief. "Some ducks in the Chesapeake," he wrote.[9] The quiet man was also a man of few written words.

While the men traveled, friends and family remaining behind in Newark read about excitement that had taken place across the river in New York City, where an elephant had broken loose from the Bowery Zoological Hall and veered through downtown streets. The beast was captured and returned to his quarters uninjured.[10] Many who witnessed the chaos could say they had "seen the Elephant."[11]

On March 3, after an overnight stay in Baltimore, the group completed its third and final day of train travel, arriving in Cumberland, where they made the transition to stagecoach. Spirits were high, with the sense of westward progress suggested by the scenery around Cumberland, nestled tight among mountain ridges and situated beside the snaking Potomac.

The same day, a member of the New Brunswick company sailing aboard the bark *Isabel* began a letter home. After twenty-seven days at sea, the ocean was finally calm enough for James Spader to write. "We were ushered at the commencement of our voyage into a troubled sea" and "have had nothing but storm, storm, storm since we left port," he wrote to his father. The seasickness and retching were so widespread among the passengers that he described the scene as "enough to sicken a horse." Almost four weeks had passed, but the *Isabel* remained "within eight days sail from New York," having crossed the Gulf Stream but still being nowhere near the equator. Even the captain was discouraged, but felt time could be made up because the "*Isabel* is a cracker to go if she has the least wind in her favor."[12]

The next day Darcy and his men encountered their equivalent of a rough day at sea. The Allegheny Mountains were before them, and the good news was that icy conditions had subsided. The bad news was that the melting of snow had uncovered a rough road surface. So sloth-paced was the travel that several of the men, including sixty-one-year-old Darcy, got out of the coach and walked. For ten miles on foot they managed to stay ahead of the horses laboring to drag the coaches through the mud. The caravan crept along, barely moving faster than four miles per hour, finally reaching Pittsburgh on the evening of March 5.[13] In Washington, President Zachary Taylor was attending his inaugural ball.

No one was favorably impressed with Charles Gillespie's part of the country. Pittsburgh was darkened with ash and soot from its ghastly iron-producing factories. It was enough to provoke Bond to write a full sentence: "There is so much coal burned here that everything is blackened by the smoke."[14] Darcy had scheduled the first organizational meeting of the group, and despite the unpleasantness of the belching city, they remained for three days to procure wagons and other provisions. They also made "a more perfect organization of the Company, which now comprises 37 men, with 11 wagons—each wagon having six oxen." On the evening of March 8 the company boarded a steamer, paying eight dollars per man for the passage to St. Louis, which would take, coincidently, eight days.[15]

For Robert Bond the steamboat travel along the Ohio was filled with social engagements, which he noted in his journal: "Landed at Steubenville about sunrise. Sent a note to Miss Wooley. She, and four other ladies honoured me with a call." The ladies were, no doubt, all eager to meet the eligible bachelor of impeccable eastern heritage. In Cincinnati he "called on Aunt Abby and Mr. H. Price." While Bond apparently enjoyed this

Skyline of Cincinnati, the nation's sixth-largest city when it was photographed in September 1848. The riverboat carrying the Newark Overland Company docked here the following March en route to St. Louis and stayed long enough for men to attend church and visit acquaintances. Courtesy of the collection of the Public Library of Cincinnati and Hamilton County, Cincinnati, Ohio.

social life, he did not neglect his religious obligations. The devout Christian took time to attend church in Cincinnati on March 11 and would again on the following Sunday in St. Louis, where he "saw a woman ride as fast as her horse could run" and realized a distinct difference between Newark and the frontier Missouri city.[16]

Reports by everyone traveling the Ohio and Mississippi Rivers from late February to mid-March that year described the waters as swift, and in some places swollen fifteen feet above normal. The pace of the Ohio's current was at some points so rapid as to "embarrass navigation very seriously," Darcy reported in a letter to a Newark newspaper. Upon reaching the confluence with the Mississippi, the steamboat turned upstream toward St. Louis and plied against the slapping current so laboriously

The side-wheeled steamers pictured are similar to those taken by the Newark Overland Company traveling the Ohio, Mississippi and Missouri Rivers. Courtesy of the
collection of the Public Library of Cincinnati and Hamilton County, Cincinnati,
Ohio.

that Darcy "watched the shores for fifteen minutes at a time without
perceiving an advancement of a foot."[17]

For the Jerseymen the route from Newark to St. Louis constituted
one-third of the distance to California, taking them through one-third of
the nation's thirty states. During this segment they had used the modern
transportation infrastructure of railroad, commercial stage, and steamboat to cover one thousand miles in sixteen days, and the trip had enlightened them to a considerable portion of the country. While Pittsburgh
was a disappointment, Cincinnati, nicknamed the Queen City of the
West, was a charm. All those passing through witnessed the commerce
that had generated its affluence. Tax dollars collected had doubled in just
seven years, and in 1848 the wealthiest man in Cincinnati (winemaker

Nicholas Longworth) had paid several thousand dollars more in taxes than anyone in Boston.[18] Cincinnati citizens were proud of their city and equally proud of its benevolence. While pro-Whig extravaganzas were held in many US cities following Taylor's election, Cincinnati celebrated by collecting $5,000 for the poor.[19]

The Darcy party arrived in St. Louis on the evening of March 16.[20] There they expected to rendezvous with Baldwin, Sayre, and others who had preceded the core group. Several of Darcy's men had disembarked before reaching St. Louis and ventured into Illinois to purchase horses. They would catch up with the company farther upriver.

Also catching up was Cyrus Currier, who was traveling alone, having left Newark by train on March 16, the same afternoon that Darcy and company arrived in St. Louis. Born in Massachusetts, Currier had resettled in New Jersey for its warmer climate, and like Darcy and Gillespie he suffered from various ailments. He owned a foundry that produced high-quality engines and machinery for which he had developed a fine reputation. Following the same Pittsburgh route as Darcy, he would reach St. Louis eleven days later.[21]

At the time of Currier's departure, a notice appeared in the *Newark Mercury* announcing passage from New York to California in less than five days. Imagine the talk about town when it was learned that an "Aerial Locomotive" was scheduled to depart for San Francisco on April 15.[22] Rufus Porter, the founder of *Scientific American* magazine, had designed a steam-powered airship, intended to hold two hundred passengers, and set the price, "wines included," at fifty dollars per person.[23] The ad prompted a Newark scientist to schedule a lecture to advise residents on the impracticality of air travel across the country.[24] Presumably, Currier did not give the matter a second thought. The airship was never built.[25]

Like Robert Bond, Cyrus Currier understood the unique experience before him and had begun recording his daily observations in a journal. He noted Pittsburgh's abundance of coal and iron. About Cincinnati he wrote, "This is a large City and the Inhabitants are busy & Enterprising." His description of Louisville was not as favorable. "This is a fine City," he wrote, "but by the looks of the buildings & people it wants enterprise & Genius to make it go ahead." As Currier viewed the north and south shores of the Ohio River, he made the intriguing analysis that "an Eastern man traveling on the Ohio can see the difference between Slave

Labor and Freeman's. I cannot give the difference in percentage but the mechanical difference is this: a Saw Mill on the Kentucky side will make 50 strokes per minute, on the Ohio side 150 and I should judge from appearances that Kentucky would be glad to get rid of her Slaves as fast as possible."[26]

In St. Louis, Currier observed that the "Father of Rivers" (the Mississippi) had breached the levees. Mud seemed to be everywhere, and streets were cluttered with debris. Once his steamer began moving up the Missouri, he made note of the very muddied water and had been surprised when he found a pitcher of drinking water in his hotel as silty and cloudy as the river he was now traveling. Missouri "natives think there is no better water in the world than this to drink," he mused in his journal. He would have to let it stand overnight for the pint of mud to settle, and only then would it be fit for drinking and permit him to take his pills.[27] Like Darcy and Gillespie, Currier believed that the cross-country journey would improve his physical condition.

Currier's wife, Nancy, was so worried about her husband that she wrote her first letter to him less than forty-eight hours after he boarded the train in Newark:

As I cannot see nor talk to you I will commence writing to you which is a great consolation but it is so lonely and desolate not to see nor hear Pa come in. Friday evening was a sad one to us all. Little Cyrus called Papa and Daddy and would hardly go to sleep at all. Mary and Osce cried when we sat down to tea and would eat but very little. I told them they must be good children and pray to God to take care of Pa and get him well and let him come back to us again.[28]

As the Darcy company regrouped in St. Louis, James Spader wrote additional news of his voyage on the bark *Isabel*. They had sighted six other ships also bound for California, but the *Isabel* soon outran them all. Temperatures were in the mid-seventies.[29] They were now gliding across the sea.

In Newark residents were invited to spend the evening of March 20 at Library Hall with "Kah-Ge-Ga-Gah-Bowh, or the Rev. Mr. George Copway, an educated Indian Chief of the Chippewa tribe." The chief was scheduled to present a lecture on the customs of tribal life, including

New York Knickerbocker and Baseball Hall of Famer Alexander Joy Cartwright Jr., circa 1885, might have played baseball while passing time in Missouri. Unfortunately, no evidence of such activity exists in his journal. Courtesy of the Hawaii State Archives.

rituals of marriage, courtship, and other sacraments, and promised "to appear in the native costume of his tribe and to sing the Missionary Hymn in his own tongue."[30] Like many of the Newark men who had just departed for California with General Darcy, Copway belonged to a fraternal lodge. The chief was a Freemason.[31]

For most emigrants, arriving in St. Louis marked their first time in a slave state. Englishman William Kelly wrote, "Slavery in the abstract and in theory is a sinful, hideous, and abominable institution." Still, after witnessing slaves working on the street, he could not ignore that those employed in the menial labor, "slaves though they be, seem a jolly, contented set, generally on the broad grin, poking fun and jokes at one another; rendering it the next thing to impossible to pity their deplorable

Cyrus Currier, circa 1885, did not mine for gold while in California. Instead he made money as a mechanical engineer. Back in Newark he thrived as a businessman and inventor by manufacturing modern machinery during the dawn of the Industrial Revolution. From John Whitehead, *The Passaic Valley, New Jersey, in Three Centuries*, vol. 2 (New Jersey Genealogical Company, 1901).

state." A few nights later Kelly was one of a few whites admitted to an "all-blacks" ball, where mint juleps and oyster patties were served while blacks dressed in white gloves and colorful turbans danced to fiddle and banjo music. Kelly noted that his entry to the affair was met with rigid scrutiny, as the partygoers believed that whites "only desire to attend to ridicule" them.[32] The Darcy men had no such experience but did comment about a large number of blacks waiting tables and taking excellent care of their needs.[33]

From St. Louis the Newark men took passage aboard the steamer *Highland Mary* for several days' travel up the Missouri River to Independence, the party's chosen jumping-off town. Here the group would acquire final food staples and other provisions and begin camp life outside the town while they waited for conditions to improve. Travel could not begin until grass along the trail was plentiful enough to sustain the ox and mule teams. Without healthy stock, the outlook for reaching the Pacific could become desperate.

Before arriving in Independence, the company recognized that their unity was as muddy as the mighty Mississippi. A dark cloud had formed over the group while in Pittsburgh, as though the grimy city had sent them off with a souvenir of its ugly skyline. Apparently, not everyone was on board with Darcy's decision to use oxen instead of mules.[34] In fact, dissension had commenced within a week of the party's departure from Newark.

Gillespie recognized part of the problem. "The company to which I belong is composed of so many important personages. They all know too much. Each one is Sir Oracle and hence a revolution which threatens to disorganize our company. For my part I keep aloof and let them fight it out knowing full well that everything will be settled in time," he wrote in a letter addressed to his sister Mary. He described the situation as "agitated" and confessed to being so disillusioned that while in St. Louis he had paid for passage to return home but remained with the group out of commitment.[35]

Those opposing Darcy favored the use of mule teams such as the ones employed when Gillespie had traveled the Southwest years earlier. Private conversations about the pros and cons of each type of beast persisted among the men as they traveled from Pittsburgh to St. Louis. Mules were known to be the preferred stock of Santa Fe traders, and there was speculation that the journey from Independence to California could be shortened from four or six months to sixty days by using mules. Fourteen of the men decided to leave St. Louis early and proceed to Independence in advance of General Darcy, and most were planning to purchase mules. Among them was the team of Cartwright, Seely, and Woolsey, who took into their mess Isaac Overton. Caleb Boylston and Joseph Doty also dropped out of the Darcy party, as did Charles B. Gillespie, who joined with Joseph and George Martin.[36] The division was widening, and it was mostly outsiders who were splintering from Darcy's Newark Overland Company.

Cyrus Currier met John W. Shaff, Augustus Baldwin, and George Sayre in St. Louis and then made his way by steamer to Independence, where on April 4 he caught up with the Darcy group just as the mules-versus-oxen crisis was playing out. The next day Currier found Darcy and the other men encamped at an old log church outside of town, where they were spending their days training ox teams, repairing guns, organizing wagons, and fine-tuning their inventories.[37] Currier, the devoted family man who preferred traveling independently, made his decision to explore options with various parties using mules. He was joined by Shaff.

The *St. Louis Republican* was unaware of the dispute when it published an article on April 9: "A company from New Jersey, styled the Newark Overland Company, are in the field, under the command of Gen. John S. Darcy. They have eleven wagons, eleven tents, sufficient mules, and provisions for six months. The company is provided with necessary maps, a field glass, compass and telescope, and each man armed with a revolving pistol, double barreled gun and rifle." Apparently the correspondent did not know about Darcy's decision to use oxen.

The St. Louis paper went on to identify the names of forty-two men and noted that both Darcy and Pennington were accompanied by servants. Among the new names on the roster were Freeman, Woodruff, and Birdsall, all of whom had joined the mess of jeweler Henry L. Johnson. The reporter included Shaff and Currier as members of Darcy's company, though both men had already split from the group in favor of mules. Absent from any mention in the list were John B. Overton and Augustus Baldwin.[38] It is believed that Baldwin returned home, possibly after receiving a letter en route from his wife, Mary, who by late March must have realized she was pregnant with their first child.

Another name would soon disappear from company rosters. Joseph T. Doty headed for home after being discouraged by the debate over which mode of travel to pursue. It was just as likely that he was homesick and frightened, as were many would-be forty-niners, by the stories "told by the Santa Fe Traders, and others who have been over the route, of Indians, and suffering by hunger and sickness." The situation was described in a letter to the *Newark Daily Advertiser,* probably written by a Darcy party member. It went on to explain that many others might have considered turning around "if they were not afraid of being laughed at."[39] Doty arrived back in Elizabethtown on April 26, leaving his partner, Caleb Boylston, scrambling to make alternate arrangements.[40]

Still, the majority of the men were optimistic about their impending travel and expressed rosy outlooks in letters home to their loved ones. They had already survived unexpected adversity in getting to Independence, the least of which was the mules-versus-oxen dispute. The difficult crossing of the Alleghenies had challenged their physical endurance, but it would pale in comparison to the hardships they would suffer later at the high elevations of the Sierra and in the nearly waterless desert basins.

On the steamer from St. Louis to Independence, Darcy and his associates had experienced a harrowing eight days that should have been a restful four-day sojourn up the Missouri. The steamer *Highland Mary* hit a snag in the river, one of the hidden bars of sediment that challenged navigators and river pilots. The vessel subsequently collided with another ship, causing serious damage to the stateroom of Newark alderman Dolph Pennington, but fortunately not to Pennington himself. The prolonged trip caused tempers to flare, and fights broke out among the passengers.[41] Altogether, their time on the Missouri devoured their patience and tarnished the luster of reaching the western boundary of the United States. In contrast, Currier's most difficult time on the Missouri came one week later, when he attempted to avoid military men on board who were demonstrative in their drinking and swearing.[42]

The fights, snags, and collision were fiascos of sorts, but soon dissipated and amounted to little more than inconvenience for the Newark men. It was a pestiferous traveler on board the steamer that raised frightening concerns when illness swiftly and violently struck two deck passengers aboard the *Highland Mary*, leaving them near death within a matter of hours.[43] Cholera, the invisible and undetectable voyager, had invaded St. Louis and caused mortuaries in the Gateway City to fill.

The medical community of 1849 understood many things about the lethal illness, much of it gathered through observation and shared analysis of the previous epidemic that had taken place seventeen years earlier. India was often blamed for being the epicenter of the disease and for launching it outward to the populous centers of the world.[44] It was known that the disease followed people and waterways, specifically "the course of rivers on which there was much traffic," the *Newark Daily Advertiser* reported.[45] This explained why St. Louis, at the confluence of two significant rivers and absorbing waves of emigrants in the spring of 1849, was one of the hardest-hit cities. To think that Cyrus Currier, a man who had embarked on a westward journey to improve his health, had drunk a pitcher of potentially deadly water!

Dr. Darcy was wise to the effects of cholera, but like the health profession in general, he did not know the exact secret of its microscopic transmittal. Still, unlike those who speculated that vegetables or lightning were the culpable conduits of the disease, he believed it to be spread through some contagion. His experience treating cholera patients in Newark in 1832 would be put to use in 1849 on the Oregon Trail, a route mapped by Capt. John C. Fremont that followed the plains-coursing Platte River, a natural channel for *cholera morbus*.

For the time being, however, the Newark Overland Company remained cholera-free during their stay in Independence, having avoided contact with the deck passengers of the *Highland Mary*. Currier's muddy drinking water had also been free of the lethal bacteria. Thus, the mules-versus-oxen dispute remained their most immediate challenge.

The meeting in Independence that led to a final split of the company became heated at times, and the exchange of insinuating remarks, coupled with man-to-man challenges, degraded the previous civility.[46] Darcy would not hear of changing his plans. His wisdom and decision-making ability had led him to the top of the medical profession, the military, and a leading transportation company. The Newark Overland Company would cross the country with teams of sturdy oxen capable of sustaining provisions and wagons across two thousand miles.

Charles B. Gillespie, who had selected mules, wrote to his acquaintances in Newark with his own account of the dispute. "You have doubtless heard that our party has been divided. The members generally were in favor of taking Mules for the journey. The General insisted upon Oxen. The question 'Mules or Oxen' produced controversy, hardly less vehement or important than the contest between the rival roses in England. The result is that five wagons have attached themselves to the mules, and expect to reach California in 60 days, leaving the oxen to drag their 'lazy length along.' They *may* accomplish the journey within 5 months!"[47] Gillespie could not resist using sarcasm to make his point.

The mules-versus-oxen split left General Darcy with twenty-four loyal men under his leadership, a number that included the two young black boys he never neglected to enumerate as part of his company. In a letter to his family on April 22, he stated that he felt the number was "enough for efficiency, expedition, entire safety, comfort, and all that relates to our welfare."[48]

After the split, relations between the parties remained respectful and cordial. One Saturday in late April, Benjamin Casterline along with Darcy's two relatives, Charles and Andrew Gray, rode ten miles to the camp of Gillespie, where they enjoyed dinner and spirits around a campfire.[49]

Like Gillespie, members of the Newark Overland Company privately employed sarcasm in regard to the other group, calling those opting to travel with Gillespie and his mules "our Jackass friends."[50]

Case closed, for now. California was beckoning.

Chapter 9

Golden California

The name "California" was made popular by a best-selling sixteenth-century Spanish novel. The book describes the mythical island homeland of Queen Califia and her Amazon followers, located beyond the distant West Indies, far from the Iberian Peninsula. The name was a natural choice for the Spaniards, who had discovered a similarly compelling region along the northeast Pacific Rim around 1540.[1] For almost three hundred years Spain laid claim to the territory whose settlement never grew beyond Franciscan missions that dotted the coastline. The famed Spanish explorers, notorious for combing the New World for treasure, failed to discover the enormous bounty of gold buried by geologic forces in the foothills of the Sierra Nevada.[2]

Mexico won its independence from Spain in 1821, taking control of Alta (Upper) and Baja (Lower) California. For the next quarter century the Mexican population was unmotivated to uproot and resettle in the remote region. The ineptness of the government, combined with citizens' lack of interest, invited the rest of the world to make claims on the resource-rich territory. Russia had been eager to colonize California for decades and had established a successful settlement at Fort Ross just eighty miles north of San Francisco. That venture had failed when the fur trading industry was wiped out in the early 1840s, ending Russia's efforts to compete for West Coast resources.

By 1846 Alta California had become ripe for annexation, and US military power stood poised to oblige. Capt. John Charles Fremont played a pivotal role.

Fremont's mere presence opened the way for controversy and theatrics. A Southerner of French descent and illegitimate birth, he possessed a reckless disposition. He had achieved fame by leading US Army expeditions in the western territories and officially mapping the Oregon Trail with the guidance of renowned frontiersman Kit Carson. Fremont best described himself in a letter detailing his attendance at an Indian feast of honor in which dog was served to him from a large pot: "Feeling something move behind me, I looked round, and found I had taken my seat among a litter of fat young puppies. Had I been nice in such matters, the prejudices of civilization might have interfered with my tranquility; but fortunately, I am not of delicate nerves, and continued to empty my platter."[3]

Fremont's bravado also propelled him into the limelight socially. In 1841 he met and proposed to Jessie Benton, the sixteen-year-old daughter of Missouri senator Thomas Hart Benton. The media reported that the powerful senator "objected to the proposition *in toto*. 'His daughter, educated for a *Prince*, was not going to marry a *Corporal*.'" The couple boldly defied him and fled to the Gatsby Tavern in Alexandria, Virginia, where they secretly exchanged their vows.[4]

Senator Benton was an intimidating, boisterous frontier politician known in Washington as an activist for Manifest Destiny, the expansion of the United States across the continent.[5] In the 1840s his home state of Missouri was situated on the western boundary of the United States. Expanding the nation's border and acquiring additional western lands had the potential to bring thousands of emigrants through his state, especially to St. Louis and towns along the Missouri River, where merchants sat waiting to supply the western movement. The accompanying economic boom would further elevate Benton's political career.

Jessie Benton Fremont, a strong-natured young woman with captivating dark features and radiant auburn hair, was as spirited as her father, much to both his delight and his displeasure. Once Senator Benton calmed down over the elopement, he used his political influence to position his son-in-law with the prestigious Corps of Topographical Engineers that accomplished two noted western expeditions by 1845. It was under the veil of another western exploration that Fremont was sent to Monterey, California, in December 1845.[6]

Alta California was then a politically confused region, with control fluctuating between alcaldes of the Mexican government and California-born rancheros known as Californios. By the mid-1840s immigrants from the United States had assimilated into the California fabric and were beginning to exert commercial and political muscle alongside the competing Mexican and Californio factions.

By the close of 1845, US envoy Thomas O. Larkin was working quietly with Californio leaders on the possibility of putting the territory under US jurisdiction. The Californios, often at odds with the Mexican government, preferred to develop the resources of their homeland with newcomers from the United States. After all, Mexico had resorted to building up California's population by banishing prisoners to this distant territory. Larkin's goal was to shift the region to an "American identity, provided that such an identity be freely chosen and that the language, customs, religion, and land titles of Mexican California be respected by the United States following affiliation or annexation."[7] The last thing Larkin and the Californios wanted was to have US military aggression play a role. The arrival of Captain Fremont aroused suspicion if not ire.

Over the next six months Fremont traversed Northern California, dismissing the territorial governor's demands that he retreat from the region. Fremont moved from Sutter's Fort far north into Oregon and back to Central California, where he allegedly received secret dispatches ordering him to proceed with a military takeover.[8] Along the way he masterfully incited local communities to rebel against their prevailing governments. On June 14, 1846, an American settlement at Sonoma succeeded in furthering Fremont's underhanded mission. Settlers there raised a primitive flag made of plain cotton with the symbols of a star and grizzly bear stained into the fabric with lampblack and pokeberry juice.[9] Without a shot being fired, they declared independence for the California Republic. In early July, US soldiers led by Captain Fremont joined the rebels in Sonoma and hoisted the Stars and Stripes alongside the Bear Flag, claiming the land for the United States. On July 7, under confused circumstances, a US flag was similarly raised at the territorial capital in Monterey. It was now understood that the territory would be taken by force.

A battle for California ensued, calling into action the US Navy under the command of New Jersey native Robert F. Stockton and additional army forces led by Newark native Stephen Kearny. In January 1847 California was surrendered in the vicinity of El Pueblo de Nuestra Señora la Reina de los Ángeles, not to ranking officers Stockton or Kearny, but to Captain Fremont.

The next round of California drama involved military infighting for the interim governorship of the territory. Commodore Stockton, who was departing for the East, had quarreled with General Kearny and left control to Fremont. Kearny believed he was rightfully in charge because he outranked Fremont, but he chose not to challenge the unpredictable Southerner. Instead he patiently waited for the arrival of the territory's officially appointed governor, Richard B. Mason. Kearny then escorted Fremont back to Fort Leavenworth, where upon arrival he was arrested on charges of mutiny and misconduct and ordered to the nation's capital.[10]

The three-month court-martial took place in the Washington, DC, armory. Lt. E. Fitzgerald Beale, who had transported the message of California gold to Washington, served as a defense witness for Fremont, while Senator Benton provided counsel. In February 1848 the military court found Fremont guilty of all charges. President Polk quickly intervened and issued the order that "Lieut. Col. Fremont will accordingly be released from arrest, and will resume his sword, and report for duty."[11]

Disgusted by the treatment from his military peers, Fremont "resigned his place in the army, upon the ground that he was not conscious of having done anything to merit the finding of the Court."[12] Encouraged by his father-in-law, Senator Benton, he made plans to rebuild his career by leading yet another western expedition.

Prior to having been escorted east by Kearny, Fremont had asked Thomas O. Larkin to purchase land for him in California.[13] This Larkin had done, but it was not a track near Santa Cruz as Fremont had expected. Instead Larkin obtained a large land grant on the Mariposas Creek in the foothills of the Sierra Nevada, still considered a desolate region. Fremont was disappointed with the choice, believing it too rocky and remote for viable farming.

Fremont headed back to California in late 1848, leading a band of explorers privately funded by associates of Senator Benton with the

Thomas Oliver Larkin, the US consul at Monterey prior to California's annexation, witnessed the gold rush frenzy firsthand. His colorful and insightful descriptions are believed to have been published in newspapers under the pen name "Paisano." Courtesy of the Print Collection, Miriam and Ira D. Wallach Division of Art, Prints and Photographs, New York Public Library, Astor, Lenox and Tilden Foundations (1552907).

purpose of locating a more direct southerly passage to California. Just prior to his departure he learned that his nemesis Kearny had contracted yellow fever and died in October. Fremont himself was courting death by attempting to cross the Rocky Mountains in winter.

Jessie Benton Fremont made arrangements to meet her husband in San Francisco the following spring and departed New York aboard the *Crescent City* on March 15, 1849, just two weeks after the Newark Overland Company had started their overland journey.[14] She was headed for Panama, the insect-infested isthmus crossing, and the crowded Pacific port where she and her young daughter would face the same delays as thousands of gold seekers. During her travels she would receive an alarming report from Lt. E. Fitzgerald Beale concerning her husband's disastrous attempt to reach California across the southern Rockies. Beale, who was again traveling from California to Washington, received the news en route and relayed it to Mrs. Fremont in Panama.[15]

The newly appointed California governor, Persifer F. Smith, had broken out of Panama's backlog a few weeks prior to Jessie Fremont's arrival. While still stranded in Panama, Smith had submitted a letter to the US consul there with the expectation that it be circulated among South and Central American nations. It amounted to a warning to foreigners that trespassing on federal property of the United States was unlawful, that taking gold from public land was the equivalent of stealing, and that such laws would be enforced during his command.[16] By March, Governor Smith was taking the reins of California's military government from Col. R. B. Mason, who must have smiled to himself and dusted off his hands as he relinquished the impossible assignment. Despite being one of the highest-ranking officers in the US Army, Smith was in no way prepared for the quagmire he found waiting for him in California.

Californians had been pushed to the brink of frustration because Washington had failed to establish any real political structure following the annexation. They had struggled through 1847 in the wake of the US takeover with four temporary military governors, including dueling Fremont and Kearny. Then had come the madness of the initial gold rush in 1848 and the influx of a population with no intention of contributing to the territory's civic stability. After a second year of congressional ineptness and failure to provide a legal framework and a formal path to statehood, residents were galvanized to take control of their own destiny.

On December 11, 1848, citizens held a meeting at Pueblo de San Jose to discuss the formation of a provisional government.

By the time Persifer Smith took stock of his new post in March 1849, Californians had already scheduled elections and were in no mood for a fifth temporary military governor. The San Francisco newspaper *Alta California* voiced support for the citizens, saying that "in the neglect of Congress, they have a right to form a government for themselves," and further rebuffed "the right of the United States to tax the people, when they give them neither government nor representation."[17]

While the citizens fumed, scores of ships continued to arrive into San Francisco Bay, California's ideal natural port, where as many as one hundred vessels sat abandoned in the crowded harbor. One year before, there had been but a single ship moored in the same location. There was no easy way to unload passengers and cargo from the steady stream of rigged and steam-powered vessels because there were no wharves.[18] There were no wharves because there was no lumber. There was no lumber because there was no manpower to mill felled trees. There was no manpower because virtually all men had been pulled by dreams and fantasy to the gold region. And the gold region was still emerging from winter, high waters, impassable roads, and dire sickness.[19]

The exploding population was entering the territory from points of origin that spanned the globe. Persifer Smith noted that Chinese, Sandwich Islanders (Hawaiians), Chileans, Peruvians, Prussians, Mexicans, French, English, and Irish outnumbered US citizens.[20] They spoke different languages, had unfamiliar religious beliefs, and practiced their own cultural rituals. Their only common ground was the hunger for wealth. With the same frustration experienced by Governor Mason, Smith realized that there was no way to enforce the temporary military rule he was expected to provide or the minimal law that remained from the remnant alcalde system. The warning he issued from Panama was laughable, and Californians were not impressed with their new leader. The situation continued to make the national news: "It appears that the authority of General Persifer F. Smith, Governor of California, has been repudiated by the people, and that his proclamation forbidding foreigners to trespass on the gold region, has been treated with disdain. We are not surprised at the reception which the proclamation met. It was a ridiculous emanation, and its publication was exceedingly silly."[21]

Governor Smith was foremost the commanding officer of the Third Pacific Army and recognized that his situation was precarious. His tenure as governor had lasted only six weeks when a subordinate officer, Gen. Bennett Riley, the sixth and last military governor of California, arrived with orders to assume the administrative duties of the territory and take over the rapidly imploding situation.[22] More harsh editorials followed:

> The discovery of gold in California, while electrifying the world, seems to have entirely paralyzed the government to which the mighty treasure belongs. There is an in-rush toward it at once of people from all quarters of the globe, but especially of countries contiguous to the Pacific, gentle and simple, paupers and knaves and felon convicts, foreigners, all, who lay their course for San Francisco and the Sacramento gold mines—the American gold mines—armed with pickaxes and spades, and washing machines, and bottles and bags in which to carry away their prizes,—without in the slightest degree troubling themselves to ask what right *they* have to enter the Dorado of another people and pick up treasures that do not belong to them.[23]

Governor Riley wisely endorsed the self-government being organized by the frustrated population of California. He issued a new proclamation calling for a statewide constitutional convention to be held in September 1849. In reality, the problem was not with Smith or Riley but with the US Congress.

Californians were keenly aware that the paralysis in Washington was due to the country's conflict over slavery. They knew that the issue was affecting their territorial status and feared that the "much vexed subject of slavery—the perpetual fire-brand of dissension between the North and South" would "prove an insuperable barrier to dispatch" and cause a delay in legislation providing them with an official government.[24] The philosophy of Manifest Destiny had agitated the situation. As US territories were being granted statehood in the 1840s—Florida, Texas, Iowa, Wisconsin, and soon California—politicians struggled to maintain a balance of voting power between the rival regional factions.

The majority of Californians opposed slavery. Still, Southerners were not ready to concede the matter. In March 1849 a Georgia man encouraged slaveholders to emigrate to California under a united front: "To be successful, we must have *strength,* which can only be secured by associating in sufficient numbers for personal security, and for the protection of private property against all ordinary encroachments." By "private property" he was referring to slaves, and he recommended that each gold seeker "shall take with him at least one, and not more than four male slaves." In reality, there was little chance of any form of slavery taking hold. The *Alta California* confirmed, "The character of emigration to California—the large preponderance of northerners—has settled the question more surely than a whole library of statutes could do, no matter how carefully prepared or how strongly written."[25]

Many reports reached the East Coast in the spring of 1849 suggesting that a state of anarchy was consuming California: "Owing to the immense number of people arriving at San Francisco, the whole country was considered in a very insecure state. There was a great want felt for the presence of an adequate military force, and for the extension of the laws of the United States over the territory, in the absence of which, much trouble was anticipated."[26] Governor Riley's September convention could not come soon enough.

The near-anarchic situation deterred no one. Every day throughout March, April, and May 1849, people arrived in San Francisco literally by the boatload. There, with no wharves, they disembarked onto tenders shuttling them to land. Some looked around and recognized the inefficiency of the situation and envisioned wharves. Some saw a city of tents growing up the hills overlooking the bay and realized the need for rooming houses to shelter the throng of newcomers. One enterprising tinsmith witnessed unequipped men rushing to the goldfields and recognized the market for tin pans.[27] In the midst of the chaos and exploding population there were entrepreneurial opportunities on many fronts.

While it seemed that California was being crushed by the weight of immigrants, another wave was amassing at staging points to the east— St. Joseph and Independence, Missouri, and Kanesville, Iowa (now Council Bluffs). And boatloads more were traveling up the Missouri River and arriving daily in these jumping-off towns. Along the way they supplied their operations from Missouri merchants, just as Senator Benton had so hoped they would when he opportunistically sent his son-in-law, John C. Fremont, to chart the course to the Pacific and open the West to settlement.

Once in Independence, eager emigrants, members of the Newark Overland Company among them, encamped on the prairies waiting for spring and the emergence of grass along the riverbanks. There were estimates that some 30,000 people were about to bolt across the prairie and merge into a single line of traffic on the Oregon Trail. As soon as conditions would permit, they would storm toward California—some led by mules, some by oxen.

John Fremont would nearly perish on his quest to traverse the Rockies to reach California over the winter of 1848–49. Jessie Fremont arrived in San Francisco on June 4, 1849, eager to confirm that her husband had, in fact, survived the disastrous crossing.[28] She was barely twenty-five years old and had spent eight tumultuous years married to the famed military renegade some twelve years her senior, during which time they had become national celebrities. Americans found the vicissitudes of their sensational lives captivating, and the media exploited any and all news about the famous couple. John Fremont's near-fatal journey to California was chronicled in the press with endless misinformation. Over the previous two years the Fremonts had rejoiced in the triumph of California's annexation and suffered from the public humiliation of a court-martial.

Finally reunited in San Francisco, their recent period of despair behind them, they would swing back to the height of elation upon learning that their remote Mariposas property was in the heart of the placer country and was indeed imbedded with millions of dollars' worth of gold.

Chapter 10

Rolling Out

Independence, Missouri, was brimming with the influx of gold seekers in April 1849. Rooming houses were filled, leaving the majority of transients to set up camp on the outskirts of town and live out of their newly purchased wagons and tents. The same held true for the other jumping-off towns of St. Joseph and Kanesville situated north of Independence along the Missouri. Each location estimated its temporary population at several thousand, promising a season of unprecedented emigration. More people were arriving every day, and no one was leaving. No grass, no travel. Impatience and discontent were growing.

Like the men of Newark, many came to the Missouri River towns intending to travel with acquaintances from their home regions. The midwestern states were heavily represented, and companies demonstrated their local pride by using catchy names, such as the Live Hoosier Company, the Wolverine Rangers, and the Buckeye Rovers.[1] The camaraderie among midwesterners was noticeable, and some described in letters home their amusement at eastern companies: "We have another large company of the F. F. V.'s [First Families of Virginia], duly attended with their servants and iced champagne; another starched set from Boston, who find their satisfaction in abusing Mr. Polk and his war, but with Yankee consistency are rushing to obtain the wealth of a country secured us by the late administration."[2] The midwesterners would have also been amused at Charles Gray's breast pin and William T. Lewis's white funeral shirt.

Charles Gillespie was similarly fascinated by the number and character of the emigrants organizing for California. In a letter to his sister he wrote,

> You would be perfectly astonished to see the crowds that are preparing to emigrate to California. The whole country is filled with them. Men, women and children, all bound for the 'Diggins.' The exodus of the Israelites is nothing to it. There are some wagons fitted up with all the comforts of a parlor, carpets, devans, mirrors, tables, and every thing else needful to take it easy. These traveling parlors are intended for the women of whom there will be a considerable sprinkling. Some of the handsomest and wealthiest ladies in the west are preparing to emigrate. Some on horseback, some on mules, others in wagons and carriages.[3]

As a population, the emigrants were mostly men of respectable finances and solid reputations. By mid-April the estimated five thousand waiting to depart from Independence were growing tired of camping and of the tedious cooking and cleaning duties that accompanied their new lifestyle. Most were not used to such chores. One newspaper correspondent observed, "The emigrants, generally, are men of enterprise and energy, and from their conduct here, I should suppose them to be of that class of our citizens that would be an honor to any country. Many persons supposed that the 'gold regions' would be overrun with gangs of cut-throats and robbers; but from observation I have come to a very different conclusion."[4] Many companies traveled with their own physician, some with the luxury of an ambulance—a wagon to house the sick and carry the company's medical supplies.[5] General Darcy's group was representative of the organized regional companies, though its medicines and such would be carried in a common stock wagon along with tools and equipment.

Not everyone came to Independence attached to a hometown company. Gold seekers who came alone or who found themselves splintered from their original group scrambled to find last-minute travel options. The Pioneer Line was a commercial enterprise with openings for 120 passengers to travel aboard spring carriages with all provisions, driving, and protection provided for a fare of $200.[6] There were also large companies forming under the leadership of men who had previously traversed the overland route, including one that would be led by Edwin

Bryant, the former editor of the *Louisville Courier* who became the the de facto authority on overland travel with his popular guidebook *What I Saw in California.*

Another organizer was William H. Russell, an egotistical Missourian who had occasional military experience and went by the inflated and unearned title "Colonel." Three years earlier Russell had been the original leader of a large overland group that departed from Independence bound for California. Edwin Bryant had also been a member of the party, and his experiences during that journey provided the material for his guidebook. After several weeks on the trail the group had split, with Russell and Bryant proceeding ahead and arriving in California by late summer. The remainder of the party lagged behind and was caught in an early autumn snowstorm while attempting to cross the Sierra under the leadership of George Donner. The grizzly fate of the Donner Party shocked the country when the story came out in the press and was a driving factor pressuring travelers in 1849 to depart early in the season.

Russell was familiar not only with the nuances of overland travel, but also with the details of California's transition from Mexican province to US possession. In January 1847 he had been with John C. Fremont during the conquest at Cahuenga and had been present at the subsequent surrender of Alta California to the United States. When Fremont became acting governor, he named Russell the territorial secretary of state, the first person to hold the office for California.

Back in Independence in April 1849, Colonel Russell was arranging to lead another wagon train of emigrants to California. Many were swayed to join his ranks after hearing him proclaim that he knew the overland trails like he knew the streets of his hometown. The idea of a large company for mutual protection and division of labor, along with a confident and experienced leader, swelled the enlistment of Russell's camp. Cyrus Currier decided to travel with Russell, as did the team of Cartwright, Seely, and Woolsey. Several of the other Newark Overland Company mule defectors, including William Emery and his son, Boylston, Shaff, and Overton, also followed Russell, who set an early departure date, hoping to gain the distinction of being the first train to move out.[7]

Currier was sharing a wagon with Newark acquaintance and coworker Stephen Dehart and Dehart's nephew Wallace Cook. Unattached John W. Shaff was the fourth member of this group. For $355 they purchased a team of six mules, which would be used for pulling the wagon, riding, and packing supplies. They had wisely selected older Spanish mules that were accustomed to being hitched and gave the men very little resistance when they practiced harnessing and driving them prior to the departure.[8] Other groups found younger American mules to be quite a handful and suffered the humiliation of being dragged to and fro across campgrounds while struggling to make the animals compliant. The work of breaking mule and ox teams by inexperienced emigrants made for many comical scenes in encampments bordering jumping-off towns. One emigrant who prided himself in horsemanship woefully admitted to being ignorant in "muleology."[9]

Other final preparations continued throughout April, providing brisk commerce for merchants and tradesmen such as blacksmiths and wagon builders. As emigrants purchased and inventoried last-minute provisions, the weather dealt a harsh blow to the temporary tent communities surrounding Independence. Heavy rain on April 12 was followed by two days of temperatures cold enough to freeze water in buckets, and then snow on April 15.[10] The unseasonable cold held spring hostage, eroded the romance of western travel, and exposed the unpleasant reality that soon would become everyday life.

Despite the hostile weather plaguing the central prairies, wagons began to roll out as early as April 16, relocating to the Missouri state line about ten miles west of Independence. The movement of the first companies was met with excitement throughout the region, and for those impatient to travel, it signaled the end of the waiting period. Englishman William Kelly's group garnered a small following and received cheers as they paraded their caravan of mule teams, with twenty-five men all attired in uniforms of white trousers with green jackets and caps. As the first companies hit the trail, they were optimistic, overloaded, and playing the odds that nature would cooperate.[11]

Right before Cyrus Currier's departure, he received a letter from his wife, Nancy, and quickly composed a reply. He rushed it to the post office, his last opportunity to utilize the US mail before working his way to the Missouri boundary and his rendezvous with Colonel Russell. The following evening he spent a restless night in a wagon that was too cold for comfort or much sleep, and he awoke the next morning feeling initiated to the hardships of trail life.[12]

Companies that remained encamped at Independence believed that waiting until May 1 to depart would guarantee that their animals could be sufficiently pastured once on the trail. General Darcy deemed it prudent to wait the extra two weeks, although most of his Newark colleagues taking mules had already made their way toward the Missouri border and the Indian Territory beyond.

Charles Gillespie moved to the state line, but once there delayed his departure until conditions improved. During these idle days he used the time to write to his family in Freeport. Across the top of a letter to his sister Mary, dated April 22, 1849, he identified his location as "14 miles from Independence on the Santa Fe Road." He described the scene:

> I am writing this about 1/2 mile from camp, sitting on a rock which is on the margin of a noisy brook that keeps singing complainingly in my ear. Birds are overhead warbling among the budding trees, and violets are peeping from the green banks on every side. . . . When in Independence I was quite unwell and I once thought I would take the homeward route but this life seems to act like a charm. I feel better than I have for months back. It is a happy yet a lazy life this being about camp without anything in particular to engage one's attention. I exercise myself and horse by taking a gallop out upon the prairies.[13]

Mary was Gillespie's twin sister with whom he maintained a close relationship and to whom he wrote frequently. After describing the delights of spring on the prairie and expressing his optimistic view of his health, he went on to write that he had separated from Darcy's New Jersey company and was with five other men outfitted with two wagons and six mules. Two of the men were George and Joseph Martin, a nephew and uncle, both younger than Gillespie. They were considerable greenhorns, and in a subsequent letter to the *Newark Daily Advertiser* Gillespie described their awkwardness in adapting to camp chores: "J. is still too nice; he spends a half hour every morning washing, brushing his hair, scrubbing his teeth, and such like things as only belong peculiarly to the chamber at home. But never mind, he will improve by-and-by, and I have no doubt before the journey is half over will be as rough, ragged and dirty as myself."[14] Like other emigrants from eastern cities, the Martins may have been appalled at the personal habits of the frontiersmen surrounding them in Missouri, who had been observed by one diarist "to pick their teeth with their tobacco knives, an operation in which they appear to take great delight, spending a pleasurable post-prandial half hour in digging out the cavities and licking the blades."[15]

Gillespie's small team, nicknamed the Jackass friends by the Jerseymen, had signed on with Missouri brothers James and Benoni Hudspeth, leaders of yet another of the larger companies taking on rogue independents and orphans from divided companies.[16] The Hudspeths had previous overland trail experience, specifically exploring and mapping the routes west from the Great Salt Lake, where they had met and guided Bryant and Russell in 1846.

Cyrus Currier soon recognized that his decision to join Colonel Russell's party had been a mistake when company bylaws were announced absent of any democratic process. Currier, a principled man of New England roots, peacefully objected to the dictatorial process, which sent Russell into a rage in which he accused the Jerseymen of disrupting his outfit. Currier and his messmates immediately withdrew from Russell's wagon train, which, despite the preemptive start, had not progressed beyond the Missouri border, having spent five days waiting for news of sufficient grass. By the time Russell rolled his wagons onto the trail on April 24, his temper had cooled enough to invite the outcasts back into the company. Currier's mess refused and watched the early-morning departure of thirty teams and 120 men disappear across the rolling prairie. Cartwright, Seely, and Woolsey were among the party, as was Caleb Boylston, who was sharing a wagon with William Emery and his son. Currier was content with his decision in regard to Russell and spent the day repairing John Shaff's gun and tending to other practical matters.[17]

Two days later Currier's mess departed at 6:00 A.M., fully confident that traveling in a small group was their best option.[18] The same day, April 26, Joseph T. Doty arrived home in Elizabeth, New Jersey, having abandoned his quest for gold and his companion Boylston, who was somewhere on the prairie with the large, slow-moving train of Colonel Russell.[19]

Like Gillespie, General Darcy moved the remainder of his Newark Overland Company from Independence to the state line to wait for a final assurance of adequate grass for their animals. The group was now strongly unified in their loyalty to Darcy and had experienced no further dissension since the mules-versus-oxen showdown.

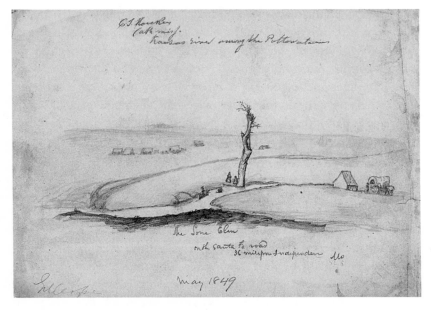

Lone Elm on the Santa Fe Trail, sketched by Charles B. Gillespie shortly after departing Independence, Missouri, May 1849. Courtesy of the Rees-Jones Collection.

In Newark friends and family anxiously awaited news of their adventuresome men, some of which was provided by Doty upon his return. Thomas Young had also decided to go back home and likewise had news of his less-than-satisfactory experience seeking El Dorado.[20] Letters from the frontier had been frequent, and the *Newark Daily Advertiser* was prompt in reporting excerpts of those shared with the newspaper by friends and family members. The flow of information was mostly one way, as the distribution of mail to moving encampments on the prairie was not easily done. While in Independence, Currier was fortunate to have received a letter from Nancy. He described its arrival as "better than its bulk in Gold."[21] There is little doubt that Darcy did not learn about the birth of a granddaughter until he reached California. Eliza Gray Darcy was born to his son, Henry, on April 17.[22]

When the first of the California-bound travelers ventured across the Missouri border onto land known as Indian Territory, the journey so long anticipated and imagined finally became a reality. They were no longer within the confines of the United States, and the vistas filled them with exhilaration. One emigrant wrote, "As I cast my eye over the broad surface of the prairie it looked like a perfect level; still it is a series of immense undulations, like the huge lazy swells of the Atlantic in a calm."[23] With similar awe Alexander Cartwright wrote of seeing "the most beautiful country diversified by every variety of scenery, in many places so quiet and exquisitely homely that we asked ourselves many times where were the saxony farm houses, the lowing herds & the waving fields of grain, that should be here," and noted that "a quiet solitude the most profound reigned supreme, no signs of life but the countless flocks of Plover."[24] There was no shortage of wonderment expressed by those with pen and paper.

The first days on the road introduced the emigrants to two obstacles that would become both routine and troublesome for the duration of their journey—river crossings and Indians. Most parties reached the Wakarusa River on the second day. Its crossing required the arduous process of lowering the wagons by rope down steep limestone banks and hauling them up on the other side. Other river-crossing hazards were quickly learned. One emigrant, swimming his horse across, nearly drowned when his mount struggled in the current and threw him into the river with his boot stuck in the stirrup.[25]

After crossing the Kansas River, Cartwright understood the disadvantages of traveling in a large party. "There has been a great deal of dissatisfaction today in consequence of the great number of waggons in our train, as an accident to one detains the whole train," he wrote in his journal. "I do not think that we shall be able to go on much longer without a division of the party."[26] Cartwright and the other New Jersey wagons would indeed separate from Russell's train and move forward together, but not as an officially organized company. Currier's mess caught up with and passed Russell's outfit, eventually meeting up with the Cartwright party. The mule defectors would continue to travel westward in parallel camps, staying in close communication and occasionally swapping members. The eclectic party of William Kelly, with its matching green-and-white attire, was also moving in close proximity to the Cartwright and Currier wagons.

The first Indians encountered by emigrants on the trail west of Independence were the Pottawatomies, who had originated in the Great Lakes region but, due to settlement and statehood, had been forcibly relocated to the northeastern corner of present-day Kansas and placed under the protection of US Indian agents. The government had employed merchants and tradesmen within the protected land to serve the tribal population. Emigrants passing through soon learned that services such as blacksmithing could not be performed without permission of the Indian agent in charge or the Pottawatomi chief, both of whom understood their power and the potential for profit.[27]

Emigrants observed that some of the Pottawatomies appeared to have French Canadian blood. Currier wrote, "They are very mixed with the French Canadian, some of them nearly White." Christian missions— Baptist and Catholic—were operating schools in the territory to educate the Natives with the intent to assimilate them into lifestyles compatible with the settled population east of the Missouri River. Many journal writers in 1849 described the unusual manner of dress adopted by the Pottawatomies. They were "attired in ill-fitting American costume; the great feature of the dress, and the one on which they principally plumed themselves, being very lofty shirt collars and projecting frills, adorned with great platter brooches of stained glass."[28] Cartwright described one who "was in shape a perfect Apollo, and sat on his horse, a beautiful & spirited animal—as though his was part of him, he was dressed in a blue 'Breech cloth,' a bandana kerchief in turban form around his head, his feet shoed with neat close fitting moccasins, while for upper dress he had about a dozen kerchiefs of different gay colors—the ends knotted together on one shoulder while the flag ends passed under the opposite arm and streamed in the wind."[29]

In his journal Cartwright declared the Pottawatomies to be "the wealthiest tribe under the protection of the United States."[30] Other accounts supported this observation: "We were in expectation of getting a supply of moccasins here, but those educated country gentlemen now deem such occupations entirely beneath them, leaving mean employments of that kind to their unenlightened brethren in the far west."[31]

The prospect of encountering Native Americans was very much anticipated by the emigrants as they crossed into designated Indian Territory and began the march across tribal lands. The reports that trickled into stateside newspapers were often exaggerated, with inflated language portraying the Indians as "savages" and "thieves." Still, the educated eastern men brought with them to the frontier a sense of concern for the Native populations. The country had been divided and human rights sensitivities had been sparked in regard to several incidents where government intervention and relocation of tribes had resulted in tragic outcomes.

The most publicized of these tragedies involved Seminole chief Osceola, imprisoned for refusing to move his followers away from Florida. When Osceola died in prison in 1838, the liberal communities reacted, particularly those with New England roots. Cyrus Currier was so moved by the injustice that he named his next child, born in 1841, after the Seminole leader. The 1850 Census enumerated no less than one hundred boys named Osceola.

Spring at last appeared on the prairie near the Missouri border, with warming temperatures and extended hours of daylight. It was good for hunting and fishing, with more food being brought into camp, but it meant coping with thick swarms of mosquitoes and other annoyances from wildlife. While there was fear that rattlesnakes would slither into bedrolls, the biting insects were far more troublesome. Travelling near the Cartwright and Currier teams, William Kelly described the discomfort: "It is a dire but inexorable necessity that compels the poor prairie traveller to pitch his tent every evening in the neighborhood of water, where, instead of finding rest, he finds the insatiable mosquitoes awaiting him, who invariably put forth their entire powers of persecution."[32]

At last grass sprouted in abundance, painting riverbanks in vibrant green and signaling the all clear for those still waiting to depart. Darcy's party had spent a month encamped and finally departed as planned on May 1, when the company of eight wagons and twenty-five men moved west beyond the US border. Despite all the preparations, the high spirits of the party spiraled into frustration in a matter of hours when two wagon tongues broke.[33] The men were forced to spend their second day camped at Point of Woods, making repairs as multitudes of wagons streamed by. They also waited there for a supply of corn to be delivered, which would supplement the grass and nourish their animals for the first week of travel.[34] Currier and others who had moved out five days earlier had also taken corn and other grain for the mules.[35] Gillespie had hired a team to drive a wagon stocked with feed to accompany them for the first eighty miles.[36]

The Newark company was again moving on May 3, the same day that Gillespie's train headed out.[37] Darcy's nephew Charles G. Gray, serving as the company secretary, had begun writing detailed entries in one of the leather-bound journals he had packed in New York. After the broken wagon tongues, Gray reported that his feet were severely blistered from walking much of the third day. May 4 brought more bad news when rain fell and turned the road into thick slop. Gray wrote that the mud was "very bad around our wagon & *in it too,* being carried in on our big boots, & everything in such a wet, cold, muddy & cheerless condition, that many of us regretted we ever started for the golden prize."[38] It was not the adventure they had all come halfway across the country to experience, and it was only four days old.

An explosion of wagons hit the trail during the first days of May, creating a traffic nightmare that thwarted forward progress. From the top of a ridge as many as two hundred teams could be seen in a continuous line marked by the dark, muddy road and the contrasting white wagon covers. From a distance some companies could be identified by the color of their painted wagons and some by canvas covers numbered or imprinted with a name or slogan.

There was more rain again on the fifth day, slowing the already crawling pace. Some wagons were mired in ruts up to their hubs, requiring stock teams to be doubled to pull them out, further delaying those behind. After a day's travel of twelve miles, Darcy's company reached the banks of the Wakarusa, where they camped for the night, pleasantly surprised to see a clearing moonlit sky.[39]

General Darcy ordered his company to rise early the next morning and cross the Wakarusa ahead of the scores of wagons close on their heels. Anxiety was mounting with the plethora of delays incurred in just five days, and there was already anticipation of a backlog at the Kansas River ferry crossing. Darcy hoped to jump ahead of some trains before the mass of wheels and hooves could further damage the trail. It was Sunday, and a number of groups would refrain from traveling in order to honor the Sabbath, but Darcy's wagons would proceed.[40] Not even the faithful Robert Bond objected.

The Wakarusa was successfully forded, and the Newark Overland Company passed into Pottawatomi country, where a better road surface improved the pace. It was warm, and the rolling vistas and the sighting of a wolf gave the men a sense of the frontier they had imagined. Temperaments improved, too. The Kansas River was ahead, and wagons were lining up to be escorted across.

The men's spirits were soaring after logging two full days of forward movement, but then they were stopped in their tracks by one of the fears of overland travel. Ironically, while waterways provided the vital sustenance of life to those on the trail, they also dealt consequences. Darcy knew immediately—cholera had struck the Newark Overland Company. It was May 10, 1849.[41]

The same evening, a world away in New York City, twenty-two people were shot dead or mortally wounded by police and military guardsmen who had been called in by a newly elected mayor to control a riot at the Astor Place Opera House. Located between Broadway and the Bowery in lower Manhattan and patronized by the city's wealthy aristocracy, the opera house was more than a venue for entertainment, it represented social standing. Around the corner was the Broadway Theater, home to actors whose fans lived in lower-class neighborhoods. Tension that had developed between the two clienteles over the years came to a head that night. Working-class fans purchased tickets to a performance of *Macbeth* at the Opera House intending to disrupt the production and avenge the reputation of their own star Shakespearian actor. Violence erupted and spilled into the streets, and there military units were ordered to fire into the crowd.[42]

Most of those killed were spectators, and one of the first to fall was a young Wall Street broker by the name of George W. Gedney.[43] News of the violence filled papers across the country, but would not reach the remote Indian Territory 1,200 miles to the west, where Gedney's first cousin Charles Gedney Gray was camped beside the Kansas River tending to his critically ill messmate Col. John R. Crockett.[44]

The Cartwright and Currier teams continued to lead the wave of emigration to California, speeding across the plains toward Fort Kearny, gaining time and miles over those who had waited for optimum conditions.

Chapter 11

Scramble to Fort Kearny

Clifornia-bound gold seekers were surprised to see a number of fine
greyhounds at the remote outpost of Fort Kearny.[1] They were kept
by some of the officers there who enjoyed taking them out for a spirited wolf hunt. However, the sporting dogs were about the only thing to
favorably impress the first emigrant parties who arrived at the military
station. Most found the facility dilapidated, with oddly formed buildings made of sod, mud, and logs—hardly a fort to most observers. A
sawmill turned by horses and mules was under construction, representing
the only productive enterprise besides the shriveling plots of vegetables
destined to fail in the sweltering months ahead. As bad as the structures
appeared, the enlisted men looked worse. Described as a shabby bunch,
"a most unsoldierly-looking lot," they were, in one observer's words,
"unshaven, unshorn, with patched uniforms, and lounging gait."[2]

In fairness, Fort Kearny had been operational less than a year and had
no advance warning that thousands would pass by and pass judgment in
1849. Three years earlier Congress had signed legislation authorizing a
series of military forts to be established on the road to Oregon to aid in
emigration to the Northwest. After briefly locating Fort Kearny along the
Missouri River, the War Department directed that it be resituated adjacent to Grand Island on the Platte River, a strategic site first envisioned
by Lewis and Clark and later by John C. Fremont.[3]

The site planned for the fort was designated as Pawnee territory. A
sixty-mile strip of land along the river was acquired by a treaty dated

August 6, 1848, "lately made by Lieutenant Col. Ludwell E. Powell, commanding officer . . . with four confederated bands of Pawnee Indians," reported the *New York Herald*.[4] The impoverished Indian nation received $2,000 in supplies, including blankets and guns, for the right to the land. The founding officers christened the post Fort Childs, but the name would change back to honor the deceased Stephen W. Kearny before the year was out. A battalion that had been appropriated approximately $15,000 was dispatched and spent several months constructing meager shelters out of the only abundant building material found on the premises—dirt. A *Missouri Republican* correspondent put his own more sensational spin on the situation: "The Battalion has now been in the service one year, and can show two buildings nearly half completed, one is a sod stable, and the other a store-house. As these buildings have only cost the United States $200,000 [*sic*] each in their incomplete state, it is difficult to say what sum Uncle Sam will have to shell out to finish them."[5]

The primary purpose for the military posts along the Oregon Trail was to protect travelers from Indians. In the immediate vicinity of Fort Kearny, those Indians were Pawnees who had agreed, by terms of the 1848 treaty, to maintain peaceful relations with whites. This effectively relegated the tribe to land north of the Platte River, forcing them into the territory of the powerful Sioux. The Sioux pushed them back, pressuring the Pawnees to remain close to the river, and thus right in the path of the westward movement. The results were tension, skirmishes, and Indian exposure to diseases carried by the emigrants. Over the years smallpox and cholera had already claimed large numbers of the dwindling tribe, and still more had perished at the hands of the neighboring Sioux and other tribes. By 1849 it was said that the Pawnees were a desperate nation, forced to beg and steal for survival. One journal writer described their plight: "The ancient *prestige* of their supremacy vanishing . . . and as their power and influence decayed, the debasing spirit of theft and treachery grew up amongst them, banishing every trace of that innate nobleness and chivalry which is still to be found in the Indian race, making the terms Pawnee and thief synonymous."[6]

The Cartwright and Currier parties reached Fort Kearny on May 11, within days of the first overland arrivals of the season. Seeing the sparse premises made Currier homesick, and he stayed only long enough to mail another letter to his beloved wife, Nancy. Like everyone entering the territory, the group was wary of the Pawnees. They began overnight guard duty to protect stock, as did other companies traveling nearby.

While emigrants initially feared the Pawnees, they soon realized the sad situation of the once-grand nation, causing one diarist to write, "The great warriors, . . . terror of the plains, turned out to be a sadly reduced starving . . . race! They begged me for bread, opened their dingy robes, and exhibited their prominent ribs and breastbones. As they were actually starving, famine might drive them to rob and break up some small party, maybe family, in the rear, and we had plenty; so I ordered a halt, gave the Indians about a peck of hard bread, half a middling of bacon, and a hat full of tobacco."[7] Others keeping journals noted the physical evidence of smallpox on the Pawnees' famished bodies.

As the California-bound wagon trains moved westward through Nebraska, a group of Sioux moved in from the north, launching an attack on the Pawnees near Fort Kearny and the Platte River. The warriors briefly attached themselves to Colonel Russell's large company. The *Missouri Courier* learned about the story and wrote of the Sioux, "Despite their amicable protestations to their fellow travellers, they were unwelcome companions, and being strongly suspected that they were only watching an opportunity of stealing the cattle belonging to the company. After two days sojourn together, the returned warriors were induced to cross the Platte and to push forward by being assured that there had already been several deaths from measles among the whites."[8] The Sioux crossed the river hastily and distanced themselves from Russell's company.

Emigrants took note of the stark contrast between the declining Pawnees and the thriving Sioux. Alexander Cartwright wrote, "The Sioux are a magnificent race of Indians, the men are tall and finely formed, with fine classic features & noble carriage, frank and open in their manner of adress, the Women, many of them the most beautiful I have ever beheld, they were principally clothed in beautiful dressed skins, some of them very richly ornamented & as white as snow, I offered one Twenty five Dollars for her dress, but met with an unqualified refusal."[9] Similar accolades about the Sioux women were articulated in other emigrant diaries.

The escalation of aggression between the Sioux and Pawnees in May and June 1849 took their focus off the transient white men. Still, there were times when emigrant parties got caught up in the hostility, mostly in support of the downtrodden Pawnees. A Sioux party of eighty warriors rode into one emigrant camp looking for Pawnees but was not told that one was wounded and hiding in a wagon.[10] Many emigrants also learned that the commanding officer at Fort Kearny was sheltering a young Pawnee boy, the only survivor of a brutal Sioux ambush of the boy's family.[11]

The Cartwright and Currier teams moved beyond Pawnee territory while Darcy and his Newark Overland Company were still passing through the land of the Pottawatomies. They were far behind on the Kansas River, where they had been forced to halt while Darcy treated John R. Crockett, who had become too ill to travel. Once Darcy realized that he was suffering from cholera and that his condition was deteriorating, he ordered the Gray-Crockett mess to be moved fifty yards away from the others. The wagon was completely cleaned, with everything removed and aired. Crockett's clothes were washed in boiling water, but the preventive measures might have been too late. Three other men were also sick. Soon Charles Gray felt his stamina flush from his system. Waves of nausea overtook him, and a violent headache forced him to withdraw from camp duties. He treated himself with a bottle of brandy and a dose of camphor, wrapped himself in a blanket, and fell into a deep slumber.[12]

Dozens of wagons passed the Newark Overland Company while they lay sidelined on the banks of the Kansas River on May 12, their third consecutive day without travel. By evening, skies had cleared—perhaps a good omen, as all men under Darcy's care had survived their debilitating bouts with cholera. With dozens of graves of cholera victims already marking the trail, the survival of all of the Jerseymen was truly miraculous. Yet while the sun was shining and physical conditions had improved, tempers and outlooks were gloomier than ever. Gray's journal entry expressed his frustration: "These past few days I have been so disgusted that if an opportunity could have offered itself I should have returned home—our wagon a hospital—up at all hours of the night—hardly a place to sleep in—all our men disputing & wrangling about the merest trifles, all my exertions to keep things in order impossible—everything used and thrown down in a filthy state—& I expected to keep it all clean."[13]

The slow travel, sickness, and filthy conditions had seriously dampened everyone's spirits. Once on the move again, Charles Gray ventured to a nearby Pottawatomi village hoping to resupply his medicine chest. He rode up to "a very *black white* man" and asked where he might purchase whiskey. The side trip was all for naught: he was told by the stranger that he was on the premises of a French Catholic mission, and consequently his request for liquor was not met.[14]

Cartwright and Currier continued to enjoy the benefits of breaking the trail and blazing the way for the gold seekers of 1849. Those parties in the lead were treated as a curiosity by Indians, who welcomed the white men to trading sessions, unaware of the thousands that would swarm their lands in the coming weeks.

The Sioux, in all their magnificence, continued to impress the emigrants. Even their well-dressed animals caught the attention of a journalist who wrote, "Their horses caparisoned in a curious but highly ornamental style: the head-stalls, rosettes, and nosebands of the bridles fringed with a light trimming of red cloth, and the saddle-cloths, which extended over the quarters and down the sides of their fine-spirited animals, elaborately worked with parti-coloured beads."[15] The emigrants sought to procure items adorned with beautiful beadwork such as moccasins and shirts. Obtaining a buffalo robe was also high on everyone's list, and astute traders learned that robes taken from a November hunt were of top quality as the animals had shed their mangy summer fur for thick winter coats.[16]

The commodity that Indians most preferred in exchange for the skins and handmade goods was alcohol, and the demand proved true across the plains, regardless of tribe. Emigrants, however, were reluctant to relinquish their own supplies and instead traded other objects desired by the Indians—specialty items such as mirrors, spyglasses, and any type of firearm.

Once on the Platte River Road, the lead teams skirted the treeless riverbanks and began to encounter geographic features unlike any they had seen in New York or New Jersey. Immense limestone escarpments created romantic vistas and were so far in the distance that dimensions seemed distorted.

The landscape, for the first time, contained vast herds of buffalo grazing in the river bottoms. Currier noted seeing "large droves of Buffaloes on the opposite side of the River. I should think their were about six Thousand, when I first saw them they looked like a young growth of wood about one mile long and 30 ft wide but as they came feeding along

I thought God had supplied the Indians with noble droves of cattle. 60 of them forded the river about 1/4 of a mile from where we were nooning." A hunt was quickly organized, followed by jubilation at bringing down two buffalo cows. The remainder of the day was spent cutting and drying the meat and finally sitting down to a dinner of sizzling steaks that they found stronger and gamier than New Jersey beef. It was May 13, Cyrus Currier's birthday, and never could he have imagined such a gift to celebrate his thirty-seven years.[17]

Timber had been plentiful for the lead parties, but as western Nebraska gave way to treeless plains, buffalo chips became necessary to sustain campfires. Chips were frequently called *bois de vache* ("wood of the cow"), and once dried they were easy to handle. The flames were surprisingly odorless, and with an inexhaustible supply in every direction, no one complained about cooking over combusted excrement.

Darcy's company was now in its third week of travel, or lack of travel, and continued toward Fort Kearny in heavy traffic. The General ordered the company to push ahead, passing an estimated seventy-five wagons, including those from Kentucky led by guidebook author Edwin Bryant, whose advice many were following.

Just when it seemed the congestion could not get any worse, the two main roads out of the most popular jumping-off towns—Independence and St. Joseph—joined, doubling the numbers of livestock, humans, and vehicles. Many companies experienced dissension, and many fragmented into smaller units on this stretch of trail. The loss of organization, combined with fatigue and frustration, increased the rate of accidents. Serious injuries from gunshots and trampling by wagon wheels became more frequent by the day, sometimes adding to the high mortality rate caused by the still-prevalent cholera epidemic. Recently filled graves were now all too common along the trail margins. Cartwright and Currier, being in the lead, were spared these images of despair. Charles Gray, however, in the middle of the emigration, found himself deeply troubled by the presence of so much death, and he confessed his feelings after observing one such grave. "I was alone, ahead of our train 2 miles," he wrote in his journal, "and as I suddenly came upon it, my mind was never so powerfully impressed with the idea of that all powerful King, to whom all shall bow—as at this time."[18]

Somewhere on the overcrowded trail within a day of the Newark Overland Company, Charles Gillespie's two-wagon contingent, the Jackass friends, jostled for position with the larger parties. They soon joined with six other wagons and made plans to stay together until reaching California.

If Gillespie was as troubled as Gray by the difficult circumstances on the trail, it was not evident in his writing. "The way from Independence this far is just lined with wagons," he wrote. "At one place at the junction of the Independence & St Joe Road for a distance of ten miles I could see one continuous line of wagons. Several of the emigrants have died and their graves now serve as landmarks in the wilderness. There has been no sickness in our company. All are well and in good spirits. There appears to be a great many women among the emigrants, some on horseback, some in wagons but the most on foot and some even driving teams."[19] Gillespie's accounts made note of more women than other diarists, who reported their presence as scarce.

While others were falling to illness, Gillespie's physical constitution seemed to benefit from the journey, just as he had hoped when he embarked on the venture. "As to my health," he wrote, "I have not been so well for years as I am at present, for the last year I was compelled to take medicine constantly, but now I have abandoned it altogether. I am satisfied of one thing at least, that if I obtain no gold, I will obtain what is much better, a sane mind and strong body. I am like Doniphan's Soldiers 'Rough, Rugged & Ready.'"[20] Forever the optimist, Gillespie wrote these words to his twin sister in a letter dated May 18, 1849, taking advantage of the opportunity to write when he encountered a team heading back to the states and offering to take mail.

During the first few weeks of travel, these trail "mailmen" were often parties of emigrants who had given up and were hightailing back to civilization. Military companies moving supplies and troops to Fort Leavenworth in Kansas were also traveling counter to the flow of emigration, as were mountain men delivering skins and pelts to centers of commerce in Missouri and delegations of Mormons going to Iowa to collect followers and assist their emigration to the Salt Lake settlement.[21] All those heading east gathered letters with the promise to mail them in the states. They also collected postage.

Not all letters made it to their destinations. Emigrants eventually became skeptical of those offering to carry mail and realized the potential for fraud at their own expense. The cost to mail a letter home from frontier territories was, on average, fifty cents, making it an easy and profitable scam. Most took the gamble anyway, as official US mail drops in the frontier territory were few and far between, located primarily at the military installations of Fort Kearny, Fort Laramie (Wyoming), and Fort Hall (Idaho).

By now the emigrant companies had settled into a daily routine. Most rose by sunrise, breakfasted on hard bread and coffee, collected and yoked animals, and rolled onto the trail. After several hours of travel they stopped for a two-hour layover referred to as "nooning," which was required more to rest the animals than people. When traffic was heavy some teams would rise and depart before sun-up in order to jump ahead of others and thus have better choices for pasturage and campgrounds in the evening. Alexander Cartwright passed the William Emery wagon early one morning several days west of Fort Kearny. When Emery's guard questioned the premature departure, Cartwright exclaimed that they were the "peep o day boys."[22] See you later!

Staying on schedule was never easy. Nothing was more aggravating than rousing from a night's slumber only to learn that livestock had strayed during the night. Hours were squandered locating animals and herding them back to camp. Oxen were easier to recapture than mules, as their lumbering gait and mild temperaments limited them from wandering as far away. Some companies had been wise to purchase a bell mare, a lead horse or mule that others naturally followed. Roundups as well as river crossings were far less complicated when mules were complacent and followed their "lead girl."[23]

The agony of losing time due to retrieving lost animals was felt by virtually every company on the trail. Animals not only strayed at night, they often panicked during violent storms and would stampede miles from camp. Cartwright and Currier narrowly escaped this predicament when a severe thunderstorm caught them late one afternoon. "The thunder rolled and the lightening blazed in one sheet of living fire, the rain descended in torrents, and hail stones as large as eggs (aye! and larger) pelted us and our poor animals—most pitilessly," Cartwright wrote in his journal. "Fortunately we had taken the precaution as the storm reached its fury to take our animals out and fasten them securely to the wheels else had we surely lost some of them, as it was they were wild with terror, and snorted and tore the earth at a furious rate."[24]

The Cartwright and Currier teams had encountered this noteworthy storm one day before reaching Ash Hollow, the Platte River Road's first indisputable landmark. There the men witnessed more than nature's ability to disburse torrents of water and crackling electricity. They saw something that Cartwright had difficulty identifying. It was "one of the grandest sights in nature, a water spout on the plains," he wrote. "It commenced some distance to the left of us, and at first was nothing but a small pillar or cloud reaching from the clouds to the earth, this pillar began traveling toward the right gradually growing large and revolving swifter until it had passed a long distance off and appeared at least one mile in circumference when it burst with a tremendous explosion, louder than the discharge of a whole park of artillery."[25] William Kelly was warned of the coming funnel cloud by a Sioux who frantically gestured for him to take cover in a thicket.[26] Cartwright's meteorological ignorance was shared by Currier, who also erroneously described the tornado as a waterspout.[27]

Darcy's company was fifty miles shy of Fort Kearny when it was forced to halt to repair a badly damaged wagon wheel.[28] All was not lost, however, as there were reports of buffalo in the area, and the men were anxious to engage in the uniquely western hunt. But the sightings of buffalo were apparently false, and there were no steaks broiled over *bois de vache* in the Darcy camp that night. Instead, a twenty-pound turkey was brought into camp for dinner. The novice hunters would have more chances for buffalo at the river bottoms ahead, where countless herds grazed. Until then, an assortment of critters such as badgers, prairie dogs, and an occasional turtle would be tasted at campfire meals.

Scores of teams again passed Darcy's group while they made their wagon repairs, and to add to the disgruntlement, a search party was required to look for a man who had not returned from the hunting trip. Baldwin was missing.[29]

As if that was not enough aggravation for Darcy, another company member found himself in hot water with the captain of a US government train of dragoons, a mounted army regiment on its way to Fort Vancouver. Foolishly, John R. Crockett had aided and abetted a deserter of the unit by providing him with food, advising him on his escape, and even offering to trade coats with him. Then, in a complete turnabout, Crockett informed the captain of the deserter's whereabouts, causing him to be arrested. Some speculated that Crockett had set up the man in order to collect reward money. Those who sympathized with the deserter were outraged at Crockett and threatened to shoot him. The dragoons were equally eager to punish Crockett when they learned of his double-crossing behavior. Charles Gray's incompatible messmate was a marked man.[30]

Crockett retreated to the wagon and hid under blankets. Meanwhile, Gray unwittingly mounted Crockett's horse, a distinct dun, which was immediately recognized by the dragoons. Gray was quickly surrounded and questioned by the soldiers, but they soon realized that he was a much younger man than the one they were seeking, and so they moved on.[31]

As the Crockett drama was unfolding, Gun Baldwin found his way back to his worried company. He had followed the trail twelve miles in the wrong direction before realizing his mistake. Some three hundred teams passed the Newark Overland Company during the myriad of fiascos that had forced them to stop.[32]

The next morning Crockett remained secluded in the wagon, still fearful of retribution, when the Newark Overland Company finally moved back on the trail. His punishment came soon enough, after a steep embankment caused the oxen to break loose and take a sharp turn. The wagon, with Crockett still aboard, tumbled down the hill spilling all the contents, destroying pots and kettles, and popping open the chest containing flour, rice, and coffee. Even Gray expressed relief when his messmate "dug his way out, unhurt, but all in a tremor and pale as a white horse."[33]

Concerned about the lost time and, more importantly, their place in line, General Darcy ordered the company back on the trail immediately. The wagon was righted quickly, with everything salvageable thrown back in randomly and "all in a heap." Gray, who was still perturbed at Crockett, became even more annoyed at the state of their wagon. During the previous day's delay he had meticulously reorganized their mess, putting it in pristine order. In an effort to lighten the load, Gray had discarded excess baggage, including heavy iron items, and even the India rubber boat they had yet to use as either a vessel or a shelter.[34] They pressed on toward Fort Kearny.

Robert Bond had been diligent in making entries in his journal nearly every day, but his minimalist writing style hardly filled the pages: "Col. Crockett arrested as a dezerter. Many wagons passed. Upset wagon. Passed Fort Kearny, Nebraska."[35] Major Meeker, the prominent Newark merchant and Bond's messmate, was also keeping a journal, typically notes regarding weather, mileage, and scenery, in much more detail than Bond's. Charles Gray was more verbose than the majority of trail writers, but like Meeker, Gray recorded mileage and noted that Fort Kearny was some 350 miles from Independence.

Neither Gray nor Meeker disclosed how the mileage was calculated, but it was most likely obtained by using an odometer, a cog-wheeled device that resembled large watch parts. Such a device was attached to a rear wagon wheel and operated by measuring rotations that were calculated into distance. They may have used a commercial product such as the trademarked Roadometer made by Mormons and first marketed in 1847, or they may have used a crudely handcrafted mechanism. Whether homemade or high-end brass, odometers were typically employed by well-organized and better-financed parties.

Despite all the delays, the Newark Overland Company was still in the first half of the emigration wave of 1849 when they passed Fort Kearny on May 24. Fortunately for Crockett, the news of his escapades had not reached the post's commanding officer, and the company moved on without further incident.

Adjacent to Fort Kearny a family of Latter-day Saints operated a store and boarding house where travelers could enjoy hospitality and home-cooked meals with offerings such as buttermilk and gingerbread. Many emigrants patronized their business primarily to purchase whiskey. Like Charles Gray, teams lightened their loads on the approach to Fort Kearny, throwing out provisions and materials that they had come to realize were not required for reaching California. As these otherwise useful items were thrown to the wayside, bottles of liquor from the Mormon store at Fort Kearny took their place.

The Darcy company pushed on through poor weather conditions to an encampment along a tributary of the Platte River. The plains-coursing Platte had come into view earlier in the day. While Bond had nothing to say, Gray wrote in detail: "This is a large river like the Missouri, water soft & yellow,—it contains large islands & in some places as wide as the

North Fork of the Platte River, one of many views sketched by Charles B. Gillespie in May and June 1849. Courtesy of the Rees-Jones Collection.

Hudson at New York, a mile; its current very strong & furious."[36] He also made note of more graves, which likely caused him more melancholy.

Charles B. Gillespie's group had moved ahead and reached the Platte three days before General Darcy's company. While Gillespie carried a journal and was attentive in taking notes for his sister, the view of the river from atop a ridge inspired him to use his pencil to sketch the continuous line of wagons disappearing into the endless horizon. Gillespie found the view irresistible and sketched it multiple times during the last week of May and on into June, when they reached the point where the Platte River divided into north and south forks.

The landscape along the Oregon Trail was now lush and green with spring vegetation. Cartwright was awed by "two beautiful varieties of mosses with small purple and blue flowers." Bond made no such entries in his diary, and Gray continued to remark on the fresh graves, focusing on death instead of the birth and rebirth of spring.

Far from the blossoming prairie, the passengers of the bark *Isabel* were enduring monotonous days at sea. To fight the boredom, spirited debates

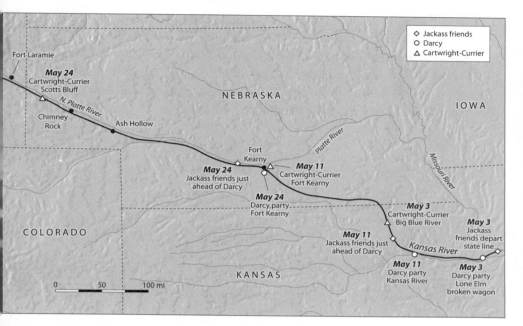

May 1849. The three groups of the Newark Overland Company and their locations on the trail. Cartography by Bill Nelson. Copyright © 2017 University of Oklahoma Press.

took place on topics such as the abolishment of capital punishment and whether Columbus or Washington was a greater historic figure. Some consumed idle hours by making rings out of ten-cent pieces, and for others watching whales and catching "Cape pigeons" helped them pass the time. As the *Isabel* navigated around the tip of South America, the winter solstice was approaching. The last hog on board was killed, and a feast was planned for the occasion. But instead of enjoying a celebration, the passengers faced panic and chaos when fire broke out from the roasting carcass.[37]

Four months behind the *Isabel,* Eliza Farnham began her westward journey, realizing her dream of leading a group of women to California, where they would provide comfort for sick and dying men who were stricken alone in a distant land. She and her three followers, destined to become angels of mercy, booked passage, coincidentally, on the bark *Angelique.*[38]

1849

On a starry night in May, Alexander Cartwright stood guard at his North Platte River camp and felt the pangs of homesickness: "My thoughts soon took the usual direction and I thought of Home, sweet home! and of my Darling wife and little ones, and breathed a silent prayer to that Beneficent Being who had said 'in the silent watches of the night I will be near thee,' for their protection & welfare."[39]

Chapter 12

Platte River Road

Violent storms continued to blow across western and central Nebraska during the fourth week of May 1849 and seemed to follow the course of the Platte River. Every emigrant on the Oregon Trail from Fort Kearny to Scotts Bluff was affected by the severe weather. Rain soaked through doubled wagon canvases, animals scattered and were lost for days, and spirits were sorely dampened. Most parties were bombarded by large hailstones, which they compared in size to chicken and pigeon eggs, with some claiming nine inches in circumference, the size of a baseball.[1]

The terrain was now changing from prairie grasslands to sandy plains marked with oddly shaped rock formations sculpted by wind and water. Lining the horizon were escarpments, appearing nearly white when catching the morning and afternoon sunlight. "We reached the top of a very high Bluff from whence the most magnificent view burst upon us, hundreds of feet below us, lay ridge after ridge of bold Bluffs in every conceivable variety of shape, their sides and tops, and the valleys between covered with verdun," wrote Alexander Cartwright, noting that some of the outcrops resembled pyramids and Turkish mosques. "The beauty of this scene I will not attempt to describe, the pencil of 'Cole' or the pen of 'Irving' alone could do it justice, its beauty and wild grandeur will never fade from my memory, neither do I think that 'twill from either of my comrades," he added, speaking of Tom Seely and Frank Woolsey.[2]

The Cartwright and Currier teams were coming into view of the spectacular sandstone formations known as Courthouse Rock and Chimney

Rock, still some eight to twelve miles in the distance, when the sky grew dark and sinister. The clouds let loose buckets of rain, soaking the caravan. Fortunately, none of the menacing clouds twisted into funnels, as one had days earlier, when it reached down and clawed the earth. Wet and chilled, the men breakfasted on cold beans and pork, which elevated their spirits if only for a brief respite. Not only was the weather deplorable, but camp life had provided additional discomforts. Seely was coping with a painful insect bite on his hand, and Cartwright was in the grip of gastrointestinal distress caused by the daily regimen of eating game.[3]

Many emigrants took time to ride to the bases of the landmark rocks but found them deceptively more distant than they had perceived. Some carved their names and initials into the soft rock. Parties passing here reached Scotts Bluff within a day, and it was on this stretch of the road that Cartwright and Currier were surprised by another weather phenomenon, a late spring snow squall. Numerous journal writers described abnormally low temperatures.[4]

On arrival at Scotts Bluff, Cartwright and his comrades encountered one of the most noted characters of the Oregon Trail in 1849, a crusty frontiersman and trapper by the name of Robidoux. Married to a Sioux woman, he operated a meager store and blacksmithing shop that would be patronized by many gold seekers over the summer. It is believed that he was Joseph E. Robidoux, the son of the French trader who founded St. Joseph, Missouri.[5]

Robidoux invited Cartwright and his messmate Frank Woolsey to spend the evening of May 24 under the roof of his primitive hut. According to Cartwright, "We passed the hours 'till one o'clock in spinning yarns of all sizes & colors, and at that hour turned in on the *hard* floor." But there was no rest for Cartwright. "Sleep refused to visit my eyes that night, although accustomed to sleep on the earth in all sorts of weather, I could not go the *stoney* couch of that night so after tossing about for a couple of hours, turned out and looked around the camp 'till day light did appear, having made up my mind to accept no more invitations, but stick to the green sward."[6]

The next day, just beyond Scotts Bluff, the first dissension occurred among the front-running mule teams when Caleb Boylston and William Emery agreed to disagree. Boylston had joined Emery and his son in Independence at the last minute after being deserted by his companion

Joseph Doty, who had headed home to Elizabethtown. But Boylston and Emery's eleventh-hour agreement went sour, and the pair disbanded. They divided their shared belongings in a settlement that left Emery in custody of the wagon and Boylston with two of the mules, which he would have to pack for the next leg of the journey to Fort Laramie. It was frontiersman Robidoux who instructed Boylston on the proper technique of harnessing the pack and adapting both mule and rider to the new arrangement. Cartwright stayed behind with Boylston to provide further assistance. In an effort to catch up with their party, they took a shortcut across the prairie, hoping to arrive at camp ahead of the wagons.[7]

The two men traveled ten miles over sand hills, delighted with the progress they were able to attain with just animals and minimal supplies. They were giddy over their success as packers until their cockiness was smacked to the ground, literally. Billy Buttons, the mule with the pack configured to Robidoux's expert specifications, was tethered to Cartwright's saddle, when suddenly the pack came unfastened and slipped between Billy's legs. The critter's orneriness erupted, and its mulish strength was enough to turn the saddle out from under Cartwright, who was thrust to the ground abruptly. Boylston's mule then bolted, sending its rider through the air to another hard landing. By the time Cartwright reached Boylston, both were reeling in laughter over their ridiculous mishap. But the humor evaporated when they looked up and saw their animals disappearing in the distance, taking with them dangling provisions and holstered firearms.[8]

Alone and unarmed, the two began to walk in the direction of their runaway mounts, retracing much of the ground they had covered over the day. Hours later they were back on the main road in the vicinity of Robidoux's post. There they found the wayward animals and Robidoux himself preparing to search for the missing riders. They confessed the details of their calamity to their host, who was thoroughly amused. Tired and not thinking clearly, Cartwright foolishly accepted an offer of coffee, jerked beef, and a swig of Robidoux's "No. 1 Brandy" as consolation. It was a poor decision following a horrible day, a bad night of sleep, and an already sensitive stomach. "That was the damnedest," Cartwright recorded. "I can compare it to nothing but 'liquid hell fire' I writhed and twisted in agony, my contortions of visage *must* have been fearful, rushing to a bucket of water, I caught up a tin cup full and tossed down my throat, but this only appeared to aggravate it, I could feel my stomach hiss as the water came in contact with the fiery fluid, God what a ten minutes of agony I endured after that bumper of No 1—it was fully two hours before I was fairly relieved from its influence."[9]

Cartwright and Boylston rejoined their train and moved on to Fort Laramie as Darcy's company began to make its way into the sand hills and rock formations of western Nebraska. The Newark Overland Company was now two weeks behind Cartwright and Currier, and the gap was widening, with the Darcy party caught in the heavy traffic of the Platte River Road.

On the crowded trail, companies were traveling, camping, and leap-frogging each other in such close quarters that they came to know their fellow gold seekers, discovering details such as where they were from and who was in charge of the different groups. The information often spread forward and backward for miles along the continuous line of wagons. A train from Jerseyville, Illinois, learned of Darcy's location and came forward with a letter from the General's brother Dr. Edward A. Darcy in yet another example of trail mail.[10]

Along the Platte River bottoms west of Fort Kearny the men in Darcy's company continued to be anxious for a taste of buffalo and began using field glasses to scan the ridges and vales. Gray wrote that the men were "all sighing for buffalo steaks," knowing that many other companies had already enjoyed the prized meal.[11] But again they had to settle for alternate fresh meat when Dolph Pennington returned to camp with only a single antelope.[12]

As with those who had passed through the vicinity earlier, the last days of May brought unseasonably frigid nightly temperatures, leaving water buckets frozen over and ropes crusty with ice crystals. Men were forced to don layers of clothes—up to three coats, plus gloves and scarves—to fend off the chill, making sleep difficult. Wolves howling all night further challenged meaningful slumber. But daylight was now bringing forth beautiful days, and the road conditions were the best of the journey, boosting even Gray's typically negative spirits.[13] He rejoiced in the solitude and beauty of a spectacular vista from atop a bluff overlooking the trail, as wagons crept along the winding river below. But his joy would not last for long.

Another severe thunderstorm struck Darcy's company on the evening of May 29 just after the men made camp. Billowing black clouds accumulated with little warning, leaving men scrambling to gather their belongings and take cover. "All the thunder, lightning & rain of half a dozen great storms seem'd united in this one. The earth seem'd to shake, the heavens were one continual glare, & the rain came down like a young deluge," Gray recorded. Huddled in wagons that rocked to and fro in the relentless gale, the men were fearful of being blown over. Tents were flattened and flapping within minutes. Everyone's heavy clothes were saturated, and a mess chest inside one wagon flooded, ruining tea and a pot of cake batter. Outside, ankle-deep ponds were forming. [14] And the storm went on for much of the night.

The men arose in the morning, aching and chilled, only to be greeted by a soggy campground and the reality that the company's oxen had scattered. None were in sight. Men with horses were sent in search of the missing cattle. After briefly scouting the prairie, one man wisely returned with an iron stove previously discarded by another company. It provided the opportunity to start a fire, otherwise futile on the soaked ground, and prepare some type of warm meal out of the remaining wet provisions. Those not hunting cattle gathered around the smoking apparatus, taking turns rubbing their hands over the rising hot air.

As breakfast was ending, the group was taken by surprise when two hefty buffaloes suddenly ran through camp, bringing forth cries of "Buffalo, Buffalo!" Two firearms were quickly grabbed and fired, but shots from one gun missed, and the other weapon was too wet to discharge at all. With all the horses away from camp there could be no pursuit, and the missed opportunity left the men aggravated and disappointed. Buffalo steaks had eluded them yet again. [15]

Darcy's party lost two days of travel after the storm. The first day was spent looking for and gathering the stray stock, fifteen to twenty of which were still missing by nightfall, at which time two men did not return to camp. The second day was forfeited herding the remaining animals and looking for the missing men. Concern spread that they had been taken by Indians, but fears dissipated when the pair showed up later in the evening. [16]

Two days earlier Charles Gray had expressed the grandeur of a vista from atop a bluff with quotes from Sir Walter Raleigh. Now the delay and poor camp conditions enveloped him in disgust. He whistled opera tunes in an attempt to shake the blues, and when that failed he shot his gun at a makeshift target. How could he have been such a fool as to journey into this desolate country, he questioned himself harshly. He sat, melancholy, took to drinking brandy alone, and vowed to return home after reaching Fort Laramie, where arrangements could be made. The alcohol began to lift his spirits, and he described the pleasure as equal to the "smile and kiss of love." As the liquor took effect, Gray evoked Shakespeare, uttering, "I let fall the curtains of my eyes & took a snooze!"[17]

By now the Cartwright and Currier teams had reached Fort Laramie, having exerted considerable energy crossing the Laramie River despite the assistance of a manned ferry operation. The nasty weather had subsided, and starlit nights and crystal-clear mountain mornings were becoming the norm. Fort Laramie was still under jurisdiction of the American Fur Company and was run by an errant Scotchman named Bruce Husband. Unlike Fort Kearny, which was a construction project when Cartwright and Currier had passed by in early May, Fort Laramie had existed for some ten years and had become the regional center for trade and commerce. The facility's location above the confluence of the North Platte and Laramie Rivers was impressive. Conversely, the downtrodden occupants, neglected structures, and disappointing trading opportunities were not. Cartwright managed to come away with fresh milk but acquired nothing else of importance.[18]

Fort Laramie was another of the points along the journey where many emigrants realized they were carrying too much weight in supplies and made the decision to expel excess contents. Out went heavy materials such as iron chains and aging provisions. With lighter loads, wagons were chopped and rebuilt to fit the streamlined baggage. Those who took this drastic measure to alleviate the burden on oxen and mules would benefit from healthier stock in the coming weeks. Those who did not would see their weary animals fail within a month's time. Currier willingly exercised the prudent measures, as did Emery, who shortened the wagon that now belonged solely to him.[19]

It was just beyond Fort Laramie that Caleb Boylston gave up mule packing and joined Cartwright's mess, which now totaled five and included Seely, Woolsey, and Isaac Overton.[20] Laramie Peak was now in view. Rising solitarily in the southwestern horizon, it was the first genuine crest of the Rockies and was like no other mountain any of them had ever seen. The North Platte River was still leading emigrants westward and would take them well into central Wyoming before giving them over to a tributary, the Sweetwater, where the waters of all creeks and freshets would begin to exhibit signs of alkali and mineral content.

Before reaching the Sweetwater, teams had to cross to the north side of the North Platte. Latter-day Saints from the newly established Utah settlement had recently begun to operate a ferry enterprise at this location. One journal writer observed, "The Mormons, always on the look-out for gain as well as glory—or salvation, more properly speaking—travelled all the way from Salt Lake, over four hundred miles, to establish a ferry, anticipating a large overland emigration, and knowing there was no other point of passing."[21] They also maintained a forge for blacksmithing services and welcomed trading with emigrant parties. In exchange for some bacon, Cartwright's mess acquired dried venison that Tom Seely used to prepare a potpie for the company supper. It was served with "milk punch," which helped revive Seely, who had nearly drowned earlier in the day. While swimming his mount across the river he was unhorsed and clung to the animal's mane as they fought through the cold current. Cartwright skipped the meal entirely due to his recurring stomach ailment.[22]

Darcy's men were again on the trail after the two-day delay spent searching for missing oxen and men—all subsequently found in good health. They were now three hundred miles behind Cartwright and Currier, just shy of the South Fork Platte River crossing and Ash Hollow.

Charles Gray was on guard duty during the early hours of June 2, and his attitude showed signs of rebounding. He wrote that the night was "delightful & for about the first time I can say it." He went on to describe the setting during his two-hour shift: "The river shining like silver in the brilliant moonlight—across it dark masses of trees & in every direction the burning camp fires of the advancing host, ever & anon the shrill neighing of the steeds 'piercing the nights dull ear,' the distant howlings of the wolves, the bright shining of the skies & the loneliness & solitariness of the scene, all conspired to render it '*decidedly romantic*'"[23]

The Newark Overland Company had taken on a new member the night before, one whose antics proved uplifting to the men. His name was Mr. Platte, a wolf pup brought into camp by Charles Hicks, who had expectations of domesticating him. The pup's playfulness was delightful, and in no time he had made friends with the dogs in camp.[24]

June 2 was the day that many of the Newark men had long anticipated. Just after crossing the South Fork, the familiar shouts of "Buffalo!" again rang out along the riverbank, and a mad dash for mounts and firearms ensued. Those on horseback took full advantage of the opportunity to gallop alongside the thundering animals as they ran up an adjacent hill. There the first of the large beasts was brought down, and soon another fell, in an operation that took less than thirty minutes. Many of the company members followed to inspect the animals, and once up close, marveled at the size of the creatures and their thick manes. While still on the ridge, the carcasses were stripped for the best cuts, and leftovers were scattered for hungry wolves.[25]

There was exuberance in camp over the day's events. Finally buffalo steaks would be broiled over a crackling campfire! And the men were delighted with the feast they consumed—all except for Charles Gray, who found the meat offensive. In his words, it had come from the *devil's kitchen.* After months of anticipation he refused to eat it.[26]

It had been only days since freezing nights and drenching downpours had exacerbated the already harsh conditions of camp life. Now the opposite extreme was taking over as temperatures soared under the hot midday sun, draining everyone's energy. Road surfaces dried and turned dusty with the constant traffic of wagons and hooves. Some of the Jerseymen at last made use of the sand goggles they had acquired on the advice of guidebooks and kept despite repeated lightening of loads. Regardless of the heat and dust, the Newark Overland Company was finally making steady progress, gaining on average twenty miles per day. They made one brief stop to trade with a small party of Sioux, during which Major Meeker obtained moccasins and others purchased deerskin britches and leggings. Gray noticed that some of the children were offspring of French trappers and wrote that they were "as fair as our home productions."[27]

General Darcy's company moved into view of the famed Courthouse Rock and Chimney Rock and experienced another violent cloudburst, similar to the one Cartwright and Currier had encountered at the same location. They were pelted by hail, which left the ground white and inspired more comparisons regarding the exact size of the ice pellets. It

Chimney Rock, a landmark along the Oregon Trail in Nebraska, sketched by Charles B. Gillespie, June 1849. Courtesy of the Rees-Jones Collection.

was the last dark, threatening sky they would see for some time. The scorching desert crossing they would endure in two months would make them long for such relief. They passed the famous rock landmarks and crossed the pass at Scotts Bluff without any mention of the colorful Joseph E. Robidoux.[28]

The Cartwright and Currier parties were now out of Sioux country, and as they moved into the territory of the Crows, they understood that warnings had been issued at Fort Laramie about potential hostilities with this tribe. Cartwright, Seely, and Emery were riding ahead of the main party when they encountered twenty Crow Indians seated on buffalo robes beside the trail. The three men stopped and dismounted, then were invited by the Natives to smoke a peace pipe. Currier and others from the party soon arrived and they also obliged the offer. Cartwright found the sage-filled pipe so pleasant that he smoked it out. A trading session followed, during which beaded necklaces were exchanged for pocket kerchiefs. Few emigrants noted such friendly encounters with the Crows. It was only a matter of hours before Currier heard gunshots in the night. He believed it was the same twenty Crows firing into the nearby camp of a company who had refused the Indians' hospitality earlier in the day.[29]

Westward progress for the Cartwright and Currier wagons was remarkably incident-free through the first week of June. Following the Sweetwater River, they reached Independence Rock, a colossal smooth turtle-shell-shaped mass whose surface was inscribed with hundreds of emigrants' initials, some dated years earlier. Currier added his name, autographing the landmark in red chalk.[30] From the base of the rock they could see the distinct crevice of Devil's Gate silhouetted on the western sky. The passage, several miles away, was a gateway for the Sweetwater River.

Days later the snow-capped crowns of the Wind River Mountains came into view, framing the northern horizon. After departing the banks of the Sweetwater for the final time, the wagons of Cartwright and Currier crested the gentle ridge known as South Pass, which divided the snowmelt of the Rockies into waters destined for both the Pacific and Atlantic Oceans. The air had thinned considerably at these higher elevations. It was the first week of June, and few teams had reached the Continental Divide so early in the season.[31]

When they arrived at the Green River, the Cartwright mess made another change. Isaac Overton was swapped for John W. Shaff, who had been traveling with the Currier team. Apparently it was a successful trade for all involved.[32]

Far to the east, the Newark Overland Company received pleasing news a day before arriving at Fort Laramie. It came to them via the makeshift communication system that had sprung up on the trail, whereby notes and cards left for friends and associates traveling behind were attached to any tree or stable structure available. Sometimes information was scribbled on bleached buffalo skulls or shoulder bones. In this fashion the men of Darcy's party learned that their Jackass friends were only a few miles ahead. With all the delays the company had experienced, the discovery that Gillespie and his "deserters" were within an hour's reach gave them great satisfaction and seemed to reinforce their belief that mules were no speedier than oxen. If intelligence had reached them regarding the whereabouts of Cartwright and Currier, they might have felt differently.[33]

The news about Gillespie's location came on Sunday, June 10, the same day Darcy ordered a prolonged noon layover. Gray interpreted that the stop was "out of *respect for the Sabbath* (thereby meaning we had some clothes to wash & some wagon repairs to do)."[34] Washing clothes was something men had to learn in the absence of women. One emigrant wrote about commencing "laundry manipulations, for the first time in our lives . . . when it came to standing bent over half a day, rubbing the clothes in our hands, trying to get out the stains . . . we thought of our wives and sweet-hearts at home, and wondered that we were ever dissatisfied with their impatience on a washing day. Had they been present, we should heartily have asked their pardon, and allowed them to scold to their heart's content."[35]

The hot days prompted men to put away their heavy woolen clothing and tall boots in exchange for lighter garments and footwear. Charles Gray blamed the changing weather for bringing on a case of rheumatism, for which the only relief was, again, his bottle of brandy.[36]

Fort Laramie was reached the next day after successfully crossing the Laramie River. General Darcy's men decided to arrive at the facility in grand fashion and hoisted a US flag to lead the way. It was somewhat of a spectacle, and members in other trains stared in confusion, uncertain whether the flag represented an actual military unit or fervent patriotism. At the fort there was no mention by Gray of abandoning the company and returning home as he had vowed earlier. He scouted the shabby structures inside the compound, mailed a letter, and then browsed some outdated New York newspapers. There would have been no word of the impending death of former president James K. Polk, and they would not learn of his passing until reaching California.[37]

When crossing the Laramie River, the General's wagon had incurred some damage and required repairs. Major Meeker remained with him at the fort late into the evening while the rest of the company went on to camp. Meeker, who spent the afternoon working on his journal, composed a long letter home that would be published by the *Newark Daily Advertiser* on August 23. In his usual businesslike manner, he provided details regarding their progress over forty-one days of travel, the reduced incidence of cholera past Fort Laramie, the routine experiences of hunting game, and the wastefulness of discarding equipment on the trail. He credited Darcy's medical expertise with saving Crockett from his bout of cholera, hailing their good fortune in having such a first-rate physician.

Fort Laramie in 1849 by Frederic Remington. Working with *Century Magazine* circa 1890, Remington created this engraving based on Gillespie's work. "From a sketch by Chas. B Gillespie MD 1849" is printed in the lower right corner. Courtesy of the Buffalo Bill Center of the West, Cody, Wyoming, U.S.A. (MS23.Rem.01081).

Boldly he predicted that they would pass the mule team of Gillespie and would reach California within sixty days, estimating a mid-August arrival. He concluded by praising their decision to travel with oxen. While Gray was ever the pessimist, Meeker's projections would prove somewhat naïve.[38]

West of Fort Laramie the road became rockier, hillier, and dustier. Whether it was because of fatigue or the effects of alcohol consumption, Gray at one point was nearly crushed under wagon wheels as the train was descending into a ravine. Running alongside the wagon, he had limited visibility and found himself pressed between the rapidly moving vehicle and a tree. The accident resulted in only minor injuries to his right leg, a narrow escape that Gray attributed to quick thinking on his part. Fortunately for him, the previous night had been cold, and the extra clothing he had donned may have provided protective padding.[39]

Snow-covered Laramie Peak impressed everyone, with an indigo sky as backdrop. It was visible all day on June 13, and, while Gray was somewhat nearsighted, he confessed difficulty in taking his eyes off it.[40] The next day, as reported in the journal of Major Meeker, the Newark Overland Company passed their Jackass friends—Gillespie's small party.[41] Gillespie himself may have been responsible for letting the larger company slip by. He had taken time off to produce a sketch of Laramie Peak, adding to his pictorial documentation. The view inspired him even though he had traveled through the Rockies in 1842, when he had taken time to draw Pike's Peak.[42]

The landscape beyond Laramie Peak was constantly changing. Exposed layers of ancient iron-rich rock were now visible across the countryside, providing scenery dominated by bright red bands. The brick-colored sediment, beaten by the constant wagon traffic, billowed into dust that painted everything red, including wagon canvases, white horses, and people. "I am a real *red man*," Gray remarked.[43] The rugged topography, more up and down than the previous sand-hill terrain, combined with the hot sun, left the men suffering a new degree of exhaustion.

Several days of arduous travel brought Darcy's company to a lush camp situated under tree canopy along Deer Creek, a North Platte tributary of fast, clear water. Despite stopping early in the day, most campsites were already filled on both banks. Finding an available spot required driving two miles up the creek, where Darcy ordered a full day of rest for both men and animals.[44] The oxen were exhibiting lameness from being driven over an abrasive road surface that had worn down their hooves. Some companies had prevented this problem by fashioning leather "ox boots" for protection, and others had wrapped hooves in tar and grease, but Darcy's men had taken no such precautions.[45] They would have to rest.

The day off fell on a Sunday, which caused Gray to quip, "Everybody else seemed to respect the day and why not we?" In the morning a "clerical looking young chap" from a neighboring train invited the men to his Sunday sermon, which Gray declined to attend, as did most of the Newark men.[46] But Major Meeker was attracted to the missionary-style lecture that convened in a grove about a mile from the Darcy camp. Meeker observed the service and reported that it was a glorious day for the transient congregation gathered "under the shade of a majestic cottonwood." Meeker, not known to be overtly pious, may have been merely curious. The death of his young son the previous summer, however, may have compelled him to seek some type of spirituality.[47] Fortunately the loss of his oldest child had failed to make Meeker a bitter man. He continued to look at the world with an open mind, willingly listening to and learning from others.[48]

Gray, who made known his skepticism regarding religion, used the idle day to take a much-needed bath in the creek and copy some notes from a guidebook about the route to the Great Salt Lake, which apparently Darcy was considering. Others went fishing with a seine, resulting in a catch of almost a hundred fish, providing a supper much more pleasing to Gray than the buffalo steaks he had found so repulsive.[49]

The oxen, having spent some forty hours recovering from sore hooves as well as necks rubbed raw from yokes, were hitched on Monday morning. After fifteen miles, the company's eight wagons stopped along the North Platte bank about ten miles below the Mormon ferry operation that monopolized the most suitable site to navigate a safe crossing. There they met other companies who were returning from the ferry with intelligence that three hundred wagons were waiting to cross, of which about fifty could be moved in one day. To avoid the delay, parties began collectively searching for an alternate crossing.[50]

Darcy's company had stopped along the river where an island split the current into a main waterway several hundred feet wide and a smaller, fordable passage on the opposite side. Due to the island, the channel was narrower than at other points upstream, forcing the water to race more rapidly. Despite the fast water, crossing to an island offered some advantages, foremost of which was secure corralling and pasturing of stock. A large train from Dayton, Ohio, had begun to move its animals and wagons to the island on a roughly constructed raft attached to ropes on both banks.[51] Conversations with this company resulted in the decision to join forces, sharing labor and experience for mutual benefit. With some luck, a successful crossing here would avoid the delays at the Mormon ferry along with the toll of $5 per wagon.[52]

A large number of the twenty Ohio wagons made it to the island by sunset, as did the oxen of the Newark Overland Company, which were moved across to a place where they would be secure for the night. During the afternoon many teams passed the makeshift operation, destined for the multi-day backlog upstream, unaware of the congestion they would find there.

The rafting process continued the next morning, a perilous endeavor considering that some forty individuals had perished crossing the river during the season, with as many as seven having drowned the previous week.[53] It was the North Platte crossing where Tom Seely had escaped drowning by clinging to his horse as it swam across.

By one in the afternoon the Ohio company was safely on the island, when General Darcy's wagon was brought forward and positioned on the raft. It moved across the rapid water without incident, leaving the remaining seven wagons to be brought over. The mess of Meeker and Bond was next, and again the operation was carried out problem-free. The amateur ferrymen were running a smooth operation, but their luck was about to run out.[54]

The first trouble came when the No. 5 wagon, belonging to the Lewis contingent and more heavily loaded than most, attempted to cross. As the raft cleared the shore and was headed toward the swift water of the channel, the wagon teetered on the unsteady craft, coming close to upsetting. Only the desperate work of the rope men on both shores along with quick decision-making by the lead raft pilot prevented disaster. The Lewis mess was grateful when the crossing ended successfully and the wagon was safely unloaded onto the island.[55]

Wind had begun to pick up in the late afternoon when the No. 3 wagon belonging to Henry Johnson's mess moved into position and waited for the empty raft to return from the island. Johnson was advised to remove the heavy canvas cover from the arched structural bows of the wagon, for fear of the cover being caught in the wind like a sail. Many before had taken this safety measure. Having watched almost twenty-five wagons over two days cross successfully, Johnson was complacent and disregarded the warnings. Alonzo Delano of the Dayton company understood the importance of removing the canvas and remarked in his journal, "One man, from New Jersey, neglected this, in spite of the remonstrances of his friends."[56] Johnson moved his wagon, sail unfurled, onto the raft. Major Meeker was on board to assist.[57]

It was a perfect storm. The wind swept across the water, snatching the canvas cover just as predicted. The wagon crashed into the water, breaking the front wheels apart and crushing the bows to which the *sail* had been affixed. Into the cold water went bags of flour, tents, gear, and the guns that had been fastened high to the bows to keep them dry during routine river fords. The fractured vehicle and its remnant contents were quickly carried downstream, where it continued to break apart as it traveled.[58]

On the island, Charles Gray had been manning the ropes and witnessed not only the wagon being overturned but also several men being knocked overboard. Frantically he began to shout, "Who can swim?" As he repeated the cry for help, one man stripped off his watch and boots and jumped into the river. He swam toward the capsized wagon with a rope in hand, hoping to secure it and bring it ashore, where some of the contents might be salvaged. Gray began to run at full speed along the shoreline, trying to keep up with the man and wreckage being propelled down the river. The swimmer managed to attach the rope to the wagon just as they reached a fortuitous bend in the river. The wagon's momentum, with some guidance by the rope, liberated it from the current and carried it toward the island shore. One rear wheel had remained attached and projected out of the water as the wagon came to rest. Gray, moments behind, went splashing into the shallow water, desperate to save anything.[59]

As Gray and others pulled wet provisions from the debris, several men who had been thrown overboard in the accident were fighting the swirling current. Among them was Major Meeker.[60]

While the Newark company was struggling at the North Platte, Cartwright and Currier had moved beyond the Wyoming border and crossed into Idaho on their approach to Fort Hall. They had chosen this route over a southern passage that would have taken them into the Mormon settlement at the Great Salt Lake, despite having met a party of Latter-day Saints who had made every attempt to convince them to travel by way of their city. There was a "widely held belief that the Mormons had adopted a deliberate policy luring emigrants through Great Salt Lake City where they could take economic advantage of them."[61]

Englishman William Kelly and his party, who had been traveling close to the Cartwright and Currier group since departing Independence, opted to visit the Mormon enclave and parted company with the other frontrunners after descending from the Continental Divide at South Pass. On their arrival at Great Salt Lake City, residents were in disbelief at seeing an emigrant party so early in the season. They were certain that Kelly had wintered at Fort Laramie until a member of his party produced a newspaper from Independence dated April 7, 1849.[62] After a brief layover among the Mormon hosts, the Kelly team moved north and once again encountered the Cartwright and Currier teams, with whom they

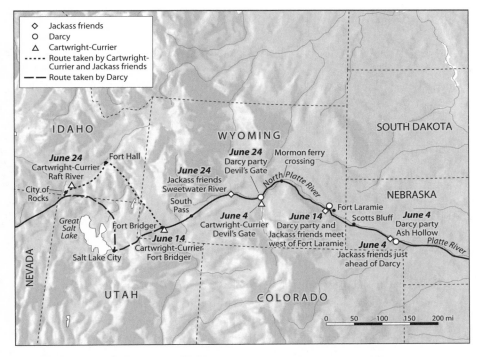

June 1849. The progress of the groups, with Cartwright and Currier taking a firm lead while Gillespie and Darcy remain within a day of each other. Cartography by Bill Nelson. Copyright © 2017 University of Oklahoma Press.

continued the journey into the basin-and-range topography of Idaho and Nevada.

The Cartwright and Currier teams experienced unprecedented success as they made their way west. They were fortunate to have had little competition for trail resources, only a handful of minor mishaps and accidents, and good relations with Indians. There was no question that if their current pace continued, they would reach California well ahead of the oxen-led Newark Overland Company and the mule-driven team of the Jackass friends. Once there, they would catch up on news from the East that was more than two months out of date.

Chapter 13

It's Summer

In February 1849, when Zachary Taylor made his preinauguration pilgrimage from New Orleans to Washington to assume the presidency, his predecessor, James Polk, was preparing to retire to a new home in Nashville. At the time, Polk had been the youngest man ever elected to the office and, at fifty-three, he was the youngest to depart the White House. He did so voluntarily, having fulfilled his promise not to run for a second term. His journey home took him over part of the same route covered by Taylor, by way of New Orleans, up the Mississippi, and across Tennessee to its capital.

Upon his departure from the Crescent City, Polk began suffering from a recurring bout of diarrhea, likely due to gallstones, but he seemed in good health when he arrived in Tennessee. He went to work on his new residence, Grundy Hill, organizing a library and employing workmen to clear the grounds. As he tended to daily activities about the estate, his upright posture made him appear hearty, defying his recent health problems. In contrast, his long gray hair made him look advanced in age and reflected more accurately his frail condition.[1]

Within weeks the chronic malady returned, and by mid-June the ex-president's physical state had weakened considerably. He remained near death for several days, with his childless wife, Sarah, by his bedside, along with his aging mother and brother, Maj. William H. Polk. He died and was buried one day later, on June 16, 1849, with Masonic rites and a copy of the US Constitution by his side.[2] The president of Manifest Destiny died having never seen any of the vast land that he had brought into the jurisdiction of the United States, including the golden prize of California.

The *Cleveland Herald* was one of the first papers to scoop the news of Polk's death, having received the bulletin via telegraph in time for publication in its evening edition on June 18.[3] Most large city papers ran the story the next day.

In Newark the sultry days of June were broken by refreshing breezes that swayed the tops of tall trees lining city avenues. Local papers ran columns describing Polk's life, career, and funeral obsequies. Politically, Polk was praised for expanding the United States beyond the Mississippi and adding four states to the Union. Newark residents also read updates about the local men who were somewhere beyond the mighty river on their way to California, which was still a US territory begging for recognition. By late June several letters from Newark's gold seekers had been received, with excerpts published in the *Newark Daily Advertiser*. Those following the story knew that the group had split into mule and ox teams and had moved out of Independence separately. The latest news had come from Charles B. Gillespie, who had sent a letter via trail mail and whose romantic verbiage may have left some wishing they had signed on: "My health continues good, and the hard labor which I daily perform gives me a good appetite for food and sleep. We have had some of the most glorious views that you can conceive—matchless sun rises and sun sets, and wide, boundless expanse of Prairie as far as the eye can reach, presenting a perfect Flower Garden."[4]

Days later the Newark paper posted a story from a *St. Louis Republican* correspondent, written at Fort Kearny just a few days after the Darcy and Gillespie teams had passed through. It was month-old news but provided a more realistic picture of the emigration. "The great majority now crossing the plains," the writer observed, "were profoundly ignorant when starting, of what was before them—had no idea of what an outfit consisted of, and in short, looked upon crossing the prairies as nothing but a pleasant trip." He described the overloaded wagons and the utter waste of throwing out valuable provisions to lighten loads. Also reported was the precise statistic that 2,527 wagons carrying an estimated 10,000 travelers had passed Fort Kearny as of May 26. Many more had arrived there with mule trains, many passed at night and were not counted, and many thousands more were still on their way from the Missouri River gateway towns.[5]

Anyone following news of the emigration to California understood that the movement was only beginning. Businessmen were still contriving to capitalize on gold mania in any way conceivable. There was no end to ideas for making fast money, such as shipping around the Horn goods they thought likely to be in demand in California. Packaged frame houses were one such item. No doubt they were unaware that Chinese exporters were engaged in a similar commercial operation.[6] There were also entrepreneurs who recognized the profitability in transporting people and products to the gold fields. Nothing was too far-fetched, except perhaps the "Aerial Locomotive" that had failed to meet its advertised April 15 departure date.

In Boston a company had organized for the purpose of promoting the use of the camels for overland travel. Numerous reports were surfacing on the feasibility of importing the animals from the Middle East due to their superior adaptability in both desert and mountainous regions. It was further proposed that the US government procure several hundred of the species for delivering the mail and transporting military caravans in the western territories. That would certainly have thrown the mules-versus-oxen debate for a loop.[7]

Other than the sudden death of James Knox Polk and the romantic stories of those crossing the country for gold, the headlines across the county remained morbidly attentive to the widespread cholera outbreak now in its third month. The epidemic was keeping coroners busy in every large US city, where it persisted as the leading killer of young and old. One part of the country free of the deadly scourge was the High Plains territory west of Fort Laramie. Emigrants who reached this point in the journey had outrun the disease.

Citizens of Newark, including the parents, wives, and children of Newark Overland Company members, were facing a summer surrounded by the deadly and unyielding illness. The gold seekers had no way of knowing how serious the threat had become to their loved ones as they moved farther away from home without the benefit of mail and newspapers. Their situation on the trail was equally precarious as they faced life-threatening perils day after day. By mid-June the least of these dangers was cholera.

Chapter 14

The Divide and the Great Salt Lake

Ten days had passed since the Newark Overland Company's near disaster at the North Platte River crossing. The chaotic events left Henry L. Johnson, a jeweler by trade, miserable and apologetic over his stubbornness in having refused advice to remove the wagon cover.[1] The decision should have been an easy one, considering the gusty conditions that persisted on the river. Not only had his decision put men in danger when they were flung into the foamy water, but he had also left his messmates without transportation and provisions. He was able to salvage a smattering of goods, some clothing, and one wagon wheel from the wreckage.[2] Fortunately everyone survived. The company lost valuable energy and time, but otherwise it was no worse for wear and moved out the next day on schedule as a team of seven wagons.

General Darcy handled the matter with his trademark dignity and wisdom. He refrained from issuing any blame and exhibited extraordinary kindness in vowing to provide the four men with food and shelter until they reached California. "These men are with us, and we will see that they share our fare on the way," he was understood to say.[3] Darcy had the ability to demand uncompromising compliance when situations dictated an iron hand, as well as the ability to act in a fatherly and compassionate manner when necessary. Darcy's company had remained intact since leaving Independence and at no time experienced any dissension that threatened the group's cohesiveness. That accomplishment, credited to Darcy, was shared by few teams on the crowded trail in 1849.

Similarly, Major Meeker had no harsh words for Henry Johnson despite having spent several fearful minutes in the North Platte's racing current due to Johnson's careless decision. Meeker's unselfish response was to assume the duty of returning ropes used in the ferrying process to their correct owners. He rode some fifty miles round-trip to ensure that each company had its rightful equipment. It was proper trail etiquette, and it was Meeker's way.[4]

Between June 19 and 29, Darcy's company moved westward at a steady pace, with no episodes of broken wagon parts or missing stock to retard their progress. They passed the paint- and tar-inscribed Independence Rock without noticing Cyrus Currier's red-chalk autograph placed there twenty days earlier. They camped just beyond the monolithic landmark, in view of a narrow canyon called Devil's Gate. Vegetation was becoming dominated by Artemisia, a distinct smelling shrub better known as sagebrush, which was consumed by almost no game except the fleeting antelope. Buffalo were notably absent, as their preferred diet of prairie grass was not found in the drier High Plains region.

The North Platte River was finally behind the Newark men when they struck out along its tributary Sweetwater River, the final east-flowing river they would follow en route to California. Yet freshwater in the region was anything but sweet, with dangerous concentrations of alkaline elements leached into creeks and pools. Such high pH levels were toxic, and many animals perished when their extreme thirst sent them rushing for a drink. It was alkali poisoning that caused the death of Faithful Joe, the lead ox of the Gray-Crockett team. Joe's loss put the men at a serious disadvantage at a time when livestock were becoming worn out while arduous mountainous ascents remained before them. Charles Gray was serving night guard when he found Joe dead: "He belonged to my mess & at present his loss is invaluable, as we cannot replace him. I didn't mourn for him, but considering our present position I shall miss him very much. Faithful Joe! Although a brute, I had hoped to have been your *companion* for many days!"[5]

Thousands of oxen and mules were lost to alkali poisoning on the trails, though some were saved by a simple administration of some type of acidic substance to neutralize the extreme base. One company doctor carried tartaric acid for such circumstances.[6] Others understood that lard or bacon fat could successfully counter the deadly effects if the animal could be corralled and forced to consume a sufficient dosage in reasonable time.[7] Faithful Joe would be the only animal lost by the Newark Overland Company over the entire journey from Missouri to California, again an accomplishment credited to Darcy's prudent and patient leadership.

Both the carcasses and the resulting stench of dead animals were now everywhere, as grass had become scarce and water more lethal. Human graves also continued to be frequent sights on the trailside margins, although, unbeknownst to most travelers, they were not always filled with human remains. Lightening loads was no longer a matter of discarding excess baggage and overstocked items. In order to reduce the burden on worn and weary beasts, it was now essential that items of greater value be left behind. Rather than leaving them exposed for pillage or ruin, companies sometimes buried articles in pseudographs and marked them with unique identifiers including false names, dates, and causes of death. The rationale was to move ahead where they could regroup and send fresh teams back to retrieve the goods. This happened rarely, but one emigrant was known to have sold the *location* of such a grave that contained a stash of liquor. Others reportedly used the false-grave measure simply to prevent both Mormons and Indians from benefiting.[8]

For the graves that genuinely contained lost comrades, the chief cause of death on the trail was no longer cholera. Typhoid and "mountain fever" had become more common fatal diseases. Accidents also took many lives, with drowning and gunshots the most common causes. On June 29 General Darcy—or more appropriately in this case, Dr. Darcy—was called on to administer to a young man who had shot himself in the leg. The wound involved a shattered knee that left no option for his survival other than amputation. Darcy was joined by a US Army surgeon, and together they anesthetized the man with chloroform and proceeded to remove his leg. The patient survived the operation, but his long-term prognosis was grim.[9]

The army surgeon who assisted Darcy was part of a regiment of mounted riflemen commanded by Maj. John Smith Simonson, a Mexican War veteran who was leading a contingent of dragoons, some fifty wagons strong, to the Bear River. Gray was interested to learn that the major's daughter was traveling with the train, as were a number of other females who were fortunate to be riding in the luxury of spring wagons, though some opted for horseback.[10] The presence of the women lifted Gray's spirits considerably. The Jerseymen traveled with the military unit for several days before leaving them encamped prior to crossing the Continental Divide at South Pass.

On the same stretch of road, the Newark Overland Company began traveling with a family from Dubuque, Iowa. John V. Berry was unwell when the parties met, and Dr. Darcy gave the man considerable medical attention, hoping to spare his young wife, Catherine, the grief of a trail-side funeral. Catherine was an educated, take-charge woman, who was as capable as her husband of managing the livestock, a pair of wagons, and their two sons, ages three and six. It was her strength and fortitude that had brought them thus far.[11]

If the women accompanying the dragoons had captured Gray's attention, Mrs. Berry may have left him with all sorts of inappropriate thoughts. As her husband struggled to regain his strength, Gray engaged in numerous intellectual conversations with the woman he described in his journal as "smart." About the same age as Gray, she was Maryland-born, the daughter of a prominent military man, and, like Gray, fond of classic literature. Among her belongings, those too valuable to be thrown out, were books including works by Shakespeare, one of which she loaned to Gray. He cherished the new acquisition even if it was to be in his possession only temporarily.[12]

There was no rest for the ailing John V. Berry when his family's two wagons combined with the seven of Darcy's company. Together they began the ascent up to the Continental Divide at South Pass. There was much anticipation in crossing into the Pacific watershed, but the summit was nothing like any of them expected. Rather than reaching a rocky crest and viewing westward-racing waters, the passage was more of a broad, treeless swale, hardly recognizable as the spine of a continent. Gray remarked that the road over the pass was one of the finest he had ever seen, comparing it to New York's Third Avenue.[13]

Once over South Pass, camp was set up along the Little Sandy River, and a day of rest was ordered. The weather was splendid and the mountain air somewhat thin at seven thousand feet but as pure as anyone had ever experienced. The Wind River Mountains to the north shone with snow-capped peaks thirteen thousand feet above sea level and were viewed in closer detail with the spyglass. Snow had been found along the trail at the higher elevations, and buckets of it had been gathered for eating, a simple treat even without cream and sugar. "Think of that ye denizens of pent up cities! snow almost in the very heart of summer!" Gray's witty remark in his journal reflected some excitement, contrary to his earlier disgust with daily hardships. He wrote in Gillespie-like fashion about the songbirds warbling in the morning and his astonishment at finding a bumblebee far from civilization, as if bumblebees were citified insects.[14]

A day off gave the men time for organizing wagons, making repairs, cleaning, and tending to livestock. Gray attempted to bathe in the Little Sandy, but found the water extremely cold—indeed, it was melted snow. "I was obliged to use a basin & towel upon the bank & felt glorious after it," he explained in his journal.

Gray finished the day by studying maps of the route, making calculations about distances, and projecting an arrival date in California. By now he knew that the General had decided to divert from the central road and visit the city of the Latter-day Saints, as did approximately 30 percent of the emigrants. The majority of wagons continued westward along numerous alternate trails and eventually passed through Fort Hall.[15] All travelers would converge on the single road near the Raft River in southwestern Idaho.

After the lazy day at the Little Sandy, the Darcy group rolled out again, making up for the lost time by covering twenty-eight miles. The difficult day stripped Gray of his lighthearted mood and again reduced his spirit to a plaintive level. He retired early, skipping dinner, but with sore feet and hands found it difficult to sleep in plummeting temperatures typical in higher elevations after sundown. No sooner had he fallen asleep than his uncle Andrew woke him, igniting a tantrum. The two got into an all-out scuffle, drawing the attention of the entire camp. Another messmate came to the aid of Andrew, and the fight continued with the younger Gray in a huge mismatch against the two larger men.[16]

Darcy was furious. The next day he took his nephew aside and reprimanded him severely for letting his ego bring out such childish behavior. Charles Gray attempted to defend himself, but he soon learned that most of the camp blamed him for the mêlée and sided with Andrew. It took two days, but he finally let go of his pride and apologized to the General for the incident and promised to avoid such conduct in the future. Gray apparently mentioned nothing of the episode when he wrote home on

July 3 but reported the journey had been more agreeable than anticipated. He mailed the letter by way of eastbound Mormons, paying fifty
cents for postage.[17]

At the Green River, the company was lined up behind twenty-five
wagons and sat waylaid for an entire day waiting their turn to utilize the
Mormon-run ferry. Brethren of the Saints mingled about the riverbanks
exciting emigrants with their specimens of California gold. It was genuine, and it was the first time any of them had seen the prize they were all
rushing to acquire.[18]

The Green River, a tributary of the Colorado, afforded one of the last
great river crossings on the trail. The Newark Overland Company spent
July 4 moving their wagons safely to the western bank, which left little
time to observe Independence Day. Many companies traveled on this day
but stopped in time to feast and fire rounds of ammunition in celebration. Loads were further lightened when rum, brandy, and whiskey were
consumed.

In the South Pacific, still nearly seven thousand miles from the Golden
Gate, the passengers of the bark *Isabel* made the most of the national
holiday. Aboard ship the "glorious Fourth" was announced with patriotic
music and the raising of colors on the masthead. The commemorative
oration delivered by New Brunswick company president Augustus Taylor awkwardly compared George Washington, "the herald of Republi-
canism," and John the Baptist, "the forerunner of Christianity," but was
overwhelmingly well received. It was certainly better than Taylor's Sunday sermons, when he is said to have preached more than once about
Jonah and the whale as the *Isabel* rolled over ocean swells with pods of the
mammoth mammals nearby. Whether the story was a personal favorite
or whether Taylor had a sense of humor is unclear.[19]

The *Isabel* was now five months at sea, sailing north toward the equator and away from the Southern Hemisphere's wintry season. The ship
captain and the company president had spent much of the voyage at
odds with one another. Their differences were petty and caused squabbles
to erupt over the silliest issues, such as Taylor wasting water when he
brushed his teeth. Often Taylor found the captain, who boasted of daring
accomplishments on the high seas, praying alone in his cabin, fearing for
his life on the stormy ocean. For Taylor, it would be written, there was no
greater moment than when the captain's wig blew off on a windy day and
was forever lost in the waters of the Pacific.[20]

The Newark Overland Company, far from any ocean, was making its way over rough terrain to Great Salt Lake City. Their route passed through Fort Bridger, a privately run trading post founded by the frontier scout Jim Bridger. Here Charles Gray went on a shopping spree, purchasing a buffalo robe, a horse and saddle, and twenty-five cigars. He then perused the grounds, and later recorded in his journal that he had seen "several squaws" and "quantities of papooses." He indicated that Bridger's wife was an Indian, but did not mention that she had given birth to a daughter three days earlier. Bridger's wife died from that childbirth, but some reports cite her death on July 4 and others claim it was not until July 13.[21]

Between Fort Bridger and the Salt Lake Valley stood the Wasatch Range, the most difficult terrain of the journey so far. Forget icy Laurel Hill in the Pennsylvania highlands. The Utah summits were precipitous and rugged, giving credence to the name Rocky Mountains, precisely what emigrants had visualized for the Continental Divide. The twisted trail was so narrow in places that drivers could not see their lead animals as they struggled with steep grades and dense shrubbery.[22]

Those who chose to visit the Mormon enclave did so to avoid the overused route to Fort Hall, as well as to recruit livestock, resupply provisions, and get a fresh start for the final seven hundred miles to the placer beds in California. Word had been spread, often by the Mormon entrepreneurs on the trail, that Brigham Young's two-year settlement was becoming an established portal for trade and hospitality. Yet suspicions ran deep in 1849, and the majority avoided any contact with the Latter-day Saints. The confrontations that had taken place in Illinois and Missouri between followers of Joseph Smith and local communities kept gold rush companies from those midwestern states away from the Salt Lake Valley.[23] Darcy's New Jersey party held more liberal views, as did other eastern companies who were not guided by the rumor and prejudice commonly expressed in the 1840s regarding Mormonism.

Seven days were required to travel from Fort Bridger to Great Salt Lake City. While arduous, the route afforded some of the most rewarding encounters and breathtaking vistas any of the men had yet experienced. They passed within a stone's throw of nesting eagles, inhaled the sweet aroma of wild roses, observed the blackened skeletons of burned evergreens, and savored trout measuring eighteen inches in length. Major Meeker took a solo climb to the crest of a craggy peak where he frightened a herd of mountain goats that scattered on his approach. A number of men explored a cave that was so large it prompted Charles Gray to declare that it could serve as a comfortable home with "a little assistance from art."[24]

The wonderment of the Rocky Mountain ascent was tempered by ever-present hardships, the most aggravating being the very poor road, an obstacle course over stumps, rocks, and logs. Wagons took a beating, and a broken wheel forced the company to halt for repairs. The misfortune at the North Platte River with Johnson's wagon had a silver lining, as the salvaged wheel was quickly put in place and travel continued.

Gray was no better off with a horse to ride than he was walking. His mount stumbled, throwing him to a hard landing that injured his leg and shoulder. A few days later the animal became mired in mud up to its belly and had to be pulled out with assistance from other teams. For Gray there was always something to complain about. Fortunately, the penny cigars he purchased at Fort Bridger helped warm him at night, but they did little to repel mosquitoes that were back again in full force, swarming campsites and tormenting the men.[25]

After a week zigzagging through the rocks and ravines of the Wasatch Range, travelers entered Emigration Canyon, where a well-defined stream directed snowmelt westward, interrupting the trail every hundred yards or so and leaving very little room on either side for wagons and horses to maneuver. Teams were required to cross the creek again and again to work their way out of the canyon. The Newark Overland Company members recorded nineteen crossings, which was the number most frequently reported by those writing of the experience, with some exaggerating a much higher number.[26]

In the afternoon ominous clouds darkened the sky, threatening a deluge, but scarcely any drops reached the ground. Thunder was still echoing angry claps through the canyon when the clouds swept swiftly from the sky, permitting golden rays to stream from above. Just as the heavens brightened, the company came to a clearing unveiling a panoramic western view. The exultation felt by the men was expressed in Gray's journal: "*Ahead* of us for some 30 or 40 miles the splendid valley of the *Great Salt Lake* bathed in golden sunshine & we could see mountain tops far *above* it, . . . whilst on our left mountains . . . were cover'd with snow & ice *almost glittering*." Crowning the vista was a faint wall of mountains in the west, causing some to mistakenly wonder if they were looking at the Sierra Nevada, keeper of the gold deposits and their intended destination. "I am free to say that such scenery cannot be often seen by man.—We were really astounded and fixed for some time in full and silent admiration," wrote one Darcy party member.[27] The silence was broken by a chorus of emotional shouts as the men realized they had reached "civilization" after thirteen hundred miles of travel through raw, sparsely populated country.[28]

The descent from Emigration Canyon continued the following day as Darcy's party covered the last thirteen miles to the Mormon community. Finally they saw the outline of a city, with blocked streets, outlying fields of planted crops, and bustling human activity. At six o'clock, the wagon train merged onto a wide thoroughfare called Emigration Street, the principle inroad to the settlement. Little Mormon boys who met the Jerseymen were immediately hired to herd and pasture the stock. Camp was set up at the base of the mountain near a commons used by the transient California-bound traffic. Once settled, men went in search of what they had anticipated most—fresh food and plenty of it, with butter, vegetables, milk, and eggs among the most savored items.[29]

Gray was still at odds with his messmates and left the camp alone in search of lodging away from his comrades. He found the campground too run-down for his liking, an odd complaint after spending seventy-five days on the trail. After scouting the town he found "a lady all to myself," with whom he arranged room and board, the "room" being a wagon on the premises. The woman prepared a spread of "*fresh fish, pot cheese, butter, green peas, rye bread & milk & buckwheat cakes,*" and Gray dined in delight "*at a table where things were cooked by a woman & everything appearing so nice and clean.*" He devoured the meal and then suffered the consequences of surprising his system with too much rich food, tossing and turning throughout the night. But he had no trouble sitting at the breakfast table the next morning and again overeating with pleasure.[30]

While Gray was away from camp, the common stock wagon that had suffered significant damage crossing the mountains was taken for repairs. The work would take several days, giving the men time to observe the population of Saints and explore the city, which was barely two years old. While Brigham Young and his followers had arrived in July 1847, most of the development had taken place in the past ten months. Great Salt

Lake City was an orderly layout of broad streets running primarily north and south. Residential districts were neatly lined with dwellings made of blue-gray adobe bricks and situated on equal-sized lots, with cultivated garden plots stretching across each backyard. Adjacent to the city were hundreds of acres of cropland, watered by an efficient irrigation system that redirected the melted snow of mountain streams.[31]

The population of the industrious town was understood by Darcy's men to be about eight thousand, the majority being US citizens. Charles Gray observed, "The people are sociable, intelligent & pleasant & the greater portion accustomed to the manner of living of the States, are in fact part & parcel of that great family, except there appears to be a tinge of fanaticism." Among the Mormon converts were men from Newark who recognized members of the Darcy party. Others hailed from such foreign countries as France and Gibraltar, and a significant number had made the pilgrimage from England. Major Meeker noted that he saw residents "indeed from almost every country on the face of the globe."[32]

The Newark men also observed a construction project underway in the city center, where masons had completed the foundation and first story of an elaborate stone building. Some described it as a church while others called it a meetinghouse.[33] There was no mention of it being another temple like the one erected in Nauvoo, Illinois, whose very cornerstone was laid by Joseph Smith. The Nauvoo structure was considered a "magnificent specimen of architecture," and after Mormons were forced to flee Illinois, the edifice was readily purchased by a Catholic mission. Fire had mysteriously gutted the temple just days before the sale was finalized.[34]

While a new place of worship was under construction, Sunday services were held under a makeshift canopied structure that Major Meeker called a "rude shed." It was actually quite substantial, measuring sixty feet by one hundred feet, constructed for the upcoming July 24 celebration of the settlement's second anniversary, which several thousand were expected to attend.[35] All California-bound emigrants were extended invitations.

A number of the Newark men went to an afternoon sermon, taking their seats among "a large assemblage, some dressed quite fashionably," according to Meeker, who was there with his messmate, the proudly religious Robert Bond. Also attending was the unapologetically unreligious Charles Gray. Music from a brass band opened the assembly, followed by business matters, community announcements, and the welcoming of visitors. Gray looked over the Book of Mormon and found that "it really *looked* about as much *like* a bible as ours, & no doubt will *do these people* about as much good." Meeker noted that the followers fully believed that their current leader, Brigham Young, whom Meeker had seen, was "as capable of performing miracles and prophesying as was the Son of God." While a number of the Newark men made fun of the occasion, Bond left with an understanding that the Mormons were people of good faith and were "very confident of salvation."[36]

The afternoon services included a series of toasts that took aim at the US government for turning a blind eye to the brutalities Mormons experienced in Illinois and Missouri, forcing them to flee the states. "Three groans for Martin Van Buren" caused laughter throughout the crowd.[37] Despite these negative sentiments, Mormon leaders had drafted a constitution and chosen a delegate to deliver the beautifully handwritten document to Washington. The delegate was preparing to depart for the nation's capital, where he expected to petition for acceptance into the Union and represent the State of Deseret in Congress. The request would generate serious opposition, especially with controversial practices such as polygamy known to exist among the Mormon population. Still, liberal newspapers would support their cause, espousing such sentiments as, "Have we not admitted New Mexico, peopled by Mexicans, adhering to Catholicism?"[38] Even Gray recognized the irony. "I look'd upon them," Gray wrote in his journal, "as the *Puritans of the 19th century*, men who had fled from persecution to a remote & distant region to enjoy unmolested their own belief."[39]

On July 16 Thomas Bullock, a clerk representing Brigham Young, made contact with the Newark men. He had begun compiling lists of the California-bound companies that had come through the Salt Lake Valley. On a blue sheet of paper the twenty-five names of John S. Darcy's company were carefully recorded, including the two young black boys brought along as servants. Samuel Kelly was among those named. Not previously listed on any company roster, he likely joined in Missouri when Augustus Baldwin, Joseph T. Doty, and Thomas Young had returned home. Written across the bottom of the page was "Newark Overland Co."[40]

General Darcy and his men spent five nights in the Mormon city, a respite from the trail that allowed time for rest and recreation. Nothing was enjoyed more than a sulfur bath at a hot-spring pool three miles

Fort Hall in Idaho, the last of the military posts where forty-niners could stop and resupply, sketched by Charles B. Gillespie, July 1849. Courtesy of the Rees-Jones Collection.

north of the city. It was so popular with both locals and emigrants that Thursdays and Fridays were reserved for females only. Meeker recognized the investment potential of the healthful water: "I would ask no greater fortune for myself than to own such a fountain of healing waters in New York or New Jersey."[41]

Gray rode out to the hot springs and found the hundred-degree water "perfectly delicious" and was pleased to be dust free after only fifteen minutes of bathing. A day later he decided to get rid of his horse. Believing that the animal was "some what dangerous to take along as he may break his leg or my neck," he traded it for a fresh yoke of oxen.[42]

On July 17, Major Meeker composed a letter about his experiences in the City of Great Salt Lake, which was subsequently published in the *Newark Daily Advertiser*. He concluded the letter with a commentary on crickets: "The Indians who inhabit this valley drive the large crickets which abound here, and which they esteem a great luxury, into the hot water, and they are soon cooked. The Indians also set fire to the grass in the vallies for the sake of crickets. By the time the grass is consumed the crickets are well roasted, and are eagerly devoured. They are about 8 times as large as crickets of the States. I have a specimen."[43]

The Newark Overland Company prepared to leave Great Salt Lake City on July 19, having utilized blacksmithing services and having fully restored their supplies and spirits. Letters were mailed, and information was collected on the northern route that would put them back on the same trail as emigrants coming from Fort Hall and the alternate northern trails. They believed they were forty-five days from California and would arrive about September 1.[44]

Charles B. Gillespie had departed Fort Hall around July 12, before General Darcy's men had reached the Salt Lake Valley. Their Jackass friends now had a clear advantage in the race for California. They would pass through the City of Rocks, the noted landmark located near the intersection of the Fort Hall and Salt Lake routes, nearly two weeks ahead of the Newark Overland team. Even more dramatic was the lead that Cartwright and Currier had gained over General Darcy's company, which by now had stretched to five weeks.

Robert Bond wrote the final entry in his journal on July 17, while still camped in the Mormon settlement. When his book was passed to later generations, someone erroneously titled it "Diary of Overland Trip to Salt Lake City."[45]

Chapter 15

July Arrivals

Morning mist from the Pacific rolled over the San Francisco hills in the summer of 1849 just as it does today. Ships teeming with anxious gold seekers were often forced to anchor outside the Golden Gate until fog lifted, yielding visibility for safe conduct into the natural port. Nearly six months to the day since its early January departure from New York, the *Ocean Bird* passed through the famed landmark on July 2, one of the first ships of the season to have sailed around Cape Horn.[1] More were following in its wake from both Atlantic and Pacific ports. Letters received back east confirmed the scene: "The anchorage was crowded with vessels and more were arriving daily. Some hundreds were expected to arrive by the month of August; a dozen or more from the Celestial Empire was daily looked for."[2]

Exactly one month after the *Ocean Bird* entered San Francisco Bay, the bark *Isabel* glided through the Golden Gate and dropped anchor alongside a hundred other sailing vessels that, together with sails furled, appeared as a sea of skeletal masts. The *Isabel*'s voyage took 178 days over 18,000 miles of ocean. New Brunswick company president Taylor and *Isabel* captain Brewer had survived each other.[3]

Once inside the harbor, few ships exited. By summer the view of the expansive bay from overlooking hillsides was blackened by scores of barks and brigs with no place to go, abandoned by crews desperate for El Dorado.[4] Excitement over reaching the port was followed by impatience,

Abandoned ships in San Francisco Bay, photographed in 1849 or 1850. Courtesy of the Library of Congress (HABS CAL, 38-SANFRA, 85-1).

as the absence of a deepwater dock meant that people and cargo had to be shuttled to shore by small crafts, a time-consuming process. Their excitement over reaching the magnificent port was tempered by the clutter and backlog impeding their path to the gilded riverbeds more than one hundred miles inland.

Many from the East Coast who had already arrived in California came by way of Panama, and Newark was well represented among these early arrivals. They shared their first impressions with hometown newspapers, describing San Francisco as an overcrowded tent city, where construction was stymied from a lack of lumber, a commodity whose prices were among the most inflated.

Additional intelligence from letters received by Newark papers reported the excess of gambling consuming San Francisco. While men lived under canvas shelters, bowling alleys and billiards parlors occupied the precious space under permanent roofs, as did countless gambling houses.[5] "It is not surprising," one reporter concluded, "that gambling should for the time prevail in the sea-port, occupied as it is by a shifting and shiftless population, of adventurers gathered from every quarter of the globe. It is mentioned as an indication of the wildness of the gambling spirit that $100,000 had changed hands at a monte bank on the turn of a single card."[6] One newcomer described the situation in letters published in the

Newark Daily Advertiser: "This is one of the strangest places in christendom. I know many men, who were models of piety, morality, and all that sort of thing, when they first arrived here, and who are now most desperate gamblers and drunkards." He also noted, "A man who does not gamble is considered a strange sort of being—one who does not drink is a perfect *museum.*"[7]

Aside from vices, everyone wrote home about the inflated prices they encountered in San Francisco's market places. In addition to lumber, vegetables brought top dollar due to demand and scarcity. There were reports of watermelons selling for eight dollars only to be turned around and sold for double the price. Real estate had increased as much as a thousandfold in two years, with lots once costing $50 able to command $50,000.[8] The only items declining in price were clothing and other durable goods.[9] All the cargo tediously unloaded one skiff at a time was piling up in the streets and, like the ships in the bay, had no place to go. Prices for those imports were driven down by the swelling supply and unavailability of shops that could control inventory.[10] "So many goods arrive," Isaac Overton would explain after his arrival in July, "that it is nearly as cheap to wear a shirt until it is dirty and then throw it away and buy another."[11]

Once in San Francisco, emigrants found that their journey to the mines was hardly over. Those who arrived with trunks and equipment realized there was no easy way to move it, and worse, no place to put it.[12] "The greatest trouble in getting around here is with baggage; they charge enormously for transportation," lamented one miner.[13] They were still far from the gold washings, located at the base of the Sierra Nevada. The only access to them was by a precious few steamers to Sacramento followed by very poor roads wending deep into the foothills and canyons. Astute businessmen recognized the unexploited market in offering services to gold hunters whose patience was worn thin by delays. Many entrepreneurs amassed fortunes by providing transportation, storage, and housing.

The *Isabel* pulled anchor on August 8 and headed inland for the last leg of the company's planned voyage to Sacramento. It was necessary to hire a river pilot to negotiate the difficult passage through San Pablo Bay, Suisan Bay, and a maze of tributaries and islands to the landing near Sutter's Fort. The experienced navigator cost the New Brunswick company an additional $550, still a bargain considering the tonnage of equipment and provisions on board that would otherwise have been abandoned due to the prohibitive cost of moving it by some other means.[14]

San Francisco's population, barely five thousand residents in June 1848, had swelled fivefold by the first of January 1849 and was expected to exceed six figures by summer's end.[15] It was changing not weekly or daily but hourly. By some accounts Americans comprised just one-tenth of the temporary residents, while other estimates went as high as one-half.[16] The incoming passengers from East Coast ports would swing the ratio to distinctly American by late August.[17] But there was no dispute that the diverse populace was overwhelmingly male, a fact not lost on the forlorn men. Seldom did women account for more than 2 or 3 percent of those listed on ship manifests. It was said that the unmarried women were besieged with marriage proposals before they could disembark ships. Discouraging news came from the *Placer Times* in late July, when it announced that the expedition of Eliza Farnham included but one unmarried prospect.[18]

Throughout July vessels continued to sail into San Francisco Bay, dispensing dreamers who then dispensed their last dollars to move themselves and their belongings to the auriferous river bars, often requiring weeks of expensive transportation. At the same time, the earliest of the overland emigrants were just beginning to scale the wall of the Sierra Nevada and spill down the slopes where they would soon meet their seafaring counterparts at the diggings. Among the first of these overland travelers were William Emery and his son, Alexander Cartwright, Frank Woolsey, Tom Seely, Caleb Boylston, John Shaff, Isaac Overton, Cyrus Currier, Stephen Dehart, and Wallace Cook, all accompanied by dependable and durable mules.

The last ten days on the trail had proven to be the most arduous for the loose-knit assortment of professionals from New York and New Jersey that comprised the Cartwright and Currier teams. About the time General Darcy's men began their sojourn at Great Salt Lake City, enjoying hot springs and buttered peas, the mule-drawn wagons of the frontrunners were far in advance, preparing to cross forty miles of unforgiving desert. For two weeks they had followed the snaking Humboldt River, covering three hundred frustrating miles over sloughs, sandy ravines, and dry lakes until they reached the point where the river simply *sank* into the wasteland. To Currier the rank odor at the Humboldt Sink was "like the stirring up of an old privy with a dash of the Salt meadows mixed with it."[19]

Once at the sink they foraged for mere spears of grass for the weary animals and collected foul-tasting water from an abandoned Mormon well to sustain themselves until they could reach the Carson River, a two-day march ahead. To avoid overexertion during the relentless midday heat, travel was planned for hours when the sun was low on the horizon or already set. For twenty hours they pushed onward, stopping only at midnight for a two-hour layover. By the time they halted at eleven the next morning, the animals were near failing, and a company meeting determined they could not go on. The party would remain in place while four men mounted the most fit horses to scout for the closest vegetation and clear water.[20] It was a prudent measure that paid off.

The scouts returned an hour later with word that a grove of trees had been spotted ten or more miles distant, indicating a substantial water source and survival for man and beast. It was decided that the stock would be driven ahead to recruit, leaving the wagons unhitched and a handful of volunteers to watch the provisions. Currier remained behind with five other men.[21]

For twelve hours they were alone in the desert, awaiting the return of replenished stock. Currier recorded the scene in his journal: "It is a dreary desolate place. As far as the eye can reach the country looks like a dried up marsh with stagnant pools in it surrounded by sandy hillocks—no bird, beast, insect or fish to be seen. We kept up courage by looking at Nature grand in desolation and in its majesty. The clear sky and the starry heavens in their splendour from Nature. . . . We quenched our thirst with what bad water we had mixed with vinegar and a little sugar."[22] At midnight the silence was broken when the herded mules returned, and at once the commotion of slapping leather, rustling chains, shouts, and brays filled the empty desert. Wagons soon rolled out for the twelve-mile trek under a half moon and a dome of twinkling stars.

As the sun broke the horizon six hours later, the contingent of wagons pulled in to camp beside the Carson River, and the reunited company rejoiced at having survived the desert crossing. They ate well, washed the layers of dust and disgusting smells from their garments, and bathed in fresh water free of stagnant chemicals. Rested and revived, they broke camp late in the afternoon and followed the Carson, moving eight miles closer to California's gold country.[23]

By midnight they had settled into another encampment adjacent to the river, where stock could graze in a green pasture throughout the nocturnal hours, watched by rotating guards. But the calm would not last. A sentry, finding that a mule had been shot with arrows, sounded an alarm, and all men turned out of tents and wagons to hunt for the culprits. None were found. Currier suspected they were Indians of "the digger Tribe, they live mostly on Roots but are very fond of Horse & mule flesh when they can get it." Upset over the loss of the animal, Currier wrote, "We left the old mule for them to eat, wishing that every mouthful of Old Ned, as he was called, would choke them."[24]

The next days were spent crossing ridges and dry lake beds, still following the general course of the Carson River, ever watchful for more Indians. Currier found the road surface curiously flat and hard, smooth as a house floor and baked like a clay pipe: "It was so hard that the mule's shoes would not dent it. The only way we could tell we were on the road was by riding ahead and finding the manure the animals had dropped that passed some days before us."[25] It was the last of the barren basin-and-range terrain they would experience.

The following day, to their relief, they entered a splendid valley they estimated to be thirty miles long and ten miles across, covered in bluegrass and clover and spotted with both icy cold and hot springs. They named it Carson Valley for the river that had delivered them into its hold.[26] The imposing Sierra Nevada lay just beyond, and they would begin ascending it on July 18, coinciding with the Newark Overland Company's last day in Great Salt Lake City.

The mountain ascent was rugged and the road nearly impassable, but believing their fortunes to lie just over the precipitous peaks, determination prevailed. Once over the mountains, companies that had been cohesive throughout the journey began to break apart as everyone hurried, mule and pack, toward the gold-laden American, Feather, and Yuba Rivers. One such company had traveled close to the Cartwright and Currier teams and was led by a "Captain Paul," who wanted to be the first overland arrival at Sutter's Mill.[27] Lagging a few days behind were the green-and-white-clad men traveling with Englishman William Kelly, whose group had remained united, less concerned about their place at the finish line.

The five-person mess of Alexander Cartwright had moved slightly ahead of their contingent by about half a day, retaining their wagon for the time being. Isaac Overton, who had joined Cyrus Currier and Stephen Dehart after being dismissed from Cartwright's mess at the Green River, decided to depart, with no objection from his latest mess. He had become so frustrated with the tedious process of unloading and reloading the wagon to maneuver up and around the crooked alpine passages that he just quit. In the vicinity of Carson Pass, amid coniferous timber and sheer slopes, he packed a single mule and set off on foot, solo.[28] Soon he fell into company with other lone trekkers, and together they walked the next hundred miles out of the formidable highlands.[29]

William Emery and his son, who had also left the group a few days earlier, abandoned their wagon as they advanced toward the 8,600-foot mountain pass.[30] Few understood the geography of the region. The eastern side of the range marks the delineation of geological uplift, hence the verticality that is so imposing on approach from the Nevada deserts. The western slopes of the Sierra are gentler, gradually descending to the great agricultural valleys of Central California. But emigrants did not understand the topography, and many gave up their wagons just when they had succeeded in dragging them almost to the top.

Currier, Dehart, and Dehart's nephew Wallace Cook were now on their own, struggling with the labor-intensive task of moving the wagon up the mountain. Like Emery and Overton, they finally realized the futility of the effort and gave it up, a difficult decision that Currier described as "like parting with an old and tried" friend. On July 20 they began to transfer their belongings to makeshift pack saddles constructed "from our cot bedstead legs and some thin boards & nails we had in the wagons." With five mules and two horses, they managed to carry the bulk of their remaining provisions and ride, not walk, the final leg to Sutter's Mill.[31]

After crossing the Sierra Nevada, called by many emigrants "the Backbone," Currier and Dehart encountered a group of Mormons traveling east to Utah. They were in need of wagons, and Dehart negotiated a forty-dollar sale of the vehicle they had left on the other side of the mountain pass.[32] Coming from the California goldfields, the land of inflated prices, forty dollars in gold dust may have seemed a modest price to those Mormons. But considering the number of abandoned wagons strewn down the eastern face, free for the taking, Dehart's deal was shrewd at the very least.

The Carson route veered south of Lake Tahoe, though no one seemed aware of the immense body of deep blue water collected in a volcanic crater. Team after team passed through forests, staring in awe at trees of gigantic proportions (now known as Sequoias), and finally, finally, they began to grasp the magnitude of their impending accomplishment. As they descended in elevation, streams grew wider, and the vegetation transitioned to hardwood and berry bushes. As they approached the diggings, the sun-kissed air warmed their exhausted bodies.

Early on the morning of July 24, 1849, Cyrus Currier's team arrived at Weaver's Creek, where they cast their gazes toward the westward-rushing water and observed for the first time men swinging picks and shoveling dirt from the rocky stream. The clanking of iron tools and sounds of heavy labor confirmed they had reached the diggings. By evening they took lodging near Sutter's Mill, a place known to local Indians as Coloma, where exactly eighteen months earlier a single nugget of gold had ignited a manic global quest. Currier penned the final entry in the journal he had kept faithfully since leaving home: "I took a glass of Porter, sat down and read the Newspaper which was a rare treat. I almost felt myself at home again."[33] It had been eighty-nine days since he had left the Missouri state line on April 26, making his mule-led overland crossing one of the quickest on record.

In an anonymous letter composed at Coloma that same July 24 afternoon, the writer described witnessing "a party of seven from New Jersey, the first party that has arrived across the mountains this season. They came about half way with wagons, but abandoned them and packed with mules."[34] It is likely that this letter was written before Currier's late afternoon appearance and referred to Cartwright, Seely, Woolsey, Shaff, Boylston, and the two Emerys.

The *Placer Times* had reported a similar event at the diggings, although not specifically Coloma, on July 14, when Michigan's Edmund Green had arrived with his partner. He would later claim to be the first emigrant to have crossed the plains.[35] John W. Shaff, writing on October 8, 1849, stated incorrectly that he had reached California on July 15 "in advance of all the trains, and was among the first from the States overland."[36] Perhaps he was referring to crossing into California at the territorial boundary, although most emigrants were clueless as to the actual location of the border.

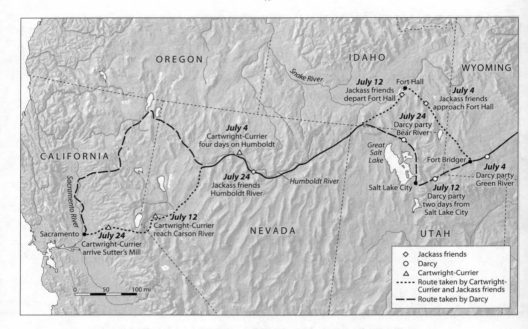

July 1849. The Cartwright and Currier teams arrive at Sutter's Mill while Darcy remains far behind, still days from the Humboldt River. Gillespie has extended his lead over Darcy. Cartography by Bill Nelson. Copyright © 2017 University of Oklahoma Press.

Shaff's letter went on to summarize his strenuous journey with a positive spin: "I have had many adventures since leaving Newark; fought the Crow Indians, and been nearly drowned ferrying in a wagon body over one of the mountain streams (but being a good swimmer, I not only saved my own, but the life of one of our company) hunted the buffalo, killed the grizly bear, crossed the Rocky Mountains, do [ditto] the Sierra Nevada, travelled miles on snow in July, was nearly killed in the Sacramento Valley by a wild Spanish Cow (by having on a red shirt) hunted and killed the elk, antelope, deer, &c."[37]

"The idea of making a fortune here in a minute is preposterous," Shaff's informative letter continued. "It is all a lottery, whether it turns out ill or well." Still, he admitted, "The gold in this country will never be dug out; it will last for ages; but the stories you hear at home are all nonsense. People have to work, and work hard for their fortunes." He closed with a simple comment: "Gambling abounds."[38]

Isaac Overton's letter to the *Newark Daily Advertiser* written from San Francisco on July 29 recounted the completion of his journey with a gentleman who had loaned him a mule to ride just for the promise of sharing company. They had ridden together into Sacramento City, arriving on July 26. Overton then sold his pack mule for $100 and spent one-quarter of the profits for passage aboard a schooner to the crowded city of tents by the bay where he expected to meet his brother. He thoughtfully mentioned the names of fellow Newarkers he had encountered and described their current endeavors for anxious hometown friends and family, including a prominent former alderman who "is here with his family and is running a scow and small boat about the harbor and making money."[39]

One person Overton had not run into was his younger brother, John, who had originally planned to travel overland with General Darcy but shifted his plans at the last minute to board the bark *Griffon* and sail via Cape Horn. Isaac Overton had inquired about the ship's status and relayed the news that the bark *Griffon* had not yet arrived. His long letter, filled with precise details for the Newark paper, included one inaccurate item: Overton believed that General Darcy and his party were expected to arrive at the mines in just ten days.[40]

Chapter 16

Sinking

The Newark Overland Company made camp on July 22, just three days' travel from Great Salt Lake City, when Charles Gray found his way to the wagon of Mrs. John V. Berry, having accepted her invitation for dinner. She and her family had been traveling with the Darcy train since mid-June, when her husband had come under the care of Dr. Darcy. Gray and Mrs. Berry shared a passion for classic literature, a rather uncommon subject on the trail in 1849. "I deem no time so happily spent as when I am reading," Gray mused in his journal. Catherine Berry likely prepared a meal of roasted prairie hens, as the fowl were abundant in the area, but for Gray it was the intellectual conversation he most savored. His journal entry made no mention of her husband, though the man had presumably regained his health during the layover at the Mormon capital, now some fifty miles behind them.[1]

Darcy's party was traveling north around the Great Salt Lake to join the majority of gold seekers who had opted for the primary Fort Hall route. They would cross the Bear River before reaching the intersection with the main road in southern Idaho a few miles south of a unique field of granite outcroppings known to emigrants as the City of Rocks. As wagon wheels and hooves pounded the parched road surface, clouds of dirt became suspended well above the travelers. The dust was inescapable, but the company pushed on in spite of burning eyes and lungs.

On July 28, nine days from Great Salt Lake City, the Jerseymen began to see "a long cloud of dust caused by the trains on the Fort Hall road about 30 miles distant" rising on the northeastern horizon, indicating that the juncture was near. When they camped the following night, they could see the flickering campfires of emigrants across ten miles of sage and sand. Nearby, the sounds of fiddles and tambourines erupted from a neighboring company—a lively performance of old familiar tunes that warmed the spirits and delighted everyone.[2]

Once the roads converged, the wagon trains were again on a single thoroughfare, moving west-southwest toward the headwaters of the Humboldt River. Each day options for food and water deteriorated. Charles Gray's health deteriorated as well. A massive fever blister had broken out on his lip, swelling half of his face and causing his jaw and teeth to throb. Dr. Darcy recommended lancing the ugly sore, but Gray steadfastly refused. As a second prescriptive treatment, the doctor had gone in search of leeches but found none in the shriveled, stagnant ponds and trickling streams along the route. Whiskey did little to relieve the pain, and Gray was prescribed morphine, which produced some relief but also caused violent headaches and nausea. As the company moved on, Gray was confined inside the jolting wagon and for hours endured intense pounding over a road often steep and littered with rocks. After several days of dreadful discomfort, the boil discharged on its own, leaving an open, oozing wound that had to be covered with a flour-based poultice to protect it from the suffocating dust. It was a miserable stretch of days for Gray.[3] He finally began to improve just as they reached a tributary creek leading to the disagreeable Humboldt River, dubbed by some the "Hellbolt."

Three hundred miles downriver and struggling with his own health problems, Pennsylvanian Charles B. Gillespie had reached the Humboldt Sink. For the past six weeks he had suffered from bouts of fever and chills, a resurgence of his old ailment, a cure for which he had believed he could attain by embarking on the cross-country journey.[4] While camped at Independence, a brief reprieve had given him a false feeling of recovery, which he proclaimed in a letter to his sister, but shortly after running into the Darcy wagons west of Fort Laramie, the malady had reappeared.

Gillespie and the Martins, George and Joseph, had separated from the Newark Overland Company in Missouri over the oxen-versus-mules dispute. They had briefly joined a larger company led by Captain Hudspeth, but Gillespie prevailed in convincing the group to go alone before starting on the trail. They had headed west across the Missouri state line with a total of six men, two wagons, and a handful of sturdy mules. When Gillespie's sickness resurfaced a month and a half into the journey, he was no longer able to provide leadership. By the time they reached Fort Hall in early July, the contingent had fallen apart, and the Martins resorted to packing with frail horses and mules, while Gillespie, in a twist of fate, became attached to a group with ox-driven wagons.[5] In his weakened condition he had taken on an aide by the name of Moody, who accompanied him across the Humboldt watershed.

During the three-week period after the Cartwright and Currier teams had moved beyond the Humboldt Sink, emigrants had learned of a lush, grassy meadow located a few ravines off the main course. News of its existence spread by word of mouth, and soon all teams diverted in its direction and spent a day pasturing animals and cutting and drying a supply of hay for the bleak forty-mile desert crossing. Upon seeing the vast waves of grain after days of barren terrain, Gillespie was astounded: "As far as I could see nothing but wheat, wild wheat, almost as high as my head, and as thick and apparently as well grained as ever I saw in a field at home!" He described the activity in his journal: "Hundreds of men busy at work making hay; some cutting with knives, others more provident with scythes; whilst their companions were gathering the green grass and spreading it out to be speedily cured by the intense heat of the glowing brassy sun. As our small caravan came rolling in, another, twice as large was just going out; their wagons piled full of hay which had been cut and cured the preceding day. Pack mules were moving off like diminutive hay stacks, nothing visible but a tail or an ear." It was an upbeat day, and spirits were soaring, even for Gillespie, whose weakness kept him from contributing much to the effort.[6]

In traversing the desert to the Carson River, Gillespie's party planned to follow the same practice as Cartwright and Currier—traveling hard at night and resting in the heat of the day when the sun was highest. Fortunately, Gillespie had his reliable horse, Dick, to ride while Moody led a miniscule mule, Mousey, which was packed with supplies. The first day they pushed late into the night and eventually stopped for a short rest near a campfire, where they met a group that was originally part of a large company from Pennsylvania. There, a most unexpected happenstance took place, when crackling and dancing ribbon-like flames shone amber light on the face of an old acquaintance Gillespie knew from Pittsburgh. Both men were elated, neither aware that the other had joined the rush for California gold, and they were amazed at finding one another amid thousands on the trail. Upon learning that his friend had lost his animals, Gillespie, in a most generous gesture, offered him the little mouse of a mule and then watched sadly as it was led away in the night.[7]

Gillespie's severe fever and chills had abated for a few days, leaving him confident of his ability to make it safely to the Carson River and to let a sicker man ride Dick while he took to foot. He later recalled, "I had made a bad calculation respecting my powers of endurance. The heavy sand was too treacherous for me. My strength was soon exhausted, and when the sun began to look upon the scene it made things entirely too hot for endurance. Fortunately I had strength enough in my arms to hold on to the rear of the wagon by which alone I was sustained and made out to struggle along."[8]

Most of the animals pulling the wagons of Gillespie's small group were holding up well and appeared capable of making it to the river ahead. But one ox was failing, and like many parties before them in similar circumstances, they came to the realization that it could not go on. The consensus was to unhitch the lone wagon and drive the healthy stock on to the water. "After a hurried consultation, I was left in charge of the abandoned wagon," Gillespie wrote. "The oxen unyoked and all but the unfortunate one like myself driven on through the sand to the yet distant Carson river there to be refreshed; and then in the near future to be brought back and draw the wagon through the desert and away to the river."[9]

Left alone in the desert with no water and no shade from the overhead blaze, not even a wisp of a cloud to block a few rays, Gillespie sought refuge in the shadow of the wagon. But he could not survive there for long. There he lay, shivering uncontrollably one minute, only to be panting and sweating the next. The swings repeated as the sun rose to its peak and began to slide toward the west, the air temperature rising every hour until it exceeded one hundred degrees. Gillespie faded in and out as he cycled through the tormenting ague.[10]

A noise approaching from the direction of the Carson River roused Gillespie from his stupor. He saw a horse—not Dick, but a jet-black steed mounted by a powerful man riding upright, coming directly toward the wagon. The horse stopped near Gillespie, and the "fine specimen of a western man" dismounted. Then a miraculous sight met Gillespie's gaze. Attached to the saddle hung not one but a dozen canteens filled with cool, sweet water! The stranger reached for a tin cup, which he filled and offered to Gillespie, explaining that he had little to spare as he was returning to his own stranded party. Gillespie relished it and blessed the man profusely. It was an act of kindness greater than Gillespie could have dreamed, and it saved his life.[11]

Twenty-four hours passed before another horse was heard approaching the wagon. This time it was Dick carrying a member of the caravan and driving four oxen. Twilight was upon them. "I mounted my gallant Dick," he recounted, "and before daylight the next morning, had crossed the desert and joined my companions, encamped on the green enameled bank of the Carson."[12]

While everyone else rejuvenated along the verdant banks of the nourishing river, Gillespie remained in the grip of a relentless fever. He was becoming desperate for a cure. "All the tonics and ante periodics that could be obtained were tried and all failed," he noted. "For two months it had alternately frozen and fried me; I was now so weak that I could not mount my horse without assistance."[13]

Gillespie momentarily contemplated a homeopathic remedy recommended by a passerby: submerging himself in an ice-cold bath. The opportunity was now at hand, with frigid water from the snow-capped Sierra flowing placidly before him. But he could not bring himself to jump in. "I verily believed the plunge would have ended me and the ague together; and so, crestfallen, and shivering," he wrote, "I downed my habiliments and like a veritable coward that I was hid myself amid some willows and there wrestled my tormentor."[14]

Companions were becoming increasingly alarmed at Gillespie's diminishing stamina, but Gillespie was about to experience a second miracle in as many days. A man from a neighboring company, just in from the desert crossing, spotted him in his willow hideout. A physician from Illinois, he queried Gillespie about the nature of his ailment and the medicines he had tried—specifically asking whether he had been prescribed quinine. Gillespie affirmed that, yes, he had swallowed ten grains with each dose. At this the doctor laughed, "You men from the east don't know how to treat the chills; we give it in tablespoonfuls." He kindly provided Gillespie with an ample dosage from his pharmaceutical supply, instructing him to take it the following morning. Gillespie complied, and the chills and fever never returned.[15] Eventually he would understand that the infirmity that had plagued him for several years was malaria, possibly contracted during travels into Mexico on his previous trip west across the Santa Fe Trail.

After two days of rehabilitation beside the Carson River, Gillespie's makeshift company faced several days of travel to reach the base of the Sierra Nevada. Ahead of them was a hard, dry lake bed, void of footprints, and the magnificent Carson Valley, with its surprising hot and cold springs that Currier had noted weeks earlier.

Waking one morning with the towering peaks before them, Gillespie and Moody decided to eliminate the wagon and pack over the mountains. They bid the men of their company adieu and with spare rations joined the march toward the wall of stone rising over ten thousand feet in the western sky.[16] From the summit, the diggings could be reached in four or five days, but they wondered how anyone managed to get to the top.

Several hours on the road brought them face to face with the sight of genuine California gold dust, shown to them by a family of Mormons who had crossed the Sierra and were heading back east. They had two wagons, one that was likely purchased, unbeknownst to Gillespie, from former company members Cyrus Currier and Stephen Dehart.[17]

Moody, Gillespie, and the horse Dick spent the day winding up canyons and traversing alpine meadows, feeling the physical exertion exaggerated at higher elevations. The Sierra seemed impenetrable, yet one by one, rifts in the mountains served as portals to the next, each taking them closer to clouds and snow and gold. They stopped for the night, knowing the final ascent could be accomplished the next day, and they congratulated themselves for not having a wagon.[18]

Moody, whose assistance Gillespie could not have done without, saddled Dick in the morning, and they began the climb, eventually coming to the tree line where wagons were being unloaded for one final ascent. There before them was the impressive spine of the Sierra, nearly treeless with exposed gray boulders and compact snow forming glacial slides. Looking carefully, they could see movement far up the slope and "began to distinguish faint black specks like crows clinging to the white glacier above," Gillespie wrote. There was no defined trail at this point, just heavily burdened emigrants and empty, weather-beaten wagons inching toward the top of what some called "the parpendicular."[19]

Lake in the Sierra Nevada, sketched by Charles B. Gillespie, August 1849. Erroneously labeled Donner Lake, it is likely Red Lake, located south of Lake Tahoe along the Carson route taken by Gillespie and his party. Courtesy of the Rees-Jones Collection.

Moody set out ahead to pilot a course. Gillespie had become short of breath in the altitude and knew the grade was too steep for Dick to carry him. But his ingenuity prevailed. "After getting my wind, a happy thought struck me," he would later write. "If Dick could not carry me, he could pull me up; and so, taking him by the tail and driving him on in advance, after half an hour's hard work and a dozen of breathing spells for man and beast, we succeeded in joining my companion."[20]

They continued to climb, with Moody leading the way and Gillespie hanging onto Dick's tail until they were hiking on snow. The sun had fallen behind the mountains, and in its absence temperatures were noticeably dropping. "Still up and up until at last we reached the summit and then what a world of glory and immensity was spread out before us!" Gillespie observed in awe. "After so many months of dreary travel; after so much suffering, so much danger, to see the promised and the longed for land before us!"[21]

Several days later they reached their destination at the dry diggings of Coloma, three weeks after the Cartwright and Currier teams had been among the season's first arrivals. Gillespie had traveled part of the incredible journey with his preferred mule teams and part of it with yoked oxen, only to arrive at his destination riding a horse. It was mid-August.

Forty miles north of Sutter's Mill, Joseph and George Martin reached the gold washings on Bear Creek "about the middle of August," Joseph wrote in a letter, "worn out with fatigue, dirty, ragged and miserable." They had parted ways with Gillespie in the vicinity of Fort Hall, where they had dumped their wagon and reorganized their provisions on three remaining mules. In need of a horse, Joseph Martin was forced to sell his watch, only to purchase a mount in poor health. While crossing mountains, the piteous creature fell dead, literally underneath Martin, leaving yet another carcass on a trail littered with fallen animals.[22]

The Martins came over the Sierra Nevada north of Lake Tahoe, having followed the Truckee River after leaving the Humboldt Sink. The northern Truckee route passed the winter camp of George Donner, who three years earlier had failed to get his party over the mountains before heavy snowfall forced them to a destiny of cannibalism. Like curious tourists, some emigrants wandered through the abandoned site where the Donner Party cabins had been ordered burned by the government. Those who kept diaries made notes of stepping over human bones, including skulls that had been sawed open for the nourishing contents. A tattered stocking still harboring the remnants of leg and foot bones was resting amid strewn scraps of household articles.[23] The Martins made no such tour of the dreadful monument.

Gillespie and the Martins were the second wave of the Newark Overland Company's former members to reach the diggings, ending their brutal cross-country trek. Meanwhile, the men with General Darcy were still weeks behind, maintaining a pace of seventeen miles per day on their approach to the smelly Humboldt Sink.

They were now in the territory of Indians known by many as "Diggers," a label perpetuated from guidebooks such as Edwin Bryant's, which Cyrus Currier noted was derived from the Natives' custom of digging roots and plants for food. They were understood to be mostly Shoshones and Paiutes and were known to wander over a large domain extending from the Sierra Nevada to the Great Salt Lake. Emigrant encounters with these Indians began along the willow-lined ravines of the Humboldt and continued into the foothills on the western slopes of the Sierra.

These Indians were known to raid emigrant camps at night to steal animals. Notes warning of this activity were left along the trail by preceding travelers, and everyone maintained a close nightly watch. Still, companies would rise in the morning to find that all of their animals had been stolen, and they were left marooned in most dire circumstances. One such company followed the tracks of their abducted oxen for miles only to find they had been "jumped off a high bank into a kind of pen from which it was impossible to get them out without ropes and pulleys, while the naked rascals who put them there could be seen dancing upon the rocks & hill tops & making all kind of jeering gestures, but taking care to keep out of rifle shot."[24]

The Newark Overland Company had resumed guarding the stock every night, heeding the warnings from other companies. "So bold had these devils become," Gray noted, that they "cut the horses from the wagon wheels to which they were tied!"[25]

The worst encounter between Darcy's company and Indians took place on this stretch of the trail. Several men had come in one evening "with a fine lot of ducks, mallard & teal, & *an arrow which was shot out of the bushes at them by Indians,*" wrote Gray. "We everyday hear many stories of their depredations & keep up a strong guard." As a result, they increased the nightly watch to four men and strictly enforced it, more so, they believed, than other companies. While some animals briefly wandered off, the Darcy camp lost none of their stock to Indians along the Humboldt margins.[26]

Not all encounters with Indians in this region involved stolen livestock, however. There were also accounts of their use of English. They were heard to utter phrases in repetitive fashion, and often used profanity, which was believed to have been learned from emigrant teamsters. One lone Indian man came into a camp looking for whiskey. When denied, he proclaimed, "White man lie. God Damn," and abruptly departed.[27] On August 6 Charles Gray wrote, "Indians have become quite plenty, every time we stop some come into camp. . . . They were young & fine looking & *could repeat after us anything we said* & when we said 'Do you know what that is, that is a shirt,' he would repeat it exactly." [28]

Some written accounts described trades between gold seekers and desert Indians. These Natives, often naked or minimally attired, were said to be covetous of certain pieces of clothing. In exchange for these prized items, they were known to assist emigrants, in some instances by helping with camp chores and in others by providing beneficial information regarding the navigation of mountain roads. Caleb Boylston, among others, confirmed that he received directions from Indians regarding the route over the Sierra Nevada.[29]

Gray described a time when a young Indian came into their camp and was very desirous of an overshirt worn by one of Darcy's men. According to Gray, he was "delighted . . . half out of his wits," when it was given to him by the man wearing it, William T. Lewis. This particular garment was the formal white dress shirt Lewis's wife, Sarah, had packed so that he would be prepared for a respectable burial should he experience a fatal mishap.[30]

The Newark men passed their hundredth day on the trail realizing that previous hardships had been minor compared to the difficulties of traveling the Humboldt River. Days were hotter, nights were colder, and dust from the alkali soil burned and irritated more so than the clouds of red dirt had two months earlier. "A deuced strange country this, I think," concluded Charles Gray. The company flour had already run low, and the last of the bacon was consumed on August 16. Of greater concern, however, was the health of a few men who had become quite ill and were experiencing the onset of high fever and tremors.[31]

Despite the sickness, a welcome relief for everyone came the next day in the form of rain, the first since torrential storms had soaked through wagon canvasses in early June. Those who were healthy exulted in the freedom of taking deep breaths and filling their lungs with spring-fresh air cleansed by the passing showers, an exercise which had become impossible in the choking dust clouds of the previous weeks.

The temporary respite was overshadowed by growing apprehension regarding the company's well-being, as more men fell ill. Job Denman, a large man and one of the strongest members of the company, had a severe case of the so-called fever. Gray noted in his journal that he had stopped by Denman's tent and "found his nervous system in a very excitable state, every part of him moving involuntarily with twitches, his fingers particularly, so much so as though he was playing on a piano."[32]

Denman glanced up at Gray long enough to notice his ornamental breast pin and asked if he could have it. Gray had just put it on, having retrieved it while reorganizing his baggage, but he took it off and used it to gently fasten Denman's shirt together. Gray walked away with a sense of dread for his companion's welfare. Denman was one of the few men in the company with whom he had not quarreled.[33]

Travel slowed as Darcy treated the sick men of his company. Anyone who experienced high body temperatures and chills after crossing the Rocky Mountains was said to suffer from "mountain fever." It was a catchall term for symptoms that had various organic derivations including infection transmitted from an insect bite; however, the illness impacting the Newark Overland Company seemed to spread, suggesting a contagion. Dr. Darcy recognized it as a "malignant typhoid."[34]

Forty-five miles from the Humboldt Sink, Darcy received intriguing intelligence pertaining to an alternate road, a cutoff to the northwest that was believed to shorten the distance to the diggings by half. The information came from a fur trader who professed knowledge of a route that emigrants had begun taking about ten days earlier due to fears that vegetation had been depleted along the main road. The reports were promising and led Darcy to believe that his party could reach their golden destination with just 150 more miles of travel. He called a company meeting to discuss their options, but the group reached no conclusions. The decision was postponed until additional information could be obtained.[35]

Charles Gray studied the guidebooks and maps, finding it difficult to understand how the new passage could shorten the distance by such a significant amount. He did not believe the reports and maintained faith in his own calculations that indicated they were still more than three hundred miles away. He was correct.[36]

By August 19 five men had been stricken with the fever, forcing the Newark Overland Company to halt for two days. They remained undecided as to their next move but watched as wagon trains moved by, expressly observing whether any were opting for the cutoff. Job Denman lingered, still seriously ill. Robert Bond was also failing.[37]

Chapter 17

The Truth about California

The summer of 1849 closed with a massive influx of foreign and American immigrants arriving in California, some disembarking in San Francisco via Panama and Cape Horn, and others pouring across the Sierra Nevada from the overland routes. Once in California, everyone's views changed. Some were enchanted by the exciting anything-goes lifestyle, while others were aghast at what seemed to be societal recklessness. Opinions were as diverse as the mushrooming population itself.

Many found California surprisingly civil and shared their experiences with hometown newspapers. "There is in no country on earth more perfect security to persons and property than here," wrote one gold seeker.[1] But for every such upbeat opinion expressed, there was one from the opposite end of the spectrum. "The state of society is not agreeable, to my notion," another newcomer wrote. "The other day I saw a man deliberately shot down in the street, and nothing was done about it: and no one knows but it will be his own turn next."[2] Most understood that there were "silly and ridiculous rumors put afloat by letter-writers from this country, for the purpose of 'making the papers sell.'"[3] And those with positive outlooks insisted, "The state of society here has been much misrepresented; you can leave anything out with perfect safety and a more peaceable and obliging set I never saw before."[4]

Attempts to describe California culture often resulted in lengthy reflections from personal experience. In a letter to the *Newark Daily Advertiser*, a former Newark resident attributed his robust health to the purity of the environment, yet he blamed much of the prevailing sickness in California on people having to sleep in open air: "The disagreeableness of the country arises from wet weather for 4 or 5 months, and extreme dry weather the remainder of the year, making the earth either muddy or dusty." About inflation, he wrote that provisions in California came at "Astor House prices." And he further mused, "If I am permitted to return home, I shall be able to spin you a long yarn, detailing those things which I have seen."[5]

Where there was unanimity regarding California life, it was all negative. Many letters home noted the 98 percent male populace, and some pleaded for action. Eliza Farnham had arrived in California with just one unmarried woman in her small group. However, she remained resolute in her mission to increase the female population and expressed her views in the *Newark Daily Advertiser*: "I hope that while our good brethren at home are bestirring themselves kindly to send out churches and clergymen, they will not forget that the best of all missionaries to such a population are resolute, virtuous, intelligent women."[6]

The poor state of the postal service was another great aggravation for the transient population. For two months in the late summer of 1849, no mail from the states was received in the majority of California towns. Like everything else, mailbags were caught in the clogged transportation process. The *Placer Times* offered this editorial on the subject:

> To the ordinary business and corresponding relations of a community, the failure of two successive monthly mails is an almost incalculable evil; but when we add to these facts the extraordinary tide of emigration, and the dismay, doubt and fear which fill that emigration at the knowledge that the pestilence and the scourge are sweeping over their homesteads, the grievance becomes utterly unbearable. Such is at present the situation of our city and district. Thousands who have just arrived among us learn with trembling that the cholera has decimated their native cities and towns, and when they turn with anxiety and fear to the only channel through which they can hear tidings of their loved ones, they are told that no mail has been received.[7]

Certainly nothing about the California experience was more universally acknowledged than the extreme amount of labor required to harvest gold. Rather than picking up nuggets on a leisurely stroll, gold was obtained by moving tons of wet dirt and rock to extract a mere handful of gold gravel. It was not what gold seekers had anticipated. Columns of eastern newspapers were full of miners' reports that described gold mining as harder than canal digging. Many were trying other businesses, and many wished they had never come.[8] Typical of the advice from those who had gone for El Dorado was the following itemization:

1st. If you can make a living at home, do not come.
2d. If you are coming to speculate, don't come.
3d. If you are coming to dig, don't come until you have had a month's experience in removing rocks to grade a northern railroad, and in digging a hole to plant a house in.[9]

Organized companies, if still intact upon arriving in California, quickly dissolved and distributed any remaining funds. At best, small groups of acquaintances remained together to work a claim, and many of those relationships ended within weeks. "This work is ruinous to clothes, and worse to one's temper," proclaimed one associate of the Newark men.[10] Similar sentiments were echoed in every letter sent home, along with an accurate comparison regarding the chances of striking a substantial deposit: it is a lottery.

While mail bound for California had ceased to move efficiently, the flow of letters to the East Coast was steady and voluminous. By late August every steamer arriving in New York from Panama was filled with thousands of letters from sons, brothers, and fathers who had gone west. Newspapers were prompt in publishing the latest correspondence for public consumption, providing those at home with an understanding of conditions prevalent in the California mines. One man working a claim on the American River wrote, "A man's life here is very uncertain. If he avoids the Indians, there is the grisly bear, the tiger, wolf, and wild cat, and rattle-snakes in great numbers: if you escape them, there is the scurvy, which is making great ravages among the miners, and the chills and fever. . . . All things are much different from what we expected; hundreds daily arrive, and after a view of the mines, leave again for the States."[11]

The rush to get out of California became just as urgent as the rush to get there had been. The trend was confirmed in newspapers: "There are many who arrive at the mines anxious for a sight of the very extreme end of the elephant's tail, which when they have seen they are content to turn about and make straight tracks for San Francisco, and from there home the best way they can get there."[12]

While various modes of travel had brought gold-hunters to California from the states, only one route was used for the return trip: the Isthmus of Panama. No one seriously considered retracing the arduous transcontinental journey, and virtually none did. Likewise, the Cape Horn route attracted no takers. Stories of tedious sea voyages and idiotic ship captains were as off-putting as those that described the punishing overland journey. The result was a large demand for bookings on one of the few steamers shuttling passengers out of the Golden Gate to Panama. By late summer those feeling disgusted and duped by gold fever found further disappointment when they learned that passage to Panama had already been engaged two months in advance.[13]

William Emery and his son were among those who could not get home soon enough. Others with whom they had traveled were similarly driven to depart. Frank Woolsey, like William Emery, looked for the fastest way back to New Jersey and discovered that it would take as long to get home as it had to reach the diggings.

Alexander Cartwright had arrived in California with Frank Woolsey and his other close friend Tom Seely. They had been in partnership since February, when they had acquired US passports. Their friendship had endured three thousand miles of exhausting travel, a remarkable feat in itself.[14]

Not only did Cartwright find the gold region deplorable, he was not well. The dysentery that had plagued him during the journey had not abated, and friends advised him to get out of California. Waiting for a vessel to return to New York via Panama was not acceptable, so he sought passage on the first ship, any ship, leaving San Francisco that would take him away. He heard about the healthy climate of the Sandwich Islands and succeeded in boarding the brig *Pacific* destined for Honolulu, half an ocean away. He had been in California less than three weeks when he sailed out of San Francisco Bay in the middle of August, about the same time that Charles B. Gillespie rode into Coloma on his trusty horse Dick.

In the islands Cartwright found a paradise greater than any amount of gold and began to contemplate building a life there and having his family join him. He had left his wife, Eliza, with their two children in New York, unaware that a third child had been conceived weeks before his departure and would be born during his absence. One can assume that he remained unaware of the impending birth, since he probably received no mail in San Francisco, as almost no one did in the late summer of 1849. Otherwise he would have likely returned to New York.

Tom Seely did not share his companions' disapproval of California, nor was he eager to leave the West Coast. Always well liked by those with whom he became acquainted, Seely possessed an upbeat, jovial personality and made friends easily. He enjoyed sharing rounds of whiskey and found the card games at gambling tables a great pastime.[15] The fast life suited him, and he stayed in California. As an experienced ship captain, he was very employable.

Caleb Boylston had been taken into the Cartwright mess after his falling out with William Emery and subsequent comical failure at mule packing. Unmarried and unattached, Boylston, too, found something intriguing in the reckless, burgeoning society he encountered on the Pacific Coast. He made no plans for a quick turnaround back to New Jersey and, in fact, would not see his homeland for almost a decade.[16]

John Shaff had joined the Cartwright group at the Green River crossing, where he took the place of Isaac Overton. With no family awaiting his return to New Jersey, he joined forces with a group of twenty men working a claim on the Yuba River.[17] Noted gold rush diarist J. Goldsborough Bruff described such unions: "They were queer affairs, those partnerships of that day. Two entire strangers would meet, and without preliminaries go to work, living and toiling together, for weeks and even months, trusting each other with their joint earnings, and dividing the same without trouble; never perhaps learning anything more of each other than simply the Christian name."[18] Shaff and his coworkers experienced little success. While his partners were incapacitated with sickness, as was widespread in the crowded camps, Shaff had never been healthier. Since leaving home he had somehow gained nearly thirty pounds in spite of the privations of traveling overland and the arduous regimen of mining.[19]

Cyrus Currier, the man of practical New England values, remained with his partner Stephen Dehart after arriving in California. Like the team of Cartwright, Seely, and Woolsey, Currier and Dehart had also maintained a cordial and respectful relationship over the course of travel.

Prior to their journey, the two men had conducted business together from the same workshop near Newark's rail yards at 290 Market Street. Dehart ran a foundry casting metal, and Currier refined the castings into machines and other tools. Before his departure for the overland journey, Dehart sent a steam engine valued at $3,000 around Cape Horn to San Francisco, costing him $330 in freight. It was one of those speculative ventures so many on the East Coast were making—to gamble in regard to products that would be in highest demand in California. Dehart hoped to return a substantial profit for his investment.[20]

Currier and Dehart spent little time in the mines and headed for San Francisco to inquire as to the whereabouts of the steam engine. Their record-setting wagon travel had been so efficient that they had reached California well ahead of it. By late August they still had not received word about when the engine would arrive, but as they viewed San Francisco's tents and learned of the lumber shortage, they envisioned a profitable way to employ the engine. They would establish a steam-powered saw-mill that would keep them on the West Coast long enough to develop the operation and deliver the first materials to the depleted market. The prolonged absence from home would be hard on Currier, whose wife and three small children were always on his mind.

Also in San Francisco, Isaac Overton pondered a line of work while he awaited his younger brother's arrival on the bark *Griffon*. On his way to the city he had come through the mining region, where he had witnessed life in the camps, and he could not imagine enduring such intense labor in one-hundred-degree temperatures. Swinging a shovel for ten hours a day merely to pay living expenses was not his dream.

Like many newcomers, Overton envisioned limitless business opportunities that could serve the escalating population, but he did not have start-up capital to get an enterprise off the ground. "If I had $1000 I would buy me a team and go to carting from Sacramento City to the mines—60 miles," he explained in a letter, believing he could clear $100 per day, a more secure income than mining. Overton, who had separated from messmates Currier and Dehart crossing the Sierra, recognized that his former companions would do well in California. "Good mechanics can do better than any other class of men without capital," he affirmed. On the contrary, Overton's former occupation with the railroad would do him little good on the West Coast. Overton would have to find employment soon if he expected to continue boarding at the City Hotel, where inflated prices were siphoning his last funds.[21]

Back in the mining region, Charles B. Gillespie's "hotel" at Weber's Dry Diggings was a crowded round tent strung up by someone calling himself an "innkeeper," an occupation that netted more in gold dust than could have been dug from the ore-rich river. The inn was located on Weber's Creek, which emptied into the Rios de los Americanos about a mile downriver from Coloma, the flourishing town adjacent to Sutter's Mill, which was considered the bull's-eye of gold country. Gillespie continued to write in his journal: "The first day we did nothing but eat, and though our landlord could only give us corned beef, warm cakes of molasses with coffee, tea, and sugar, still this was a feast to half starved emigrants like ourselves and our host thought we done ourselves more than justice for he charged us each an additional quarter for emptying a half pint bowl of molasses: our appetites had not yet come down to the usual prices." The next day he and his partners purchased mining tools for use in unearthing their fortunes, "expecting that every stroke of the pick would expose untold of wealth to our astonished eyes."[22]

During Gillespie's first futile day overturning the river bottom, not a single speck of anything glimmering or yellow was discovered. Like most novice and impatient treasure hunters, he and his partners concluded that they had chosen an unlucky spot and abandoned the site the next day to seek another location, again toiling in the hot sun with poor results. And so the pattern continued day after day, chasing the elusive wealth only to circle around to the original diggings to see some other laborers gathering gold in the precise spot where they had failed. Many first-time miners wasted valuable time prospecting for the mother lode rather than tediously excavating and washing each scoop for the handful of flakes that would eventually total a respectable day's wages. Gillespie's group would occasionally have a good day, which only served to keep them at the game, guaranteeing that the cycle of prospecting and moving camp would go another round.

Throughout the fall of 1849 Gillespie made his livelihood roaming from Coloma to Weber's Creek, Hangtown, and "Kelsey's dry diggings," experiencing the highs and lows of mining and witnessing the waves of emigrants rolling in to join the circus. Hardly any place on earth could compare to the diverse and unpredictable hillside camps of California's gold mining towns. Gillespie befriended a family of Chileans with whom he communicated as easily as he did with a Frenchman and his daughter, thanks to his gift for languages and his Butler, Pennsylvania, education. While the placers were not yielding Gillespie a substantial profit in gold, he realized there could be a bona fide bonanza in capturing the unique and colorful stories of life in the mines. He began to write and sketch.

One Sunday in Coloma, Charles B. Gillespie wandered the streets observing miners, some of whom had come into town to worship the saloons and gambling tables with their sacrificial gold. His words captured the scene. "The street was alive with moving crowds of men passing, and repassing, laughing, talking and all appearing in the best of humor," he wrote. "Negroes from the Southern states, swaggering in the expansive feeling of runaway-freedom; Mulattoes from Jamaica were trudging arm in arm with Kanakas from the Sandwich Islands; Peruvians and Chilians were claiming affinity with the swarthier Mexicans." The carnival-like procession of international travelers continued, with Gillespie recognizing Americans as "Yankees" and complimenting California's northern neighbors by calling them "genial Oregonians." After itemizing a host of Europeans, he described Chinese immigrants as "a few celestials with their pig tails, and conical hats," writing that they "appeared like the ghosts of those strange pictures that so took our boyish fancy when studying the geography of the East."

Last, Gillespie noted "a sprinkling of Indians, the only indigenous creatures among all these exotics." He went on to write,

A group of half a dozen of Indians especially attracted my attention; they were strutting about in all the glory of newly acquired habiliments—but with this distinction, that one suit served to dress them all. The largest and best looking Indian had appropriated the boots and hat . . . without any other article of apparel. . . . Another had lost himself in an immense pair of pantaloons, a third sported nothing but a clean white shirt with ruffled bosom; a fourth flaunted a blue swallow tailed coat bespangled with immense brass buttons; a fifth was decked with a flashy vest; and the sixth with nothing to hide his nakedness but a black silk handkerchief, which modestly would have tied around his loins, but which the custom of his whiter brethren impelled to knot around his neck. Thus, what

would have served but one white man, just as effectually accomo-
dated six Indians.[23]

The observations Gillespie recorded about the happenings in Coloma
on that Sunday would provide readers with pages of amusement decades
later. But another encounter, also in the town where the tailrace at Sutter's Mill coughed up the golden egg, had far more historical significance.
It was again a Sabbath morning when Gillespie wandered away from
Coloma's freewheeling activities to pay homage to the site where the first
glint of ore had caught the eye of John Sutter's construction foreman,
James W. Marshall.

Walking slowly along the millrace, Gillespie turned pensive. He would
later record in his journal how a "moralizing vein of thought stole over me
and I saw, and felt the realization of the oft repeated saying that events but
trifling in themselves often produce the most stupendous consequences.
One year ago and this region was a wilderness—now how is it?"[24]

Gillespie understood that the growth and progress in California was
unprecedented, like nothing the modern world had experienced in such
a short period of time. In a matter of months the land had been transformed from one inhabited by Indians, Californios, and a sprinkling of
immigrants to one populated by people from around the globe. The contemporary network of roads and bridges now linking neophyte towns
and villages seemed to have risen by "enchantment," Gillespie wrote.[25]

An excited voice coming from high above shook Gillespie from his
thoughts. Looking up, he realized the man was speaking to him and
seemed to be waiting for an answer to some question. "'Come up here'
exclaimed the stranger in a half pleased and energetic manner, 'come up
here under the shade of these two pines, and I may tell you more than
you are aware of about this place.'"[26]

Gillespie climbed the embankment, and the stranger motioned him to
sit down beside him. The two men exchanged pleasantries, with Gillespie
explaining that he had recently arrived from Pennsylvania, while the man
shared that he had been in the West for a number of years. Then he made
a curious statement: "If it hadn't been for me Californy would be still a
wilderness." And he followed up with, "Maybe you don't know me?"[27]

It was none other than James Marshall himself. Gillespie then listened
while Marshall recounted the events of that early January morning in

This sketch of James Wilson Marshall by Charles B. Gillespie, circa 1849 or 1850, is a rare image of a man who refused most attempts to capture his likeness. Marshall's faint signature is written across the bottom. Courtesy of the Rees-Jones Collection.

1848, when he found gold below the mill, and of traveling to meet John Sutter at his fort near Sacramento, where the two evaluated the material to ascertain its identity. Gillespie took notes as Marshall spoke, and he obtained consent to sketch the ordinary-looking man. Marshall acknowledged his approval of the likeness by signing the portrait.[28] A few years after this encounter, Marshall began refusing to allow his likeness to be captured, making Gillespie's sketch one of very few from the era. Photos of Marshall come from later in his life.[29]

Gillespie was appreciative of the opportunity to hear Marshall's reminiscences. "I thanked him heartily for his condescension in narrating a history so entertaining, and one which but few have had the opportunity of hearing," he would later record. During the long conversation Gillespie came to know Marshall as a solitary man who had become somewhat soured by his own misfortunes. Having lost his livelihood when thousands overtook California's rivers and canyons, Marshall had expected some reward for the discovery. He had asked for 640 acres surrounding the mill, an amount equal to the claims given to settlers in Oregon. At the time of his encounter with Gillespie, Congress had not acted on the request.[30]

Marshall, a New Jersey native, was also lobbying to secure his identity as the discoverer of gold and to set the record straight regarding the sequence of events following the fateful day in January 1848. Embellished accounts of the event had begun circulating amid the worldwide frenzy, with an array of individuals claiming to have played a major role. Gillespie's notes remained in his personal papers for many years before they were shared with the public in *Century Magazine*.

North of Sutter's Mill, in the vicinity of Grass Valley, Gillespie's former companions George and Joseph Martin spent two weeks in a mining camp without making enough in gold dust to pay living expenses. After finding his way to San Francisco, Joseph Martin composed a letter, later shared with Newark readers, in which he counted himself among those not enamored with California: "San Francisco is a miserable place to live in: the gambling houses get the most of the miners' gold. They are numerous and are open night and day, being specially crowded on Sundays, and the gambling is almost universal. It is not an uncommon thing to see a Spanish woman betting 70 to 100 ounces on a single card. The statements of various writers, making a Paradise of this country, is a very rich joke."[31]

Martin's letter provided valuable information for those at home who anxiously awaited news from the Pacific Coast. He announced the arrival of the bark *Griffon* on September 16 with passenger John B. Overton and conveyed the latest intelligence on the whereabouts of General Darcy's party by explaining that from "Sacramento . . . he was 400 or 500 miles back, and . . . had taken the road to Oregon on account of the grass."[32]

One month later Martin provided a follow-up letter, this time with a grave announcement: "A young man named Cook, from Newark, who came through with Dehart died this morning at the hospital."[33] In fact, Wallace Cook had not made it to the hospital in San Francisco before succumbing to dysentery aboard a steamer from Sacramento. Stephen Dehart was with his nephew, caring for him to the end. In Newark, Wallace Cook's mother was inconsolable after hearing of her son's death, which she first learned about from the newspaper account.[34]

There was additional information in Joseph Martin's correspondence that would devastate those following the progress of General Darcy's party: "We have heard from the Darcy party, which is on Feather River. Two of the party, Messrs. Bond and Denman, are dead. Dr. D's young man, A. Jobes, is very low, and it is thought will not recover. The Doctor, I understand, is much affected by the death of his unfortunate companions."[35]

In late August, Californians were just receiving the news of another death, that of ex-president James K. Polk. Ceremonial observances were carried out in the streets of cities and towns across the territory some two and a half months after obsequies had taken place in the states.

Chapter 18

Dead Last

Joseph Martin's information was correct. The Newark Overland Company had taken a cutoff due to concerns over depleted grass at the Humboldt Sink.

General Darcy hardly understood that they were going almost to Oregon when he had made the decision in late August. If they had stayed on the old route for another day or two, they might have learned about the large meadow nearby with its abundant tall grass for all. Instead they had encountered a frontier character who recommended the unproven course.[1] A few days earlier a diarist in another company, Alonzo Delano, had recorded that "an indefinite tale was circulated among the emigrants, that a new road had been discovered, by which the Sacramento might be reached in a shorter distance avoiding altogether the dreaded desert; and that there was plenty of grass and water on the route. It was said, too, that on this route the Sierra Nevada Mountains could be crossed with but little difficulty."[2]

Six of the seven New Jersey messes departed the Humboldt River on August 21, believing that the decision to veer off the regular trail would give them an advantage in distance and resources. One wagon team remained behind with Job Denman, who was too sick to travel.

For two days they moved onward, mostly at night, through a dry ravine to a barren stretch of desert, missing entirely one of the few watering spots, called Rabbit Hole Springs. The crossing was comparable to the forty-mile run to the Carson River, with life-sustaining resources equally nonexistent. The difference, and a significant one for those who had opted for the alternate road, was the lack of an emerald-banked river with fresh mountain water on the other side. "Instead of avoiding the desert, instead of the promised water, grass and a better road," Delano wrote, "we were in fact upon a more dreary and wider waste. . . . We had been inveigled there by false reports and misrepresentation."[3] More desolate terrain and stagnant alkali pools awaited them when they finally camped. It was the Black Rock Desert, aptly named for "deposites of lava & the whole surface . . . cover'd with ashes," according to Gray's description.[4]

At dawn on August 24, the lone aft wagon with Job Denman arrived in camp. Denman was near death, with signs of mortification showing in his blackened lips and extended abdomen. By noon he was dead, and preparations for his burial commenced amid grief and silence. Scarce timber was gathered for a makeshift coffin and headboard, upon which was inscribed "Job Denman, Aged 23 years, N.J." Gray noted that the gravesite would show "the traveller the resting place of one, who little thought ever to have laid his bones so far from home & kindred." He continued the journal entry with details of the solemn affair. "We took a few locks of his dark & waving hair & then consigned him to his eternal Sleep. All our own men & several strangers follow'd him to the grave at which the Gen'l made a few excellent & appropriate remarks."[5]

There was hardly time to grieve. Robert Bond was also in the grips of the fatal illness believed to be typhoid fever. Major Meeker was caring for his messmate and had gently moved him from the wagon to a borrowed tent to minimize his discomfort. Poor Bond agonized throughout the night of August 24. In the morning he was examined by Darcy, who knew he would not survive until nightfall. The Newark men spent the day constructing another coffin and excavating a burial site a few feet from Denman's.[6] The mood was somber, with conversation more scarce than clean water and green grass.

Just past three in the afternoon Bond expired, and the funeral ritual afforded to Denman the previous day was repeated. Again emigrants from neighboring companies paid their respects during the service conducted by General Darcy. Bond was thirty years old and, according to Gray, had "*professed* to be a follower of the meek & holy Jesus & well did he acquit himself in the calling."[7] The diary Bond had kept, with its minimal wording and its final entry written at Great Salt Lake City, would be sent home to his sister in New Jersey.

That evening Gray opened his journal to a blank page in the back, where he penned a list of his earthly possessions and instructions attesting his last will: "Should I die, or be killed, it is my wish that my uncle Andrew J. Gray will have this book presented to my father & mother. All & every description of property belonging to me I wish him to sell & convert into money and pay the same to my brother Henry Peters Gray. General Darcy will also be so kind as to see that my effects are sold & not squander'd or given away & the money received for them & paid over as devised." The items included his gun, a team of oxen, a buffalo robe, some gold and silver, and his quarter share of the wagon along with clothing and equipment. Further specifications directed that a loan of $30, which he had advanced to the company and had been recorded on the company's books, be collected as part of his estate. At the bottom, just above his initials, "CGG," he wrote four more words, underlined twice: "*and I owe Nothing.*"[8]

Hours after Bond's funeral, the Newark men encountered a band of Mormons traveling to Great Salt Lake City from California, where they had witnessed thousands of gold seekers arriving by sea. Despite the influx, they confirmed that gold was still plentiful, a breath of good news that raised the spirits of Darcy's company, still grieving over the losses of Denman and Bond. At daybreak the next morning the Newark Overland Company left their deceased comrades side by side in a forsaken cemetery near the disappointing watering holes called Black Rock Springs.[9] One month later prolific diarist J. Goldsborough Bruff recorded passing two graves not far from a sulfurous pool where he had observed "the tail and 1 hind foot of an ox sticking out."[10]

Thirty miles along the trail Darcy's company met a military unit that, like the Mormons, was traveling east. They were coming not from California, but from Oregon, which may have been the Jerseymen's first clue that the so-called cutoff was taking them far to the north.[11] Rather than getting closer to the gold region of Central California, they were getting farther away. Most emigrants who selected this road believed they were taking a newly charted course over the Sierra Nevada on a more direct line to the Sacramento and Feather Rivers. Instead, they were on the

38.

August 25th 1849.

Should I die, or be killed, it is my wish that my uncle
Andrew J Gray will have this book presented to my
father & mother, All & every description of property
belonging to me I wish him to sell & convert into
money and pay the same to my brother Henry Peter
Gray. General Darcy will also be so kind as to
see that my effects are sold & not squandered or given
away & the money received for them & paid over as
devised.

I own as follows :—

1/4 th of the wagon & fixtures. provisions &c &c
1/4 th of 6 oxen, bought by us together
1 yoke (2) of oxen of my own. bought at the City of the G.S.Lake
2 bags of clothing
1 haversack of do
1 bag of blankets (4 of them)
1 overcoat
1 Buffalo Skin
1 water proof cloth
1 axe
1 Canteen

First page of the last will and testament of Charles G. Gray, written shortly after the
deaths of two company members in the Black Rock Desert of northwestern Nevada.
Courtesy of the Huntington Library, Art Collections and Botanical Gardens (HM
16520).

39.

1 double barrel gun + apparatus for do.
$25 — in gold + silver in my belt, in my haversack
and $30 + upwards my due from the New Jersey Overland
Co., which I have advanced on their account, + for
the correctness of which see the books of the C——
and I owe Nothing.

C. G. G.

Cancelled Novem'r 15th 1849.
Sacramento City
Cal.ª

Second page of Gray's last will and testament, which he canceled in Sacramento several months later. Courtesy of the Huntington Library, Art Collections and Botanical Gardens (HM 16520).

Applegate Trail, first blazed in 1846 as an alternative way to homestead-
ing opportunities in the Willamette Valley. However, the intelligence of
a cutoff was not entirely unfounded. Thirteen miles from the Oregon
border a new road finally branched off the Applegate heading in a southerly direction. This road had been charted by Peter Lassen in 1848 with
the intention of offering emigrants another option for reaching the gold
country, coincidently passing by his ranch and trading post.[12]

While back at the Humboldt juncture, Gray had estimated a final 350
miles of travel to reach their journey's end by way of the main road, their
target destination being the mining area of the Yuba River. After driving
nearly one hundred miles on the northwestern cutoff, he learned from
the eastbound military personnel that they were still 350 miles away. Gray
confided that the latest calculation had them "out of gear," as most of the
company had calculated being within two weeks of the mines. Further
dampening their mood, Darcy's men were warned of dangers from hostile Indians in the northern Sierra.[13]

One week after starting on the cutoff, also known as the Oregon
Road, the company moved beyond the Black Rock Desert and entered a
steep-walled defile called High Rock Canyon and then began to ascend
into mountains. Finally they reached snowmelt, almost too cold to
drink—and almost too late, as the effects of swallowing the water from
putrid hot springs had taken its toll. Seven men were suffering from
having drunk bad water from hand-dug desert wells. Gray, who had
just completed his last will and testament, was one of the sickest. He
agonized from extreme pain in his side, so serious that Dr. Darcy again
administered morphine to allow him to rest with some comfort. On
September 1 the company was forced to halt to permit Gray and others
some time to recover.[14]

Doped on painkillers, Gray remained quite ill for another week, during which time he was confined in the wagon while the company moved
forward. His condition was blamed on his having consumed lead-tainted
water, causing stricture of the intestines. It was the same ailment that had
ruined Darcy's health the previous year, prompting him to undertake
the overland journey to restore his vigor. Darcy's young attendant, Ash
Jobes, who had provided Darcy with priceless care during that illness,
watched over Gray during the nine days that he was too sick to ingest
anything of substance. Andrew Gray worked with Ash night and day to

insure that his nephew's needs were met. Dr. Darcy instructed them to wake him any time he was needed or for any reason that Charles might ask for him.[15]

Propped up inside the wagon, Gray was unaware of the departure of the Berry family, who left the company after being offended by remarks made about their children by one of Gray's messmates, likely John R. Crockett. The Shakespeare volume that Catherine Berry had loaned to Gray remained with him during his sick days in the wagon and provided much-needed diversion to his discomfort: "Need hardly say it was worth its weight in gold to me, reading it in the wagon when the road was good. I read it nearly through & found it as I have for the *100'th time, a most delicious treat.*"[16]

Buried in blankets, Gray was barely cognizant of the moment the company crossed the Sierra, having reached the 6,000-foot crest, which would later be named Fandango Pass. The milestone was just south of the Oregon-California territorial border, far from the gold-bearing rivers where emigrants, who had traveled near Darcy's party but had not taken the cutoff, were now arriving. Once over the pass, the company camped at Goose Lake before moving to the Pitt River (now Pit River), a tributary of the Sacramento.[17]

On September 8 the Newark team awoke to discover that "Indians had eluded the guards & seized 11 head of cattle." With a number of men ailing, sixty-one-year-old Darcy and one other man formed the search party. At six o'clock in the evening the General returned to camp driving all the cattle, which had been found abandoned by their captors in a canyon some thirteen miles away.[18]

It had been a week since the Newark Overland Company had almost reached Oregon. They were now in California but, like other emigrants on the cutoff, had no clear understanding of their location. They were seriously off course, zigzagging along a route not well established and not identified in guidebooks. More twisted trails lay ahead, winding past volcanic peaks and over dry lake beds. But for poor advice they would have already reached their destination.

Charles Gray's illness had begun in the Black Rock Desert, where temperatures exceeded one hundred degrees. By the time his condition improved, he emerged from convalescence amid a misty and magical timberland. Gray was finally able to mount a horse, allowing him to conserve his strength over the mountainous terrain. His ravenous appetite was a sign of his recovery, but his spirits remained low.

Incentive for Gray to get out of the wagon was the failing health of his messmate John R. Crockett, with whom Gray managed few, if any, cordial exchanges. Their mess was particularly dysfunctional, in part due to the personality differences of the two men, and sharing the inside of the wagon would have been unpleasant for both. But they were about to be faced with an extraordinary situation.

Overnight on September 10, Crockett's mare surprised the company by giving birth to a colt. She had somehow survived the rigors of the desert crossing, mountain ascents, and shortage of food and water, all while pregnant and while thousands of other animals had died from the stress of these hardships. Darcy ordered their mess to remain together while Crockett cared for the mare, sending the rest of the company ahead to make camp. They reunited late in the evening with mare and foal in tow.[19]

Confusion regarding the route lingered for many of the wagon trains trapped on the cutoff, but optimism began to emerge with talk of a 150-mile homestretch. Those hopes were dashed when they learned from members of a pack-mule expedition traveling north that Peter Lassen's ranch was still 175 miles away, with Sacramento City another hundred miles beyond, and further that the road was very poor. The northbound expedition had been employed by the government to survey a passage for a potential railroad route through the Sierra. The scout hired to guide them over the mountains was none other than Peter Lassen.[20]

Lassen was the trailblazer of the labyrinthine trail that had been advertised as a cutoff to the diggings. Danish by birth, he had immigrated to the United States two decades earlier, first settling in frontier Missouri. Following early pioneers, he had then made his way to California, where he became acquainted with John Sutter, who favorably advised him on procuring land from the Mexican government. Lassen looked to follow Sutter's success by establishing a trading center in California's northern interior but was never able to match his mentor's achievement.

Darcy, learning that Lassen was nearby, ordered two Newark men from camp to find him and obtain clarification of the unmapped course. They returned not with the requested information but with Lassen himself. Late into the night he entertained the men around a radiant campfire, recounting captivating stories of success in the mines and exaggerating the quality of the road ahead.[21]

The next few days, however, were downright miserable. The trail that Lassen had described as "not a bad one for a mountain road" turned out to be the worst of the journey, putting undue stress on already fatigued wagon parts. The coupling bolt on the Gray-Crockett wagon snapped, seriously damaging the fore axletree, while another wagon suffered similar damage, both incidents costing time in repairs. While sidelined, a more disturbing situation developed: the mare was so protective of her foal that her behavior had become vicious. With all the hardships already impeding the company's progress, an unmanageable animal could not be tolerated. The solution was to shoot the colt, leaving a feast for some lucky wolf or wildcat.[22]

As if that weren't enough, more hindrances came when rain turned to ice overnight, stifling campfires, which in turn led to a cold breakfast. And they remained lost in the dizzying maze of forest trails roughly following the Pitt River. The complications of the cutoff added several hundred miles of unnecessary travel for all those who had believed the route's merits, falsely advertised by Lassen and his agents.

For the Newark Overland Company the most costly situation was just developing. General Darcy's health was beginning to fail, which he attributed to "inflammation of the bowels." But word around camp was that scurvy, a painful debility brought on by months without vitamin-C-bearing fruits and vegetables, was eroding his constitution. Darcy's faithful protégé, Ash Jobes, was also ill. He had begun to experience chills and fever, and as his health declined he could no longer provide assistance to his father figure. Darcy now had to rely on others for care. When the company reached the headwaters of the North Fork Feather River, finding ample pasture there, the decision was made to rest. In the vicinity were dozens of other parties, however, and their rowdy nighttime behavior, with barking dogs and popping pistols, was disruptive to the sick men, Gray noted.[23]

Peter Lassen, meanwhile, had also become unwell and left the exploring party to return to his ranch. Encountering the Newark camp on his way back, he entertained the men once more with tales of California life. Spinning the stories with much optimism, he explained there was so much sickness in the mines that being delayed in arriving there could only be an advantage. Gray, for one, wasn't buying it and wrote in his journal that Lassen gave *"as favourable a view of it as he can & at the same time have regard for the truth."*[24] Lassen lived life with a devil-may-care attitude. Indeed, even his illness was fortuitous, as the government expedition with which he had been employed suffered fatal losses from an Indian ambush just after his departure, an event that would eventually make national news. The *Newark Daily Advertiser* reported in December, "Capt. Wm. H. Warner, a valuable US officer, lost his life 27th September, while ascertaining the feasibility of a rail road to Oregon. . . . Capt. W. fell dead pierced with poisoned arrows."[25]

An ugly incident took place among the Newark men during the last week of September, probably exacerbated by the multitude of bad luck the company had already encountered for much of the month. A serious dispute broke out between the General's aides and his kinfolk, involving a lost ox and what was perceived as childish behavior by both Andrew and Charles Gray—conduct considered so out of line that Darcy stepped in and severely reprimanded his brother-in-law and nephew. Both Andrew and Charles were incensed at the General's failure to support their viewpoint, and Andrew finally made it clear that they *"had the very highest respect for him & he knew it well,"* adding that they, *"were ready & willing at all times to serve him, but didn't wish any high handed measures from his officers."*[26] The confrontation stressed not only Darcy's fragile condition, but also personal relationships.

Statuesque firs and junipers with diameters as wide as wagons lined the mountainous road, along which progress slowed to a paltry ten miles per day. Sickness and splintering wagon parts contributed to more delays, during which rations ran short, requiring additional bacon and flour to be procured at exorbitant prices. Colorful trout were bountiful in streams and deer plentiful in the forest, and when time permitted these could be obtained to supplement the daily provisions. But nothing in the food supply provided medicinal value to counteract the effects of scurvy.

A wide desert crossing projected to be ahead prompted prudent measures to cut and cure grass and fill canteens and kegs. The "desert" proved not to be treeless, sandy flatland but instead a stretch of dense forest void of any edible ground cover. Lassen's ranch lay forty-five miles on the other side of it, with a series of ridges in between that would require careful navigation and would drain the last of everyone's fortitude.

Cresting a high mountain ridge to a vale known as Steep Hollow proved difficult. The axletree of General Darcy's wagon broke for the third time, and he ordered the company to move forward without him. Now, just twenty miles from Lassen's ranch, many companies were leaving wagons behind, some with notes declaring that they would be retrieved, others simply abandoned. Carcasses of oxen and mules, so pitifully close to surviving the depraved journey, were distributed along the trail. The Newark Overland Company nearly lost Old Jim, one of the company's favorite oxen, who fell in his yoke from pure starvation. The company's last remnants of hay were presented to him, along with water and any branch or twig that could be gathered. The all-out effort paid off, and the brute survived. The company then laid by, waiting for Darcy to catch up, and watched as scores of destitute packers shuffled along, begging for scraps to sustain them to the ranch.[27]

By late September the state of the emigration, particularly of those on the northern cutoff, began to alarm Governor Smith, who appropriated $100,000 to aid those still fearfully late in crossing the mountains. A government train taking cattle and provisions to struggling travelers passed Lassen's ranch just prior to Newark Overland Company's arrival.[28]

The teams of Darcy's company had become separated and straggled along the trail, with three wagons pushing forward and the remaining four escorting the General in the rear. None of them reached Lassen's before the end of September. Darcy remained weak but was still able to raise his ire when the two black servants, both named John, lost his prized horse. The company's precarious situation precluded any effort to stop and search for the valuable animal. The four trailing wagons finally crossed Deer Creek, where Lassen's much-anticipated ranch was located, and joined the three messes already encamped there. It was here that Charles Gray found Catherine Berry and her family, all well, having arrived a few days earlier. He returned the Shakespeare volume that had provided him with hours of escape while sick in the wagon. It was October 3, a month later than they had expected to arrive at the diggings on the Yuba River, a cascading tributary of the Sacramento.[29]

Lassen's ranch, consisting of three buildings, was a hub for emigrants resupplying before continuing on to the mines. Meat of many kinds was abundant and consumed in large quantities by famished overland travelers. Wild grapes that lined the banks of Deer Creek would begin to arrest and reverse the ravages of Darcy's scurvy. He had become emaciated, and his ankles were badly swollen.[30]

The company would remain and rest at Lassen's for some time—all but Charles Gray, who was called on by Darcy to return to the highlands and search for his horse. Gray had no choice but to oblige, noting that "for no other man in California would I do it, so immediately taking my buffalo robe & one pair of blankets, some pork, a small bag of crackers & cracker dust & pair of holster pistols, I mounted & went my way, vex'd out of all character at such a stupid piece of carelessness & that he didn't send those to hunt him who had lost him." It was a four-day odyssey, backward into the Sierra Nevada, resulting in mission accompli and a moment of redemption and glory for Gray: "The General was delighted at the recovery of his horse & thank'd *me many times for the great service I had render'd him.*"[31]

Upon his return Gray was surprised with developments in the company's structure that had taken place during his absence. Rising on the morning of October 7, he learned that his mess, including his uncle Andrew, along with the men of another mess had decided to part with General Darcy and seek mining opportunities sixty miles north on the Trinity River near Redding. Gray was confounded by his uncle's disloyalty and confronted Andrew, reminding him that "*it was the understanding with us that we were to go to California with the Gen'l whether any one else went or not*" and noting that "*our intention was to be & stay & work together & assist & take care of one another.*"[32] Andrew Gray's decision may have been provoked by Darcy's tongue-lashing two weeks before, but regardless, the alliances were set, with seven men planning to move north pending the finalization of business matters. (The seven are believed to have been Crockett, Andrew Gray, Lewis "Gun" Baldwin, Dolph Pennington and his servant John Rowe, Abram Joralemon, and Moses Canfield.) Charles Gray would remain with the General.

As company secretary, Charles Gray took charge of the bookkeeping details. He wrote in his journal that he took "*a long time in making out the shares & dividing the gold dust which we received for our common stock wagon & tools, & apportioning it among so many.*" An article of dissolution was drafted for the Gray-Crockett mess, signed by all, with Charles Gray collecting his one-quarter interest.[33] Combining those assets with profits from the sale of his three oxen, Gray found his finances to be quite sufficient.

During the final day at Lassen's ranch, Gray learned about the death of ex-president James Polk.[34] The blackout of news during five months of overland travel was beginning to lift.

Darcy's remaining contingent of four wagons departed the next morning, heading south and destined for the last march to the Yuba River. Fifteen men had stayed with the General, among them Major Meeker, Benjamin Casterline, three members of the Lewis family, Henry L. Johnson, Ash Jobes, William Donaldson Kinney, and Darcy's servant, John Hunt.

Gray, now without a mess, had the privilege of riding the General's horse while Darcy traveled in his wagon, not because of his health, which had stabilized, but in order to care for Ash Jobes, who had shown no signs of improvement for the greater part of two weeks. In fact, Ash's condition was bizarre, as though constant fever had affected his brain. "*Ash is crazy all the time & acts like an idiot,* talking in the most incoherent & disconnected style," Gray noted in his journal on October 11. Further degradation was observed the next evening: "He raved all night incessantly, calling upon every body & everything & presented a mournful picture of the power of his disease. In appearance he is much changed—his eyes wild & glassy, his flesh colour gone—his head hot & he unable to walk, reeling about like a drunken person & every way almost a wreck of mind & body."[35] Much of Darcy's time was devoted to Ash, whose deterioration forced another halt. Meeker and the Lewises moved on without them, intending to leave roadside messages regarding their whereabouts.

For three days the care of Ash Jobes consumed those in camp. Gray dedicated himself to the effort, remembering Ash's "constant attention to the General during his severe illness last year & his kindness to myself but a few months ago." But Ash remained in jeopardy. "*At night myself & the Gen'ls negro boy* slept at the door of the tent into which Ash had been removed, & all night we were kept awake by his repeated efforts to get out of the tent & at one time almost succeeded. . . . Poor boy! we shall wait for you and attend you though the gold lay in glittering masses beneath our feet."[36]

On October 16, believing Ash to be well enough to travel, Darcy moved sixteen miles to the Feather River, where they learned of mining activity a few miles upstream. Finally they could say they had reached the diggings, but it was hardly the grand arrival enjoyed by Cartwright and

Currier three months earlier. And the circuitous route through the Sierra Nevada was not yet over. The next day they followed the river only to find many branching trails and not a trace of a note from Meeker and Lewis. "Amid these forks & turns we don't know where we are, or where we are going," Gray lamented, recognizing the utter confusion.[37]

As they traced and retraced their steps looking for the Yuba River trail, they witnessed Indians along a riverbank spearing salmon, some as large as twenty pounds. Gray wrote in his journal, "We tried to buy a salmon for ourselves, but money was of no value in their eyes, nothing but shirts, coats or blankets would answer. . . . So we went to the bank & held up an old red flannel shirt. . . . Two other Indians came wading through the river with the half of a fine fish, weighing about 10# & for which we gave him the shirt." Gray observed other Natives making acorn bread and fishing on the riverbank. He noted their simple lifestyle, "Civilization probably not yet having been so far carried by missionaries & other medling emmisaries as these remote & *heathenish* lands," and then added, "and God be praised for it."[38]

As travel continued to Rose's Ranch beside the Yuba River, Darcy's health continued to be a concern, and they happened to encounter an Englishman who had served as a surgeon aboard a British warship, where he had treated many cases of scurvy. In an inebriated state—actually, "about as near drunk as he well could be," as Gray wrote—the physician examined Darcy, confirming that scurvy was the cause of Darcy's swollen ankles. To mitigate the pain, Darcy had been wrapping the inflamed joints with strips of muslin, successfully limiting the swelling. Stoically he had endured the physical pain while maintaining the duties of leadership, but those who had not seen him for six months would have been shocked at his appearance. Beginning the journey in March weighing 230 pounds, he had wasted to 159, his six-foot-two frame fearfully gaunt.[39]

Seven days passed with no sign of Meeker and Lewis. At last, on October 21, the parties reunited after discovering that Darcy's group had apparently leapfrogged the others on a side trail and gained fifteen miles on them. Together they searched for a mining location on the Yuba, a river they found to be deep and rocky, with its fast current moving over boulders creating a constant song of rushing water. Along the banks a few cabins had been constructed by those who intended to spend the winter—some set up as shops, others as boardinghouses. Along the river sunburned men toiled with pans and rockers. The transient community was about eight hundred strong, mostly men. For several days Darcy's fifteen loyal followers scouted the Yuba for a permanent camp, eventually settling for a site on the north bank near Howard's Bar.[40]

The privations of the overland journey were finally behind the Newark Overland Company. After six months of wearisome travel their bodies were spent and spirits disheartened. They had survived, but the toll was greater than any of them had expected. Two were dead.

In the days ahead, after encountering miners who had traveled around Cape Horn and spoke of their experience, Gray regretted his decision to take the overland route. "They had a very pleasant passage," he wrote in his journal, "plenty to eat & leisure to read & amuse themselves as they pleased, whilst we have suffer'd everything, cold, heat, almost starvation, constant & unwearied labour, toil, dust, contentions, disputes, accidents, death—the devil!" Or so he understood.[41]

In fact, the sea voyage had not been so easy, but the experience had somehow mellowed in the minds of the seafarers after weeks of arduous labor digging for gold. Indeed, one miner reevaluated his experiences, declaring that he thought he "saw the Elephant" when coming around the Horn, but now he concluded, "It was not the real Simon—HE lives here."[42]

Chapter 19

California Begins, 1849 Ends

Every day the Newark men met acquaintances from New Jersey who shared news of the world and of home. Charles Gray was particularly curious about New York's Astor Place Riot, which had occurred so close to his Manhattan residence, though in his journal he expressed no awareness of his cousin's tragic death. Everyone had questions about the cholera epidemic that had swept the country after they departed Independence, and a journey to the post office in San Francisco was an urgent priority. While in San Francisco, they witnessed the local scene, including the rush by recent arrivals to obtain passage back to the states.

The most newsworthy event in California in October 1849 was the Constitutional Convention in Monterey, where delegates assembled to draft a founding charter for a state government, even though California was still a territory. A constitution may have seemed presumptuous, but other states had taken similar measures prior to being admitted to the Union.[1]

The deliberations in Monterey concluded with a celebratory ball on the evening of October 13. Copies of the proposed constitution were sent to printers for immediate distribution throughout the territory. "It embraces the best features of that of the State of N.Y.," praised the Newark paper, "and is creditable to the Territory. Besides the absolute exclusion of Slavery, it provides that all officers, judicial and executive, are to be elected by the people." Among other enlightened measures noted in the document was the statute granting married women the right to own property independent of their husbands, perhaps an enticement for women to consider California. While progressive in regard to women, the authors of the constitution also found it necessary to prohibit men from dueling, mandating the loss of voting rights and the right to hold public office as consequences.[2]

Elections were scheduled for one month hence, November 13, to accept or reject the constitution. Also on the ballot were candidates for governor, lieutenant governor, and other state officials, again presumptuous as those positions hinged on the passage of the proposed constitution. Candidates for office quickly surfaced and wrangled for support and publicity.

News of the constitution and pending elections eventually reached the Yuba River camp, where Darcy's men had commenced their mining operation. William Donaldson Kinney had joined Darcy as an official stakeholder of the business. Henry L. Johnson was named foreman, indicating that his poor judgment at the Platte River crossing was not a factor in Darcy's decision. Unfortunately for Charles Gray, everyone was partnered, leaving him without companions to work a claim, and no one seemed inclined to include him. After a week spent wandering neighboring camps, selling his gun and excess baggage, doing laundry, and killing time with other chores, Gray decided to accompany the General on an excursion to Sacramento City to procure provisions and retrieve goods that had been shipped around Cape Horn to San Francisco. The messes of Major Meeker and the Lewis family were also going to Sacramento, leaving one wagon and a core team of workers behind at the mining camp, which they affectionately named Darcyville.[3]

The jaunt to Sacramento was poorly timed, as drizzling rain began on November 1, the morning of their departure. The sixty-five miles of travel should have taken two or three days in good weather, but the muddy roads had the viscosity of jelly and were prohibitive for the movement of animals straining to pull empty vehicles that were stuck up to the hubs. The trip back, with wagons fully loaded, would be a colossal challenge. As they moved out of the Sierra foothills across the pancake-flat Sacramento Valley, days and nights were passed inside wagons, with dripping canvas covers flapping incessantly, leaving everything downright soaked. On November 9 they arrived at their destination one mile south of the confluence of the American and Sacramento Rivers. There, the settlement founded by John A. Sutter resembled a bustling military encampment, and Darcy described it as having "the frailest kind of shantees, and rags or tents, with a fluctuating population of 6 or 8,000 souls, grown up during the past season like a mushroom."[4]

The commercial waterfront abutting the swollen Sacramento River was similar to San Francisco's crowded bay, with a forest of rigging, including that belonging to the bark *Isabel* occupying prime mooring space adjacent to the main business corridor. The New Brunswick men who had remained with the *Isabel* received General Darcy with the heartiest welcome. Darcy's health had improved while at Lassen's ranch, where wild grapes and berries were added to his diet, but his appearance was nonetheless alarming. His dramatic weight loss had reduced him in flesh by nearly one-third. Those anticipating Darcy's arrival in Sacramento had grown concerned for the doctor after weeks had passed without the company arriving. The New Brunswick friends offered him a stateroom aboard the *Isabel*, which Darcy gratefully accepted.[5]

Upon their arrival in Sacramento, Major Meeker and Benjamin Casterline secured passage on a steamer to San Francisco with the mission of retrieving the company's mail and goods sent from home. During their absence Charles Gray explored Sacramento, the town he nicknamed "Ragdom" after the tattered blankets and canvases strung between trees as makeshift shelters. He browsed the local gambling houses and watched as drunken miners carelessly tossed obscene quantities of gold onto piles of already-wagered nuggets. Later he perused a general store where excessive prices were charged for limited quantities of produce "of the most miserable character." With a keen interest in the fine arts, Gray noted the presence of a theater.[6] In fact, the Eagle Theater's recent opening had received a favorable review, at least in terms of its patronage. The *Placer Times* reported, "This house opened . . . to a full, and we may add, fashionable house, for the 'dress circle' was graced by quite a number of fine looking well-costumed ladies, the sight of whom was somewhat revivifying."[7] Weeks later the reviews waned, and the paper recommended that a comedy act be employed by the establishment.[8]

Another entertainment venue had opened in San Francisco days before Meeker and Casterline arrived. For a three-dollar entrance fee patrons were treated to a night of daring equestrian tricks by costumed

Long lines at the San Francisco Post Office created anxiety for many forty-niners, including Casterline and Meeker who were sent to fetch the company mail in November 1849. Courtesy of the Library of Congress (LC-DIG-pga-06296).

riders, acrobatic dancers on a tight rope, antics of a clever clown, and the showmanship of a very obedient, if not sagacious, horse named Adonis. Joseph Rowe's Olympic Circus had arrived in California and was filling seats at an amphitheater on Kearny Street before the last of the overland travelers had scaled the Sierra. Local reviewers praised the circus for providing amusement at a time when the tedium and uncertainty of a long, wet winter was approaching.[9]

Meeker and Casterline failed to return from San Francisco as quickly as Gray and the other impatient company members anticipated. The situation of the US mail was still floundering, with four steamers having arrived from Panama with nothing for the post office. Speaking for the disgruntled public, an editorial in the *Placer Times* proclaimed, "It is certainly one of the most outrageous grievances that ever any people suffered, to be so long deprived of the receipt of the regular mails from the United States." Editors suggested that a private enterprise take charge of managing the mail and urged citizens to become involved.[10]

The San Francisco Post Office, manned by an overwhelmed staff, was located at Pike and Clay Streets, where the small building was readily recognized by long lines of frustrated patrons snaking out the door. Meeker and Casterline's mission was further complicated by a Pacific Coast drencher that was vividly described in the *Alta California:*

> On Saturday morning, at an early hour, despite the straight-downwardness of the rain and the muddy, slippery, contemptible condition of the streets, a multitude besieged the Post office for letters. . . . Lines were formed, stretching down a slippery hill to the distance of eighty feet from the office. Shoulder to shoulder stood men from every part of the United States. . . . Not unfrequently would persons remain in the ranks for three and four hours. Places near the window were sold for five and ten dollars. All this was done in a rain, to bear up against which would have tried the fortitude of even Oregonians.[11]

After hours waiting in line, many were disappointed when they were turned away without precious letters from home. Trail mail, which had cropped up spontaneously along the remote overland roads, had afforded a more efficient postal system than presently existed on the Pacific Coast.

Meeker and Casterline eventually picked up the mail that had made it through the backlog. While in San Francisco they had the opportunity to view the city, which was in a more advanced state than when Cartwright, Overton, Currier and others from their original group had passed through in late summer. The evolution was hailed in many letters home. It was not just growth but the rocketing pace of building that garnered attention: "The canvass tents, which but a few months ago occupied some of the most central and valuable business locations, are giving place to substantial buildings of wood and brick; and it is astonishing with what rapidity these improvements are made. You may, on one day, see a canvass tent occupying a lot, and before the sun sets on the next day, the tent has vanished, and a two story frame building occupies its place."[12]

For speculators the news was still good. A letter to the *Newark Daily Advertiser* reported, "Many, six months ago, believed that the excitement in real estate would subside before this time, but it is as great as ever, and the city is spreading on all sides, and before long the business men will be located more in the centre of the city plot, they being now mostly near the landings."[13] There were also newly constructed wharves, which aided greatly in moving merchandise from ships. City corridors remained filled with unclaimed goods. Slowly these were being moved to consigners and markets, but loaded drays were so stifled in the slippery, mud-filled streets that mules charged with moving them appeared to be in perpetual motion.[14]

Charles Gray anxiously awaited Casterline and Meeker's return, fighting boredom by venturing into Sutter's Fort on the outskirts of Sacramento. Swiss native Capt. John A. Sutter had established the fort a decade earlier after rightfully procuring from the Mexican government a vast tract of land in California's interior, where he envisioned a thriving center of commerce with cultivated land, productive mills, and skilled craftsmen. It was inside the adobe-walled structure of the fort that James Marshall had revealed the handful of pea-sized gold to Sutter and the two had secretly tested the ore for authenticity. Unfortunately, the discovery of gold was not a windfall of wealth for Sutter, who was helpless to prevent his land from being swarmed by thousands who took up residence with no clear right of title. The enterprise he spent years building was visibly spinning into neglect.

The day after Gray's visit to the fort, Darcy had the privilege to meet and dine with Captain Sutter at the Sacramento City Hotel on another damp, windy evening. It was November 13, 1849, the Election Day on which Californians would choose state officials and approve the constitution. Darcy had been invited to the evening festivities by fellow New Jersey native and acquaintance Peter Halstead, who was running for a congressional seat but would not fare well with voters.[15] Captain Sutter was on the ballot for governor but would only pull 16 percent of the vote, losing to judge Peter H. Burnett, a recent transplant from Oregon. The rain was a large factor in what was considered to be a poor electoral turnout, but the constitution was overwhelmingly approved, with some 12,000 votes in favor and a mere 800 dissenting. A mixture of entertainment and politics dominated the large gathering, the first such event attended by Darcy since his farewell gala in February. Back at his tent, Charles Gray dined on pickles, dates, and whiskey.

After days spent eagerly awaiting the return of Casterline and Meeker with the mail from home, Gray felt a slap of dejection when only ten letters and twenty newspapers were delivered to him. He had expected so much more, yet he managed to find some satisfaction in reading them over and over during yet another rainy day. A bigger blow came the next day when he learned that the possessions he had sent aboard the *Orbit* before leaving New York were not among those retrieved. Lost was the carefully packed trunk of goods he had prepared to begin his life in California. Anxious to find his possessions, he was compelled to part with three gold eagles (ten-dollar coins) for the thirty-dollar steamer fare to San Francisco, where he would search for them among the masses of unclaimed goods lining the streets.[16]

In preparation for his venture Gray shaved and cut his hair for the first time in seven months, although he soon complained of being cold without it. Suspecting he would not return to General Darcy's mining operation on the Yuba, he purchased for his uncle two bottles of fine Madeira as an expression of gratitude. The two spent their last night together playing cards on the *Isabel* and consuming a bottle of whiskey. The General saw his nephew to the steamer the next morning, where his parting words left young Gray overwhelmed with emotion as he hurried aboard: "*Good bye, my son, & if you cannot do anything in the city, my tent is your home as long as I am in California!*"[17]

The day-long voyage to San Francisco made Gray feel more like he was in New York than California, and in his journal he compared the Sacramento River to the Hudson and noted his surprise at the ship's decor of Brussels carpets, rosewood finishes, and "mahogany bedsteads with canopies of silk & silver & gaudy enough to entertain an emperor!" On arrival in the city, Gray went to a boardinghouse patronized by "Jerseyites," many of them acquaintances. He identified the proprietor as "Overton," not specifying if it was John B. or older brother Isaac. Here Gray's accommodations for the night were even less appealing than the rain-soaked tent he occupied in Sacramento. He described the disagreeable night as one in "a perfect garret—on the third floor, 30 of us 'gentlemen in difficulties' turned in—some drunk & to me who for 7 months & upwards has not slept under a shed or in a house, as hot as a small hell—there we laid (not slept) all night, like a dozen cats curled up in a tub."[18]

The next day Gray sought and obtained employment as a clerk in a consignment house, where he was offered a small private room. He walked the city hoping to learn the whereabouts of his goods shipped on the *Orbit,* only to be mired in "mud to an extent no *Atlantican* can conceive of," halfway up to the tops of his boots. Certainly, no refined East Coast woman would have donned heavy footwear and shortened her skirt as was required in California. Roughly quoting Byron's *Don Juan,* Gray described the population as coming from "all places under the canopy of heaven of every clime, complexion & degree." He completed his tour of the city by paddling out to observe sea lions, then settled into his new quarters, preparing to begin work in the morning.[19]

Gray's final entry in his journal noted his unexplainable twenty-seven-pound weight gain over the course of hardships and sickness for nearly eight months. Surprisingly, it was almost the same increase that was realized by John W. Shaff. Gray lamented the difficulty in giving an accurate description of California: "I could write down for a long time many stories & accounts which would *only* however appear *impossible* & incredible, so I shall make a wholesale remark of it & say that take the *Arabian Nights, add* to them *Gullivers Travels* & then *multiply them* by *Baron Munchausen* & the product will be *California!*"[20]

Gray closed the journal he had faithfully maintained, writing with a hint of uncharacteristic optimism: "That the events, the trials & dangers of our campaign may at some future day afford amusement (small though it may be) to several of my valued friends & relatives, as well as to *myself* is my wish & hope." He canceled his will. He would never return to the Yuba River. [21]

Cyrus Currier's associate Stephen Dehart was in San Francisco about the same time as Gray. He was there to take possession of his steam engine, which had finally arrived in early November after being detained outside the harbor due to dense fog. On top of the $330 he had paid to have it shipped around Cape Horn, it cost him another $1,850 to have it transported twenty-seven miles south of San Francisco to the ranch of Charles Brown. Various water-driven sawmills had operated on the property known as Brown's Redwoods (now Redwood City) but had faced repeated outages from either too much or too little water flow. The use of steam power would guarantee steady, year-round operations and income. Dehart sold two shares interest in the engine, receiving a handsome profit, and kept the third share for himself.[22] Currier was hired to configure the steam engine to run the mill machinery, earning $500 for his mechanical expertise.[23]

Despite having received no mail from home, Currier continued to write to his wife in Newark. He considered California to be a healthful climate and said that the sores in his mouth and throat were clearing up and that the outbreak of boils all over his body were beginning to heal, believing they were the "last of the old disease." He was optimistic about completing his work by January, at which time he would return home. "I get as home sick as ever and my mind is constantly thinking of you and the children. I long for the time to come when I shall see and embrace you once more. . . . God grant this may find you and the Children well," he said in closing, advising her to "draw money from the Shop as you wanted and make yourself as comfortable as possible."[24]

Nancy Currier had received the most recent correspondence from Cyrus on December 10 and hurriedly mailed a reply, knowing that the mail to California was seriously backlogged. "I received your letter of Oct 31 yesterday and never did I feel more greatful to the kind Dispurser of all events than when reading your letter," she wrote, joyous to hear that her husband's health had improved since his previous letter a month earlier. Nancy and the children were all well, having experienced no symptoms of cholera or smallpox, which had recently claimed victims in Newark. She told Cyrus that they bathed every day and encouraged him to do the same.[25]

The letter from Nancy continued with events from the home front, in particular the anguish suffered by Wallace Cook's mother and the family's surprise that Stephen Dehart had not returned home immediately after his nephew's death. Details about the children followed, with "Osce" being singled out for his notoriously mischievous character, which included telling everyone that his Pa was bringing home a pound of gold. On the subject of gold, Nancy put in her request: "And while your hand is in bring me enough for a set of teeth." [26]

On November 28, General Darcy sat down with pen and paper and began composing a letter to a friend back home, later shared with the public via the *Newark Daily Advertiser,* in which he provided a detailed analysis of the exhausting journey and his first impressions of California's mining region. Regarding the overland crossing he concluded, "The route on paper looks very well; the books of Fremont and others make out, it is true, a long, but romantic, and very interesting journey. We found it a most tedious, laborious, vexatious, and wholly destructive and unsatis-factory route. Every day almost produced incidents to mar our comforts and to require our best efforts to maintain kindly feelings among our-selves and the thousands of others who thronged the entire route for 23 or 2400 miles."[27]

The long letter, some fifteen or more handwritten pages, was intended to convey advice and intelligence, just as Darcy had promised well-wishers when he departed Newark. He assured those who had declined to join him on the transcontinental trek that they had chosen wisely and advised anyone contemplating the journey to think again. The first half of the letter covered matter-of-fact observations relating to the overland route, describing the likes of Indian encounters and bad water. The sec-ond part related facts about the current California economy, with much attention on prices and wages. The published version did not mention the deaths of Bond and Denman.[28]

Darcy communicated his pleasure at seeing the steady movement of steamers between Sacramento and San Francisco, a sign that transporta-tion was becoming routine and reliable. He related the encounter with the ill-fated government party surveying a railroad route through the Sierra, expressing disbelief that such an endeavor was being contemplated: "I have been utterly astonished at the folly of the projected Railroad from the Missouri to the Pacific. The line of road would cost in grading an immense amount, and 1700 miles would not furnish a stick of timber to make the road, nor fuel enough to run one train over that barren district. No accumulation of business could ever be expected on the line, nor could the road, if made now, free of charge, pay its current expenses. It will never be made."[29] Unbeknownst to Darcy, who still served as presi-dent of the New Jersey Railroad, a national convention had recently met in St. Louis to consider the feasibility of connecting Missouri to the West Coast by rail.[30] *It would be built.*

As 1849 was coming to a close, those in the mining communities and throughout Central California faced additional storms, with gale-force winds and downpours severe enough to inspire thoughts of ark build-ing. Somehow the deluge did not prevent a fire from breaking out in the commercial district of San Francisco, where damage to newly framed structures was estimated to exceed $1 million. Many transient residents had never witnessed such a conflagration. "You should have seen it burn," wrote one eyewitness. "The buildings, being of light material, very readily ignited and burned with a fury I have never seen equaled." Noting the impact to the healthy gambling industry, the observer continued, "The fire broke some of the Monte Banks in the hotels, but they start like mushrooms at every step."[31]

While flood and fire wrought havoc in the city, the *Alta California* published upbeat news reflecting one sign of progress: "Yesterday no less than twenty-five females arrived in different vessels from New York, New London and Mazatlan—some of them married, but others still in their spinsterhood."[32] It was indeed a bountiful occasion as the San Francisco harbormaster had recorded only 677 females among the 24,333 arriving ship passengers since April 1849.[33]

On December 21, another example of California's progress was taking place in San Jose, where lawmakers, who had been elected just one month earlier, gathered to hear the first annual message of Peter H. Burnett, sworn in the day before as the new territorial governor. The transition of power from military-appointed governor Riley to populace-elected governor Burnett had succeeded with but one small hitch: Governor Riley was not present. Apparently after Riley's gracious effort to journey to San Jose for the event, no one bothered to tell him the appointed hour of the inaugural oath. Some blamed it on the weather.[34]

Both houses of the new legislature convened to hear Governor Burnett outline his vision for California's future. In his address he urged the senators and assemblymen to recognize the extraordinary opportunity they had before them to establish California's civil and criminal codes of law. "What shall be done *now*," he articulated, "cannot be touched or changed *hereafter*, but at great cost and inconvenience. . . . California is now in a position to adopt the most improved and enlightened code of laws to be found in any of the states."[35]

The governor's commitment to constitutional power and his recognition of the opportunity to build a progressive government were evident in his message. Yet one recommendation stood awkwardly in contrast to the overall forward nature of the address. At the October convention, delegates had unanimously banned slavery "so that the people of California are once and forever free from this great social and political evil." Yet despite unquestionable opposition to slavery, delegates had deliberated the idea of excluding all blacks from the state, a measure that almost passed until its ramifications were fully digested. In his opening statement Burnett revisited the merits of limiting entry into the state, strongly recommending that lawmakers make this California's legacy. His argument was based on the denial of suffrage to free persons of color. "If we permit them to settle in our state, under existing circumstances," he argued, "we consign them, by our own institutions, and the usages of our own society, to a subordinate and degraded position; which is in itself, but a species of slavery."[36]

Californians would not buy the governor's viewpoint nor would the *Alta California* editors, who blasted the governor's ideology as prejudiced. The newspaper editorial further questioned what right anyone had or did not have to make this decision for any class of people. Why, they argued, were free blacks from the United States alone recommended for exclusion and not convicts from Australia or other undeserving foreign immigrants? But the *Alta* stopped short of suggesting suffrage for free men of color, knowing such a policy would reflect negatively on California's bid for statehood.[37]

In Sacramento, the future state capital, the river was flowing fast and high as holiday festivities commenced despite the unforgiving climate. At the City Hotel, a Christmas Eve ball enlivened spirits while the well-to-do, showcasing all their finery, turned out to exchange compliments "with all the cordiality and good feeling which characterizes the epoch in other lands," the *Placer Times* reported.[38]

While Christmas Eve was rejoiced in town, General Darcy spent a quiet evening in his *Isabel* stateroom composing another personal letter confirming that he was "enjoying comfortable accommodations and the liberality of friends that knows no bounds." He went on, "I am fast recovering health, flesh and strength—have gained 26 pounds in weight since I arrived at this place." He reported that the season remained plagued with rain: "All the low lands for many miles around this city, and many of the shanties, tents and some houses, are in or under water; and ferries are temporarily established in some of the streets. The deck of our bark is now full 16 feet higher than when I first came on board of her." Darcy expressed his commitment to rejoin his company on the Yuba, where he expected to fulfill his mission to mine gold. He conveyed plans for returning home, believing he would most likely remain over the next year, and promised, "In all my movements I shall have due regard to health."[39]

Darcy remained a guest on the *Isabel* through December and into January, while a number of his party wintered at the Yuba River camp, with W. Donaldson Kinney, the Lewises, Thomas Fowler, and Ash Jobes among them. Unlike Pennsylvania native Charles B. Gillespie, who flitted from claim to claim, the Newark men wisely established a structured camp and worked together methodically to produce a modest but successful output, reflecting Darcy's modus operandi of patience and prudence. During the General's brief stay observing the Yuba mining camps he had witnessed that "a large share of them are constantly running from one locality to another, and spending their time in trying to find places where they can soon realize fortunes without gathering one fourth what they could if they would be satisfied with reasonable success." Each of the Newark men was making about eight dollars per day at Darcyville, with expectations that the yield would triple once quicksilver could be procured and applied to the process of separating gold from rock.[40]

By early December Isaac Overton had succeeded in obtaining passage home and was out of California, but he was not the first of Darcy's original company members to return to the states. William Emery and his son had already fled the West Coast, and on December 7, 1849, they disembarked from the *Crescent City* in New York, where William declared that "no amount of money would induce him to undertake the same journey again."[41] Also traveling aboard the *Crescent City* from Panama were Col. D. B. Crockett, brother of John R. Crockett, and Lt. E. Fitzgerald Beale of the US Navy, who fifteen months earlier had arrived in Washington with the official message of the gold discovery. Most noteworthy of the passengers on board the *Crescent City* were young cousins Alexander Liholiho and Lot Kamehameha from Honolulu, both future kings of the island nation who would eventually rebuff US attempts to annex their tropical principality. The current king, Kamehameha III, would soon appoint Alexander Cartwright to the position of Honolulu fire chief, insuring that the New Yorker would become a permanent resident of what were then named the Sandwich Islands. Cartwright's son and namesake would one day marry into the royal family.[42]

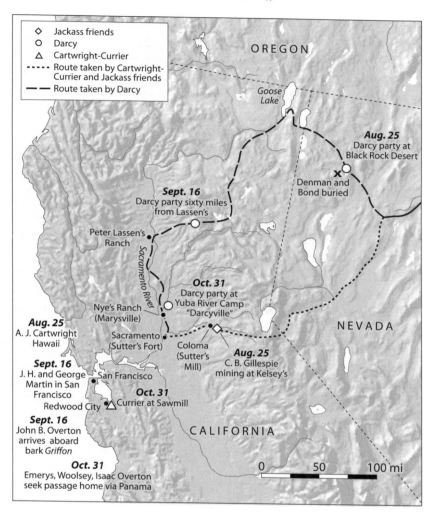

August to October 1849. Former trail mates scatter upon arriving in California, while Darcy's group struggles to complete the journey. Cartography by Bill Nelson. Copyright © 2017 University of Oklahoma Press.

Three weeks after Emery's return, Frank Woolsey sailed into New York harbor on the *Empire City,* crossing the waters he had navigated so many times.[43] Following Woolsey was Isaac Overton, who reached home in mid-January.[44] Both men would resume their professions in the transportation industry, Overton with the railroad, Woolsey as a ferryboat pilot. Overton returned to New Jersey without his younger brother, who had arrived in San Francisco on September 16, 1849, with the joint stock company on the bark *Griffon*. John B. Overton, like many, saw a world of opportunity in California and had no intention of leaving without attempting to make his fortune. Like so very few, he would become a millionaire.

The men who had departed Newark the previous March with plans to follow General Darcy across overland trails to California would never forget their tumultuous journey. While the men with mule teams claimed superior speed in reaching their destination, it was not the preference of stock animals that determined their fate. It was the choice of passage across the formidable Sierra Nevada that separated those who arrived safely with sustained health from those who reached California fearfully late in the season, emaciated and disheartened.

Before 1849 ended, three men, Robert Bond, Job Denman, and Wallace Cook, all thirty years of age or younger, had perished. Four others had returned to New Jersey after a brief stay in California, and one was starting a new life on an island in the Pacific. For the remaining Jerseymen 1850 was dawning, and most were still pursuing their dreams of golden wealth, either by mining ore in the rivers and canyons or by providing supplies and services to others who chose the backbreaking occupation. It was crystal clear to all that success was exactly as John W. Shaff had declared, a lottery.

PART III

After 1849

Chapter 20

Achieving Wealth, Going Home, 1850–1851

On January 1, 1850, Californians said farewell to favorite son Col. John C. Fremont who was boarding the steamer *Oregon* for Panama. The colonel was now Senator Fremont, one of two appointed to the US Congress ten days earlier by legislators in San Jose. At the time of his departure Fremont was keenly aware of the vast gold deposits on his Mariposas property. In a letter to his father-in-law, Thomas Hart Benton, he confirmed that his property contained "a gold mine . . . which in magnitude and wealth exceeds anything of the kind ever found in California."[1]

Joining Fremont, who was on his first trip to Washington since his court-martial in February 1848, was fellow senator William M. Gwin, also appointed by the newly elected California legislature. Gwin, a former US representative from Mississippi, had been in California only seven months, having arrived the previous June on the same congested steamer out of Panama taken by Jessie Benton Fremont. While both men were appointed by the legislature, Gwin won the draw giving him the six-year term, leaving Fremont with a two-year commitment. Even so, Fremont commanded the attention of the press, most recently with reports that he was the richest man in the world.[2] Jessie Fremont, also a favorite of zealous journalists, accompanied her husband to Washington, making news when she fell seriously ill in Panama and delayed their arrival.

Two years had passed since January 1848, when gold had been quietly discovered at Sutter's unfinished sawmill, initiating the mobilization of wealth seekers from across the globe. There had been be no abatement of the emigration to California and, in fact, the pace would increase in 1850. Once again, companies of middle-class American men would dominate the movement, though some differing groups gained the public's attention. A New Orleans newspaper learned of one such group and reported, that "an association of colored men for the purpose of mining in California" was due to set sail from New York in late January.[3] Perhaps nothing captured more attention than the sight of camels that had been imported for experimental use by the military on the western frontier. After arriving in Baltimore, they were to continue to Independence, where one hundred Texas Rangers would escort them to California.[4]

Despite the plethora of stories about the severe hardships of overland travel and the swearing of repudiations by those who made the trip in 1849, the number planning to cross the continent in 1850 would rise nearly 60 percent. Before the next California rainy season, 50,000 emigrants would follow the Platte, Sweetwater, and Humboldt Rivers to the now-crowded banks and bars of California's gold-rich rivers. Those who were destined for California in 1850 would find a much different state of affairs than those who had arrived the previous year.

In Missouri a forty-five-year-old husband and father of three was one of those planning the overland journey to California in 1850. His name was David Meeker, older brother of Major S. H. Meeker, and he would emigrate from Missouri with a team of oxen, no doubt at the recommendation of his younger brother. David Meeker had been in Missouri more than a decade, having fled New Jersey after causing embarrassment to his family, for which he was ever regretful.[5] He had pledged to live a worthy life, never forgetting the failures of his youth, and welcomed the opportunity to reunite with his brother. His wife, two young daughters, and an infant son would remain in Missouri until he was settled and arrangements could be made for them to join him in California.

Major S. H. Meeker, who had been an accomplished merchant in Newark, declined the opportunity to join General Darcy's mining operation on the Yuba River. While in San Francisco retrieving the mail in November, he had explored business opportunities with fellow New Jersey acquaintances, which led to a prime Sacramento storefront dealing in provisions, imported liquors, and tools. Meeker was correct in thinking the gold rush would continue in 1850, and established his shop in a central and opportune commercial location just two blocks off the heavily trafficked waterfront. Customers browsing Meeker's shop would find Monongahela whiskey, sugar, oysters, and English cheese, all shelved alongside an inventory of mining essentials, such as drilling equipment, canvases, tinware, and mercury (better known as quicksilver). Major Meeker smartly advertised his merchandise for sale "on very liberal terms," meaning the store accepted gold in almost any form.[6]

Business was vigorous at Meeker's store, which was spared much of January's heavy flooding. The shop had become something of a head-quarters for Jerseymen, who flocked in for news from home with the arrival of each mail steamer. Occasionally Meeker was able to offer issues of the *Newark Daily Advertiser* to his news-famished clientele.

Like S. H. Meeker, Stephen Dehart was engaged in a successful busi-ness venture, the Redwood City sawmill, and advertised in late January the availability of lumber by sale or contract.[7] The resupply of the com-modity into the depleted market would bring prices down sharply and would equally affect the price of imported wood products. One business-minded undertaker, who had sent large quantities of coffins around Cape Horn after realizing the severe shortage of lumber on the West Coast, would see the value of his investment jeopardized by the new availability of local lumber.[8] The scenario was typical of California markets, which changed as frequently and dramatically as the diverse population.

Dehart and partner Cyrus Currier had hoped to be home by the first of the year, but were detained due to unexpected complications in bring-ing the steam-powered mill to full functionality. In a January 27, 1850, letter to his wife, Currier explained

> You may be disappointed in not seeing me as soon as you expected. I was in hopes 2 months since to have had the mill all agoing before this and to have been ready to sail in the Steamer that conveys this letter but it has rained so much here for the last 3 months we could not get along as fast as I wished to. . . . Some times it rains so hard that it is impossible to get from here to San Francisco. The rain raises the Streams so high that they cannot be forded and the roads so muddy that a horse cannot travel.[9]

Currier had received two letters from Nancy in recent weeks. Mail service had improved since mid-January, when a new US mail agent was appointed to address the deplorable state of postal service in California.[10] Currier was delighted in finally hearing from his wife and replied, "I received your letters of Oct 14 and Nov 12 and it done my heart good to read them. I did not sleep much the night that I received them for I was reading of them half of the night. The other half I imagined myself with you and the Children." Currier had also received letters from his Newark business partner, who expressed his concern about the financial state of affairs at the Market Street shop, stating that he was contemplating mortgaging part of the property in order to make ends meet. Currier gave instructions to Nancy, affirming his complete trust in her judgment: "I think you will have to act as my Attorney and counsult with some of my friends what is best to do. I shall send you five hundred dollars in Gold dust which you can let Mr Davis have the whole or part as the case requires or none at tall if you think he can get along without it until I return."[11]

The letter closed with sentiment from Currier intended to comfort his wife in his absence:

> It is hard for You and me both, for me to stop here so long. I want to be with you and the Children but have stoped in hopes to earn money for yours and my benefit also the Childrens. I am comfortably situated considering all things. We have plenty to eat and drink. My health is good. I look at my old Shoulder Braces and Supporter hanging up in the Tent and Hope that I shall never be under the necessity of wearing them again. I shall speed the Time as fast as possible to my return and God grant we may have a happy meeting.[12]

Meeker and Dehart were two of the 1849 arrivals who found success as entrepreneurs in the growing commercial centers of Sacramento and San Francisco, where the pace of development was dizzying. Other aspects of California life were beginning to settle down and take shape, with the election of local officials and the adoption of a constitution. Californians were finally benefitting from the structured government that they had so desired and collectively worked to establish, despite the assault on their homeland by thousands of outsiders. Communities were transforming into towns and cities with societal structures such as court systems, schools, and churches. An aristocracy was also forming and catching up with the eastern cities, with cultural attractions such as a "Venetian Night" masquerade ball and performances by Henri Herz, a world-renowned composer and concert pianist who arrived in California in the spring of 1850.[13] Daguerreotype artists were opening shops, providing customers with the opportunity to have photographs taken in fashionable clothing as well as mining attire. New restaurants, not just saloons, were offering quality dining, including fine cuisine prepared by Chinese proprietors.

Sacramento and San Francisco were not alone in experiencing unprecedented growth. Across the state flourishing new towns such as Marysville emerged at strategic crossroads, primarily serving the swelling mining population. Marysville, located at the juncture of the Yuba and Feather Rivers, was incorporated in January 1850 from the purchase of Nye's Ranch, a popular way station for the emigrants of 1849 and the place where the Newark Overland Company had rested in October. No sooner were town lots surveyed than they were sold and resold, often turning profits many times the original purchase price.

General Darcy's camp on the Yuba was located fourteen miles upriver from Marysville, close enough for the Jerseymen to see the boomtown materialize. Upon their arrival in the fall they had taken over a discarded claim that was now turning a solid profit. Early winter flooding had subsided, allowing the men to work steadily throughout February, and the operation gained an enviable reputation for above-average success.

Company member William T. Lewis, who worked in the capacity of hauling rather than mining, managed to get in on the Marysville land speculation and realized enormous profits in a short span. While Lewis reaped significant financial success from his real estate dealings, luck was fleeting in California, and he soon saw his windfall diminish when he fell seriously ill, requiring expensive medical care and hospitalization in San Francisco. By April he was making plans to rejoin his wife and four daughters in New Jersey and to return to the Ohio homestead he had left two years earlier.[14]

Ash Jobes, the young man so favored by Darcy, was not as fortunate and became the fourth member associated with the General's overland expedition to succumb to fatal illness. Never having fully recovered from the sickness that plagued him during the latter part of the journey, Jobes's

health again declined, leaving him critically ill as he and his companions waited for spring flooding to subside at the Yuba River claim. On
the evening of April 7, 1850, Henry Ashfield Jobes, having just turned
twenty-four, died in the Darcyville camp. He left behind his bride of
fourteen months, Catherine, who was residing in Newark with Darcy's
wife and daughter. The death of his young office assistant devastated the
General, whose grief, due to his fondness for the young man, was understood by all.

The news of Jobes's death reached Newark through William T. Lewis,
whose arrival on the *Crescent City* from Panama on May 27, 1850, was
noted in the *Newark Daily Advertiser.* Lewis informed the paper that
Darcy had tended to Jobes and had "employed every means within the
power of medical skill to restore him, but without success." Lewis had
departed San Francisco just five weeks earlier and had expected to make
the trip with Stephen Dehart, but business matters had detained Dehart
at the last minute. According to Lewis, Dehart, who had realized enormous profits at the Redwood City sawmill, was determined to make the
next steamer out of the Golden Gate.[15] Dehart's partner, Currier, would
also soon depart California and reunite with Nancy and his three children, ending the painful separation about which he had so often written.

Unlike Nancy Currier, Sarah Lewis had not received letters from her
husband during his journey to California, leaving her concerned that
he had perished and been buried in his gentlemanly white shirt. Upon
his unexpected return to his mother-in-law's Newark residence after a
fifteen-month absence, he was met by one of his daughters, who did not
recognize him. When Sarah realized that the man at the door was William, she fainted.[16]

Just prior to Lewis's return in late May, Alderman Dolph Pennington
and traveling companion Abram Joralemon disembarked from the *Cherokee.*[17] They had spent just enough time in California to understand that
their success was at the sole discretion of Lady Luck. They came through
Panama about the same time that an eighteen-foot anaconda was discovered along the isthmus crossing.[18] Pennington returned with his young
black servant, John Rowe, who was identified on the ship manifest as a
twelve-year-old by the name of Penfato, likely a misspelling by a shipping
agent or just a nickname.[19] They were all part of a second mass migration,
this time of men returning home from the goldfields in droves, with the

vast majority deposited in New York City from steamships running regularly to and from Panama.

An Englishwoman visiting New York in the spring of 1850 witnessed the diversity of humans parading the streets. She was aware of the difference between newly arrived foreigners in their native dress and those who were returning home from California in miners' garb. "Their hair, in some instances, hangs nearly on their shoulders, in others it radiates away very respectfully from the skull, as if controlled by some mysterious centrifugal force of the brain within," she noted. "In the name of fortune, whence are they? They look intelligent, resolute, self-confident—in the name of fortune, indeed! for perhaps these men, at the moment you are half-pitying them, half-wondering at their forlorn and destitute appearance, are worth millions of money, and to-morrow, they will shine out in all the splendour of a New York exquisite's toilette. They are returned Californians, just landed, come to enjoy in 'the States,' the golden fruits of their toils, their perseverance, and their industry."[20] Sarah Lewis may have been less shocked that her husband had suddenly shown up alive than she was at his unrecognizable appearance.

By the summer of 1850 only half of the original Newark Overland Company remained scattered in California. Alexander Cartwright sailed back to San Francisco from Honolulu for a brief stay, during which time he likely rendezvoused with several of his New Jersey acquaintances, perhaps meeting with some of them at Major Meeker's Sacramento headquarters. Cartwright made journal entries during his June 1850 voyage and took down the mailing addresses for Meeker and his trail companions Thomas Seely and Frank Woolsey.[21] Not mentioned in his journal was baseball, although he may have been influential in introducing the sport to California. Games would become a common sight in San Francisco's city plaza in the coming months.

A number of the gold seekers who returned to their homes in the spring of 1850 arrived in time for their whereabouts to be documented by federal census workers. Among those counted was the Newark Overland Company secretary and journal writer Charles G. Gray. On July 17 he was identified in the New York City household of his parents, where he shared the residence with his sister, Julia Cone, her husband, John, and infant son, Charles. Gray was listed as twenty-eight years old and unemployed.[22]

Despite having obtained work in San Francisco, Gray had found no contentment in California and presumably made no more friends than he had during the overland journey. In New York City, however, he would soon find lifelong companions in William H. and Abby Tyler Oakes, with whom he became acquainted in the city's art community through the connections of his brother. The Oakeses were from Boston, where William had established himself as a distinguished music engraver. His talented wife, Abby, was making a name for herself as a landscape artist, one of few women to attempt such a career in the mid-nineteenth century. Charles Gray would spend the next four decades of his life with the couple.

As census workers went door to door during the summer of 1850, the nation was abruptly cast into mourning upon the sudden death of President Zachary Taylor, who succumbed on July 9 after a brief but severe attack of gastroenteritis described by his doctors as *cholera morbus*. It was not believed to be the strain of Asiatic cholera that was reaching epidemic levels in some US cities. Instead, speculators blamed Taylor's illness on having eaten tainted fruit, notably cherries consumed with chilled milk, during the Fourth of July celebration in Washington. At the time that Taylor was stricken, contentious debates over slavery and statehood were raging in the House and Senate chambers, where most politicians were initially unaware that the president was gravely ill. California, with a population now greater than Delaware and Florida, was at the forefront of the congressional brawl. Honorary pallbearers at Taylor's funeral included Missouri senator Thomas Hart Benton and Taylor's presidential opponent, Lewis Cass. Millard Fillmore assumed the presidency.

A few weeks later former California territorial governor Richard B. Mason, who had been promoted to brevet brigadier general, passed away after falling victim to cholera. The *Newark Daily Advertiser* proclaimed, "He will be remembered . . . as the officer whose report of the gold discoveries in California first created a confidence in the wonderful wealth of that region."[23] After influencing thousands to journey west, he had died in St. Louis, the city at the crossroads of the western emigration and a breeding ground for the resilient disease.

In California citizens awaited news of statehood, as census officials had the daunting task of counting a transient population. From boomtown to dry canyon, they gathered numbers well into September and October.

Sacramento waterfront, late 1849. The three-masted ship in the center may be the *Isabel*, Darcy's winter home 1849–50. According to a passenger, the *Isabel* was moored at the water's edge with an awning covering the entire deck. The side-wheeled steamer on the right is the *Senator*. Courtesy of the Mariners' Museum, Newport News, Virginia.

Identified at Darcy's mining operation on the Yuba River were his partner W. Donaldson Kinney and Newark Overland Company members Lewis "Gun" Baldwin, James Lewis Jr., and foreman Henry L. Johnson. Thomas Fowler and Benjamin Casterline were likely with them, but neither was recorded, nor was Darcy himself.

Enumerated among Sacramento's population were merchant S. H. Meeker and his brother David, who had just arrived from Missouri. While census takers painstakingly recorded names, ages, and occupations across the state, many of the Jerseymen were not found. Known to have remained in California throughout 1850 but not listed were Caleb Boylston, John W. Shaff, George D. Sayre, Thomas W. Seely, and John B. Overton. There was also no mention of John R. Crockett, surprisingly—the former Newark fire chief was hard to miss with his boisterous personality.

Moses Canfield was another of the original company who failed to show up in the California census. This was not such a surprise, as his wife had not heard from him since his departure nearly eighteen months earlier. A jeweler by trade, Canfield was one of those gold rush idealists who embraced the anonymity of life far from home. His family would never hear from him again.[24]

A handful of the members of the New Brunswick Company had also stayed in California, where the bark *Isabel,* their ship and General Darcy's winter quarters, would be sold at auction in August 1850 for a mere $5,000, less expenses charged by one company member for overseeing the vessel's maintenance. After an initial $700 investment per member, the organization's books were closed out with a distribution of $39.50 to each shareholder.[25]

Pennsylvania native Charles B. Gillespie remained in California, where he continued to write stories for publication. Unbeknownst to Gillespie, his previous publisher from the *Western Literary Journal and Monthly Magazine* had run into serious legal trouble in New York City. The publisher was a sensationalist writer known by the penname Ned Buntline, and his articles had fueled the gang hysteria that led to the Astor House Opera Riot and deaths of twenty-two citizens in May 1849. After serving a brief prison sentence for his role in the riot, Buntline resumed writing by plagiarizing some of Gillespie's earlier stories from the frontier. In an April 11, 1850, article the *Newark Daily Advertiser* recognized the fraud, citing Buntline's deception and giving Gillespie due credit for his work.[26]

Aside from literary writing, Gillespie found occasional work as a newspaper correspondent, reporting on the California legislature, which made him an eyewitness to contentious political maneuvering regarding California's admission to the Union.[27] The Southern states did not want a large territory free of slavery to become a state. By the end of the summer of 1850, Californians were becoming exasperated with congressional indecision regarding statehood.

Not until Henry Clay stepped in with a diplomatic compromise did the Senate finally pass the bill to admit California. Only six Southern senators voted in favor—former Texas president Sam Houston and five from sympathetic border states. But September arrived and House members were still bickering, paralyzed in part by political righteousness and the need to balance slave states with free states. The size of California was an issue, and a suggestion was put forth to divide the state into a southern half, which would permit slavery, and a northern half that would adhere to the voter-approved antislavery constitution. Already disgusted with congressional ineffectiveness, Californians were outraged at the attempts to dictate their governance. There was more indignation when it was learned that Utah, "a miserable, sparsely populated, unimportant and insignificant fraction of our possessions on the Pacific side of the continent," according to the *Alta California,* had been granted a territorial government.[28]

Nearly a year after the Newark Overland Company's arrival in California, autumn was again about to turn dry breezes into wind-whipping, wet storms. In San Francisco, every ship arriving from Panama was expected to bring word of statehood. When the mail steamer arrived on October 7, 1850, with disappointing news that Congress had again failed to pass the final legislation, the *Alta California* responded with scathing words: "They bluster about disunion, and talk of a Southern Confederacy to intimidate the weak minded; and even on the floor of Congress resort to gross misrepresentations, and absolute falsehoods, to achieve their ends. . . . Let the House admit California and the whole Union and the world would see that Georgia would not dare put in force her traitorous and revolutionary doctrines, even if it was the will of her inhabitants, and that all the clamor was but the blustering of political demagogues, struggling for notoriety."[29] Still, there was optimism that the bill would pass before the end of the legislative session.

Eleven days later, on October 18, as the steamer *Oregon* navigated the Golden Gate passage into the port of San Francisco, crew members mustered on deck, loading and firing cannons to announce the ship's arrival. The flashes of gunfire and sounds of heavy ordinance raised alarm on shore. Those with windows overlooking the bay and those able run into the streets for a glimpse of the harbor strained for a view of the commotion. Patriotic banners streaming from the *Oregon's* masts confirmed what many had been anxiously awaiting: California had been admitted to the Union. Jubilation erupted in the streets of San Francisco as citizens raised flags and fired brass cannons from the city plaza.[30]

A parade was organized, with marshals attired in uniforms of light blue, silver, and gold, followed by army regiments, sailors from warships, foreign dignitaries, police, firemen, marching bands, and even a brigade of Chinese participants dressed in crimson satin and displaying banners with their native pictorial lettering. Drawing the most attention was a flatbed wagon carrying thirty young boys in matching outfits representing the thirty US states and one little girl with a headband of red roses proudly representing the thirty-first entry to the Union. In the evening fireworks were set off above the fog-shrouded bay where ships below honored the event with displays of blue lights.[31] Similar celebrations were repeated across the state as the news spread to neighboring coastal towns and inland to the mining districts.

The statehood legislation had finally passed the House on September 7, with President Fillmore signing it two days later on September 9, the date set for future annual celebrations of statehood. In Washington, Senators Gwin and Fremont promptly swore their oaths and took their appointed seats in Congress. The quest for statehood was over.

For Charles B. Gillespie, reporting for a California newspaper, it was one of many historic events he would observe during his lifetime. General Darcy's loyal contingent witnessed celebrations at their mining camp on the Yuba River.

S. H. Meeker and other Newark men celebrated California's statehood in Sacramento, the future capital. David Meeker had arrived from his overland journey during the first week of September 1850, just days before California gained its statehood. After a brief time working the riverbed for gold, he took full-time employment at his brother's shop, where a flood of new gold seekers was providing brisk business.

While many were continuing to arrive in California's placer region from the 1850 season of overland travel, many of the previous year's arrivals were preparing to return to their homes and families in the East. By December claims were becoming unworkable due to seasonal high water, prompting operations to close and shifting priorities for some to a winter trip home via the isthmus. Among those bound for Panama were several of Darcy's company who had spent a year tediously collecting gold particles from the Yuba River at their site east of Marysville. The abandoned claim that they had taken over upon their arrival had become increasingly efficient with the aid of quicksilver to extract the gold. W. D. Kinney sent some of his profits home to his father, who proudly informed the *Newark Daily Advertiser* of the company's success.[32] They were on track to return home with modest fortunes.

General Darcy and W. Donaldson Kinney arranged travel together and would be followed weeks later by Benjamin Casterline and Gun Baldwin. Mining foreman Henry L. Johnson decided to remain at the camp, perhaps, like Moses Canfield, to avoid returning to his monotonous marriage in New Jersey, preferring to revel in the freedom of less judgmental California society.

Darcy arrived in Sacramento from the Yuba River camp in early December and spent several days enjoying the hospitality of New Jersey acquaintances with whom he wined and dined as he prepared for the journey home. On the afternoon of December 12 he boarded a steamer for San Francisco. Along the levee, just two blocks from the thriving consignment shop of S. H. Meeker, a crowd gathered to see Darcy board the vessel amid a hail of cheers and wishes for safe travel. Although much smaller than the farewell that sent him off to California, it was no less heartfelt. Tempering the sadness of Darcy's departure was the understanding that he would return to California in the spring.[33]

After a two-day stay in San Francisco, Darcy boarded the steamer *California* and sailed for Panama. On the passenger list following Darcy's name was an entry for "C Gray," but it is not known whether or not it was Darcy's unpopular nephew who was traveling with him. The General reached Panama's western port after encountering harrowing gale-force winds off the coast of San Diego, which caused him to give sincere reflection to the conundrum of overland-versus-sea travel.[34]

John R. Crockett had left California just ahead of Darcy and Kinney, crossed the Isthmus of Panama, and then boarded the *Prometheus,* reaching New York in mid-January. Crockett shared the news with the *Newark Daily Advertiser* that Darcy planned to depart Chagres on or about January 13 aboard the *Falcon.*[35] Crockett would return to his partnership with his brother Caleb, producing oiled silk and japanned muslin, commodities for which Newark was becoming a manufacturing center.

Darcy's return was anticipated throughout Newark, but there would be no fanfare to mark his arrival. Darcy and Kinney slipped into New York's port on the evening of January 24, 1851, and quietly proceeded to their homes and families.[36] When friends and associates were finally able to reunite with the two, they found Darcy looking robust and healthy, but Kinney appeared aged and exhausted. Caroline Meeker relayed these observations to her husband, Major Meeker, along with news that the General would not be returning to California after all.[37]

Weeks later, on the afternoon of February 18, telegraphs in New York clicked with projections that the steamship *Crescent City* would arrive around 5:00 P.M. Among the 218 passengers on board was Benjamin Casterline, whose eleven-day voyage from Panama included stops in Kingston, Jamaica, and San Juan, Puerto Rico.[38] Benjamin would reunite with his young wife, Eliza, and resume his old job at his father's grocery store, which had moved from Broad to Ferry Street during his absence.[39]

A month later, Gun Baldwin was welcomed back to Newark after two years away from home.[40] Baldwin would similarly renew his former employment following his father, a well-respected gunsmith.

Charles B. Gillespie joined the exodus from California and packed his bags in early 1851. Once again he sketched scenes of his travels and spent time filling pages in his journal with publishable works, including a poem with a prophetic message that his wandering days were over. Gillespie was nearing thirty and perhaps felt a calling to settle down. Sailing out of the Golden Gate aboard the *Adrian,* he sketched the landmark aperture and coastline from the Pacific side. The illustration depicted a sailing ship, blown forcefully by coastal winds, leaning dangerously in a foamy sea. From calmer tropical waters off Panama's western shore he captured the twin towers of a seventeenth-century cathedral inside a walled city with a backdrop of distant jungle mountains. The two contrasting images became part of a family collection of gold rush sketches.[41]

Once across the isthmus, Gillespie boarded the *El Dorado* for his voyage home from the bewildering El Dorado of California.[42] After touching Staten Island overnight on April 11, Gillespie's vessel reached New York City the next morning. He disembarked and stopped for breakfast at a Greenwich Village boardinghouse before booking a room for the night at Tammany Hall. Once settled, Gillespie hit the streets of New York, first visiting a men's clothier, where he transformed himself from California miner to East Coast writer. Next he purchased a theater ticket and, with his updated haberdashery, spent Saturday night at a Broadway show.

The following morning he ferried to Newark to meet old acquaintances and reunited with artist Rembrandt Lockwood, with whom he spent much of the next week immersed in artistic pursuits and frequenting local galleries.

Gillespie began the final leg of his journey home to Freeport, Pennsylvania, on April 23, traveling via Philadelphia and Harrisburg and arriving in the wee hours of the morning two days later.[43] Time would tell if he was ready to settle down as he had articulated:

And now with tall masts bending free,
And sails that clasp the wind,
Our vessel ploughs the tropic sea,
A foaming trail behind;
And wander forth we'll never more,
No, never more we'll roam,
Should we but meet the friends of yore,
The loving hearts at home.[44]

In regard to staying home, Caroline Meeker had been correct when she had written to her husband that General Darcy would not venture back to California. He did not return to the Pacific Coast in the spring of 1851—or ever. Once home, Newark's beloved doctor settled back into his multifaceted life, resuming his medical practice and taking on additional responsibilities with the railroad. In April, at a meeting of steamship and rail executives in New York City, Darcy was selected chairman of a committee to develop a transportation exhibit for the World's Fair planned for 1852 (which actually took place in 1853).[45] He accepted the honor but continued to decline repeated pleas to run for public office.

After two years away from their families, the men who had accompanied Darcy to the Yuba River and followed him home in early 1851 resumed their normal lives. They were among a mere 10 percent of gold seekers who actually achieved wealth mining California river bars with picks, rockers, and quicksilver.

Benjamin Casterline would invest his California profits in a sizable New Jersey farm, where he and Eliza would raise six children. William T. Lewis, having recovered from his serious illness, put his money in Ohio land, where he returned with his wife and four daughters and where he would see Sarah give birth to another four girls. Neither Lewis nor Casterline would ever travel far from home again, which was typical of many of Darcy's company.

As some men returned home, others were captivated by California's charms—its seemingly limitless opportunities and unrestrained societal freedoms. At least a dozen men of the Newark Overland Company remained California after the exodus of forty-niners in late 1850 and

Ohio homestead and family of William T. Lewis, circa 1884. His wife, Sarah, who insisted he take a white shirt for burial, is pictured in the center with a black bow at her neck. Courtesy of the Jean Heuman family.

early 1851. More than half of them would become lifetime California residents:

Caleb D. Boylston

Joseph H. Martin

Moses Canfield

Stephen Harris Meeker

Andrew J. Gray

John Brewster Overton

John Hunt

George D. Sayre

Henry L. Johnson

Thomas Seely

Thomas Fowler

John W. Shaff

Like the men from New Jersey, Eliza Farnham found the prospects and independence of California life enticing. The educated woman who had perhaps defied the odds in making it to the West Coast with her own visions and dreams settled her husband's estate, which provided her with a two-hundred-acre ranch near Santa Cruz. With her two sons she began farming the property she appropriately named Rancho La Libertad.

Chapter 21

1850s
Success and Loss

By 1851, it was downright confounding why anyone, in fact some 50,000, would take to wagons to reach California overland when the route via Panama had improved so much that the journey could be completed in just five weeks. New York and San Francisco were connected via Central America, with regular steamer routes on both east and west coasts. And there were dramatic modernizations across the isthmus where American entrepreneurs had descended on Panama, establishing accommodations and guide services for the jungle crossing. Talk of a railroad had begun.

Taking advantage of the improved transportation infrastructure were Stephen Dehart and W. Donaldson Kinney, both of whom ventured back to California within months of their return to New Jersey, presumably for business interests they left behind. In early 1851 the journey still involved seriously crowded steamers, with sleeping space on deck at a premium, although there were fewer backlogs in booking travel. To cross the isthmus, travelers spent several days meandering along the jungle-canopied Chagres River, staying overnight at still-primitive hotels that dotted the inland passage. Moving westbound, passengers transitioned from the comfort of stern- or side-wheeled steamers to small, raft-like boats worked by Natives using long poles to move upstream until the river was no longer navigable. At this point, coastal mountains separated travelers from Panama City, and conveyance by organized pack-mule train was required to traverse the angular, muddy terrain. The improved transportation services allowed more opportunity to observe the exotic wildlife and lush tropical foliage along the route.

Dehart, whose return to California preceded Kinney's, completed his business by late spring and departed San Francisco for New Jersey on May 17, 1851.[1] While General Darcy had closed the door on going back to the West Coast, his mining partner Kinney returned, despite poor health, and reached Sacramento just prior to Dehart's departure. There Kinney rendezvoused with S. H. Meeker at the Sutter House hotel before continuing north to the Yuba River camp, where he took lodging on the north bank around the area of Parks Bar (also called Sicard Flat). By the end of May, Kinney was organizing a Whig Party in the region with fellow New Jersey miner Henry L. Johnson, Thomas S. Myrick (whose 1849–55 letters would later be published), and Judge John V. Berry, who had traveled overland part of the way with the Newark Overland Company and whose well-educated wife, Catherine, had become a favorite of Darcy's nephew Charles Gray.[2]

Despite some normalcy taking hold in California, those returning to pursue business and participate in the state's development could easily see the differences between the East and West Coasts. Meeker, a prolific letter writer (he claimed that he composed as many as ten letters a day), sent details praising California life to a Newark friend he called "Captain." After describing the rapid improvements in steamers plying between Sacramento and San Francisco, Meeker wrote, "The progress of civilization and refinement is equally visible in other quarters. A few months since we considered ourselves fortunate to get enough of hard bread and bacon spread out on a barrel head for a table, and a beverage *called* coffee sweetened with dark Chinese sugar for drink." That, plus occasionally a little whiskey, he added. But things had changed: "Now an abundant supply of game and excellent vegetables are daily served up to us with all the proper appointments, and the frequent arrivals from the Islands and China bring us a variety of the Chinese tropical fruits."[3]

While others discouraged their associates at home from venturing to California, Meeker was forthright with his optimism. "You hint at a desire to be here and try your luck at hunting," he wrote to his friend. "I have frequently wished with all my heart that you were, and when I tell you that Huge Grizzlies, Elk, Deer, Panthers, Wild Cats, Wolves,

Antelope, Geese, Ducks, Pelicans and many other kinds of game have been killed this winter within one mile from the spot where I am writing, and that the river abounds with the finest Salmon I ever saw, besides a variety of other choice fish, I fancy that you will almost feel like packing up for an excursion to the El Dorado." Meeker continued, stating his belief that the climate was healthful, and further advised his friend, "But seriously, Captain, should your throat or lungs trouble you again let me urge you to come to the valley of the Sacramento where such diseases are wholly unknown notwithstanding many are living here who have suffered from them at home."[4]

Meeker was thriving in California, where his brother had joined him in business. In the same letter he suggested that his time in California was permanent by implying that he considered himself part of the new population: "We are a fast people and it is not too much to predict that some parts of this country will in less than two years equal in Splendor and luxurious living any part of the World." Referring to the state's development, he added, "Both the desire for it and the gold to pay for it exist here in a great degree."[5]

Meeker had one more enticement in regard to California: "The Ladies are coming too!" He hinted that his wife would soon join him. "I have partially consented that Mrs. M—— should try California life and climate for a while." He signed the letter affectionately, "Harry," his nickname derived from his middle name.[6] Indeed, Caroline Meeker would find California like no place on earth, much to her husband's utter dismay.

One of the "ladies" who had already come to California was Newark socialite Anna Maria Plume, daughter of highly regarded War of 1812 veteran Col. John Isaac Plume. Her brother, John V. Plume, had arrived in June 1849 on the steamer with the esteemed passenger list including both Senator Gwin and Mrs. John C. Fremont.[7] Plume had been one of the first to establish a banking operation in San Francisco and had profited enormously from early land speculation with city lots. Anna Maria Plume, being of high social standing, was one of the most eligible single women to arrive in San Francisco. And her successful suitor was none other than W. Donaldson Kinney, also from Newark and also of impeccable heritage, who may have headed back to California with designs to pursue Colonel Plume's eldest daughter. The marriage took place in San

Francisco on August 20, 1851, and was subsequently reported in the *New York Times*.[8]

Kinney and his bride made their home in San Francisco, where he engaged in the business of tanning leather. Earlier in the summer he had become one of the charter members (No. 329) of the 1851 Committee of Vigilance organized by citizens to curtail the lawlessness that was spreading across the city. Kinney was the only member of the Newark Overland Company to sign the organization's doctrines, which he did in San Francisco on June 9, citing a business relationship with Burgoyne and Company, the banking house of John V. Plume.

Newly married Kinney was putting down roots in San Francisco while another of the Jerseymen was preparing to depart California and return to Newark, where he too would soon marry. Heeding the call to settle down was John W. Shaff, one of the first to arrive overland in 1849. He had left California in late 1851, having spent a short time in the mines, before disappearing into the frontier fabric. Shaff picked up his mail regularly in Sacramento, where he likely frequented the Newark headquarters at Major Meeker's consignment shop. Within months of his return to New Jersey he married Harriet Francisco on February 10, 1852, and opened an accounting business at 102 Mulberry Street. Settling down, however, would prove much more difficult for Shaff than crossing the plains in a covered wagon.

It is believed that while still in California John Shaff had obtained work as a ship's purser, keeping the account books on a passenger and mail steamer with regular runs between San Francisco and Panama.[9] As Major Meeker had noted, the steamship industry was one of the best examples of California progress. Shaff's overland messmate Tom Seely had also found employment, becoming well known on the rivers as a steamer captain, charged with safely navigating the snags and bars that complicated the transportation system. Seely was one of the first hired when steamship companies began regular service, moving miners and equipment from the Bay Area to the inland gold rush centers. In February 1851 Captain Seely's steamer *Union* was running routine trips between San Francisco and Stockton, and passengers held him in the highest regard, often speaking of his gracious and polite manner.[10] His reputation was second to none.

Back in Sacramento, Meeker's business continued to thrive as the former Newark umbrella maker rose to the ranks of local prominence. He became involved with the city's Whig Party, representing Sacramento's First Ward, fulfilling his civic duties by promoting party members for state offices and raising funds to build a levee along the seven-mile waterfront so susceptible to flooding.

Public finances were also needed to deal with squatters who had organized, with the assistance of the opposing Democrats, to force issue over land titles. The squatters, or "settlers" as they fashioned themselves, questioned the legality of current deeds and had all but ruined John Sutter, who had abandoned his fort and much of his property granted under Mexican rule a decade earlier. As a member of the Whig Party, Meeker found himself opposing the squatters. By September, Meeker's party was referring to its organization as the Whig Vigilance Committee, although it was not associated with the 1851 Committee of Vigilance based in San Francisco.

By December 1851 Major Meeker had become the target of Democratic bullying, with insinuations that he had misappropriated money while serving as a fund commissioner with the Common Council. Coming to his defense were the editors of the Whig newspaper *Sacramento Daily Union,* who praised Meeker's character as being "ambitious and noble" and one "that can only be attained where the heart is pure, and the mind in all its conceptions is honorable and just." The editorial recognized Meeker's obligation to serve his community, noting that he was practically forced into the public position, and expressed hopes that the "unimpeachable" Meeker would not be disturbed by the reckless and dishonest criticism.[11] Like his mentor, General Darcy, Meeker would resist running for political office, preferring to support causes through private generosity.

At the close of 1851 the California population was estimated at 255,000, having more than doubled in just one year. Skyrocketing growth continued in all corners of the state and in all aspects of the emerging society. In San Francisco the well-to-do, such as the Plumes and the Kinneys, were enjoying a lavish new theater named for the most famous performer on the planet, Swedish songstress Jenny Lind. The theater's October opening had coincided with Lind's arrival in New Orleans, where swelling crowds greeted the superstar amid pandemonium. Lind's American concert tour was sponsored by entertainment promoter Phineas T. Barnum, who had done everything to hype the star with huge name recognition. Not only were theaters being named for her, so were lines of perfume and ferry boats. Her rapid rise to stardom roughly paralleled the rush for California's gold, and she would flee the spotlight as quickly as many of the gold seekers bolted for home. Lind's marriage in February 1852 ended her meteoric career.

Like San Francisco, Sacramento experienced exploding growth in 1851, with few benefiting more from the influx of people than S. H. Meeker. It was in Sacramento that he spent his third New Year's Eve three thousand miles away from home, and his second with business partner and brother David. He prepared a basket of his finest imported products, gathering French Heidsieck Champagne, cans of peaches and oysters, and a "firkin" of Goshen Butter (a specialty of New York's Hudson River dairy industry) from the selection of goods stocked on his store shelves. Meeker rose early on New Year's Day and deposited the basket on the doorstep of the *Sacramento Daily Union* office along with a note wishing them prosperity and happiness in the coming year.[12] The gift was an expression of appreciation for the support the editors had given to him over the allegations regarding misuse of public funds. The paper reciprocated by publishing Happy New Year salutations to their favorite merchant.

The next year, 1852, was an election year, and presidential politics began heating up between the Whigs and Democrats. Millard Fillmore would fail to gain his party's nomination and go down in history as one of the few US presidents never elected to the office. It was the beginning of decline for the Whig Party, which would once again turn to a military hero from the Mexican War, Gen. Winfield Scott, for its candidate. The Democrats seized the opportunity afforded by Fillmore's unpopular presidency and nominated yet another veteran of the Mexican War with a gamut of political credentials, alcoholic lawyer Franklin Pierce of New Hampshire.

For S. H. Meeker, 1852 would bring continued growth in his business, but by year's end he would be stricken by severe financial loss. In June he moved his store from Front Street to the southwest corner of Second and K Streets in the heart of Sacramento, where a substantial brick building described as one of the most elegant and spacious of the downtown square had been erected at a location considered unsurpassed in the city. On Saturday, June 19, the doors of Meeker's new store were opened to the public when he hosted an open house for his clientele. The *Sacramento Daily Union* predicted that Meeker, their friend and respected merchant, would reap a large share of public patronage. During the event, the paper reported, "an immense quantity of substantial edibles were consumed, and choice wines 'punished' by an innumerable number of visitors."[13]

Days after Meeker's grand opening, the nation lost one of its most eminent statesmen when Henry Clay, former Speaker of the House, secretary of state, and three-time presidential candidate of the Whig Party, died of consumption (tuberculosis) in Washington. It was June 28, 1852, some twenty years after John S. Darcy had publicly greeted Clay in Newark's city park and bequeathed to him a carriage crafted by local artisans. Senator Clay's diplomacy in the summer of 1850 had been pivotal to California's admission to the Union. After news of his death reached San Francisco by steamer five weeks later, memorial celebrations in his honor were planned across the state.

Sacramento officials set aside Thursday, August 12, for remembrances of Clay, with a ceremonial processional to take place in the city center, where businesses were requested to remain closed, with flags lowered to half-staff. Recognized as a Whig standard-bearer, Major Meeker was selected as a parade marshal, with orders to report to the Orleans Hotel at eight-thirty on the morning of the solemnities. Prior to gathering with other marshals and organizers, Meeker stopped by a shop on Front Street to pick up a pink sash, trimmed in silver and adorned with black rosettes, that would identify him as an official.

A representative funeral hearse pulled by four white horses was escorted to and from the American Theater by a host of dignitaries, among them military units, fraternal organizations, Knights Templar, the Benevolent Hebrew Society, firemen, merchants, and mechanics, with a Chinese delegation taking up a position in the rear. The thirty-minute procession took place under spectacularly sunny skies and with a huge turnout owing to both respect for Clay and the closing of gambling houses for the day.[14]

One month later Sacramento prepared for another public event. The city was host to an agricultural and horticultural fair during which the finest specimens grown in California soil were showcased. Hundreds, including children from local schools, visited the exhibits over the two-week event that commenced in late September. Meeker was asked to serve on two judging panels that would select the best entries, which would entail not simply recognition but also monetary prizes. As a merchant who sold fresh produce, Meeker participated in choosing the superior potatoes, onions, pumpkins, cabbages, and turnips in the vegetable class. His other panel, categorized under "Fine Arts," was assigned to evaluate artistic presentations using flowers and fruits.[15] A huge success, the event closed in early October, at which time Meeker turned his focus to New Jersey.

Caroline Meeker had agreed to come to California, at least for a visit. She may not have understood that her husband was in California for good, although it was clear when the *Sacramento Daily Union* reported, "Mr. Meeker has won for himself hosts of friends by his gentlemanly demeanor, liberality and public sprit, and although his departure will be regretted, we have the assurance that he will soon return with his family, to dwell permanently among us."[16] Apparently there were differing opinions between S. H. and Caroline Meeker. The children would not accompany their parents to the Pacific Coast, but instead remain in the East, probably at the Rye, New York, estate of Caroline's parents.

The couple had suffered the devastating loss of their oldest child in 1848, months before Major Meeker departed for California. Both parents grieved alone, and the major's absence had now stretched to nearly four years, a long separation in their eleven years of marriage. Cracks in the relationship would continue to develop, and California would prove no place to repair the marital rift.

On a late October Saturday, as pedestrians maneuvered along the waterfront shops of Sacramento's levee, Meeker boarded a steamer to begin his journey home to New Jersey, bound for the Isthmus of Panama for the first time. He reached Newark about the time loved ones were gathering around tables overflowing with Thanksgiving feasts. Unfortunately he would not have much time to savor the joys of a heartfelt reunion.

The steamer *Philadelphia* arrived in New York on December 10 with the latest California news, approximately five weeks old, which was published in New York and Newark newspapers the following day.[17] It is unclear whether Major Meeker had received personal correspondence from his brother David with details of the night of devastation in Sacramento or if he only learned of it when reading the published reports.

It happened on the first Tuesday in November, Election Day 1852, when Sacramento inspectors were up late, counting ballots collected from

On Election Day 1852, Sacramento went up in blazes as captured in this Hugo Nahl watercolor. The successful business of S. H. Meeker suffered substantial damage in the fire while he was three thousand miles away visiting family in New Jersey. Hugo Wilhelm Arthur Nahl, *The Fire in Sacramento*, 1852. Watercolor on paper, 4.563 x 7.13 in. Courtesy of the collection of the Oakland Museum of California. Oakland Museum of California, Gift of Concours d'Antiques, Art Guild (A77.112).

citywide polling places earlier in the day, mostly cast for Whig candidate Winfield Scott. In a millenary shop, where the proprietor, Madame Lanos, maintained an inventory of ladies' bonnets, collars, and dressmaking patterns—items made from cotton, silk, paper, and straw, all very flammable materials—the first spark had ignited. It was two blocks from Meeker's large store. With the focus on the election, there was some delay in responding to the fire, so the flames, fanned by winds from the levee, spread rapidly from store to store. When the fire jumped the street and consumed the Crescent City Hotel, there was little firefighters could do but evacuate the local hospital and deliberately explode buildings in an attempt to create a firewall. The conflagration was out of control. Block after block went down to ash and ruin.[18]

The following morning, November 3, the *Alta California* reported a population strangely cheerful and undaunted by the latest destruction, many having survived the devastating flood of January 1850.[19] One lone building was left standing, the remarkably fire-resistant Lady Adams

Hotel (still standing today), constructed just months earlier of brick brought around Cape Horn from Germany. Major Meeker's new building, while also made of brick, was otherwise a shell filled with flammable soft goods. His damages were first estimated at $40,000, but when fully realized were raised to $75,000, placing them among the greatest losses of businessmen in Sacramento.[20] By the time Major Meeker learned of his losses in mid-December, significant rebuilding was already underway throughout the city.[21]

Five weeks and three thousand miles separated Meeker from hands-on attention to his business in California. As Christmas festivities rolled into New Year's Eve celebrations and 1853 was about to break the horizon, Caroline and S. H. Meeker said their good-byes to New Jersey friends and family and boarded the steamer *Georgia* for the nine-day voyage to Panama.[22]

With a writing style as eloquent as her husband's, Caroline Meeker articulated the scenes of her journey in a letter to her sister-in-law in which she mused about the transition to a warmer climate: "Imagine if you please a voyage but ten days from a northern latitude, where all was frost, and cold, bound with the ice kings fetters, and then turn to a scene more like enchantment than reality, and you can faintly picture to yourself the delight, and astonishment I felt, as the magic scene burst upon me."[23]

Her wonderment continued once on the Chagres River, where Natives propelled her boat as they moved deeper into the exotic jungle paradise: "Elegant water lilys, white as the virgin snow, reared their proud heads above majestic leaves of brightest green, clusters of orange, and scarlet blossoms almost too bright to gaze upon, greeted us. . . . Parrots of most brilliant plumage flitted from bough, to bough, monkeys revelled in their native wildness, and butterflies the most gorgeous I ever beheld sported in the gentle breeze."[24]

While travel across the isthmus had improved with American influence, it was still primitive, and the Meekers were exposed to their share of difficulties enduring Panama's rugged topography and sometimes lawless culture. Caroline called it the bitter with the sweet: "The terrors of the isthmus no Pen can paint, the danger, annoyances, fatigues cannot be described, it must be traveled to be appreciated. Its mountain Passes, so narrow, deep, and dark, its steep precipices, its deep mud holes, and its stubborn mules, but faintly portray its difficulties. The change one experiences in leaving the Chagres river, to the mule travel, can most aptly be compared to leaving heaven to pass through purgatory." She mentioned little improvement when they began the descent from the mountainous terrain and caught sight of the glittering Pacific before entering the walled city of Panama.[25]

The Meekers remained for a week in Panama's western port, where Caroline found "the most hated, jaded, specimens of humanity we could well imagine." Finally they boarded the steamer *Oregon* for San Francisco, thinking the worst was behind them. But Caroline's letter intimated a sense of desperation when she wrote, "We had a still more formidable foe to contend with, and one from where there was no retreat. Two days out, yellow fever of the most malignant kind broke out amongst us, and once a week had passed, seventeen of our number were consigned to the briny deep. . . . The steamer was very small, between five and six hundred souls on board, weather intensely hot; the sick and dying stretched upon the deck at our very feet, was a scene to appal the stoutest heart."[26]

Another woman on board the *Oregon* hailed from frontier Missouri and was likely less affected by the hardships of crossing the isthmus and surviving the noxious sea voyage than Caroline. Elizabeth Meeker, wife of the major's older brother David, had also agreed to try California life with her husband and had joined her in-laws en route to San Francisco.[27] As a farm girl, she was no doubt more prepared to adapt to California life than was the refined Caroline.

The Meekers arrived in San Francisco on February 3, 1853.[28] Like many who entered the Golden Gate, Caroline could only describe the expansive bay as "magnificent." Yet her first two months there would do nothing to sell her on making the Pacific Coast her home: "For the present I can but say that we are all well, and pretty well contented, though I find California any thing but home. I think I shall know how to appreciate my home more than ever, if I live to return to it and yet I have not been sick an hour, and have gained seven pounds since I arrived." And with that she closed, requesting that her letters remain strictly private.[29]

Nothing had gone Major Meeker's way since he had judged vegetables and flower arrangements at the agricultural fair in October. The destruction to his property in the Sacramento fire and the failure of his entire family to join him permanently in California was not how he had planned to start the new year. And now his wife's first impressions of the West Coast were anything but positive. By the time Meeker reached home in mid-February, there was more tragic news out of Sacramento.

On December 12, 1852, fellow Newark native Andrew J. Gray (youngest brother of Mrs. John S. Darcy) had died at the age of thirty-seven in Yolo County, across the river from the Sacramento waterfront. Only months earlier he had been in apparent good health at the Yuba River with Henry Johnson, who was still running a mining operation near the original claim. General Darcy, a father figure to his young brother-in-law, had learned of his death in January when the *Newark Daily Advertiser* announced the latest intelligence from California brought by the regular mail steamer.[30] Andrew had been only a few years older than his nephew and overland trail messmate, Charles Gray, with whom he had maintained a strained relationship.

Barely three months after the death of Andrew Gray, the family suffered the loss of oldest sister Eliza Gray Darcy. She died in Newark on March 12, 1853, at the age of sixty-one, survived by her husband of forty-three years, John S. Darcy, three grown children, and a growing cache of grandchildren.[31]

Charles Gray may not have been at his father's New York City residence to mourn the deaths of his Aunt Eliza or Uncle Andrew in early 1853. After returning from California, he had begun a personal association with acclaimed music engraver William Oakes and his wife, Abby Tyler Oakes, a transplanted Boston couple well ensconced in the art community of New York City, where Charles Gray's older brother was a major player. William Oakes had made his way to California in 1852, first associating with the *Marysville Herald* before forming a business relationship with the *San Francisco Daily Evening Bulletin.*[32] Charles Gray may have traveled back to California in the early 1850s, as some records exist that suggest employment and travel, but it is most likely that he remained based in New York City with Abby Tyler Oakes, while her husband established himself in San Francisco.

Opportunities in California continued for those like William H. Oakes, who came to the state with spirit and determination to succeed. Not all enterprise, however, was taking place in the commercial centers of San Francisco and Sacramento. Up and down the placer-laden rivers and canyons, many ex-miners realized that a stable trade or industry far exceeded the lottery of arduous digging. Such was the experience of John B. Overton, who had bid farewell to his homeward-bound brother, Isaac, in 1849 and set out to conquer his share of California's promise.

The Overton brothers had been orphaned at a young age when their father, a conductor for John S. Darcy's New Jersey Railroad, tragically lost his life while on the job. They consequently grew up under the care of court-appointed guardians, not always together, until they were able to share a home in Newark before being enticed west by gold fever.[33] Isaac, who had been one of the first to arrive in California in 1849 and one of the first to hightail it home, preferred the security of a job as railroad ticket agent in New Jersey. Younger brother J. B. felt there was nothing to lose in taking risks and settled in California. Despite the three-thousand-mile separation, the two remained close and in touch, reconnecting in 1856 when J. B. returned to New Jersey for a visit.[34]

While J. B. Overton's mining efforts were successful, his earnings seldom outpaced his spending. Finally he managed to save enough to open a store on the Middle Fork of the Feather River, deep in the Sierra foothills, well northeast of Marysville.[35] A permanent population with a growing demand for goods and services was taking hold in the region that had been designated Plumas County. The store launched Overton on a successful career path following in the footsteps of S. H. Meeker, not only in commercial success but also in prominence and respect in his community.

As smaller gold rush towns were vying to establish themselves commercially, the major import and export activity continued to converge on California's largest city, and the resulting wealth was forming a privileged society. After suffering substantial financial losses in November's fire in Sacramento, merchant S. H. Meeker opened an office on Clay Street in San Francisco. Perhaps he had in mind to restore and expand his business, or it may have been an astute measure to appease his wife. The San Francisco social world was far more advanced than Sacramento's and possessed elite standards more in accord with those of a New Yorker accustomed to the crème de la crème. S. H. and Caroline Meeker took up residence on Washington Street above Powell on the northern slope of Nob Hill, a location that afforded a bay view.[36] The core of Meeker's business, however, remained in Sacramento, which is where he spent most of his time, again away from Caroline. In contrast, Elizabeth Meeker made her home in Sacramento with her husband, David, where she was adjusting well, content with all her new life had to offer.

Major Meeker's ploy, if it was such, was working. Caroline Meeker began to recognize that San Francisco was exhilarating. Elegant balls, theater engagements, and soirees, all more mysterious and more casual than any that could have taken place in proper New York City circles, captivated many who had never before experienced such social freedom. What may have been considered underground in the East was almost the norm in San Francisco, where anyone drawn into the realm was essentially free from repercussions.

Caroline Meeker began to settle in and embrace the status she held as the wife of a leading merchant. Her husband's propensity for business seemed limitless, even in the wake of the fire. The Sacramento store had recovered and was once again thriving, with its market share of quality imported products. In San Francisco, Meeker's reputation was climbing, and by late summer Caroline had adjusted to the comings and goings of her new life. It was not just the gaiety of an active social calendar but the simpler customs of a blended population. She delighted in the opportunity to display her artistic needlework, entering embroidery samples in the 1853 Agricultural and Horticultural Fair, a statewide event growing in popularity and this time held in San Francisco.[37] With things seemingly working so well, the Meekers began to contemplate arrangements for the children to join them within the coming year. It appeared the family was headed for a lifetime in California, for better or worse.

In September 1853 another high-profile San Francisco couple with New Jersey roots was boarding a steamer bound for Newark, now a journey reduced to four weeks, with services across Panama more streamlined than ever. W. Donaldson Kinney and Anna Maria Kinney departed after two years of living in the Bay City, possibly after learning that her father, Colonel Plume, was seriously ill. They would never return to California.

W. D. Kinney and his wife arrived in New Jersey two weeks before tragedy would strike one of his fellow gold seekers from 1849. Cyrus Currier's beloved wife, Nancy, the woman who had been so worried about the well-being of her husband during his sixteen months in California, died on October 28, 1853.[38] The brief obituary did not mention the cause of death, but according to the family Bible, her death was due to complications from giving birth to a son, George, who would survive only a few months after his mother's death.[39]

Unlike the Meekers, whose relationship was privately strained, or the obviously troubled marriages of Henry L. Johnson and Moses Canfield, the Curriers had felt true devotion to one another, which was expressed lovingly in their letters. With three children to raise, the youngest now five years old, Cyrus Currier faced the coming years as a widower. His loss was unfathomable.

John S. Darcy, who had also buried his wife in 1853, was emerging from his grief by contemplating politics. At sixty-six years of age, Darcy was about to reverse his longtime reluctance to run for public office. He would accept the Democratic Party's nomination to campaign for a congressional seat representing New Jersey. The political climate of 1854 was stormy, with an ever-deepening divide between proponents of antislavery and those who supported states' rights, specifically the right of each state to determine its own laws, even laws regarding human rights. The ideological argument broke clearly along regional lines, with the southern states becoming more resolute in the fight for their sovereignty and constantly threatening disunion.

There were questions why General Darcy, at his advanced age, would venture into such hostile arenas as running a political campaign or holding public office. The *Newark Daily Advertiser* found Darcy's decision inconceivable and held nothing back in its October 9, 1854, editorial:

> On the venerable Dr. Darcy's account, not our own, we regret he has not persisted in declining the Democratic nomination. . . . Had he chosen years ago to aspire to office, it would have been better judged and more suitable to his time of life. Now, when age should have allayed, not stimulated an appetite for political promotion, it is really surprising, indeed almost incredible, that he should be willing to leave the quiet of domestic life, and the prosecution of a useful and laborious profession, in which he has spent his days and earned an enviable reputation, and for what?[40]

While the newspaper was aligned with the opposing party, it is debatable as to whether the sentiment expressed was partisan or represented public consensus.

Not only was Darcy inexperienced in professional politics, he was running against an incumbent with equally stellar credentials, and one with a family name that had dominated New Jersey's highest offices for decades. Alexander C. M. Pennington would go on to win a second term in Congress, defeating Darcy at the polls in November 1854. The General would not repeat his mistake in regard to seeking office, but remained committed to supporting the Democratic Party. In 1856 he would again travel west on the Ohio River, as he had in 1849, this time to serve as a delegate at the party's national nominating convention in Cincinnati, where James Buchanan would be put forth as the party's presidential candidate.

While California was steadfastly antislavery, it was somewhat insulated from the heated debates being waged east of the Mississippi, and consequently the state's politics remained focused on economic and social development. With the gradual demise of the Whig Party across the nation, many members were turning their allegiance to the American Party, also known as the Know Nothings. Other Whigs were aligning themselves with the newly established Republican Party, which supported an antislavery platform. Among the Republicans was John C. Fremont, a southerner by birth and California's most noted public figure. His fame would garner him the party's first presidential nomination, and he would square off in 1856 against Democrat James Buchanan and ex-president Millard Fillmore, representing the Know Nothings. Buchanan, with a unified party backing him, would have no problem taking the majority of votes to become the fifteenth US president.

S. H. Meeker and his brother David were considered old-line Whigs, having come of age at the time when the party was established by Henry Clay and John Adams. With a home and business in San Francisco, S. H. became affiliated with the American Party in that city. David, solidly based in Sacramento, had a more difficult time letting go of his Whig roots and may well have been the last candidate elected to office under the Whig banner when he defeated a Know Nothing for alderman of Sacramento's Second Ward in 1855.[41]

David Meeker was a pillar of the community, devoting his time and energy to such public service efforts as the construction of roads and to such progressive causes as education for minorities. As city councilman he coauthored an amendment to permit black children to be educated in public, if separate, schools, a piece of legislation that was vetoed by the mayor before Meeker and an associate forced a second vote. Arguing that blacks in the community were paying taxes and should equally benefit from such funding, Meeker successfully persuaded fellow councilmen that it was a matter of justice to override the veto. Siding with Meeker on the issue were antislavery advocates and future railroad magnates Charles Crocker and Mark Hopkins.[42]

Though not as savvy as his brother, David Meeker was well respected in business and would form a brief business relationship with another future railroad magnate, Leland Stanford. The partnership was reviewed favorably by the *California Farmer and Journal of Useful Sciences,* where it was reported, "The house of Stanford & Brother & Meeker of Sacramento, may be looked upon with pride as a house of great business capability and integrity, with ample capital to back it."[43] The Meeker and Stanford families would eventually be tied by the marriage of David Meeker's son Henry Harris Meeker and Leland Stanford's niece Jane Stanford. David Meeker managed to remain dedicated to family and public service, showing little interest in elite social circles.

Just the opposite was true for younger brother S. H. Meeker and his often-distant wife. In March 1854 Caroline traveled alone back to the East Coast, where she reunited with her children, Minnie and Heyward.[44] Some months later she returned with them to San Francisco, apparently with the desire to settle permanently. They arrived in California on January 29, 1855, having crossed Panama weeks prior to the opening of the new time-saving railroad that sliced across the isthmus.[45] They would move to a new home, also on Nob Hill, located on the southeast corner of Pacific and Mason.[46]

Caroline's husband continued his business interests in Sacramento while shifting his inventory toward imported liquor and fine wines in San Francisco. Meeker & Company became the sole supplier in California and Oregon of wines produced by noted American winemaker Nicholas Longworth, who was originally from Newark but had built his wine industry in the Ohio River Valley. The *California Farmer and Journal* also approved of this business arrangement: "No better or more worthy house could have been selected than that of Meeker & Co., as they are among the pioneer merchants of California, one of the earliest houses, passing through fire and flood unterrified and unshaken, and their trade and acquaintance are as widely extensive as any house in California, and

GOODWIN & CO. and MEEKER,
IMPORTERS AND WHOLESALE DEALERS
— IN —
Foreign and Domestic Liquors,
No. 121 FRONT STREET, corner of Oregon,
SAN FRANCISCO.
FINE WINES, BRANDIES AND GIN, IN BOND.
LONGWORTH'S WINES,
SOLE AGENTS OF
Max Sutaine & Co., Rheims, celebrated "Cabinet Champagne."

Major S. H. Meeker became the exclusive West Coast importer of wines produced in Ohio by Nicholas Longworth, a fellow Newark native considered the "Father of American Grape Culture." From *Colville's San Francisco Directory, 1856–1857* (San Francisco: Monson, Valentine, 1856). Courtesy of the San Francisco Public Library.

their reputation and credit as high as any firm need desire."[47] The store in Sacramento would gradually be taken over by David, with S. H. Meeker turning his interests full time to the importing business in San Francisco.

Unlike his brother, who was following a modest life in Sacramento, S. H. Meeker was drawn to the finer rewards his hard work had earned. One of his passions was horses. Major Meeker was known to own some of the finest-bred horses in California, and he kept them for both pleasure and sport. He was often recognized riding a beauty of a sorrel colt—together they formed a striking silhouette that spoke of wealth and status. Harness racing was his sport of choice, with Frank Forrester, his handsome gray trotter, taking top honors in the 1856 State Agricultural Fair, performing so well that a hefty $2,000 price was negotiated for his sale.[48]

While enjoying the high life, Major Meeker protected his spotless reputation with clean living and exemplary conduct. Caroline, however, was rumored to be involved in an improper relationship with a Capt. Ed Gorham, taking advantage of her husband's long absences when he was tending to business matters in Sacramento. Those with a keen eye for such illicit activity may have noticed that Gorham had returned from the East at the same time as Mrs. Meeker, not only departing New York with her on the steamship *George Law* but also arriving in San Francisco listed on the same manifest of the *Golden Age* in January 1855.[49] The logistics indicate they would have crossed the isthmus together on coinciding itineraries. Gorham was known in San Francisco as one of the originators of the 1851 Committee of Vigilance, having had the distinction of being the third signer of the organization's charter. Major Meeker was acquainted with him casually through political circles.

The 1851 Committee of Vigilance had all but disbanded by the mid-1850s, although lawlessness was still lurking. In May 1856, San Franciscans were stunned by a street shooting so premeditated and deliberate that it was considered an assassination. A member of the city's Board of Supervisors had pulled the trigger, killing a newspaper editor who was about to publish reports damaging to the supervisor's reputation. Mortally wounded was James King of William (he added "of William" to his name, in reference to his father, for uniqueness), who had seven months earlier founded the popular *San Francisco Daily Evening Bulletin*. The cold-blooded shooting on one of San Francisco's central commercial thoroughfares led to the reemergence of the Committee of Vigilance in 1856.

At the time of the shooting, William H. Oakes was working with James King of William for the *San Francisco Daily Evening Bulletin*. Known as a music engraver, Oakes had come to California four years earlier, and had previously worked in the newspaper industry. Two months before the assassination of his friend and colleague, Oakes's wife and son had joined him in San Francisco. Making the trip to California with Abby Tyler Oakes and her young son was Charles G. Gray, who, despite having worked only occasionally as a clerk, had the luxury of traveling with a servant. A fellow passenger on board, also arriving in San Francisco on March 3, 1856, was young Englishman Eadweard J. Muygridge, who had yet to make a name for himself—and his innovative photography—in the world of fine arts, though his reputation would rise quickly in San Francisco.[50]

Whether or not Muygridge chose California as a destination because of an association with Gray and Oakes is uncertain. He may well have crossed paths with them in New York City where Charles Gray's brother,

Henry Peters Gray, was an accomplished artist whose works were displayed at the National Academy of Design. Also exhibiting at the academy in 1854 was Abby Tyler Oakes, one of a handful of women accepted to showcase her talents at that level. Her pleasing landscapes hung among some of the finest nineteenth-century paintings.[51] If Muygridge had not encountered Gray and Oakes in New York City's art coteries, they would soon become acquainted in San Francisco. Within months of his arrival Muygridge opened a bookstore and arranged to sell the quality engravings produced by William Oakes.

In San Francisco, Charles Gray took up residence with William and Abby Oakes on Geary Street just up from the main Market Street promenade.[52] If Gray was engaged in any gainful employment while in San Francisco, the business directory made no mention of it. Conversely, Abby Oakes had come to California to work, specifically to paint. She quickly began to locate sites around the Bay Area to capture on canvas, undeterred by the frontier vigilantism and the murder of her husband's associate just after her arrival in San Francisco.

Women who came to California in the 1850s understood that the freedom available to them was far and away greater than anywhere in the United States. Nowhere else were women so readily accepted as entrepreneurs, property owners, and even artists. The unconventional nature of the society was embraced by those who found the progressiveness refreshing. Those who did not approve of it left.

Caroline Meeker would leave California, but her reasons for doing so were more complicated. By July 1857 it was clear that her marriage was dysfunctional and that her dalliances could damage her husband's reputation. She returned to Rye, New York, with her two children and moved in with her parents. Her father, John Griffen, a successful farmer and livestock breeder, was building a lavish estate located at Mamaroneck, overlooking Long Island Sound. Details of the failed relationship likely remained hidden from the family. S. H. Meeker would keep in touch with his father-in-law, at least regarding business ventures, as his investments in California included both wheat and specially bred hogs imported from the Griffen property in Rye.[53] The Meekers would not divorce.

California in the 1850s proved hard on relationships, as evidenced by the Meekers' strained marriage, along with countless others in which one or both partners had been lured there by the state's unbridled culture.

The very nature of a man who would travel overland in a wagon for the prospect of instant wealth, or a woman who would sail thousands of miles from her home and family, is evidence of a yearning for adventure and a rejection of the confines of a routine life. From the Newark Overland Company, the Canfields, Johnsons, and Meekers all fell victim to the spell.

John W. Shaff fared no better. Perhaps he should have stayed in California. By 1856 the man who embarked on the cross-country adventure in 1849, and who likely authored the *Newark Daily Advertiser* letter in May of that year exclaiming that he would go on to China if his wanderlust was not satisfied, found himself trapped in a mundane marriage with two children and a daily routine of adding numbers on accounting book columns.[54]

Faced with a monotonous life to which he was not adjusting, Shaff opted for a drastic change that allowed him to provide for his family while attempting to drain the last of the restlessness from his system. The bookkeeping skills he practiced everyday qualified him for service with the US Navy in the role of purser's clerk, a professional position considered a "forward officer," similar in status with sailmakers, gunners, and boatswains. In 1856 Shaff signed on for a three-year commitment with the USS *Portsmouth* under the command of Andrew H. Foote, whose orders were to join the East India Squadron.[55] John W. Shaff was going to China after all.

Built in Portsmouth, New Hampshire, the *Portsmouth* was a striking wooden sloop-of-war, with billowing sails cascading from tall masts, bow-to-stern gunnery decks, and an intimidating bowsprit pointing the way. The ship had seen service in the Mexican-American War before being stationed to protect San Francisco Bay during Fremont's erratic conquest of California in 1846.

Departing the East Coast in May 1856 bound for Asia, the ship and crew rounded Cape Horn in late summer in the wintery seas of the Southern Hemisphere. It was the journey Shaff had not taken in 1849, when he had opted to travel overland. Ninety-four days after setting sail from the states, the *Portsmouth* reached Batavia (now Djakarta, Indonesia) on its way to China. Once in Canton they met armed resistance and were forced into an amphibious assault and brief occupation of the city before defeating Chinese garrisons in a fiery gun battle. They had found themselves caught in the start of the Second Opium War but managed to limit their involvement to the single skirmish.

The *Portsmouth* was ordered to return from its Far East expedition after spending two years touring ports in Java, China, Siam (now Thailand), Singapore, and Japan. It reached its home base of Portsmouth, New Hampshire, in June 1858, having lost fourteen crewmen, primarily from disease. Shaff was released from his commitment in April 1859 and returned home to his wife and two children in Newark, where he resumed his accounting business. Time would tell whether his restless spirit had been calmed or whether it would be a lifelong condition.

Shaff's delight in exploration and adventure had been unmistakable in the letters he wrote during his 1849 gold rush trek, when he expressed the excitement of the West with optimistic and colorful stories. In stark contrast, Charles Gray's writings from the overland journey revealed chronic frustration, as though he was on the brink of depression much of the time. Once in California, his journal entries continued to reflect his negative mood. The two men shared the same occupation of bookkeeping but nothing else, and even in that single commonality they were opposites, as Gray seldom practiced his profession. How odd then that a decade later John Shaff was living in Newark, starving for fulfillment, while Charles Gray was a resident of San Francisco surrounded and stimulated by the fine arts culture he craved.

Financial success and personal relationships for the men of the Newark Overland Company continued to evolve throughout the decade following 1849. Darcy remarried in 1855, again to a woman named Eliza, a widow who not only caught the General's eye but also certainly captured one of Newark's most eligible bachelors.[56] Likewise, Cyrus Currier found another love in Charlotte Axford, whom he wed in 1857.[57] The couple would be blessed with two children, many grandchildren, and the celebration of thirty-five wedding anniversaries together. Both Darcy and Currier maintained enviable stability in their careers as well as their fortune in finding suitable mates a second time around.

Like Darcy and Currier a number of the men progressed steadily in the years following their gold rush days. William T. Lewis found himself in the desirable position of having a new railroad line traverse his Ohio property, thanks to wife, Sarah, who agreed to the business arrangement while he was in California. He plotted out the village of Lewis Center just north of Columbus, built a new home for his family, and enjoyed life as the town proprietor, all while keeping horses and hounds for fox hunting. He would on go to become a respected horse breeder.

Others were unsettled, as was the case for Darcy's former mining partner W. Donaldson Kinney. The once energetic man who had successfully engaged in business and politics while in California grieved the loss of his young wife, Anna, in 1856 after a long, debilitating illness. Kinney took up residence with his widowed mother and managed the family hardware business in Newark alongside his brother. His grief over the loss of his wife lingered years longer than Darcy's and Currier's.

Not all uncertainty resulted in disappointment for the once confident gold hunters. Pennsylvania native Charles B. Gillespie, an optimist at heart, wrote about settling down when he sailed back to New York in 1851. It did not happen. As the decade progressed he remained unmarried and uncommitted to any career as he continued to pursue a cavalcade of passions. Perhaps inspired by his bout with malaria on the trail in 1849 and his chance cure by quinine provided by a passing doctor, Gillespie entered the Philadelphia School of Medicine in 1858. Upon graduating he began a medical practice serving his hometown, Freeport.[58] He continued to paint and sketch and write. Life was good.

And then there was Tom Seely, the freewheeling messmate of baseball enthusiast Alexander Cartwright. Seely had obtained employment as a riverboat captain shortly after arriving on the Pacific Coast. In 1856 the California Steam Navigation Company named Seely captain of the SS *Senator* when it began its twice-monthly coastal service between San Francisco and San Diego, with stops in San Luis Obispo, Santa Barbara, and San Pedro.[59] If Seely had found San Francisco and all of its freedoms something of a paradise, he found Southern California, with a population of affluent, party-hosting rancheros, truly heaven on earth. Life was really good.

Chapter 22

Mechanics, Southern Hospitality, and Disunion

D uring the summer of 1857 citizens of San Francisco witnessed the construction of a large edifice on a vacant lot along Montgomery Street that gradually consumed the entire block. Built as a temporary structure, it was visually grand, laid out using a Greek-cross plan with a central dome ninety feet in diameter, upon which flew a US flag of still only thirty-one stars. Additionally, corner turrets sported flags representing colors of various nations, graciously loaned to the organizers by the US Navy. The building's striking appearance was deceiving because the roof was mere canvas.[1]

Earlier in 1857 the Mechanics' Institute of San Francisco had distributed a circular announcing a fair to promote "every department of industry; works of art of every variety; choice specimens of ingenuity and skill; . . . in short, whatever nature or art can contribute, curiosity discover or ingenuity devise."[2] The Pavilion, as it would become known, would house artistic handiwork, uniquely West Coast products, and state-of-the-art mechanical devices submitted for exhibition by a local population eager to showcase California's progress.

The Mechanics' Institute had been formed in 1855 "to encourage citizens of the industrial occupations to gather, study and exchange ideas," and it had "for its object the establishment of a Library, Reading Room, the collection of a Cabinet, Scientific Apparatus, Works of Art, and for other literary and scientific purposes."[3] Its ranks were soon filled with the

Pavilion of the First Industrial Exhibition of the Mechanics' Institute of San Francisco. Charles Gray submitted one entry to the fair in September 1857. Courtesy of Mechanics' Institute Archives, Mechanics' Institute, San Francisco, California.

prominent men whose industry and labors qualified them for membership, including Eadweard Muygridge, whose interest in photography was becoming his passion. Muygridge selected items from his art and book collections for presentation at the first annual fair.[4]

Cavernous inside, the Pavilion covered 20,000 square feet, all of it needed for exhibits in 1857, as more than nine hundred individuals registered one or more items for display. There were forty-five exhibit classes, each with multiple categories, including steam-powered wagons, beet sugar, innovative carpentry, leather goods, California wine, painting and drawing, pumps and windmills, and even dentistry.

Muygridge's acquaintances Charles Gray and Abby Tyler Oakes also registered items for the exhibit. Gray had continued living with the Oakeses on Geary Street, just blocks from the Pavilion, in an arrangement that may have included some type of modest employment managing the couple's affairs, in particular those of Mrs. Oakes. He had arrived in California with her in March 1856, when she reunited with her husband after a four-year separation. Two months after their arrival, the shocking assassination of James King of William in San Francisco had led to a partnership between William Oakes and Muygridge, who had arrived on the same ship as Mrs. Oakes and Gray. Commemorative portraits of the deceased King of William, produced by local artists, were engraved by Oakes and offered for sale at Muygridge's recently opened Montgomery Street bookstore, with both men referenced as publishers of the acclaimed likenesses.[5]

Abby Tyler Oakes took little time to capture the attention of San Francisco's art community with her own creative works. In September 1857 she submitted six oil paintings and a crayon sketch to the inaugural Industrial Exhibition of the Mechanics' Institute.[6] Displayed inside the Pavilion alongside hundreds of other items, her work quickly drew favorable attention, and she was among the most commended local artists.

The exhibition opened on September 8, a Tuesday. Several thousand patrons streamed into the Pavilion each of the first two days, and no fewer than five hundred attended on any of the subsequent fifteen days of the fair's duration. In all, more than 30,000 visitors would attend. Teachers, public school students, clergymen, and members of the press were granted free admission. Gas lighting and nightly musical performances enticed paying attendees to surrender fifty cents each to enter the elaborate tent structure, where a tower clock greeted them in the main hall. In the center, under the airy dome, was a large marble fountain, around which there was ample space for mingling.[7]

Browsing the exhibits, visitors could see items recognized with non-monetary prizes awarded for each category and special silver medals given for ingenious new inventions or for significant improvements to existing technologies. A miniature portrait by Charles Gray's brother, Henry Peters Gray, possibly of Charles himself, was honorably noted by the judges but not recognized with any awards, as the artist was not a Californian. E. J. Muygridge entered three chrome lithographs and a set of imported books, which were similarly singled out by the reviewing panels for their excellence. In the category of landscape oils, Abby Tyler Oakes was awarded the show's highest merit for two paintings considered the best of their class.[8]

The Mechanics' Institute had included a call for the "the delicate and beautiful handiwork of women" when the fair was announced, expecting the likes of fine embroidery, hair ornaments, pickled fruits, and artificial flower arrangements.[9] The women of San Francisco did not disappoint, filling the traditionally female categories with scores of high-quality specimens. Yet they also came forth with numerous paintings, drawings, and sketches, many submitted by girls and unmarried women who had produced their works as students of fine arts. An accomplished artist for more than a decade, Abby Tyler Oakes was a rare breed in the profession—a wife and mother who challenged her male counterparts with exceptional talent. She was known to sign her work "Mrs. A. T. Oakes," making clear her gender and marital status, but unconventionally using her own initials instead of those of her husband.

Merchant S. H. Meeker was neither an artist nor mechanic, but probably attended the well-advertised event. After his wife had left in July with the children, Meeker had moved to the Oriental Hotel for room and board. The hotel was only blocks from the Pavilion, and it was just across Market Street from the residence of Charles Gray. The two former associates of the 1849 overland journey likely crossed paths regularly.

Also based in San Francisco was Capt. Tom Seely, with living quarters aboard the SS *Senator,* which was routinely docked at the Broadway and Pacific Street wharves. Seely likely missed the fair and its pageantry, as he was known to be waylaid in Los Angeles, suffering from gout.[10] His reputation as a steamboat captain had soared over the years. He had first risen to public attention while based on the inland waterways commanding the steamers *Union* and *Bragdon,* and his popularity continued to grow after transitioning to the *Senator* in 1856. The affable Seely was a recognized and favorite citizen in both San Francisco and Southern California.

Seely loved the gambling tables, rounds of fine liquor, and the company of party-loving companions. According to certain stories, he would disembark the *Senator* at San Pedro, turning over command of the steamship to his first-mate officer for completion of the final leg to San Diego. San Pedro was twelve miles from Los Angeles, then a village barely one-tenth the size of San Francisco but home to the Bella Union Hotel, a social hot spot where Seely routinely enjoyed card games and drinking. After several days Seely would rejoin his vessel and crew on its return trip back up the coast. Maybe he used the excuse of gout, or maybe he just used his authority to partake in these side trips. Either way, no one complained.

In May 1858 Seely managed to elevate his reputation further when he made the *Senator* available to the citizens of Los Angeles for an excursion to San Diego. They were to be the guests at a grand ball hosted by the residents of that city.[11]

Separated by 120 coastal miles, Los Angeles and San Diego were worlds apart in 1858. With the development of San Pedro for shipping, Los Angeles was becoming infused with business traffic, yet it was by no means competition for San Francisco as the population center of California. San Diego, meanwhile, remained a sleepy outpost where the US Army's Third Artillery occupied an old mission and less than one thousand permanent residents comprised the town.

Seely and other organizers spared no expense to make the two-day event memorable. Carriages, some sporting six-in-hand prancers, assembled at the Bella Union Hotel at two o'clock on Thursday, May 20, 1858, to transport passengers to the *Senator*. In the evening the steamship would weigh anchor and begin its journey down the coast under calm, silvery skies. The *Los Angeles Star* described the scene: "The moon shed her silver light on the peaceful waters, and disclosed in bold relief the towering mountains of the coast. Music added its sweet influence to enhance the charms of nature."[12]

By daylight the *Senator* lay in the picturesque San Diego Bay, where the excursionists got their first look at the town, which they found surprisingly sparse and far less populated than expected. Seely assisted everyone ashore, where the guests were treated to a tour of the mission grounds and gardens and entertained with a full-dress parade by the San Diego Guards. At five o'clock everyone was ushered back to the *Senator*, where Seely hosted a festive dinner for passengers and local residents. Champagne flowed freely, and guests found tables elaborately decorated with castles, ships, armies, and angels, all made of confectionary frosting and placed amid colorful jellies and iced treats. The main fare was a representation of sea, sky, and land, with abundant servings of fish, fowl, and game. The *Los Angeles Star* noted the details and praised "Capt. Seely dispensing his hospitality with that ease and grace with which no man can excel, and but few equal."[13]

But the event was not over. At nine o'clock guests were transported back into town to the Gila House, with Captain Seely paying particular attention to the comfort of the women. Dancing in a grand ballroom went on into the wee hours of the morning, pausing only for another meal served just after midnight. As the sun broke around six in the morning,

The steamship *Senator*, captained by Thomas Seely, transported mail and passengers between ports along the California coast. In 1863 it carried Seely's body back to San Francisco for burial. Courtesy of the Mariners' Museum, Newport News, Virginia.

the assemblage made their way back aboard the *Senator*. A rolling sea met the passengers on the voyage up the coast, confining most to their staterooms. Carriages met the party at San Pedro and returned everyone to the Bella Union. "Thus terminated an excursion fraught with pleasure and delight to all—throughout the whole of which Capt. Seely relaxed not for a moment, his anxious endeavors to promote the comfort and happiness of his guests, commending himself more strongly, if that were possible, to the respect, esteem, and affection of all classes of our citizens, for his affability, courtesy and attention to his guests, his unbounded liberality, and his princely hospitality," concluded the *Los Angeles Star*.[14]

The overindulgence was hardly over. During the return trip, gentlemen of the excursion, so enamored by Seely's generosity, had called a meeting on his behalf. In the Ladies' Saloon, unoccupied by the women due to the current rough seas, gentlemen of the excursion yielded the floor to one another for prolonged orations praising the hospitality of the captain. A committee was formed to draft resolutions expressing their gratitude, intending that they be published in Los Angeles and San Diego newspapers. "Resolved, Capt. Tom Seely *this*." "Resolved, Capt. Tom Seely *that*." And so on almost endlessly, but concluding, "Resolved, That we enshrine Capt. Tom Seely in our hearts as a model of every attribute which marks the accomplished office, the true-hearted man, the affable gentle man—in a word, 'God's nobleman.'"[15]

There was more. Two weeks later, on June 8, another grand ball was held, this time hosted by citizens of Los Angeles in honor of Seely. Again, an elegant meal was prepared by a local chef, and it was accompanied by an abundance of choice wines. An excellent band entertained, and Seely and his well-to-do worshippers again enjoyed dancing until dawn.[16] Could the captain's life get any better? Seely would never leave the California coast.

In contrast, California's luster was wearing off for a few of the original members of the Newark Overland Company still residing in the state after nearly a decade. Some decided to leave the Pacific Coast and return to the East to settle, marry, and start families.

Henry L. Johnson had made some attempts to return to his family in Newark, possibly to convince his wife to join him on the West Coast. Ship manifests indicate that he sailed from Panama to New York in 1853 and again in 1855. The US Census of 1860 reports him with his family in New Jersey on June 8, 1860, and also in Marysville, California, seven weeks later, on July 30, which was entirely possible considering the improved service between New York and San Francisco. However, throughout the 1850s the Newark City Directory listed Johnson as in *California*, indicating that he was not conducting business locally. Sometime in the early 1860s he was dropped from the listing all together, while California voter registration rolls placed him as a resident of Yuba County. After transitioning from a career as a jeweler in Newark to a mining supervisor in Brown's Valley, Johnson eventually became a farmer. His family would never join him in California.

Fellow Newark jeweler Moses Canfield made no effort to reunite with his family. He took up his profession making watches and other jewelry in the Sierra foothills until 1859, when fire destroyed the shop he maintained at Chipp's Flat.[17] Like Johnson, Canfield turned to farming as his livelihood. He would eventually share a residence with three Chinese men.

After nearly a decade in California, Caleb D. Boylston, the man who had endured the mule-packing fiasco with Alexander Cartwright in 1849, returned home and joined his widowed father on his farm in Elizabeth, New Jersey. The move east was permanent. Within a year of his return he married and began a successful career as a brick and stone mason. Six children followed.

Any number of former Newark Overland Company members who were back in New Jersey in late 1858 may have gathered for a somber event in early December. At the age of forty-four, James A. "Dolph" Pennington succumbed to the deteriorating illness of the lungs, tuberculosis. Unknown by that term in the mid-nineteenth century, Pennington's obituary identified the cause of death as "hasty consumption." He had rapidly declined after mid-October, but he may have been struggling with the disease for fifteen years.[18] Considered a frail man, Pennington had endured ill health since the 1840s, when, around the age of thirty, he was forced to retire from his jewelry manufacturing partnership. Taking part in the formidable journey across the country in 1849 may have been inspired as a remedy for his poor constitution, similar to the situations of Gillespie, Currier, and Darcy, who all believed such an adventure would restore their vigor. Pennington seems to have been in full health during the trip—hunting antelope, crossing mountains, surviving capsized wagons in rushing waters—yet he did travel with a personal attendant, possibly because of his physical shortcomings.

Perhaps in another attempt to battle his recurring illness, Pennington had become involved with local sporting clubs that were growing in popularity among Newark's social classes. Cricket was Pennington's sport of choice, and his participation belied his weakened constitution. As late as 1856 he was active in the Newark Cricket Club, allowing a vacant lot adjacent to his Elm Street property to be used for local competitions.[19]

After his return from California in early 1850, Pennington had resumed his role as alderman for Newark's Tenth Ward, having been reelected in absentia. Still, he struggled to overcome his frailties, and except for civic obligations he remained at home, away from occupational demands. Well-respected, Pennington served his district in the New Jersey state legislature for one term in 1855–56. The *Newark Daily Advertiser* would remember him as one who "was always a member of the Democratic party, and an active sympathizer in every plan which looked to the largest liberty of the people with regard to the free exercise of their social, political and moral impulses."[20] Dolph Pennington had hailed from a political dynasty. His grandfather and uncle had both been governors of New Jersey, and his uncle would become US Speaker of the House, eventually leaving office on the day of Abraham Lincoln's inauguration.

On the evening of December 7, 1858, the day after Pennington's death, fellow Newark city councilmen met to draft resolutions honoring the man they described as "a fearless, faithful and incorruptible public servant," one who possessed "marked perseverance in whatever he deemed to be right." They resolved to attend the funeral the next day as a unified body, and they would assemble an hour before the service and proceed in a convoy of carriages to Pennington's late residence. [21] After the eulogy, they joined a large cortege that made its way to the First Presbyterian Church burial ground. There Pennington was laid to rest while a local choral society harmonized on the dirge "Silent Is the House of Mourning."[22]

Certainly General Darcy paid his respects to Pennington. The two men shared a lifelong allegiance to the Democratic Party, with common threads of compassion and liberality binding their political philosophies. Of the same persuasion was overland trail mate Benjamin Casterline, whose father had served with Pennington on the Newark Common Council from the same ward and same party. Local gunsmith Gun Baldwin was another with close family ties to Pennington.

During the year following Pennington's death, threats of disunion accelerated, with fears mounting that a nation of independent states could not remain united under one central government. Sentiments were clearly geographical, with North versus South at the brink of an emotional, economical confrontation. A few states sandwiched in between were faced with playing both sides.

In California similar lines were surfacing, although much less distinct than those east of the Mississippi. There were Southern sympathizers in Southern California, where landowners, many with families who had controlled large tracts for generations, related to an economy based on agriculture. There was also a large local population that had emigrated from Texas and Arkansas that was in control of various political offices and judgeships. In Northern California the population, whose center radiated from San Francisco, along with the seat of government in Sacramento, remained staunchly against slavery, as did the still-active gold mining region. In reality, however, as evident in the elegant balls in Los

Angeles and inspiring art exhibits in San Francisco, Californians were far removed from the high-stakes tension about to break on the other side of the continent.

In 1858 music engraver William H. Oakes closed shop in San Francisco and returned to New York City.[23] Charles Gray, the onetime secretary of the Newark Overland Company and journal keeper extraordinaire, remained in California with Oakes's wife, artist Abby Tyler Oakes. It seemed an odd relationship. She was flourishing in her career and submitted thirteen paintings to the Second Annual Mechanics' Fair shortly after her husband's departure. Gray had begun dabbling in art himself and submitted two of his own creations, one listed as an oil painting and the other as a painting on iron.[24] In 1859 Abby Oakes was one of several artists known to complete works depicting the Yosemite Valley, specifically Vernal Falls.[25] Auction houses in San Francisco consistently advertised her paintings for sale.

Gray and Mrs. Oakes returned to New York City during the summer of 1860, when the nation was focused on the upcoming presidential election.[26] Political conventions nominated candidates, followed by the splintering of the Democratic Party, with the new parties hosting additional conventions and nominating more candidates until no less than four men eventually won a substantial number of electoral votes in November. Lincoln's rise to the presidency could not stop the nation from breaking apart. In fact, it served as a catalyst. Military confrontation began a month after his inauguration, which took place in front of a still-domeless, almost naked-looking Capitol building on March 4, 1861. Regiments for both the Union and Confederacy filled quickly.

Over the next year six of the Newark Overland Company men would join a hometown military unit. Half of them—Birdsall, Freeman, and Woodruff—had been in Henry L. Johnson's mess, the one whose wagon had capsized in the unforgiving current of the North Platte River. The other three were Gun Baldwin, C. B. Gillespie, and John R. Crockett. In addition, John W. Shaff again signed on for a stint with the US Navy, renewing his position as a clerk aboard a Union vessel. Woodruff was the only one to join the Confederate forces.

All these men would encounter strife far greater than they had on their grueling march across the country in 1849. None of them would die on the battlefield.

Lewis B. "Gun" Baldwin
Sergeant, New Jersey Second Volunteers, Company K
Enlisted May 30, 1861

Charles B. Gillespie
Captain, Pennsylvania Seventy-Eighth Infantry, Company F
Commissioned September 10, 1861

Joseph Freeman
Saddler sergeant, New York Eleventh Cavalry Regiment, Company G
Enlisted January 3, 1862

John R. Crockett
Captain and assistant quartermaster, US Volunteers
Commissioned July 28, 1862

Daniel S. Birdsall
Private, Connecticut Sixteenth Infantry, Company C
Enlisted August 24, 1862

John W. Shaff
Paymaster, US Navy, USS *Wabash*
Enlisted 1862

David B. Woodruff
Private, Second Georgia Battalion, Macon Volunteers—Floyd Rifles,
    Company C
Confederate States Army (CSA)
Enlisted April 1861

Chapter 23

The Civil War and Three 1863 Deaths

The scene on the Ohio River was dramatic late in the afternoon of October 21, 1861. Six steam-powered riverboats moved westbound at a brisk pace, each with black smoke venting from tall stacks and multiple decks outlined by tightly picketed railings holding back throngs of rubbernecking passengers.[1] The wharves along Louisville's riverfront were also crowded, filled with local citizens, mostly women and children, who were hoping catch a glimpse of the excitement, even a bit of history, after news had buzzed throughout the community that the vessels were in sight.[2] They had learned that Union troops were approaching the city, where they would enter the confused border state of Kentucky and march to an encampment to await further orders.

The chartered steamers carried the three regiments of Negley's Brigade—the Seventy-Seventh, Seventy-Eighth, and Seventy-Ninth Pennsylvania Volunteers, with Gen. James Scott Negley himself aboard the flagship *Sir William Wallace*.[3] Each of the vessels carried about five hundred soldiers, scores of horses, and the supplies and paraphernalia required to support military life.

Those on the Fifth Street docks who had come to witness the spectacle were treated to a show. After the riverboats passed Six Mile Island, east of Louisville, they pulled alongside each other and continued to steam toward the city in a six-abreast formation.[4] Visible from the shore were glints of gold reflecting from the spit-and-polish brass of cannons lining

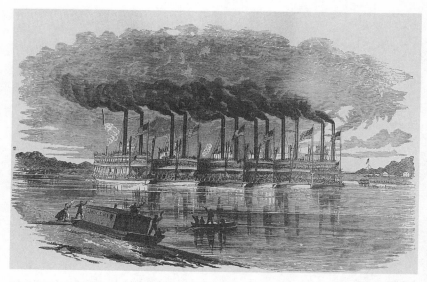

Six steamers that carried Negley's Brigade on the Ohio River as they approached rebel territory in Louisville, Kentucky, October 1861. Capt. Charles B. Gillespie's men of Company F, 78th Pennsylvania Regiment, were among the troops on board. *Frank Leslie's Illustrated Newspaper*, November 16, 1861.

the lower decks. A US flag flew front and center atop each of the steamers, forming a skyline of stars and stripes, an unintended yet subtle message of unity.[5]

The recently recruited men on board were both apprehensive and curious about the welcome they would receive in a state with significant Southern sympathies, one that still permitted slavery. When artillery was spotted on the southern shore, their trepidation heightened, especially when the ordnance suddenly fired. But the Union regiments quickly realized that the thunderous boom was a salute in honor of their arrival. The welcoming Kentucky crowd cheered.[6]

Three days earlier Negley's regiments had been encamped in Pittsburgh, preparing for a final parade and military exhibition before Pennsylvania governor Andrew Curtin. From their temporary outpost, the brigade assembled, in full military dress and accoutrements, and marched through the city to the Monongahela House, where the governor was quartered with a host of top Union officers. Curtin was there to present each regiment with a standard of colors, gifts from the state to be carried with the units at all times. It was expected that the flags would be inscribed with every battle fought and, at the conclusion of the conflict, returned to the statehouse in Harrisburg for preservation.[7] It was further expected that they would be returned in short order.

The governor's mission was twofold. He was also meeting the troops to announce the location of their first assignment, still a mystery to the three thousand soldiers. The men were anxious for this news, but Curtin prolonged his words. He stated first that they would *not* be going to Missouri, and they would *not* be going to western Virginia. At last he proclaimed they were bound for "Kentucky, where the rebels were now laying waste, with fire and sword, to the property of Union men—and not only Union men, but citizens of a loyal State." He continued his dramatic oration, declaring that their duty was "to defend the loyal citizens of Kentucky . . . from the enrage and robbery of the rebel hordes who had invaded her soul."[8] In truth, the rebels were Kentucky residents. The Union troops were about to become the invaders.

The governor concluded with a deluge of highly patriotic remarks, which were followed by brief speeches from General Negley and each of his commanding officers, who stepped forward to accept the flags from the state of Pennsylvania. The final words were instructions for the troops to prepare for their pending departure. The skies were threatening as the ceremony closed.[9] Dr. Charles B. Gillespie from Freeport, well traveled and well educated, witnessed the pageantry as captain of Company F, Seventy-Eighth Pennsylvania Volunteers.

The next day the brigade marched to the Monongahela wharf, where six steamships, consigned to transport them to Louisville, awaited.[10] They pulled away from the docks at dusk in dense fog.[11] Once again Gillespie was heading west on the Ohio River.

Several days earlier, Gillespie had taken part in two ceremonies that would forever change his life. On October 12, 1861, he had sworn an oath of allegiance to the US government as he and his company of twenty-four men officially mustered into the rank and file of army life. He was commissioned as a captain, agreeing to a three-year commitment.[12] Charles B. Gillespie had found another new career.

The second ceremony had occurred the following day, October 13, when Gillespie stood before two witnesses at the Sugar Creek Catholic Church. Beside him was his bride, Irish-born Susan Brunker, a music teacher who had recently settled in Freeport to train young students.[13] She was twenty-one and had fallen in love with the multifaceted town doctor nearly twice her age. The couple would slip away for a brief honeymoon while Gillespie's Company F boarded a car of the Allegheny Railroad, bound for their encampment in Pittsburgh.[14] Charles B. Gillespie had finally found a wife.

It was sometime in early August, two months before these life-altering ceremonies, that Gillespie had first realized the nation's unity was truly threatened. Union losses at the Battle of Bull Run in Manassas, Virginia, had inspired Gillespie to raise a company of young men from the fields and shops around Freeport. The youngest was eighteen, the oldest forty-five, and their occupations included farmer, teacher, mechanic, and miner. Gillespie was so unfamiliar with military practice that he purchased an old flintlock musket to rehearse drills by himself—at home, late at night, in front of a mirror.[15]

The embarrassing retreat by federal troops at Manassas had awakened everyone to the threat of a viable confederation of Southern states, prompting calls on governors across the country to requisition troops for the US Army. The request for troops arrived in California by Pony Express in early August, and the response was immediate, although Southern California continued to harbor sympathies for the secessionists. According to the *Sacramento Daily Union,* the regiments recruited were expected to protect the overland mail routes and contain "the schemes of Texas and her confederates," assignments they dutifully fulfilled despite the desire to participate in more crucial activity in the East.[16]

While California cavalrymen made their way to protect western interests and Pennsylvania troops entered Kentucky, New Jersey sent its volunteers into the most intense confrontations south of the Potomac. Participating in the First Battle of Bull Run (fortunately for their pride, only as a reserve unit) was a regiment from New Jersey that had been formed just after Lincoln's call for 75,000 troops in April, following the exchange of gunfire at Fort Sumter. Mustering into Company K of the New Jersey Second Infantry was gun maker Lewis B. Baldwin, one of the men with whom Gillespie had departed Newark on March 1, 1849, destined for the California goldfields.[17] They were the first of the former Newark Overland Company to sign up to defend the Union.

While Baldwin and Gillespie had enlisted within the first months of the war, they were not the first of Darcy's forty-niners to take up arms, but they were the first for the *US Army.* It was the opposing Confederate

States Army that had enticed one of the gold rush associates of Baldwin and Gillespie to volunteer within days of artillery fire in Charleston's harbor. David B. Woodruff made a commitment to his local regiment, the Floyd Rifles, representing his adopted hometown of Macon, Georgia.[18]

Woodruff had become a prominent citizen in Macon, having utilized his carpentry skills to build an extensive lumber-planing mill and factory, specializing in windows and door sashes. Despite his Connecticut upbringing, he chose to defend the sovereignty of the state where he had developed his business over seven years. He signed on not to defend slavery, as his very lucrative company had achieved success without slave labor, but to defend a state's right to govern itself free from the oppression of a bullying central government. After all, it had been only eight decades since the United States was formed on the same principle. So passionate was Woodruff about the Southern states' right to secession, he was considered the first person, not just in Macon, but in the entire state of Georgia, to hoist the Stars and Bars of the Confederate flag (one crafted by his wife in a single night) above his door.[19] The war would ruin him financially.

Eventually two more men with whom Woodruff had traveled to California in 1849 made commitments to serve Uncle Sam, two who had shared with him the close quarters of a covered wagon and the loss of that wagon in crossing the North Platte River. Joseph Freeman mustered into a New York cavalry unit, while his brother-in-law Daniel Birdsall enlisted in an infantry regiment from Woodruff's native state, Connecticut. Woodruff's former messmates would oppose him in the nation's bloodiest war.

Birdsall was one of the men who responded to Lincoln's July 1, 1862, directive requesting an additional 300,000 men to volunteer for military duty. For fifteen months the Union generals had failed to quell the Confederates, forcing the president to reassess the dire state of the fractured nation. A last-minute Union triumph at Shiloh in April 1862 had seemed promising, but elsewhere the rebel defenses could not be put down. At no place were more regiments and battalions assembled than in Virginia, where Union officers struggled for victories, and the tensions teetered on the brink of apocalypse.

In the spring of 1862 the obvious Union strategy was to capture the Confederate capital at Richmond by marching troops southward from the Maryland border as well as by invading from the Chesapeake Bay with an amphibious assault at Hampton Roads. It should have worked. But cagey Confederate generals were able to continually outmaneuver and downright outsmart the Army of the Potomac. By the end of June 1862 the months-long Peninsula Campaign ended when seven final days of fighting failed to break Confederate resistance. The rebels had saved Richmond. Lincoln was left with no other choice but to refortify his army and escalate Union efforts, hence the call for 300,000 more men and Birdsall's enlistment.

The Seven Days Battles had begun on June 25, 1862, just east of Richmond, where the tidal waters narrow to streambeds and snake into the open farmland of the fertile Piedmont. On the third day a costly battle erupted near Gains Mill (now Gaines Mill). Behind the Confederate lines was the Second Georgia Infantry Battalion, including Company C, the Floyd Rifles from Macon, Georgia. David Woodruff had reenlisted with his company after the first year but had been requisitioned to Florida, where his carpentry skills were needed to construct a saltworks facility for the Confederate government.[20] The reassignment kept Woodruff from direct combat with former gold rush associate Sgt. Lewis B. Baldwin, whose volunteer unit was part of the Union forces flanked in opposition to the Confederate army, fresh under the command of Robert E. Lee. At Gains Mill the day went as poorly for Baldwin as it did for the rest of the Union forces.

Two weeks later, on July 9, 1862, the *Newark Daily Advertiser* reported on the casualties suffered by the local New Jersey regiments. Listed by company were those killed, wounded, and missing. Under the heading "Second New Jersey Company K missing" was the name Lewis B. Baldwin.[21] A company muster roll filled out shortly after the battle stated simply, "Killed in action June 27 at Gains Mills, Va."[22]

Ten days later, on July 19, a meeting was organized by citizens in Newark in response to President Lincoln's call for additional troops and the sobering news of local war losses. The outpouring was considerable, the *New York Times* reported: "A large, highly respectable, and extremely patriotic assemblage of the citizens of Newark, N. J., was held in the Park of that city last evening for the purpose of strengthening the hands of the Government in the existing crisis. The occasion seemed to be made quite a holiday; the National flag greeted the eye in every quarter, while the determined resolution to do all that men and money can do to put down the unholy rebellion, was made most apparent."[23] An official committee was then formed to facilitate the recruitment of more volunteers and to raise monetary contributions to aid in the cause. Among the thirty-some vice presidents named to carry out the organization's resolutions was proud and patriotic John R. Crockett.

Crockett was swept up in the fervor of defending the Union—just as he had been passionate over the election of Zachary Taylor and other Whig candidates, and just as he had been zealous over the rush for gold in 1849. It was his nature to proclaim his causes with a sword over his head and an all-out charge forward. There was no doubting his enthusiasm for any effort to which he pledged his loyalty. But at sixty years of age, no one expected him to be so impassioned as to sign up for military duty.

Although familiarly known as Colonel Crockett, a title not necessarily earned through military service, he was commissioned as a captain and assigned the title of assistant quartermaster, US Volunteers. He signed the acceptance of his commission on July 29, 1862, and, like everyone else who joined the Army of the Potomac, he was sent to Virginia.[24] He left New Jersey immediately and proceeded to Hampton Roads to report to his commanding officer, unprepared for the climate of the Virginia Peninsula in August, known for its sliceable humidity and sauna-like temperatures.

A month later Crockett lay infirm on a mere speck of an island in the middle of the James River called Rip Raps (now Fort Wool). The facility was part of Fortress Monroe, the only Union-held army post *anywhere* in a Confederate state. The island's strategic location, where the James River meets the Chesapeake Bay, provided an evacuation route for sick and wounded soldiers, allowing Crockett to be removed to the Armory Square Hospital in Washington, DC. Although shaking from chronic fever, his hand was steady enough to compose a letter dated September 3, 1862, stating that he had "accepted the commission, not understanding the nature of its duties." He requested that his resignation be tendered due to his illness, noting that the brigade surgeon supported him. Two days later Secretary of War Edwin Stanton approved and personally signed Crockett's release.[25]

Meanwhile, there was news regarding Sgt. Lewis B. Baldwin. It was eerily similar to the situation in May 1849, when two overland journals had chronicled, "Baldwin is *missing.*" At that time, search parties had been dispatched over a two-day stint along the Oregon Trail, and widespread concern consumed the Newark Overland Company regarding his fate. Once again, in 1862, the gunsmith went missing but surfaced mostly unscathed after a two-day absence. Far from spending his days lost on the Nebraska prairie as in 1849, Baldwin had been captured by Confederate forces and taken to Richmond, where he managed to escape and, to the utter surprise of his fellow soldiers, rejoin his unit still camped in the Virginia countryside.[26] The subsequent muster roll of Company K counted him present and made the correction, "Erroneously reported killed at last muster."[27]

By the time Crockett had enlisted and resigned and Baldwin had escaped rebel capture, Captain Gillespie had experienced a legion of war's unpredictable turns, albeit much different from the events in Virginia. After arriving in Louisville in October 1861, Gillespie's regiment had been assigned to the command of Gen. William T. Sherman—the same man who had helped spark the gold rush with his scientific observations and writing when he was military lieutenant governor of California in 1848.

From Louisville, Gillespie's Company F had marched south, meeting little resistance, to an encampment at Munfordville, Kentucky, where they settled in and focused on protecting a strategic pontoon bridge on the Green River. There, in January 1862, the Pennsylvania regiment faced a stark reminder of war when the body of Gen. Felix Zollicoffer was carried through the camp under a flag of truce.[28] The Confederate general, killed during a skirmish, was being returned to the CSA.

In February 1862 the regiment received orders to move into Tennessee. The mission was to drive a wedge into the heart of the Confederacy, through which communication and supplies could be transferred. The Seventy-Eighth would be in charge of protecting these lines and maintaining order—Union order—along the way. Keeping the peace had not been difficult in Kentucky, where residents of the border state struggled with allegiance. The situation for Kentuckians was best described by one of Gillespie's men who attended a local church service. He observed that when prayers were given for the rebel causes, Union supporters refrained from standing and sat quietly, and the respect was reciprocated when the Unionists stood and asked for blessings for their own.[29]

Efforts to break camp for the move to Tennessee were hampered by two inches of snow that made for slushy ground and numb feet, yet the men were ecstatic over the change of venue. They headed for a newly built railroad bridge to cross the Green River, with flags flying and brass horns of the regimental band belting out "Dixieland."[30] It was a spontaneous moment of jubilation in the midst of drab army life, if only for a moment. Not far to the west a major battle was brewing at Fort Donelson.

Finally adjusted to his role as military leader, Gillespie had turned down offers for promotions, believing his duty was to lead the men he recruited from his hometown. Despite his humility, he was often included in elite circles, those of the highest commanding officers, even sidetracking nine miles with Col. William Sirwell for a guided tour of Mammoth Cave while on the advance to Nashville.[31]

By March 1862 Gillespie's health had once again become problematic, or so the records suggest. He requested and was granted sick leave to return to Freeport, apparently having convinced his superiors that his chances for recovery were greater at home than in the wintry Tennessee field camp.[32]

It is curious, though, that one would have traveled so far if truly incapacitated by a severe illness. Is it possible the captain was actually homesick for his bride, Susan? Once back in Pennsylvania and reunited with his wife, an unconventional decision was made that resulted in Mrs. Gillespie packing her bags. She would not part with her husband again and was determined to accompany him back to the war front, where she vowed to support Company F in the capacity of nurse, but more likely her motivation was to look after her husband.[33] In truth, Susan Gillespie spent most of her time in Nashville among friends and away from the cruel sights and sounds of the battlefield. Gillespie's letters suggest that other military wives had also traveled into the South with their husbands.[34]

Despite all his efforts to remain with his men, Gillespie was named provost marshal of Pulaski, Tennessee, upon his return to active duty in May 1862.[35] The new assignment, some seventy miles south of Tennessee's capital, would separate him from most of his unit for an extended time, but it would give him more opportunity to spend time with his wife.

As provost marshal, Gillespie had the supreme judicial authority of the town—judge and jury for all civil and military cases. Overall Gillespie found the citizens of Tennessee as conflicted as those in Kentucky regarding support of the Confederacy. He wrote in May 1862, "The inhabitants are in great tribulation the Union army is amongst them, and their own sons, brothers and friends are exiled." Still, he believed, "There is a Union feeling dormant among the people, and if they could only assure themselves . . . of the certainty of our triumph, . . . they would come out openly. Should their army be defeated at Corinth, they will all return to their Allegiance of this I have no doubt."[36]

Gillespie's most troublesome dealings as provost marshal involved the havoc wrought by the plundering Confederate general John Hunt Morgan. He wrote to a friend, "I am just now put in possession of the finding of a court of enquiry to assess damages in the case of a Union Merchant of this city whose goods were taken and distributed by John Morgan the Guerilla chief a few days since. The court has assessed $1263.88 upon the city which I am to have collected."[37] A native Kentuckian, Morgan had first opposed secession. He would be remembered as the renegade Confederate officer who led raids across the Ohio River into Union territory.

All is fair in love and war, it is said. By summer's end in 1862, when Baldwin went missing and Crockett begged to go home, Susan Gillespie learned that she was expecting their first child. It seems like a perilous situation, to be pregnant in a war zone, but many in the western theater believed that the hostilities could not last much longer. In April the Confederate army had lost a significant battle at Shiloh, also known as Pittsburg Landing, located just one hundred miles to the west of Pulaski. It was one of the costliest battles of the war to that point and was almost another Union failure due to poor decisions by General Grant. Ultimately it was a disaster for the Confederacy. Killed was Albert Sidney Johnston, the highest-ranking Confederate general and confidant to Confederate president Jefferson Davis.

Within forty-eight hours telegraph lines across the country communicated the breaking news of General Johnston's demise, including grim specifics of how he had been shot while riding across the battlefield to rally his troops and had subsequently bled to death. Thanks to the new transcontinental telegraph completed in October 1861, Californians were now only days behind the latest reports. The telegraph had rendered galloping postal ponies obsolete after just eighteen months of service.

Johnston's death was of great interest in California, where he lived prior to joining the Confederate army. One year before his death he had resigned his position as commander-in-chief of the Pacific Division, US

Army, citing the need to return to his neglected property in Texas. In fact, Johnston had been organizing a small band of rebels for Confederate service and, with the aid of local sympathizers, slipped out of Los Angeles bound for the Southern states. Speculation about his loyalty and whereabouts had been widespread at the time. After his death the *Sacramento Daily Union* was gracious in its remembrance of Johnston and made note that "he left his wife and children in Los Angeles, and under the stars and stripes in this loyal State. They have remained there undisturbed while he has been commanding rebel armies and fighting the battles of rebellion against the Government he has so long served and to which he intrusted his family."[38]

Other than eagerly following the telegraphed news reports and supporting their local military men stationed at posts on the western frontier, Californians felt little impact of the war. The handful of Newark Overland Company men who had made their lives in the state after arriving a dozen years earlier continued their successful careers with no threat of financial ruin. In May 1861, S. H. Meeker had agreed to serve the California State Militia as assistant quartermaster general, but there is no evidence of his having joined a Union regiment.[39] The following year he retired from his lucrative business to enjoy the fortune he had amassed importing liquor and speculating in regional mining ventures. Meeker & Company was left in the hands of his longtime partner and Newark native A. Richards Baldwin (no relation to Gun Baldwin).[40] At the time, Meeker was considered one of the wealthiest men in San Francisco.

The carnage in the East continued into 1863. Despite the blockading of Southern ports by Union warships along the Atlantic Coast, and the nuisances of Confederate ironclads, S. H. Meeker set his sights on sailing home to New Jersey. Perhaps he believed it was time to see his aging mother and his distant wife, not to mention the two children he hardly knew.

At nine o'clock on the morning of April 13, 1863, Meeker made his way to San Francisco's Folsom Street wharves to sail for Panama, having taken measures to post public notices regarding his business contacts during his absence. So popular was Meeker locally that his departure was headlined in San Francisco newspapers. The *Alta California* reported, "Major S. H. Meeker leaves this city to-day on the *Golden Age* for his former home, in New Jersey. He is a true type of the California merchant, and has, since his arrival here in '49, always maintained a character for energy, enterprise, and sterling integrity. His many friends in California, whilst they regret even his temporary departure, will be the more pleased to welcome him home again, after a brief sojourn amongst the scenes of his boyhood."[41]

Another newspaper suggested that Meeker was not well: "Mr. Meeker revisits his early home after an absence of some ten years; he goes to meet his kindred and friends, and to regain his health and strength by a change of climate and scene, made necessary by long years of assiduous attention to his business here."[42] There seems to have been a prevailing belief in the mid-nineteenth century that long-distance travel, albeit strenuous, could cure one's ailments.

Meeker's Panama-bound steamship sailed out of the Golden Gate into the Pacific just one day behind the *Senator*, which was still under the command of the popular Capt. Tom Seely and still sailing twice a month between Northern and Southern California. When the *Senator* was at port in San Luis Obispo, Meeker's ship sailed by in the open ocean, still some ten days or more from Panama City. Meeker was not well.

Seely, on the other hand, was in splendid form and headed to yet another social engagement. At San Pedro on April 27, 1863, when preparing for the return trip to San Francisco, Seely had agreed to host a party on the *Senator* for guests of Phineas Banning, a local shipping entrepreneur. The docks at San Pedro were too shallow for the ocean-going steamship, requiring passengers to be tendered to and from on a smaller vessel. For the shuttle service, Banning supplied his tug, which was routinely used to convey passengers and freight to steamers in the harbor. It had been recently purchased, inspected, and renamed the *Ada Hancock* after the daughter of Banning's close friend, Union general Winfield Scott Hancock (who was making his way to Gettysburg, Pennsylvania, at the time). Around five o'clock in the afternoon nearly sixty people boarded the smaller *Ada Hancock* to shuttle to the *Senator*. Banning, his wife, and their two small children were among them, as were a number of people returning from an excursion to the Colorado River. As always, Captain Seely tended to the women, captivating them with his flirtatious conversation.[43]

Some say it was a sudden squall that sent the *Ada Hancock* careening off balance, allowing cold water to rush into its steam chambers. Years later a great swindling caper involving a Wells Fargo messenger, a local loan shark, and a large quantity of gold taken on board would be blamed, citing gunshots between the two feuding men and an errant bullet that struck the boiler. The blast was instantaneous. For the crew on board the *Senator* anchored offshore and for acquaintances on the wharves waving farewell, the sight was horrendous. Bodies and body parts went flying. The *Los Angeles Star* described the scene with little restraint: "The mutilations of poor humanity were awful. Bodies were brought ashore without heads, or arms or legs."[44]

The boiler explosion of the *Ada Hancock* was California's most significant civilian marine disaster in an era when steamer travel had come to be regarded as safe and uneventful. Twenty-six were dead, and almost all of the survivors suffered injuries, many severe and life-threatening. Escaping without harm were the two small Banning children. The *New York Times* reported that they had been "saved from the wreck by 'Darkness,' a colored servant girl of Mrs. Banning, who displayed undaunted courage and rendered great assistance to numbers of others." The heroism of Darkness was reported in newspapers throughout the country, although some refrained from using her name.[45]

The loss of life included:

- the eighteen-year-old son of the Confederate general killed at Shiloh ("That noble boy, the young, ardent, gallant Albert Sidney Johnston, the darling hope and stay of a widowed mother," lamented the *Los Angeles Star*; "Where is she to turn for consolation in all this wide, wide world?"[46])
- two ranking Mormon missionaries on their way to the Sandwich Islands to further the cause of the Latter-day Saints
- Wells Fargo messenger William Ritchie, later suspected of spurious intent, who lived for two hours
- J. L. Bryant, captain of the ill-fated *Ada Hancock*
- Fred Kerlin, nephew of E. Fitzgerald Beale, the man who had carried the official reports of gold to Washington in 1848; nephew and uncle had most recently been employed caring for the US government's herd of retired camels at Fort Tejon, just north of Los Angeles[47]
- William Fessenden Nye, a Harvard graduate, native of Newark, and son of a steamboat captain who was as famous on Atlantic Ocean crossings as Seely was on the Pacific Coast

Fort Drum Barracks, where the bodies of Capt. Tom Seely and other victims of the *Ada Hancock* explosion were taken, is located adjacent to the port of San Pedro. This photo, showing a camel in the foreground, was taken within months of the disaster, circa 1863. Courtesy of the Drum Barracks Garrison & Society.

Unquestionably, the most significant loss of the dreadful explosion and the name that headlined papers from Los Angeles to San Francisco was that of Thomas W. Seely. "Among the dead we find the best men of the community—Captain Seely, in noble generosity, whole heartedness, in all the attributes that distinguish the highest type of manhood, who could compare with him?" the *Los Angeles Star* questioned in a grievous tone.[48] Seely had been struck in the head by a section of the fragmented boiler, and his body is believed to have shielded that of Mr. Banning's. Within minutes an engineer had reached Seely floating in the tide and desperately cradled his captain's head above water, hoping he could be saved, but Seely was already dead from a severed jugular vein.[49] His body was one of the first recovered.

Three days later the *Senator* steamed into San Francisco Bay, returning her captain for a hero's burial. Along the San Francisco wharves nearly all the vessels in port paid respect to Seely by displaying flags at half-mast, including the sloop-of-war USS *Saranac*.[50] The gesture by a military vessel was an exceptional honor to a man who had not served the US Navy.

The *San Francisco Daily Evening Bulletin* published a fact-based obituary, less emotional than those of the Southern California papers, describing Captain Seely as a native of New York, forty-two years of age, and unmarried. It included details about his funeral arrangements and subsequent burial at the gardenlike Lone Mountain Cemetery less than a mile from the Golden Gate. His tombstone would reflect the reputation that Seely had cultivated during his lifetime: "As an efficient seamen, a firm friend and generous companion he had no superior."[51]

Word of Seely's death was beyond the reach of S. H. Meeker, who was beginning the passage across Panama, a country still years away from telegraphic technology. Meeker arrived at the isthmus in rapidly declining health, so weak that a litter was required to carry him to the Atlantic steamer, with care being administered by a circle of friends. The jungle of Central America, laden with tropical illnesses, was no place for a sick man. Upon reaching New York on May 7, 1863, he was taken to the Fifth Avenue Hotel to receive immediate medical attention. Family members gathered. He was dead within thirteen hours.[52]

Meeker's obituary indicated that he was not alone when he took his last breath, but did not specify whether any of his immediate family members were with him—his brother, his elderly mother, his estranged wife, or his children. His widow, Caroline, prevailed in selecting a burial site in the Griffen family plot on her father's expansive estate in Mamaroneck, New York. His body would be conveyed to the cemetery by train after services at Manhattan's Church of the Transfiguration on May 11, 1863.[53]

The news of Tom Seely's death had hardly faded from the San Francisco papers when editors were again writing about one of their esteemed citizens lost in the prime of life. While Seely and Meeker were remembered as early pioneers, few may have realized that both of the successful and highly respected men of their community had started for California in 1849 with the same overland company.

Notice of Meeker's death took eight days to reach West Coast newspapers. A telegram had been sent on May 9, 1863, to his business partner, A. Richards Baldwin, who at the time of the transmission was away from the city. Upon returning to San Francisco on May 16, Baldwin received the private correspondence and immediately felt concern about its authenticity. Wired one day after Meeker's death by either Caroline Meeker or her representatives, and lacking any tone of mournfulness, the message read, "Did Major Meeker leave in San Francisco a will of later date than that found amongst his papers in New York?"[54] Perhaps Mrs.

Meeker was worried about a possible codicil that would eliminate her bequest—that after a six-year separation she might receive nothing.

But there was no such codicil. Meeker had left half of his estate to his wife and the other half to his two children. They were the only beneficiaries of his wealth, estimated at more than $214,000 (an economic status equal to more than $43 million in early twenty-first-century dollars).[55] In addition to her spouse's assets, Caroline Meeker was about to inherit the massive compound of her father, who died two weeks after her husband and was buried in the same family cemetery beside the freshly dug grave of Major Meeker.[56]

A world away from the financial dealings of a wealthy New York widow and the political detachment of California, Tennessee had become a battleground of the rebellion almost as bloody as the once-pastoral fields of Virginia. But the circle of life continued. A baby girl, Rosetta Mary Gillespie, had been born April 23, 1863, in Nashville, as Union troops were beginning to amass for a six-week-long siege of Vicksburg, Mississippi. Captain Gillespie had moved from Pulaski to the company headquarters thirty miles from Nashville. He must have received word that his wife was in labor because he submitted a request for a five-day emergency leave on April 22, citing that his wife had "taken suddenly and dangerously ill." He arrived at her side late on Friday, one day after the birth, having been granted a leave of only forty-eight hours.[57]

"Sue was delivered of a fine daughter on last Thursday and is getting along remarkably well," he wrote to his twin sister, Mary. "The child is large and healthy. Sue says she will name her after her mother and you. . . . Sue has been fortunate in meeting with some old tried friends and making new ones. She could not have been better attended at home." Gillespie also apprised Mary of the latest events at his camp outside of Murfreesboro and speculated that Company F would endure heavy marching in the coming months.[58]

The Seventy-Eighth Pennsylvania, in fact, would be on the move before summer's end. Its direction was southeast to Chattanooga, where the main railroad line was considered as strategically advantageous as the Mississippi River at Vicksburg. After spending much of their two-year army service on patrol and provost duty, Gillespie and his men were heading toward military confrontation and greater danger than anything they had yet experienced during the war. And they were moving farther away from Nashville, where Susan and baby Rose were left behind.

Susan Gillespie had reason to be anxious. She was far from home with an infant child, living in enemy territory, and concerned about a husband now in harm's way. When the battle at Chickamauga raged in mid-September 1863 and reports swelled papers with news about a decisive Union defeat, she could only have agonized, knowing that the Pennsylvania troops were heavily involved. Even if she had known that Company F had remained mostly in the rear, she would still have had reason to worry. The Seventy-Eighth was part of column on its way to slash and burn Georgia with General Sherman.

Captain Gillespie understood that he had left Susan and Rose in a formidable situation. Writing from the Chattanooga headquarters in early October 1863, he asked for a twenty-day leave of absence to take his wife and infant back to Pennsylvania, claiming, "My wife is now mentally deranged after a long spell of sickness and is amongst entire strangers in Nashville."[59] Gillespie must have understood the art of exaggeration in composing military leave requests, having previously used the terminology "dangerously ill" to describe Susan's labor. His leave was granted.

Twenty days later, on October 22, 1863, with his family safely home, Gillespie spent his last night in Freeport before returning to his regiment in Chattanooga. He composed a letter to close friends in which he declined a dinner invitation for the following evening, explaining the need to rush back to Tennessee. He closed the correspondence emphasizing that he was "one who loves country more than party, and who hates the rebel as he does the devil." The letter was signed, "Truly yours, Chas. B. Gillespie, Captain 78th Penn'a Vols."[60]

The same evening that Gillespie penned the letter and prepared for his morning departure, widespread grief swept over Newark, New Jersey. At the age of seventy-five, John S. Darcy was dead from a stroke.[61]

The outpouring for Darcy was so tremendous that it took four days to prepare for the funeral. Colleagues in the medical profession met and drafted resolutions in honor of Darcy and arranged to attend in a delegation. They also agreed to wear badges of mourning for thirty days.[62] Throughout the region, Masonic lodges made plans to participate and posted notices in the *Newark Daily Advertiser* specifying the hour and location to congregate: "The members . . . are hereby summoned to . . .

attend the funeral of our late brother." One notice from the Kane Lodge was signed, "by order, W. Donaldson Kinney"—Darcy's former business partner from the Yuba River mining operation.

The funeral was set for Monday morning, October 26, 1863. After a Newark court had adjourned on Saturday, the prosecutor of the pleas had sent a tribute to the *Newark Daily Advertiser* that included this statement: "That the Court should testify its appreciation of such a man, by adjourning on the day of his funeral, will answer the great ends of their existence more than pursuing their ordinary routine of duty." He further justified the adjournment by saying it was so that "all might be enabled to attend the funeral ceremonies of that excellent man, notwithstanding the pressure of the public business," and he clarified that the special honor for Darcy was "not because of his station, his wealth or of any worldly greatness, but because of his intrinsic virtues."[63]

At eight o'clock on Monday morning the doors of Darcy's residence at Ten Cedar Street opened to a throng of anguished people who had come to pay their respects. An almost continuous line of visitors had formed to view the body, which was remarkably preserved and "appropriately attired in a black wrapper with quilted breast and cuffs, gathered with a cord and tassel," the *Newark Daily Advertiser* reported. The viewing procession went on for hours until it was necessary to proceed to Grace Episcopal Church for the services.[64]

From Cedar Street, a hearse carried the burnished silver-trimmed coffin down Broad Street, escorted by Masons in full regalia and medical professionals dressed in mourning attire. Family and friends followed in carriages. Bells tolled. Shops remained closed. Mournful residents lined the street. Flags flew at half-staff, including those on the ferries docked in the harbor nearby, boats that would normally be scuttling back and forth across the bay. The entire city of Newark stood by and grieved.[65]

A large crowd was already assembled at the church awaiting the arrival of the cortege. In attendance from Trenton was the New Jersey governor, who sat alongside people from all ranks of society. The procession to the Rosedale Cemetery in Orange followed, and there Darcy was buried with full Masonic rites.[66]

A headline feature in the *Newark Daily Advertiser* detailed the obsequies and the tributes paid to Darcy, emphasizing that the funeral was attended by citizens of all classes, reflecting Darcy's genuine sense of equality. The article listed the prominent mourners who came from across the state and closed by quoting a local judge who felt some reason to share personal details about Darcy's faith in God. He began by explaining, "Those who loved him had one great regret concerning him, that a man of so warm a heart, and such lively sympathy with his kind, was not a regular attendant upon religious ordinances and a professed believer in the Christian religion." The judge assured the public that Darcy's "deathbed was one of hope and happiness. Before he left this world he expressed his belief in his Saviour, and died in full hope of a happy resurrection."[67]

John S. Darcy had lived long enough to see the Emancipation Proclamation issued on January 1, 1863, but he died before the Civil War ended and the Union was restored under one flag. Five men who had once departed New Jersey for California under Darcy's leadership continued to serve in army units as 1863 came to a close. Three of them were heading toward Georgia.

Loyal to the Confederacy, David Woodruff would remain in charge of the saltworks plant in Florida for the duration of the war, keeping him out of direct armed conflict.

Joseph Freeman, the saddler sergeant for Scott's 900, the Eleventh New York Cavalry, was unable to complete his full term. He was discharged for medical reasons on March 1, 1864, as his regiment was boarding ships to reposition from duty along the Potomac River to service in the Gulf of Mexico.[68] In a letter written in early 1863, Freeman accurately predicted that the war would last another two years.[69]

Charles B. Gillespie completed his three-year commitment as captain of Company F, Seventy-Eighth Pennsylvania Volunteers, after marching through Georgia under command of General Sherman. He was mustered out on November 4, 1864, having never accepted a promotion, and returned safely to Freeport, where he was reunited with Susan and their eighteen-month-old daughter, Rose.[70] He carried home with him an assortment of sketches he made while camped near Lookout Mountain, Tennessee.

None of the New Jersey men saw more significant military action than Gun Baldwin. His New Jersey regiment was engaged in the most infamous campaigns of the war, including the First and Second Manassas (Bull Run) engagements, the Peninsula Campaign, and Antietam, where they formed a line opposite Confederate troops just north of the

Company F, Seventy-Eighth Pennsylvania Volunteer Infantry, at Lookout Mountain, 1864. Captain Charles B. Gillespie pictured far left, hand on hip with sword. Courtesy of the Rees-Jones Collection.

Dunkard Church. In 1863 they were at Chancellorsville, where Confederate general Stonewall Jackson was lost, then moved north to Gettysburg, where they held a reserve position. Their orders the next year took them back to Virginia, where they saw fighting at Wilderness, Spotsylvania, Cold Harbor, and Petersburg. In 1865 they chased General Lee and his dwindling army to the foothills of the Blue Ridge Mountains.

On the evening of April 9, 1865, while camped four miles from Appomattox Courthouse, the New Jersey regiment "received news of the unconditional surrender of Lee's army, which caused the wildest enthusiasm and heartfelt joy among the troops."[71] Sgt. Lewis "Gun" Baldwin was not with them. On May 6, 1864, unable to escape a second rebel capture, this time at the Battle of Wilderness, Baldwin was again a prisoner of war. For nearly ten months he suffered through dire conditions at Confederate prisons, first at Andersonville, Georgia, and later in South Carolina. Finally paroled in late February 1865 at Goldsboro, North Carolina, he was fortunate to have survived imprisonment but unfortunate to be a very sick man. He was taken to a military hospital in Annapolis, then released to the care of his brother, a physician in Newark.[72] His five-foot-eight-inch frame was so emaciated that friends were shocked to see his almost skeletal appearance.[73]

Daniel Birdsall, brother-in-law to saddler sergeant Joseph Freeman, had been the last of the Newark Overland Company men to enlist in August 1862. A few weeks later at Antietam, his Connecticut regiment raised their rifles for the first time, so inexperienced that casualties were high. Over the next year they moved south into the Carolinas. In April 1864 his company was assigned to a federal stronghold at Plymouth, North Carolina, where the Albemarle Sound reaches its most inland point. Confederate ironclads overtook Union vessels and captured the garrison, where Birdsall and his fellow soldiers, outnumbered five to one, were all captured by rebel forces.

Birdsall was taken to Andersonville Prison, arriving just weeks before Gun Baldwin. Andersonville was a twenty-six-acre compound constructed as a stockade to hold about 10,000 prisoners. The inmate population had swelled to three times that number, creating a breeding ground of pestilence and scourge. Compounded by starvation and exposure to Georgia's climate, nearly 30 percent of those imprisoned at Andersonville died. Daniel Birdsall perished on October 28, 1864, from "scorbutus"—scurvy—the same ailment that caused John S. Darcy to waste away during the last months of the 1849 overland journey.[74] Birdsall was subsequently buried in the adjacent prison cemetery.

Birdsall's final resting place was forty miles from Macon, where his one-time 1849 messmate, David Woodruff, returned home from Confederate service a few months later and began to build a new career. So successful was Woodruff over the next decades that the fruits of his labor would become acclaimed in cities throughout the South.

Chapter 24

Impact and Aftermath

A nineteenth-century Christmas in New York City conjures images of penny-sized flakes gently falling in canyons of multistory brownstones, whose ledges and architectural details are dressed in fresh snow. The amber glow of firelight peeking from windows is the only color amid a spectrum of silver and grays. Along a residential thoroughfare, the silhouette of a sleigh pulled by a lone horse can be pictured gliding silently over fresh tracks.

Such was not the case on December 25, 1865. The sky was as blue as the Mediterranean Sea, and the sun blazed as brightly as it had during the desert crossing that baked the gold seekers of 1849. Nature seemed to be expressing her pleasure that two crusty West Point generals had met at a Virginia farmhouse eight months earlier and signed a surrender ending the War between the States. The December sunshine seemed a divine declaration that four years of gore and destruction were over.

It was a glorious day to celebrate the birth of Christ in the nation's grandest metropolis. And so it happened that in the heart of an upscale Manhattan neighborhood a young man who had returned to his family from gallant service to the Union received a heartfelt gift from his father. It was a portrait of the dashing soldier himself, resplendent in his military uniform, complemented with polished sword, brimmed hat angled smartly over his face, and epaulets depicting his rank as first lieutenant. The signature in the corner read "HP Gray '65 NY / For Christmas."[1]

Brought up in his father's progressive New York City fine arts community, Henry Peters Gray Jr. had attended a prestigious military academy and suspended his studies at age seventeen to enlist into the army. Upon completing his military commission at the war's end, he had rejoined his parents at their urban residence in New York, where he would finish his education and eventually obtain lifelong employment with Tiffany and Company.[2]

The young soldier's uncle, Charles Gray, lived nearby, still residing with artist Abby Tyler Oakes and her husband. The threesome had been living in the city since their return from California just prior to the war.

On that magnificent Christmas Day of 1865, another affluent New Yorker was spending the holiday far from home, having disembarked a steamer the previous day after weeks of travel. Arriving from Panama aboard the SS *Constitution,* Caroline Meeker and her two children had stepped onto a San Francisco wharf and gazed up at a city, once their home, that was now hardly recognizable to them.[3] A decade of progress had transformed the once raucous municipality into a world-class center of commerce and culture. Perhaps the only thing that remained unchanged was the abundance of gambling houses, open to the public even on Christmas Day and serving eggnog to voracious patrons.[4]

Caroline Meeker had traveled to California to claim her husband's estate, half of which would transfer to her and half of which would be split between her children, Minnie and Heyward.[5] Her husband, S. H. Meeker, had left lucrative assets in real estate and mining that would secure his family's place in privileged society for the rest of their lives.[6] Caroline would remain in San Francisco for nearly six months, overseeing the sale of prime city lots and settling local investments. She had no intention of retaining any business interests on the West Coast. Whether or not Caroline was a guest of her brother-in-law David Meeker is not documented. He had moved from Sacramento in the preceding years to live and work in San Francisco.

During her last weeks in California, in May 1866, Caroline Meeker and her children took part in an extraordinary excursion into the High Sierra. Their destination was far south of the point where her husband had crossed the same formidable range seventeen years earlier. Specifically, it was a glacially carved valley known at the time as Yo-Semite.

While the ugly war had raged in the East, tourism to Yosemite had begun to take shape. By 1866 there were far more resources and amenities for visitors than when Abby Tyler Oakes had ventured there to paint landscapes in 1859. Pleasure trips to the scenic, granite-walled valley were becoming a must, almost a status symbol, for the well-to-do, and this was clearly within Caroline's budget. Making the trip in May afforded the best and worst of conditions. Rapidly melting snow was filling creeks and rivers with rushing water and transforming those that spilled over cliffs into breathtaking waterfalls, but the excess runoff also muddied roads to the point of impassability, forcing reroute after reroute and tedious delays.

Hotel advertisements enticed privileged travelers, promising, "No pains will be spared on the part of the proprietor. . . . The table will always be spread with the best of everything the market affords." Even in the remote mountain canyon this included "wines, liquors, and cigars."[7] There is no question that Caroline Meeker and her children were treated to the best accommodations on their tour. Accompanying her to Yosemite were Leland Stanford, her husband's one-time business partner and California's former governor, and his wife.[8]

Caroline and her children left California forever in June 1866, returning to a home in New York City, where they would live among the city's fortunate class.[9] Wealth and status had not prevented Caroline's life from being a series of highs and lows, nor would it secure her future from such vicissitudes. Indeed, fifteen months after her return from San Francisco, enriched with the assets bequeathed to her that few could boast, Caroline Meeker suffered the devastating loss of twenty-one-year-old daughter Mary Deale, known as Minnie to her family and friends.[10] Once again Caroline dutifully planned funeral services at Manhattan's Church of the Transfiguration and arranged for mourners to take the train to Mamaroneck, where carriages would transport them to the family cemetery.

One year later, in November 1868, Caroline sailed for Europe as Mrs. F. S. Thomas, having remarried in the wake of her grief.[11] Son Heyward joined his mother and stepfather. Like excursions to Yosemite, extended vacations across the Atlantic were increasing, with the distraction of the war slipping well into the past.

A few months earlier Abby Tyler Oakes had embarked on a similar voyage to France, Germany, and Italy, where she intended to study with master painters to refine and expand her skills.[12] Charles G. Gray witnessed and signed her passport application, but there is no evidence that he sailed with her to Europe.[13] Shortly after Abby Oakes returned to the United States in 1869, Gray purchased from his sister property that was located on West 24th Street in New York City.[14] The address would be the home of Gray, Abby Oakes, and William H. Oakes for at least the next fifteen years.

The gold rush of 1849 propelled participants to an array of life experiences, some as a direct result and some as destiny would dictate. Personality, fate, and luck all played a role in determining subsequent accomplishment, hardship, happiness, and heartbreak for those once inflicted with gold fever. There is no better testament than the lives of the seven men who had chased the dream in 1849 and later volunteered to fight during the Civil War.

So unlucky was Daniel Birdsall that he perished while enduring horrific conditions at Andersonville Prison, never seeing the end of the war or returning to his Connecticut home. Likewise, Gun Baldwin never recovered from his imprisonment. For five years after the Union victory and his release and return to Newark, Baldwin struggled to restore his deprived body. He traveled to Florida seeking a more healthful climate, but to no avail. He succumbed to his weakened condition in August 1870 at age fifty.[15]

John R. Crockett, who managed only a month of service as a commissioned captain in 1862, died in July 1867, although not necessarily of the illness he had contracted in Virginia. The former Newark fire chief, onetime mayoral candidate, and parade enthusiast left a legacy of patriotism. By nature he was front and center at every headlining event, not just participating but leaping headfirst at the call. He was buried with the rites and honors worthy of a lifelong Mason.

A more ordinary life followed for Joseph Freeman, who also suffered from an illness that cut short his cavalry service. Returning to New York City, he invested well as a restaurateur only to suffer loss when fire broke out on the premises in 1869.[16] He rebuilt the business successfully until poor health got the best of him. He died in January 1873 before reaching his sixtieth birthday, having provided well for his family. As with Crockett, fellow Freemasons were called to honor their deceased comrade, and additionally for Freeman, Knights Templar and Grand Army of the Republic members came to mourn his passing.[17]

John W. Shaff was a man whose spirit of adventure kept him in constant search of fulfillment. He went west to California in 1849, then far east to China in 1856, and south to the Confederacy in 1863. Perhaps a risk taker by nature, he survived all the perils of such worldly travel only to fall off a train near the Bergen, New Jersey, "deep cut" in 1866. The accident badly mangled his left leg, necessitating amputation.[18] Fate would leave him toiling as a bookkeeper and in the end penniless, living in the confines of a soldiers' home, where he spent his last decade.[19] He died in 1890, having never reconciled with his wife and family.

Then there were two soldiers possessing spirits so strong and buoyant that neither the difficulties of their gold rush quest nor the brutalities of the battlefield could vanquish them. They were kindred spirits in optimism but enemies in war.

After mustering out of military service, Charles B. Gillespie, the captain of a Union company, returned to his birthplace where he resumed the practice of medicine. He and his wife were blessed with seven more children, all born in the peace of their home rather than a distant war zone. In 1870 he took his family to Wirt County, West Virginia, where an oil boom was making headlines. He returned home empty-handed only to learn of trouble in Rome for his cherished Catholic Church, and in a sincere letter to the Vatican offered to raise a papal army. Nothing came of his offer, but his name was soon put forth for a congressional seat. And so he remained Charley Gillespie from Freeport, Pennsylvania, always eager to be part of the action wherever it might be.[20]

Life finally settled for Gillespie when he developed a passion for chemistry as it applied to health and healing, and he began to practice his medical profession more as a druggist than a physician. The fortuitous prescription of a dose of quinine along the Carson River in August 1849, which had ended Gillespie's lingering malaria, may have triggered a curiosity in curative compounds and eventually led to his steady vocation. It was a positive outcome that correlated directly to his gold rush days.

Painting, sketching, and writing continued to be the mainstays of Gillespie's idle hours. He honed the stories of the gold rush that he had so colorfully articulated in his journal, turning them into articles for literary periodicals such as *Century Magazine,* whose readers were treated to the tales of "Sunday in Coloma" and the creek-side interview with nugget-discoverer James Marshall. The adventures of the forty-niners were becoming a popular subject for publishers as the fiftieth anniversary of the historic overland emigration approached. Talented writers like Gillespie, who could spin a glorified story of the times, were in demand.

Prior to Gillespie's gold rush experience he had made the acquaintance of artist Rembrandt Lockwood, whose renderings of religious visions might have inspired Gillespie to sketch while on the trail in 1849. Through Gillespie's association with *Century Magazine,* some of his artwork provided inspiration for famed western artist Frederic Remington, who arranged to use Gillespie's depiction of Fort Laramie to produce his own hand-colored woodcut, appropriately annotating the work "from sketch by Chas B Gillespie 1849."[21]

Gillespie's Civil War regiment had participated in General Sherman's March to the Sea, which crossed Georgia in 1864 and became storied for the Union army's torching of town after town in its path. Spared from conflagration was Macon, home to Confederate veteran David B. Woodruff. While Woodruff's adopted city had survived, his business did not.

Like Gillespie, Woodruff had traveled in 1849 to California, where he failed at mining but succeeded in observing and learning from the experiences put before him. He returned east via a yearlong exploration of South America and relocated to Georgia, where he married the daughter of a prominent businessman, also a transplanted northerner. Prior to the war, Woodruff developed a thriving enterprise supplying custom lumber products for residential and commercial construction.[22] His partner was his youngest brother, who could not support the Confederacy and returned to Connecticut about the time David enlisted in 1861. Fortunately the conflict did not splinter the family. After the war, David's older brother joined him in Macon, and within a few years the duo was landing lucrative contracts to design and engineer large-scale municipal projects as the South rebuilt its infrastructure. They were in the right place at the right time.

Woodruff's status as an architect soared across the South, and his expertise was in demand from Macon to Savannah. The reputation of Woodruff's character also soared. He became a member of the Knights of Pythias, a fraternal organization chartered by an act of Congress and founded on honor and loyalty, whose membership included US presidents

David Benjamin Woodruff, from progressive Connecticut stock, found success in the construction business in Macon, Georgia, in the 1850s. When the Civil War broke out he supported the Southern cause and joined the Confederate States Army. From *Pythian Knighthood: Its History and Literature* (Cincinnati: Pettibone, 1888).

and Supreme Court justices. By 1878 Woodruff held the rank of supreme chancellor, the highest office of the national organization.[23] Achieving success after recovering from failure and loss defined Woodruff's life.

Both Gillespie and Woodruff lived to see the twentieth century, and both seem to have been forever blessed with conviction and sureness.

Capt. Thomas Seely, with his jocund personality and love of partying, may have enjoyed a life immersed in social engagements regardless of where he lived. However, had he not made the decision to join two companions for the venture to California, he would not have obtained employment with a steamship company on the West Coast. That fork in the road placed him at the site of one of California's deadliest maritime disasters, the boiler explosion of the *Ada Hancock,* which took his life in an instant. Fate, bad luck, and personality, in his case, were all rolled into one.

After reaching California, Tom Seely's compatible overland companions, Frank Woolsey and Alex Cartwright, followed opposite paths as their lives progressed through the second half of the nineteenth century. Little could they have imagined when they applied for passports together at New York City's customhouse in February 1849 that after five months of travel they would never see one another again. Both men outlived Seely by decades.

Woolsey returned to the East Coast after spending only enough time in California to wait for a steamer to Panama. Initially he rejoined the family business, managing the ferry operation between Jersey City and New York. Within a few years he established a ship chandlery and contemplated opportunities with the Pacific Coast steamship industry. His close friend Seely would have been an excellent contact, but no associations appear to have materialized, and it is doubtful that Woolsey ever returned to California. In 1859 he became involved in a speculative real estate venture with several partners. A large tract of farmland was purchased south of Jersey City, where the investors envisioned an upper-middle-class suburb. The Civil War disrupted their plans, but the town of Bayonne was born of this endeavor, and Woolsey's name will forever be linked to its history.[24]

For two decades Woolsey built a solid career and business, all while supporting his mother and three sisters. The assets he listed on the 1870 census exceeded $35,000, well above his peers and most of the former Newark Overland Company. Economic depression hit the country in 1873, and Woolsey began a financial slide that required selling property and eventually his business. His last years were spent living in the New York City home of a niece. There he fell ill suddenly and died in March 1888. Coincidently, his deathbed was only two blocks from the home of Charles Gray in midtown Manhattan.

While Woolsey lived a predictable life in the shadow of his childhood home, Alexander Cartwright was a world away having chosen to dwell in an island retreat. After he departed for California in 1849, he never again saw his parents or the vacant New York City lots where he had once played baseball.

Like Woolsey, Cartwright had left California in 1849 so quickly that most of his one-time Newark Overland Company associates were still on the trail. His departure was prompted by the chronic dysentery from which he had suffered for most of the journey. It was recommended that he convalesce in the tropical climate of the Sandwich Islands, and he sailed for Honolulu in August just weeks after his record-setting arrival date at Sutter's Mill. Once rejuvenated, Cartwright expected to make his way back to New York via China and other ports of the Far East. But that never happened.

The Pacific island paradise so captivated Cartwright that he soon decided to stay among the people and striking scenery of the Hawaiian archipelago created from volcanic eruption. It took two years for his family to join him, including daughter Kate Lee, born after Cartwright's departure from the East Coast in 1849. Tragically, the little girl died just days after meeting her father for the first time when the family arrived in Honolulu in November 1851.[25]

Various career opportunities came his way, and Cartwright became one of Hawaii's most respected citizens. Early on he was named Honolulu fire chief, and he subsequently served as advisor to the Hawaiian royal family and was appointed consul to Peru. He joined the local Masonic lodge and enjoyed witnessing the growth of baseball as a favorite pastime among local communities. He only left the islands for a few trips to San Francisco before his full life ended in 1892.

Six months after Cartwright's death, one of his overland traveling companions, Cyrus Currier, died in Newark. Mourned by the close-knit family he so cherished, Currier had turned his foundry business over to his sons, who continued the reputable operation. Transcripts of the letters between Currier and his first wife, Nancy, remain with the family today.

The life of journal writer Charles Gedney Gray also came to an end in the 1890s. He died in New York City on September 1, 1897, at the home of his sister, Julia Gray Cone. A half century later the two volumes containing his overland diary were donated to the Huntington Library in San Marino, California, where they were eventually discovered by Thomas D. Clark, historian from the University of Kentucky. Clark published the journal in 1976 with an introduction and historical annotations.

Gray's living arrangement with William H. and Abby Tyler Oakes ended sometime in the early 1890s. Abby Oakes lost both her husband and son to tuberculosis and subsequently spent the next years traveling between homes in Boston and Florida.[26] In her later years she had moved beyond painting, focusing her attention on writing poems and plays, with which she had limited success. Gray's remaining years were spent at the residence of his sister. There are no records to confirm whether or not he ever accompanied Abby Oakes to Massachusetts or spent time at her winter residence near St. Augustine, where she died in 1898 less than a year after Gray.[27] Details of their forty-year association remain obscure.

Caroline Meeker also died in 1898. She and Abby Tyler Oakes were progressive, well-to-do women who shared the experience of living in two of the most exciting cities in the United States, San Francisco and New York, and the privilege of vacationing in Yosemite and Europe. They also shared the heartbreak of outliving the all of the significant men in their lives and, sadly, all of their children.

By 1900 only seven of the men of the Newark Overland Company had survived to see the dawn of the twentieth century. They had lived to witness the fiftieth anniversary of their historic migration west and to be celebrated as forty-niners. The anniversary coincided with the discovery of gold in the Klondike region of British Columbia, where once again men were rushing for the precious metal, this time by a treacherous journey through Alaska's tundra.

Benjamin Casterline was nearly broke when he died in December 1900, a widower who had too often lent money to friends and acquaintances who never repaid him.[28] Charles Hicks and Thomas Fowler passed away quietly in 1904 and 1908 respectively, having lived modest, ordinary lives.

Gillespie and Woodruff died nearly one year apart. Woodruff was visiting his Connecticut birthplace when he died suddenly on July 22, 1906. Gillespie passed away in his lifelong home of Freeport, Pennsylvania, on August 3, 1907. A number of newspapers and periodicals published detailed biographical obituaries of the two men.

The 1849 gold rush provided a path for members of the Newark Overland Company to pursue extraordinary lives. Only the small contingent

According to family legend, "he crossed rivers on horseback." Benjamin Casterline, circa 1895, was one of seven Newark Overland Company members to see the 50th anniversary of the historic 1849 gold rush and the turn of the twentieth century. Courtesy of Edith Smeaton Kennedy, great-granddaughter of Benjamin Casterline.

that remained loyal to General Darcy on the Yuba River and worked methodically at the same claim, day after day, succeeded in obtaining gold. Among them were Lewis Baldwin, Benjamin Casterline, Darcy's partner W. Donaldson Kinney, and the Lewis contingent of Thomas Fowler, William T. Lewis, and James Lewis Jr. These men all returned to the East and were known to have accumulated "modest fortunes" during their two years mining in California. For some, life thereafter was mostly ordinary, the newfound wealth quickly evaporating due to lackluster investing and sometimes due to poor business decisions, as in the case of Casterline.

John B. Overton's life, however, was never ordinary. He was the only member of the Newark Overland Company to achieve the status of millionaire. After spending years in the gold-rich country of California, Overton made his way to neighboring Nevada, where a vein of silver known as the Comstock Lode had thousands rushing to the eastern slopes of the Sierra. Yet it was neither gold nor silver that brought Overton his millions. It was the most elementary of compounds: water.

Chapter 25

The Last Scandal

John B. Overton was once described by old friends as being a "jovial, genial, freehearted man who was the head and front of every escapade, daredevil exploit and project for fun in Jersey City." Indeed, he had organized a club of fellow young men who engaged in youthful pranks and relished each other's steadfast camaraderie. His fun-loving nature was combined with an acute sense of leadership and boundless energy. When barely into his twenties, he claimed the responsible position of chief engineer of the Jersey City Fire Department and became an officer in the state militia, garnering him the lifelong title of captain.[1]

It is a testament to a man's character that he can overcome the hardships of a deprived childhood. Overton's mother died from complications of childbirth when John was a boy only four years old. Her death left his father with five children to raise. Because Nathan Overton traveled as a conductor on John S. Darcy's New Jersey Railroad, he could not be home with his children and was forced to apprentice the boys to tradesmen. After two years of abuse, young John B. Overton fled from his arduous indenture and struggled on his own until his father found him and was able to send him to a proper school. But his life in academics ended quickly when Nathan Overton was killed in a train accident. All five children were then placed under the guardianship of the state.[2]

John "J. B." Overton and his brother, Isaac, his senior by three years, endured years of separation until they were reunited as young men and shared a residence in Newark. J. B. had taken a job with the New Jersey Railroad. When gold fever struck, the brothers jumped at the opportunity and made plans to join Darcy's overland company. Both were identified as departing with the group on March 1, 1849.[3]

Several weeks later the name of John B. Overton had vanished from the roster of the company. He had, in fact, opted at the last minute to sail via Cape Horn aboard the bark *Griffon* as a member, or more likely as a substitute member, of a joint stock company. Once again he was separated from his brother, Isaac, who had started west with Darcy's New Jersey contingent.

They would see each other again in September 1849, a continent away, in the wild and unpredictable port of San Francisco. J. B. would become enthralled with California and its seemingly endless possibilities for success, while Isaac was eager to return to his home in New Jersey and his steady job as a railroad ticket agent. And so again the brothers would part ways.

For nearly two decades the younger Overton clawed his way to success and prominence in the Sierra foothills of Plumas County, a jurisdiction that existed only because of its proximity to gold. A dry goods store, a sawmill operation, and numerous terms as county clerk placed him among the leading citizens of Onion Valley.[4]

Back in Newark, older brother Isaac built a stable life as an agent for the Erie Railroad, and in 1862 he married a Morris County woman.[5] Within a few years, however, the relationship had soured. To escape the failed marriage, Isaac Overton returned to California and joined his brother who was now located in the town of Quincy in Plumas County.[6] Despite spending most of their lives apart, the bond of brotherhood kept them close, and the reunion after nearly eighteen years was a bittersweet reminder of their previous years apart. Mrs. Isaac Overton filed for and was granted a divorce in 1870 during her husband's absence from New Jersey.[7]

In that same year, 1870, events compelled J. B. Overton to uproot and abandon the Plumas County community where he had built a solid reputation. Along with Isaac he moved to San Francisco, where he tried a variety of entrepreneurial endeavors, including work in the brokerage business.[8] Isaac, true to his steady character, took modest employment as a clerk. Back in Plumas County, thirty-six-year-old Hiram Clemons married a young woman named Adele, still in her teens.

It wasn't long before J. B. learned about employment opportunities in western Nevada, where a deposit of silver ore known as the Comstock Lode had been enticing wealth-seekers for nearly a decade. Two stock-brokers named James Flood and William O'Brien, possibly brokerage associates of Overton's, were dabbling in mining stock investments and may have encouraged Overton to take his skills to the Washoe Valley east of the Sierra Nevada. Whatever the source of the opportunity, Overton made his way to Virginia City and early in 1871 was hired by the Gold Hill and Virginia City Water Company to oversee the operation of supplying water to the bone-dry region.

In Plumas County, Adele Clemons gave birth to a baby boy named Jay. Shortly thereafter J. B. Overton hired her husband, Hiram, to be his chief foreman.[9]

With his brother leaving for Nevada, Isaac Overton returned east to his familiar occupation in the railroad industry. Perhaps avoiding his ex-wife, he went south to Georgia and spent a number of years with the Brunswick and Western Railroad.[10]

Since 1860 the Comstock Lode had been yielding significant silver ore. The lack of water around Virginia City had limited not only the mining process but also the population of those employed by the mining industry. Without a source of water, the extraction of ore would reach its mechanical limit. J. B. Overton teamed with a German engineer to structure a combination flume-and-pipe system that would direct water some seventeen miles from the highland watersheds just above Lake Tahoe. The concept of transporting such a volume of water over so many miles was almost inconceivable. It was not just the distance, it was the topography. Water had to flow down the mountain with enough pressure to carry it over the Washoe Valley and up the adjacent mountains where the Comstock was located. Difficult. Beyond the technical obstacles, it could not happen unless the company could secure legal rights to the water.[11] And so, enter a man unafraid of pushing the envelope, John B. Overton, graciously described by the Virginia City *Territorial Enterprise* as someone "of tireless energy and limitless resources, who devotes himself with a remarkable self-sacrificing spirit and zeal."[12]

Little is documented about how Overton managed to persuade intelligent, enterprising men to sell their land's most vital natural resource, but once the rights were acquired, construction began with all-out abandon.

In late July 1873 gates opened, releasing water into the newly completed system. When the water reached Virginia City, fireworks were set off in celebration of the engineering accomplishment, along with "music, parades, and cannon booms from Fremont's abandoned howitzer."[13]

Overton's success supplying the Comstock with water was a severe loss to local ranchers and landowners. Litigation over the water rights would flood the local courts for years to come. It was said of Overton, however, that "he was able to subdue all opposition in an overbearing but charming way." Another recollection of Overton made a more amusing observation, stating that his "ability to appropriate water, claimed or unclaimed, was equaled only by his knack of attracting the ladies, attached or single."[14]

The stock brokers Flood and O'Brien, with whom Overton likely became acquainted while in San Francisco in 1870, went on to partner with two savvy miners, James Fair and John Mackay, who knew the Comstock well and provided insider information to the finance men. In 1875 the foursome struck one of the largest veins on the Comstock and instantly became the wealthiest men on the West Coast. When they formed the Bank of Nevada, J. B. Overton was named one of the trustees.[15]

The Gold Hill and Virginia City Water Company would be run by Overton's formidable hand for more than three decades. He would amass a fortune and achieve a reputation unequalled on the Comstock. He also managed the Sierra Nevada Wood and Lumber Company and through this association developed the logging town of Overton, California (now Hobart Mills).

Through the management roles Overton held in these companies, he gained a business reputation that was unparalleled. The *Territorial Enterprise* said that he "superintends personally the minutest details, apparently with the ability to be everywhere at all times, infusing his own indomitable energy into the men employed on the work." The paper noted that he was "the especial terror of the shirkers."[16]

Overton's renown was not limited to his business management. He would be remembered as having owned "one of the handsomest saddle horses available," as "an entertaining conversationalist, a natty dresser, and a ruthless competitor," and, unquestionably as "one of the most sought after bachelors on the Comstock." Indeed, his reputation with women was legendary.[17] A former employee was said to have "expressed great concern because a good friend of his permitted his daughter to go about with John Overton."[18] And Overton was known to travel with not just one but several young women at a time. On an "excursion for San Francisco . . . to hear Paderewski, the pianist," J. B. Overton was accompanied by "Miss French, Miss Lamb, and Miss Amelia Kline," the *Nevada State Journal* reported.[19] If women were not mentioned in such news briefs about Overton, it was his wealth: "J. B. Overton, the Nevada County millionaire and mining man is at the Russ in San Francisco."[20]

When the history of the Comstock water supply was written, Overton's full name was given as "John Bear Overton."[21] He was a towering, imposing bear of a man, and that's how he was known. In fact, his middle name was Brewster, from his prestigious Long Island, New York lineage. "Brewster" appears on his California voter registration, his application to the Society of California Pioneers, and his membership records in Masonic Lodges. Yet on the Comstock, he was John Bear Overton.

In addition to the water and lumber companies, Overton helped establish the Virginia City Electric Company in 1887 and took on another supervisory role there. In June 1888 Virginia City was illuminated with electric light. Another cofounder of the utility, employed as company secretary, was Overton's brother, Isaac, who had joined him in Nevada sometime in the mid-1880s. The brothers would part only one more time. In August 1894 Isaac Overton died at the age of seventy-three in Virginia City, of "general debility," having been hospitalized for the last three months of his life.[22]

Back to Overton's reputation with women, in particular one named Adele Clemons. Over the years it was widely speculated that her son, Jay, had been fathered by Captain Overton. This circumstance might explain his abrupt departure from Plumas County around 1870. Rumor says that Overton convinced Hiram Clemons to marry the pregnant teenager. If so, it proved to be a workable solution for all parties involved. Surely Hiram Clemons was rewarded with a lifelong job serving as Overton's chief foreman. The arrangement was no secret. Overton's "offspring was well known in the community." Overton was a frequent visitor in the Clemons household over the years, and the men remained friends until Hiram Clemons died in 1904.

The following year Overton retired and left the Comstock to spend his retirement in Seattle. Of course, he sailed to the Pacific Northwest "in

Capt. John B. Overton, millionaire, Virginia City, Nevada, circa 1890. Courtesy of the Special Collections, University of Nevada, Reno Libraries (UNRS-P1987-19-1).

the company of two attractive young sisters."[23] In February 1905, prior to boarding the ship for Seattle, Overton drafted a will in his own hand in case he met disaster sailing north along the Pacific Coast. In it he named a number of his women friends as heirs to modest bequests. Overton's rumored son, Jay Clemons, was assigned as executor and the primary beneficiary of the vast investments in property and banking institutions.

In spring of 1909, Capt. J. B. Overton, the former gold rush pioneer and dominant figure of the Comstock suffered a stroke in Seattle. He returned to Reno over the summer, where he convalesced at the Clemons home. On September 26, 1909, Overton was stricken with a second and more severe stroke, which he did not survive. He died at Jay Clemons's Reno residence.[24]

Headlines from Los Angeles to San Francisco to Salt Lake City, and especially those of the local newspapers in Nevada, declared the death of an original Comstock pioneer. Tributes were widespread, with praise and admiration for the man whose ingenuity and drive had brought water and enterprise to Virginia City and surrounding communities.

In August 1910, eleven months after Overton's death, his name again returned to the headlines. Four women and one man who had been named as beneficiaries in his will filed a lawsuit for collection of their inheritances. When Overton's will had been probated in October 1909, the millionaire's estate was appraised at a paltry $100.[25]

Just as Overton had manipulated water rights for the Virginia City Water Company, he had shrewdly restructured his investments in favor of Jay Clemons. His reasons may have been twofold. As a trustee and investor of the California Safety Deposit and Trust Company, Overton was liable to lawsuits when the bank encountered serious solvency issues in December 1907. In fact, just three days after the announced bank failure, Overton had moved a large block of stock in the Oakland Traction Company to Clemons.[26] By selling and transferring investments to Jay Clemons, Overton protected his assets from legal recourse. Secondarily, he likely intended Clemons to be the sole beneficiary of his wealth.

Litigation over the Overton estate went on for three years, during which the judge ruled that Clemons, as executor, was barred from testifying. One interesting piece of information was made public in the proceedings when a sworn witness described Jay Clemons as the adopted son of John B. Overton.[27] The father-son relationship had been rumored for many years.

Finally, in July 1913, a district court judge declared that Jay Clemons held stock that should have been itemized as assets in the estate of J. B. Overton, and the judge directed that the five plaintiffs be awarded their money. Clemons immediately appealed the verdict.[28]

On September 5, 1914, the Supreme Court of Nevada declared a new trial for the Overton estate. Another year would pass before the second trial would begin.

Chapter 26

The Last Funeral

On December 18, 1912, the sting of a winter chill met Mrs. Caleb D. Boylston and her two daughters as they proceeded to the hillside cemetery north of Elizabeth, New Jersey. The cold ground had been prepared to receive the remains of her late husband, a mason by profession, father of six, and one of the adventuresome men who had crossed the country for gold in 1849—a true forty-niner. Not far from Caleb Boylston's final resting place was the grave of another of the Newark Overland Company, William Donaldson Kinney. The former partner of John S. Darcy had been dead some sixteen years before Boylston's passing.

The three women were the only remaining members of their immediate family. As they stood at the gravesite for the burial at Evergreen Cemetery, their gaze likely wandered to the markers of previously deceased family members—a son, grandson, brother, nephew.

Boylston's nearly ninety-one-year lifespan had allowed him to witness great strides in transportation—from travel by covered wagon, to the transcontinental railroad that John S. Darcy believed would never be built, to the advent of flight on a blustery Carolina sand dune in 1903. Boylston also lived to see the United States become a nation of forty-eight states, with Arizona completing the contiguous configuration in January 1912, eleven months before he died.

Four years after Boylston's death and seven years after the death of Capt. John B. Overton, Jay Clemons, the man believed to be Overton's

C. D. BOYLSTON DEAD AT 91.

One of the Forty-niners Was Descendant of First American Physician.

Caleb Dudley Boylston, one of the few remaining men who crossed the plains to California in 1849 when the gold discoveries there excited the country, died on Monday at the home of his daughter, Mrs. Abbey Wood Smith, 452 St. Nicholas Avenue. He was 91 years old.

Mr. Boylston was born in Elizabeth, N. J., and was the eighth in descent in direct line from Thomas Boylston, who sailed from Staffordshire, England, in 1635, in the ship Defense. The family settled in Massachusetts, clearing a farm afterward known as Breed's Hill, which was the scene, 140 years later, of the Battle of Bunker Hill, and which one branch of the Boylston family sold later for $5,000 to be the site of the Bunker Hill Monument.

The great grandfather of Mr. Boylston's great grandfather, Thomas Boylston, a son of the original Thomas, who was born in Brookline in 1645, was the first native American physician. His son, the celebrated Dr. Zabdiel Boylston, made the first attempts to inoculate against smallpox, and in 1721, long before Dr. Jenner's discovery of vaccination was given to the world, he inoculated his own six-year-old son.

In 1849, when he was 27 years old, Mr. Boylston and a companion started overland from New York for California with a mule team. The journey occupied months, and the other man gave up, but Mr. Boylston kept on. He made friends with the Indians, who escorted him over the desert.

On his return to the East, in 1859, he married Anna Johnson Vandervoort of Linden, N. J. She and two of their six children, Mrs. Smith and Mrs. S. G. Lawrence of this city, survive him.

Caleb D. Boylston's obituary. *New York Times*, December 18, 1912.

biological son, won his appeal, closing the litigation over his father's estate and clearing the way for his sole inheritance.[1]

Ninety years after the gold rush, Alexander J. Cartwright was enshrined as a member of the Baseball Hall of Fame in Cooperstown, New York, for his contributions to the advancement of baseball in the 1840s.

Lewis Center, Ohio, founded by William T. Lewis on a portion of his land, is today a thriving upscale community north of Columbus and remains a lasting namesake for a man with eight daughters and no sons. Lewis had stayed with General Darcy in California and was among the small contingent that successfully mined the claim on the Yuba River. The wealth he achieved in California may have provided the financial security to develop Lewis Center.

In 1964 the well-written journal of Charles G. Gray's tumultuous overland trek caught the attention of Thomas D. Clark while researching at the Huntington Library in California. His transcription of the two leather-bound volumes was published in 1976 as *Off at Sunrise*. Clark believed that Gray lived his life working a desk job in New York City and never learned about Gray's return to California or his relationship with William and Abby Tyler Oakes. For some reason, Clark erroneously identified Gray's middle name as "Glass."[2]

The gold bullion lost during the explosion and sinking of the *Ada Hancock* that killed Capt. Tom Seely, and estimated to be worth as much as $125,000 in 1863 dollars, has never been recovered.

Appendix A

Newark Overland Company Members

BALDWIN, AUGUSTUS
Born September 22, 1825, Bloomfield, New Jersey, to William Brown
Baldwin and Harriet Pierson Grover. Married Mary A. Prior, six
children. Died November 10, 1899, Moultrie, Florida.
Clerk, bookkeeper, farmer.
Returned from Missouri early April 1849.

BALDWIN, LEWIS BROADWELL "GUN"
Born August 20, 1819, Newark, to Aaron Baldwin and Anna Gould.
Married Amanda Ogden, two children. Died August 15, 1870, Newark.
Gunsmith, Civil War soldier, POW Andersonville.
Returned March 15, 1851, aboard *Crescent City.*

BIRDSALL, DANIEL S.
Born around 1825. Married 1) Rachel Freeman, two children; 2) Eliza S.
Sears, no children. Died October 29, 1864, Andersonville Prison, Georgia.
Hatter, Civil War soldier, POW Andersonville.
Returned November 28, 1851, aboard *Brother Jonathan.*
Brother-in-law of Joseph Freeman, nephew of Henry Johnson.

BOND, ROBERT
Born around 1819, Lyon's Farms, New Jersey, to David Bond and Rebecca
Osborn. Unmarried. Died August 25, 1849, Black Rock Desert, Nevada.
Occupation unknown.
Never returned (died en route).

Boylston, Caleb Dudley
Born January 1822, Elizabeth, New Jersey, to Nathaniel Boylston and
Abby Wood. Married Anna Johnson Vandervoot, six children. Died
December 16, 1912, New York City.
Farmer, brick and stone mason.
Returned 1859.

Canfield, Moses "Moss"
Born May 10, 1814, Newark, to Thomas Canfield and Mary Sheperd.
Married Sarah A. Massie, seven children. Died after 1880, California.
Jeweler, farmer.
Never returned (remained in California, abandoning family in New
Jersey).

Cartwright, Alexander Joy, Jr.
Born April 17, 1820, New York City, to Alexander Joy Cartwright Sr.
and Ester Burlock. Married Eliza Van Wie, five children. Died July 12,
1892, Honolulu.
Clerk for brokerage firm, bank teller, bookstore owner, bookkeeper, fire
department chief engineer, advisor to Hawaiian royal family, consul to
Peru, member Baseball Hall of Fame.
Never returned (went to Sandwich Islands in August 1849 and made
Honolulu permanent residence for himself and family).

Casterline, Benjamin M.
Born December 26, 1826, Newark, to Mulford W. Casterline and
Harriet Samson. Married Ann Elizabeth Titus, seven children. Died
December 22, 1900, Rahway, New Jersey.
Grocer, farmer.
Returned February 18, 1851, aboard *Crescent City*.
Great-great-grandfather of *Jersey Gold* coauthor Margaret Casterline
Bowen.

Cook, William Wallace
Born around 1830. Unmarried. Died October 23, 1849, San Francisco.
Occupation unknown.
Never returned (died on steamer between Sacramento and San
Francisco).
Nephew of Stephen Dehart.

CROCKETT, JOHN ROBINSON
Born February 19, 1802, Newark, to James Crockett and Lydia Pierson.
Married Jane Pierson, six children. Died July 7, 1867, Newark.
Fire department engineer, merchant of patent leather and oiled cloth,
Civil War assistant provost marshal, holder of US patent no. 35740.
Returned January 22, 1851, aboard *Prometheus*.

CURRIER, CYRUS
Born May 13, 1812, Salisbury, Massachusetts, to Moses Currier and
Nancy Stevens. Married 1) Nancy Maria Roper, five children; 2)
Charlotte Axford, two children. Died December 6, 1892, Newark.
Steam engine mechanic, owner of machine shop and foundry, manu-
facturer of brass and iron works and machines for hat, jewelry, paper,
leather, and oiled cloth industries.
Returned May–June 1850.
Business partner of Stephen Dehart.

DARCY, JOHN STEVENS
Born February 24, 1788, Hanover, New Jersey, to John Darcy and
Phebe Johnes. Married 1) Eliza Gray, three children; 2) Eliza Bowne
Hinchman, no children. Died October 22, 1863, Newark.
Doctor, US marshal, president of New Jersey Railroad, general in New
Jersey Militia, US congressional candidate.
Returned January 24, 1851 aboard *Falcon*.
Brother-in-law of Andrew J. Gray, uncle of Charles Gedney Gray.

DEHART, STEPHEN
Born around 1804, New Jersey, to John Dehart and Jane Dodd. Married
Phoebe Quinby, three children. Died July 2, 1873, Coldwater, Michigan.
Machinist, farmer.
Returned June 24, 1850, aboard *Crescent City*. Went back to California
in 1851 to settle business interests.
Uncle of William Wallace Cook, business partner of Cyrus Currier.

DENMAN, JOSEPH "JOB"
Born October 14, 1825, New Jersey, to Calvin Denman and Eleanor
Parrot Lewis. Unmarried. Died August 24, 1849, Black Rock Desert,
Nevada.
Occupation unknown.

Never returned (died en route to California).
Probably nephew of William T. Lewis.

DOTY, JOSEPH TOBIAS
Born August 31, 1828, Somerville, New Jersey, to Tobias Hall Doty and
Mary Kerr. Married Susan D. Storms, one child. Died October 26, 1853,
Elizabeth, New Jersey.
Farmer.
Returned from Independence, Missouri, arriving back in Elizabethtown
April 26, 1849.

EMERY, DAVID
Also identified as William Emery Jr.
Born around 1833, New Jersey, to William Emery and Clarissa [surname
unknown].
Occupation unknown.
Returned December 21, 1849 aboard *Crescent City.*
Son of William Emery.

EMERY, WILLIAM
Born around 1812, Warren County, New Jersey. Married Clarissa
[surname unknown], multiple children. Died after 1880, possibly in
Peoria, Illinois.
Contractor, merchant.
Returned December 21, 1849, aboard *Crescent City.*
Father of David Emery.

FOWLER, THOMAS PAYNE
Born October 1831, New Jersey, to Charles A. Fowler and Catherine
Payne. Married 1) Lucetta Clark, no children; 2) Hannah M. Pierson,
one child. Died January 20, 1904, Rahway, New Jersey.
Coal dealer.
Returned after remaining in California eight to ten years.
Brother-in-law of William T. Lewis.

FREEMAN, JOSEPH
Born October 10, 1815, New York City, to Marshall Freeman and Sarah
Ross Annin. Married Mary Folsom, eight children. Died January 15,
1873, Hudson County, New Jersey.
Merchant, restaurateur, Civil War saddler.

Returned about 1851.
Brother-in-law of Daniel Birdsall, nephew of Henry Johnson.

Gibbons, A.
Few details were found. He is known to have been with George Sayre in California in late 1849.
Occupation unknown.
Return unknown.

Gillespie, Charles Bonaventure
Born October 15, 1820, Donegal Township, Butler County, Pennsylvania, to Neal Gillespie and Barbara Duffy. Married Susan Brunker, eight children. Died August 3, 1907, Freeport, Pennsylvania. Lawyer, doctor, writer, artist, Civil War captain of Pennsylvania Seventy-Eighth Infantry.
Returned April 12, 1851, aboard *El Dorado.*

Gray, Andrew J.
Born January 7, 1815, Morris County, New Jersey, to Jacob Gray and Pheba Ward. Unmarried. Died December 12, 1852, in Yolo County, California.
Occupation unknown.
Never returned (remained in California as permanent resident).
Brother-in-law of John S. Darcy, uncle of Charles G. Gray.

Gray, Charles Gedney
Born January 1, 1821, New York City, to George Washington Gray and Julia Ann Gedney. Unmarried. Died September 1, 1897, New York City.
Clerk, bookkeeper.
Returned about February 1850. Went back to California where he lived in San Francisco from 1856 to 1860.
Nephew of John S. Darcy and Andrew J. Gray.

Hicks, Charles
Born around 1824, New Jersey, to Jason Hicks and Rachel Lefevre. Married Catharine Wilson, three children. Died May 5, 1908, Masonic Home, Burlington, New Jersey.
Clerk, grocer, merchant.
Returned December 9, 1850, aboard *Empire City.*

APPENDIX A

HUNT, JOHN
Born around 1832. Probably died before 1880, California.
May have worked as a hostler (caretaker of horses).
Did not return to New Jersey with General Darcy and likely remained in California (evidence suggests that he married an Indian woman, and if so, he lived and raised a family near Shasta, California).
Servant to General Darcy.

JOBES, HENRY ASHFIELD "ASH"
Born February 22, 1826, New Jersey, to John H. Jobes and Anne Hunt. Married Catherine Gallagher, no children. Died April 7, 1850, "Darcyville," Yuba County, California.
Assistant to John S. Darcy.
Never returned (died in California, having never fully recovered from his illness contracted on the trail).

JOHNSON, HENRY LEWIS
Born around 1813, New Jersey. Married Phebe Annin, five children. Died December 21, 1876, Yuba County, California.
Jeweler, miner, farmer, mining foreman at Yuba River camp.
Evidence indicates he returned to New Jersey for brief visits in 1855 and 1860. Residency in California became permanent after 1860, while family remained in New Jersey.
Uncle to Daniel Birdsall and Joseph Freeman.

JORALEMON, ABRAHAM J. "ABRAM"
Born January 21, 1812, New Jersey, to James Joralemon and Gitty Spier. Married Hester Terhune, seven children. Died August 27, 1885, Belleville, New Jersey.
Butcher.
Returned May 8, 1850, aboard *Cherokee* with Dolph Pennington.

KELLY, SAMUEL
No details are known about this individual recorded with the Darcy party by Mormon clerks at Salt Lake City. The name "Kelly" is mentioned once in Meeker's journal, corroborating his existence in the company.

KINNEY, WILLIAM DONALDSON
Born March 22, 1816, Newark, to Abraham W. Kinney and Elizabeth Donaldson. Married 1) Anna Maria Plume, no children; 2) Prussia Catherine Peshine Trenor, no children. Died July 12, 1896, Newark. Family hardware business, John S. Darcy's business partner at Yuba River camp, member of San Francisco Vigilance Committee of 1851. Returned January 24, 1851, aboard *Falcon*. Resided in California from 1851 to 1853.

LEWIS, JAMES, JR.
Born around 1793, Morris County, New Jersey, to James Lewis and unknown mother. Married Eleanor Parrot Smith, two children. Died before 1870.
Farmer.
Returned about 1851.
Cousin of William T. Lewis.

LEWIS, WILLIAM T.
Born around February 1810, probably in Hanover, New Jersey, to Lawrence Lewis and Hannah [surname unknown]. Married Sarah Elizabeth Fowler, eight children (all daughters). Died December 8, 1875, Lewis Center, Ohio.
Stage driver, horse breeder, land developer, town proprietor, postmaster.
Returned May 27, 1850, aboard *Crescent City*.
Cousin of James Lewis Jr., brother-in-law of Thomas Fowler, probably uncle of Job Denman.
Great-great-grandfather of *Jersey Gold* coauthor Gwendolyn Joslin Hiles.

MARTIN, GEORGE WELLS
Born around 1829, New Jersey, to "Captain Martin" and Sarah W. Died before 1900.
Bookbinder.
May have returned December 21, 1849, aboard *Crescent City*.
Nephew of Joseph H. Martin.

MARTIN, JOSEPH H.
Born around 1828, possibly Ohio. Died around 1892, possibly Kern
County, California.
Occupation unknown.
May have returned December 21, 1849, aboard *Crescent City*.
Uncle of George Martin.

MEEKER, STEPHEN HARRIS
Society of California Pioneers lists him as Samuel H. Meeker from
Connecticut, errors attributed to a posthumous application.
Born around 1817, New Jersey, to Obadiah Meeker and Jerusha Cook
Harrison. Married Caroline Rogers Griffen, three children. Died May 8,
1863, Fifth Avenue Hotel, New York City.
Umbrella manufacturer, liquor merchant.
Made California his permanent home, returning East to visit family in
1852 and 1863.

OVERTON, ISAAC OUTCALT
Born April 13, 1821, New Brunswick, New Jersey, to Nathan Overton
and Jane Outcalt. Married and divorced Helen M. Colbath, no
children. Died August 14, 1894, Virginia City, Nevada.
Railroad ticket agent, accountant, clerk.
Returned January 15, 1850, aboard *Cherokee*.
Brother of John Brewster Overton.

OVERTON, JOHN BREWSTER
Born April 13, 1824, Allegany County, New York, to Nathan Overton
and Jane Outcalt. Unmarried. One son likely. Died September 27, 1909,
Reno, Nevada.
Miner, hydraulic engineer, water company superintendant.
Sailed to California via Cape Horn aboard bark *Griffon*.
Returned only to visit in 1856 (remained in California and Nevada as
permanent resident).
Brother of Isaac Overton.

PENNINGTON, JAMES ADOLPHUS "DOLPH"
Born November 14, 1814, Newark, to James Wheeler Pennington
and Lucretia Shoulders. Married Charlotte B., no children. Died
December 6, 1858, Newark.

Farmer, Newark alderman, jeweler, cricket player.
Returned May 8, 1850, aboard *Cherokee* with Abram Joralemon.

RICHARDS, JOHN C.
Possibly born January 2, 1823, New Jersey, to Aaron Richards and
unknown mother. Died February 18, 1851, Newark.
Occupation unknown.
Believed to have left California early, returned by way of New Orleans,
where he resided until shortly before his death.

ROWE, JOHN
Last name may have been Rowe, Rose, or Room.
Born around 1838.
Returned May 8, 1850 aboard *Cherokee* with Pennington. Listed on ship
manifest as "Penfato."
Servant to James A. Pennington.

SAYRE, GEORGE DAVIS
Born July 7, 1824, New Jersey, to Moses Sayre and Mary Ogden
Bigelow. Married Maria Brittain, one child. Died September 8, 1893,
Baltimore.
Merchant, jeweler.
Returned December 28, 1857, aboard *Northern Light*.

SEELY, THOMAS W.
Born around 1821, Orange County, New York. Unmarried. Died
April 27, 1863, San Pedro, California.
Steamship captain.
Never returned (remained in California as permanent resident).

SHAFF, JOHN W.
Born 1828, New York. Married Harriett Francisco, two children. Died
February 2, 1890, soldiers' home, Newark.
Bookkeeper. Spent three years aboard USS *Portsmouth* on expedition to
China and other ports in the Far East, 1856–59. Civil War naval officer
aboard USS *Wabash*. Lost leg in train accident.
Returned about December 1851.

WOODRUFF, DAVID BENJAMIN
Born April 23, 1829, Orange, Connecticut, to John Woodruff and
Betsey Hotchkiss. Married Adelia Scattergood, two children. Died July
22, 1906, Connecticut.
Architect, builder, Confederate States Army (CSA) engineer.
Returned via South America in 1851.

WOOLSEY, BENJAMIN FRANKLIN "FRANK"
Born January 7, 1812, Milton, New York, to William Woolsey and
Lucinda [surname unknown]. Unmarried. Died March 8, 1888, New
York City.
Ferry boat captain, ship chandler.
Returned December 26, 1849, aboard *Empire City*.

YOUNG, THOMAS
Details unknown. Believed to be middle aged in 1849.
Returned April 1849, without completing the journey to California.

Appendix B

Travel Groups and Messmates

NEWARK OVERLAND COMPANY (MAIN CONTINGENT)
Members who remained with General John S. Darcy

Wagon 1
John S. Darcy YR

Wagon 2
S. H. Meeker
W. D. Kinney YR
Robert Bond
Charles Hicks

Wagon 3 **
Henry L. Johnson YR
Daniel S. Birdsall
Joseph Freeman
David B. Woodruff

Wagon 4
Dolph Pennington (7)
Abram Joralemon (7)
Moses Canfield (7)
Benjamin Casterline YR

Wagon 5
William T. Lewis YR
James Lewis Jr. YR
Thomas Fowler YR
Job Denman

Wagon 6
Andrew J. Gray (7) YR
Charles G. Gray
John R. Crockett (7)
Lewis B. Baldwin (7) YR

Wagon 7
Samuel Kelly (7)
Ashfield Jobes
John Hunt
John Rowe

Wagon 8
Common stock wagon

** Wagon lost crossing North Platte River, June 19, 1849
(7) Members believed to have separated from Darcy to mine in vicinity of Trinity, California, October 1849
YR Men known to have mined at the Yuba River Camp and acquired "comfortable fortunes"

Appendix B

CARTWRIGHT-CURRIER TEAM
Men who separated in Independence, Missouri, preferring to travel with
stock mules, and were subsequently among first overland travelers to
reach Sutter's Mill (July 24, 1849)

Alexander J. Cartwright   Cyrus Currier   William Emery
Thomas W. Seely   Stephen Dehart   David Emery
Frank Woolsey   Wallace Cook   Caleb Boylston **
Isaac Overton *   John Shaff *

*   Swapped at Green River
**   Joined Cartwright mess at Scotts Bluff

JACKASS FRIENDS
Men who teamed with Charles B. Gillespie and left Independence
with two mule-driven wagons and six members, nicknamed the Jackass
friends by Darcy members. The contingent fell apart en route.

Charles B. Gillespie   George Sayre *
Joseph H. Martin   John Richards *
George W. Martin   A. Gibbons *

*   Unconfirmed, but believed to be members of the mess

MEN WHO MADE ALTERNATE ARRANGEMENTS
John B. Overton: last-minute travel plans put him on bark *Griffon*,
departing by sea in mid-March 1849
Augustus Baldwin: returned home from Missouri
Joseph T. Doty: returned home from Missouri
Thomas Young: returned home from Missouri

Appendix C

A Discussion of Firsthand Accounts
of Company Men and Their Wives

The first-person voice of the Newark Overland Company, captured with pen during the cross-country travel and the early days in the mining region can be attributed to twelve men—more than one-quarter of the membership. Their words are recorded in six journals and more than forty letters, some intended to be strictly private, and others written for public interest and shared in the *Newark Daily Advertiser*. Letters from two wives provide additional voices and perspectives from the home front. Another ten written items express sentiments from the company men who participated in the Civil War. The authors are listed below according to the amount of their writing.

CHARLES B. GILLESPIE

Letters: nine private, six published in *Newark Daily Advertiser*, two
    military
Journals: August 1, 1849–October 25, 1849; December 20, 1850–April 24,
    1851

Certainly, the largest variety of personal voice came from Charles B. Gillespie, whose letters and journal entries were written as much for entertainment as for information. Rather than recording weather, mileage, and scientific observation, Gillespie wrote narratives of trail encounters and of the circus atmosphere he found in California. His story-like accounts contain few dates, which explains why citations from his journal are referenced by page number instead of date. The 1849 overland journal entries were rewritten on larger letter sheets, but the journal of his return home in 1851 appears to be the original four-by-six-inch leather-backed volume.

Nearly forty years after the gold rush two of Gillespie's forty-niner stories were published in *Century Magazine* (1890–91). He also sent many of his sketches to *Century*, and they were shared, in turn, with noted artists of the time. Frederic Remington produced an engraving of Fort Laramie based on Gillespie's work (see p. 122). The locations and dates he wrote on some of the original sketches are misidentified, and this may have been done while Gillespie was working with *Century*. For example, one sketch is labeled "Falls of the Columbia River," another "Donner Lake," neither of which were on Gillespie's route to California.

CHARLES GEDNEY GRAY
Letters: two or three published in *Newark Daily Advertiser*
Journal: May 1, 1849–November 19, 1849, plus two pages of notes
   February 26, 1849–April 30, 1849

Charles G. Gray was the most prolific diarist of the Newark Overland Company. Considered the company secretary, Gray kept daily notes of their progress, often adding plaintive comments regarding trail life. Examination of Gray's two volumes reveals remarkably clean writing, absent of crossed-out words or other corrections. This, along with the concise page numbering and the consistency of each entry, suggests that Gray, like many who kept trail records, copied his work once in California, taking care to preserve the authenticity. Gray did not refrain from topics such as religion and his passion for literature. When referring to his comrades, he often refrained from mentioning anyone by name, a trend found in many contemporary diaries, perhaps done in consideration that their words might one day be made public. Private letters, on the other hand, spoke more freely. Gray's journal is currently in the possession of the Huntington Library in San Marino, California, where it was transcribed and annotated by Dr. Thomas D. Clark and published as *Off at Sunrise* (Huntington, 1976). Not included in Clark's work were the entries prior to May 1, 1849, which appear to be an afterthought on Gray's part, further suggesting that he may have rewritten the account after reaching California.

CYRUS CURRIER
Letters: two private to wife Nancy, one published in *Newark Daily Advertiser*
Journal: March 16, 1849–July 24, 1849

Nancy Currier
Letters: three private to Cyrus

Newark mechanic Cyrus Currier's letters to his wife, Nancy, along with a daily journal provide a different flavor of firsthand account. His diary entries were fewer than Gray's, due in part to his record-setting overland journey, which covered the distance in four months and one week, while Gray's entries were made over six months. As a writer, Currier struggled with punctuation and spelling (which was often phonetic), but his New England practicality comes through loud and clear. The letters between Cyrus and Nancy reveal a trusting relationship, with Cyrus progressively supporting and encouraging his wife to manage the family finances and make her own decisions in his absence. Their concern for each other's health and well-being is expressed lovingly in every correspondence. Typical of private letters, Cyrus and Nancy mentioned names freely, clearly identifying the activities of fellow travelers. A microfilm copy of Currier's original handwritten journal along with a transcription of the work is available in the Wyoming State Archives in Cheyenne. The current whereabouts of the original is unknown.

Stephen Harris Meeker
Letters: four published in *Newark Daily Advertiser* (1849–50), three
    private (1851–60)
Journal: May 24, 1849–July 18, 1849, published in *Newark Daily
    Advertiser*

Caroline Meeker
Letter: one private to sister-in-law

Caroline Meeker's feminine perspective and detailed descriptions of her first journey to California, including the perils of crossing the Isthmus of Panama, were written to her sister-in-law, from whom she requested privacy. On the contrary, her husband's words were likely written for public consumption, as his journal accounts of the trail (through July 18, 1849) and observations of the Mormon settlement in Salt Lake City were published in the *Newark Daily Advertiser*. Even S. H. Meeker's private letters seemed to anticipate a wider readership, and he described California life both vividly and quantitatively. While Meeker clearly kept a journal and some entries found their way to the *Newark Daily Advertiser*, no journal has been found. It is very possible that it perished in the fire of 1852 that destroyed his Sacramento business.

John S. Darcy
Letters: eight published in *Newark Daily Advertiser*

The voluminous letters of John S. Darcy were also shared with the *Newark Daily Advertiser*. Darcy wrote detailed summaries of the journey, including the idle days in Independence, the layover in Salt Lake City, and latter months wintering in Sacramento. Editors may have chosen to edit Darcy's accounts, as the deaths of Bond and Denman are not included in the published record.

Alexander Joy Cartwright Jr.
Journal: April 24, 1849–June 5, 1849

The journal of Alexander Cartwright is held in the Bernice Pauahi Bishop Museum in Honolulu and has inspired speculation and controversy concerning its authenticity. It has been suggested that the copy is not in his handwriting and was rewritten decades after 1849 to promote Cartwright's role in baseball history. While baseball was not a focus of this book, the document's legitimacy is important to the research. Evidence suggests that Cartwright's journal *was* rewritten, particularly with his introductory page describing his arrival in California, which would have only been written post-travel. It appears that Cartwright himself, like Gray, made a clean copy of his journal shortly after completing his journey. Following the entries of his overland travel in 1849, Cartwright made daily notes of his voyage back to California in June 1850, supporting an 1850 provenance for the journal. More compelling clues that Cartwright rewrote the journal soon after 1849 are the "address book" entries in the back of the volume. One address, for example, is that of S. H. Meeker in Sacramento, where he resided only prior to 1855. If the rewrite of Cartwright's journal was done decades later, why would addresses from the early 1850s be included? Furthermore, beside Meeker's name and several others, in different ink and handwriting, is the notation "Dead"—suggesting that Cartwright updated the address list over time. Meeker died in 1863. The decades-later theory raises another question: why would entries for dead men be made, only to be crossed off?

Appendix C

Robert Bond
Journal: March 1, 1849–July 17, 1849

Another Newark Overland Company diarist was Robert Bond, whose words were disappointingly sparse. Yet, in his few words, Bond provided names when Gray and others did not. By cross-referencing, it was possible to connect individuals by name with situations discussed in other journals. Where Gray wrote entries about a missing man, Bond's simple "Mr. Baldwin lost till noon next day" connected the pieces of the puzzle. Bond's entries ceased after the company's stay in Salt Lake City, and then within a month he was dead. The journal made its way back to his family and later to the Western Americana Collection of the Beineke Rare Book and Manuscript Library at Yale University.

Joseph H. Martin
Letters: three published in *Newark Daily Advertiser*

Joseph H. Martin sent letters to the *Newark Daily Advertiser*, giving grim details of the journey and of California life. He wrote with a degree of disgust and melancholy and broke the news of Wallace Cook's death.

John W. Shaff
Letters: two or three published in *Newark Daily Advertiser*

John Shaff wrote from Independence, Missouri, where he gave a clue that Augustus Baldwin had turned back for home, and from California, where he described it as a place of adventure, recounting abundant wildlife and rampant gambling.

Isaac Overton
Letters: two or three published in *Newark Daily Advertiser*

Isaac Overton's letter from Independence, Missouri, suggested that he was departing with Cartwright, Seely, and Woolsey. On arrival in California he wrote a matter-of-fact report of his final days crossing the Sierra Nevada and provided news of Darcy's whereabouts and observations on San Francisco. The *Newark Daily Advertiser* printed Overton's letter, identifying him by his initials. However, a common printing mistake (swapping "I" and "J") led some to believe that it was penned by John

Overton, not Isaac. Research confirmed that John Overton had not yet arrived in San Francisco when the letter was dated.

AUGUSTUS BALDWIN
Letters: one private to wife Mary

The private letter from Augustus Baldwin to his wife, written during the first week of travel to Missouri was never meant for anyone but Mary. It was personal, colorful, and shared names, providing the best record of the trip from New Jersey to Missouri.

W. DONALDSON KINNEY, BENJAMIN CASTERLINE, OR
LEWIS B. BALDWIN
Letters: one or two published in *Newark Daily Advertiser*

The *Newark Daily Advertiser* published letters identified as having been shared by a Newark resident whose son was with the Darcy company. By default this would have been W. Donaldson Kinney, Benjamin Casterline, or Lewis B. Baldwin. The most likely author was Kinney.

JOHN R. CROCKETT
Letters: two military, Civil War

JOSEPH FREEMAN
Letters: one private, Civil War

Notes

Bond Diary   Bond, Robert, Diary, 1849. Yale Collection of Western Americana, Beinecke Rare Book and Manuscript Library, Yale University.

Cartwright Journal Cartwright, Alexander Joy, Jr. "Journal of a trip across the Plains from Independence to San Francisco via South Pass, Rocky Mountains, and the Sierra Nevada." MS Doc 55, Bernice Pauahi Bishop Museum Archives, Honolulu, Hawaii.

Currier Journal Currier, Cyrus. "Journal to California by the Northern Overland Route from Newark, State of New Jersey." H-77. Wyoming State Archives, Cheyenne.

Currier Papers Currier, Cyrus and Nancy, Letters and Bible records. Private collection of Nancy Currier Dorian and Ewen Currier McEwen.

Gillespie Journal Gillespie, Charles B., Journal, 4 August–25 October 1849. Copy given to authors on 25 February 2014 by great-grandson Richard M. Rogers.

Gillespie Papers Gillespie, Charles B., Papers, journals, letters, sketches and paintings. Copies given to authors on 25 February 2014 by great-grandson Richard M. Rogers.

Gray Journal   Gray, Charles G. "Journal of an Overland Passage from Independence Missouri to San Francisco, California in 1849." HM 16520. Huntington Library, San Marino, California.

PROLOGUE

1. *New York Times*, 18 December 1912.

2. Ibid.

3. Plot diagram, Lot 4, Section A, Evergreen Cemetery, Hillside, New Jersey, copy in authors' possession; *New York Times*, 31 December 1926.

Chapter 1

1. *Newark Daily Advertiser*, 21 November 1848.
2. Ibid.
3. *Arkansas State Democrat*, 21 January 1848.
4. Young, *Sketch of the Life*, 368.
5. *Newark Daily Advertiser*, 22, 24 November 1848.
6. Ibid.
7. Ibid.
8. Ibid.
9. Ibid.
10. Shaw, *History of Essex and Hudson Counties*, 1:224.
11. *New York Herald*, 17 September 1848.
12. *Californian*, 15 March 1848.
13. Sutter and Marshall, "Discovery of Gold in California."
14. *Californian*, 19 April 1848.
15. *Newark Daily Advertiser*, 2 December 1848.
16. Ibid., 11 December 1848.
17. Ibid., 24 October 1848.
18. Ibid., 1 November 1848.
19. *Baltimore Sun*, 28 November 1848.
20. *Newark Daily Advertiser*, 9 December 1848.
21. Ibid.
22. *Newark Mercury*, 10 February 1849.
23. Ibid., 30 January 1849.
24. *Newark Daily Advertiser*, 19 December 1848.
25. Ibid., 2 December 1848.
26. *Daily National Intelligencer*, 4 December 1848.
27. Ibid.
28. Ibid.
29. *North American and United States Gazette*, 14 September 1848.
30. *New York Herald*, 17 September 1848.

Chapter 2

1. *Trenton Federalist*, 27 September 1824.
2. Ibid.
3. Ibid.; Wickes, *History of Medicine in New Jersey*, 225–26.
4. Pitney, *History of Morris County New Jersey*, 1:49–50.
5. Wickes, *History of Medicine in New Jersey*, 226; John S. Darcy to Timothy J. Darcy, 28 October 1851, Timothy J. Darcy Papers.
6. John S. Darcy to Timothy J. Darcy, 28 October 1851.
7. Lee, *Genealogical and Memorial History*, 1:328–29; Johnson, *George Washington the Christian*, 86–88.
8. Halsey, *History of the Washington Association*, 17.
9. "John S. Darcy," 100–101.
10. Shaw, *History of Essex and Hudson Counties*, 1:193–94.

11. Ibid.

12. Lee, *Genealogical History*, 1:329.

13. Urquhart, *History of the City of Newark*, 1:489.

14. "John S. Darcy," 100–101.

15. *New York Spectator*, 25 November 1833.

16. Urquhart, *History of the City of Newark*, 2:819–20; *Newark Daily Advertiser*, 13 June 1835.

17. Shaw, *History of Essex and Hudson Counties*, 1:194.

18. "New Jersey Colonization Society," 151–52; "Forty-Seventh Annual Report of the American Colonization Society," 33.

19. Nestell, "Case of Strangulated Inguinal Hernia," 179–81.

Chapter 3

1. Wickes, *History of Medicine in New Jersey*, 227.

2. Gillespie, "Prairie Sketches No. 3," 59; Gillespie biography and 1841–42 sketches, Gillespie Papers.

3. *Butler Citizen*, 6, 8 August 1907; Blanchard, *Progressive Men of the Commonwealth of Pennsylvania*, 1:163.

4. Beers, *Armstrong County Pennsylvania*, 1:157; Smith, *History of Armstrong County, Pennsylvania*, 409.

5. *Butler Times*, 6 August 1907.

6. C. B. Gillespie, "Leaves from My Journal," January 1845, 153.

7. Ibid.

8. Ibid.

9. Ibid., 154.

10. Gillespie biography, Gillespie Papers.

11. *Butler Citizen*, 8 August 1907; *Butler Times*, 6 August 1907; Harris, *Harris' General Business Directory*, 28, 116.

12. "Rembrandt Lockwood's Painting of the Last Judgment," 185–86; "Rembrandt Lockwood," *Art & Architecture of New Jersey*, Richard Stockton College of New Jersey, www.ettc.net/njarts/details.cfm?ID=2, accessed 4 November 2011.

13. Gillespie typescript, "Correspondence of the Morning Post, Harrisburg, January 21, 1848," Gillespie Papers.

14. Karl [Charles B. Gillespie], "(Correspondence of the Worthy Visitor) Newark, New Jersey, July 5th, 1848," Gillespie Papers.

15. *Newark Daily Advertiser*, 1 December 1848.

Chapter 4

1. *Boston Courier*, 1 January 1849; *Daily National Intelligencer*, 20 December 1848.

2. Phillips, *Historic Letters*, 33–34; *Daily National Intelligencer*, 14 November 1848.

3. *Newark Daily Advertiser*, 4 January 1849.

4. *Newark Mercury*, 13 February 1849.

5. *Newark Daily Advertiser*, 27 January 1849.

6. Ruiz, "The Argonauts."

7. *New York Herald*, 3 February 1849.

8. *Milwaukee Sentinel and Gazette*, 3 February 1849.

9. *Boston Courier*, 1 January 1849.

10. *Newark Daily Advertiser*, 3 January 1849.

11. Ibid., 9 December 1848.

12. Kull, "New Brunswick Adventurers of '49," 13; *Newark Daily Advertiser*, 8 January 1849.

13. *Newark Daily Advertiser*, 5, 10, 17, 24 January 1849.

14. Ibid., 23 January 1849.

15. Ibid.

16. Ibid., 17 February 1848.

17. *Arkansas State Democrat*, 29 December 1848.

18. *Newark Daily Advertiser*, 23 January 1849.

19. *New York Herald*, 30 December 1848.

20. *Newark Daily Advertiser*, 23 January 1849.

21. Ibid., 24 January 1849.

22. 1850 US Federal Census, S. Ward City of Newark, Essex County, New Jersey, 30 August 1850; Jobes/Gallagher Marriage Record, Newark, Essex County, New Jersey, 13 February 1849.

23. Gray Journal, 13 October 1849.

24. *Newark Morning Eagle*, 2 March 1849.

25. *San Francisco Daily Evening Bulletin*, 25 May 1891; Clark, *National Register*, 132. Spelling for Captain Obadiah Meeker Sr. is also found as "Obediah."

26. Holdredge, *House of the Strange Woman*, 57; *Brooklyn Eagle*, 29 October 1841.

27. *North American and Daily Advertiser*, 14 March 1844; Pierson, *Directory of the City of Newark for 1849–50*, 159.

28. Peshine, *Peshine Family*, 58.

29. Shaw, *History of Essex and Hudson Counties*, 1:224; Lee, *New Jersey as a Colony and as a State*, 5:17–21.

30. Shaw, *History of Essex and Hudson Counties*, 1:193–94.

31. *Newark Daily Advertiser*, 23 October 1863.

32. Ibid., 13 July 1896.

33. Ibid., 24 August 1870.

34. Pierson, *Directory of the City of Newark for 1848–49*, 73.

35. *Newark Daily Advertiser*, 19 April 1848.

36. Ann E. Casterline, 1850 US Federal Census, New Jersey, Ward 5, City of Newark, Essex County, 11 September 1850; Casterline/Titus Marriage Record, Hopewell Township, Mercer County, New Jersey, 27 September 1848.

37. Flynn, *History of St. John's Church*, 40; Urquhart, *History of the City of Newark, New Jersey*, 2:665–66.

38. Jobes/Gallagher Marriage Record, Newark, Essex County, New Jersey, 13 February 1849.

39. Urquhart, *History of the City of Newark, New Jersey*, 2:666.

40. Henry Ashfield Jobes, Baptism Record, St. Paul's Church, Newark, New Jersey, 16 January 1849.

41. *Newark Daily Advertiser*, 16 February 1849.

42. Kull, "New Brunswick Adventurers of '49," 13, 16.

CHAPTER 5

1. Stuart-Wortley, *Travels in the United States*, 1:283.
2. Cartwright Journal, 24 May 1849; *Newark Morning Eagle*, 2 March 1849.
3. William Woolsey, 1850 US Federal Census, Jersey City, Hudson County, New Jersey, 16 August 1850.
4. US Passport Applications, State of New York, 21 February 1849, National Archives and Records Administration.
5. Stuart-Wortley, *Travels in the United States*, 1:284–85.
6. Ibid.
7. *New York Times*, 12 December 1901; Alexander J. Cartwright, US Passport Application, State of New York, 20 February 1849, National Archives and Records Administration.
8. Nucciarone, *Alexander Cartwright*, 6–8.
9. Ibid.
10. *North American and United States Gazette*, 10 February 1849.
11. *Daily National Intelligencer*, 27 August 1849.
12. *Boston Daily Atlas*, 25 August 1849.
13. Ibid., 11 August 1849.
14. Cartwright Journal, front page.
15. Flint, *A Peters Lineage*, 61; Gray Journal, 10 May, 23 June, 19 November 1849.
16. Flint, *A Peters Lineage*, 61; Will of Jacob Gray, 2203N, New Jersey Archives, Trenton.
17. Gray Journal, 8 May 1849; Bond Diary, 8 May 1849. "Mess" refers to a group living out of the same wagon and sharing provisions with an agreed-upon division of labor.
18. Flint, *A Peters Lineage*, 60–61.
19. Gray Journal, 7 October 1849.
20. Ibid., 19 August, 24 September 1849, Gray's will, dated 25 August 1849, located on the last two pages of the journal.
21. Oral history of William T. Lewis family, Lewis Family Papers.
22. Charles B. Gillespie to My Dear Sister, 18 May 1849, Gillespie Papers.

CHAPTER 6

1. Unless otherwise noted, information for this chapter comes from *Newark Morning Eagle* and *Newark Daily Advertiser*, 20 February 1849.
2. *Newark Daily Advertiser*, 2 March 1849.

CHAPTER 7

1. Unless otherwise noted, information for this chapter comes from Augustus Baldwin to My Dear Mary, Cincinnati, Ohio, 27 February 1849, private collection of Marian Wilkin Fleming.
2. Smith, *President Zachary Taylor*, 154.

3. *Cleveland Herald*, 24 February 1849.

4. Bowen, *A Blind Man's Offering*, 340.

5. Greeley, *Recollections of a Busy Life*, 557–59.

Chapter 8

1. *Newark Morning Eagle*, 2 March 1849.

2. Ibid.; *Newark Daily Advertiser*, 29 March 1849.

3. Price, *Family Record*, 16–17; Ricord, *History of Union County*, 1:438; Urquhart, *History of the City of Newark*, 2:965.

4. Gray Journal, 24–25 August 1849.

5. *Newark Daily Advertiser*, 13 December 1848.

6. Canfield, *A History of Thomas Canfield and of Matthew Camfield*, 97.

7. *Newark Morning Eagle*, 2 March 1849.

8. Ibid.

9. Bond Diary, front page, 2 March 1849.

10. *Newark Daily Advertiser*, 2 March 1849.

11. "Seen the Elephant" was a phrase common in the mid-nineteenth century, largely referring to seeing or taking part in something extraordinary, as in having a once-in-a-lifetime experience (in a positive context) or surviving an extremely difficult situation (in a negative context).

12. *Sentinel of Freedom*, 8 May 1849.

13. *Newark Daily Advertiser*, 29 March 1849.

14. Bond Diary, 3 March 1849.

15. *Newark Daily Advertiser*, 29 March 1849.

16. Bond Diary, 9–18 March 1849.

17. *Newark Daily Advertiser*, 29 March 1849.

18. Ibid., 17 March 1849.

19. Ibid., 2 December 1848.

20. Ibid., 29 March 1849.

21. Currier Journal, 16–27 March 1849.

22. *Newark Mercury*, 12 March 1849.

23. Unruh, *The Plains Across*, 100.

24. *Newark Daily Advertiser*, 19 March 1849.

25. Unruh, *The Plains Across*, 100.

26. Currier Journal, 20–30 March 1849.

27. Ibid.

28. Nancy M. Currier to Dear Husband Dear Cyrus, 18 March 1849, Currier Papers.

29. *Sentinel of Freedom*, 8 May 1849.

30. *Newark Daily Advertiser*, 19 March 1849.

31. Denslow, *10,000 Famous Freemasons*.

32. Kelly, *Across the Rocky Mountains*, 1:35, 37.

33. *Newark Daily Advertiser*, 13 April 1849.

34. Ibid., 10 May 1849.

35. Charles Gillespie to My Dear Mary, 1 April 1849, Gillespie Papers.

36. *Newark Daily Advertiser*, 13 April 1849; Cartwright Journal, front page.
37. Currier Journal, 27 March, 4–5 April 1849.
38. *Newark Daily Advertiser*, 27 April 1849.
39. Ibid., 13 April 1849.
40. *New Jersey Journal*, 1 May 1849.
41. *Newark Daily Advertiser*, 20 April 1849; Bond Diary, 21–29 March 1849.
42. Currier Journal, 31 March 1849.
43. *Newark Daily Advertiser*, 20 April 1849; Bond Diary, 24 March 1849.
44. *Cleveland Herald*, 13 November 1848.
45. *Newark Daily Advertiser*, 17 November 1848.
46. Bond Diary, 16 April 1849.
47. *Newark Daily Advertiser*, 5 May 1849.
48. Ibid., 10 May 1849.
49. Ibid., 17 May 1849.
50. Gray Journal, 10 June 1849.

Chapter 9

1. *Daily Picayune*, 26 January 1894; Polk, *The Island of California*, 121–32.
2. *North American and United States Gazette*, 9 December 1848.
3. Bigelow, *Memoir of the Life of Public Services of John Charles Fremont*, 40–41.
4. *Emancipator & Republican*, 7 March 1850; *New Hampshire Statesman*, 31 December 1847.
5. Starr, *California*, 64–66.
6. *Emancipator & Republican*, 7 March 1850; *Daily National Intelligencer*, 15 May 1846.
7. Starr, *California*, 64.
8. *Boston Daily Atlas*, 15 February 1848.
9. *Californian*, 13 February 1847.
10. *Daily National Intelligencer*, 2 September 1847.
11. *Vermont Chronicle*, 1 March 1848.
12. *Cleveland Herald*, 26 February 1848.
13. *Scioto Gazette*, 9 May 1850.
14. *Daily National Intelligencer*, 19 March 1849.
15. Ibid., 31 May 1849.
16. *New York Herald*, 3 February 1849.
17. *Boston Daily Atlas*, 4 June 1849.
18. *Newark Daily Advertiser*, 13 August 1849; *Californian*, 23 February 1848.
19. *Newark Daily Advertiser*, 6 August 1849, 24 July 1849.
20. *Boston Daily Atlas*, 25 June 1849; *Newark Daily Advertiser*, 15 August 1849.
21. *New York Herald*, 19 May 1849.
22. *Boston Daily Atlas*, 25 June 1849.
23. *North American and United States Gazette*, 1 March 1849.
24. *Californian*, 21 October 1848.
25. *Greenville Mountaineer*, 20 April 1849; *Alta California*, 7 June 1849.
26. *New York Herald*, 17 May 1849.

27. *Newark Daily Advertiser*, 15 August 1849.
28. *Alta California*, 7 June 1849.

CHAPTER 10

1. Mattes, *The Great Platte River Road*, 15.
2. *Milwaukee Sentinel and Gazette*, 23 May 1849.
3. Charles B. Gillespie to My Dear Sister, 22 April 1849, Gillespie Papers.
4. *North American and United Stated Gazette*, 27 April 1849.
5. Bruff, *Gold Rush*, 4.
6. Gordon, *Overland to California*, 30; Unruh, *The Plains Across*, 101.
7. Currier Journal, 16 April 1849; *Newark Daily Advertiser*, 1 May 1849; Cartwright Journal, front page.
8. Currier Journal, 9–16 April 1849.
9. *North American and United States Gazette*, 31 May 1949.
10. *Newark Daily Advertiser*, 1 May 1849; Currier Journal, 12 April 1849; Gray Journal, 14 April 1849; *North American and United States Gazette*, 27 April 1849.
11. Kelly, *Across the Rocky Mountains*, 37, 44.
12. Currier Journal, 14–16 April 1849.
13. Gillespie to sister, 22 April 1849.
14. *Newark Daily Advertiser*, 17 May 1849.
15. Kelly, *Across the Rocky Mountains*, 41.
16. Gillespie to sister, 22 April 1849.
17. Currier Journal, 21–24 April 1849; Cartwright Journal, 24 April 1849.
18. Cartwright Journal, 26 April 1849.
19. *New Jersey Journal*, 1 May 1849.
20. Nancy Currier to Dear Cyrus, 20 May 1849, Currier Papers.
21. Currier Journal, 14 April 1849.
22. Lee, *Genealogical and Memorial History*, 1:329.
23. Kelly, *Across the Rocky Mountains*, 47.
24. Cartwright Journal, 27 April 1849.
25. Kelly, *Across the Rocky Mountains*, 63.
26. Cartwright Journal, 26 April 1849.
27. Kelly, *Across the Rocky Mountains*, 51–52.
28. Ibid., 53.
29. Cartwright Journal, 27 April 1849.
30. Ibid.
31. Kelly, *Across the Rocky Mountains*, 53.
32. Ibid., 77.
33. Bond Diary, 1 May 1849; Gray Journal, 1 May 1849.
34. Gray Journal, 2 May 1849.
35. Currier Journal, 17 April 1849.
36. *Newark Daily Advertiser*, 17 May 1849.
37. Ibid., 12 November 1849.
38. Gray Journal, 3–4 May 1849.
39. Ibid., 5 May 1849.

40. Ibid., 6 May 1849.
41. Ibid., 10 May 1849.
42. Ranney, *Account of Terrific and Fatal Riot*, 5–6, 7–9, 29.
43. Ibid.
44. Gray Journal, 10 May 1849.

CHAPTER 11

1. Decker, *The Diaries of Peter Decker*, 75.
2. Kelly, *Across the Rocky Mountains*, 78.
3. Mattes, *The Great Platte River Road*, 168–69.
4. *New York Herald*, 17 September 1848.
5. Mattes, *The Great Platte River Road*, 168–71.
6. Kelly, *Across the Rocky Mountains*, 75.
7. Bruff, *Gold Rush*, 17.
8. *Missouri Courier*, 12 July 1849.
9. Cartwright Journal, 19 May 1849.
10. Delano, *Life on the Plains*, 48–49.
11. Decker, *The Diaries of Peter Decker*, 75.
12. Gray Journal, 10 May 1849.
13. Ibid., 12 May 1849.
14. Ibid., 13 May 1849.
15. Kelly, *Across the Rocky Mountains*, 96.
16. Ibid., 88.
17. Currier Journal, 13 May 1849.
18. Gray Journal, 17 May 1849.
19. Charles B. Gillespie to My Dear Sister, 18 May 1849, Gillespie Papers.
20. Ibid.
21. *Newark Daily Advertiser*, 16 June 1849.
22. Cartwright Journal, 20 May 1849.
23. Kelly, *Across the Rocky Mountains*, 43, 54.
24. Cartwright Journal, 19 May 1849.
25. Ibid.
26. Kelly, *Across the Rocky Mountains*, 105–8.
27. Currier Journal, 19 May 1849.
28. Gray Journal, 19 May 1849.
29. Bond Diary, 19 May 1849; Gray Journal, 20 May 1849.
30. Gray Journal, 21 May 1849.
31. Ibid., 22 May 1849.
32. Ibid., 20 May 1849.
33. Ibid., 23 May 1849.
34. Ibid., 21 May 1849.
35. Bond Diary, 20–23 May 1849.
36. Gray Journal, 24 May 1849.
37. Kull, "New Brunswick Adventurers of '49," 18–22. "Cape pigeon" is another name for the Cape petrel.

38. *Liberator*, 25 May 1849.
39. Cartwright Journal, 19 May 1849.

CHAPTER 12

1. Gray Journal, 6 June 1849; Kelly, *Across the Rocky Mountains*, 107–8.
2. Cartwright Journal, 19 May 1849.
3. Ibid., 4, 17–18 May 1849.
4. Ibid., 24 May 1849; Currier Journal, 24 May 1849.
5. Bruff, *Gold Rush*, 594–95.
6. Cartwright Journal, 24 May 1849.
7. Ibid., 25 May 1849; *New Jersey Journal*, 1 May 1849.
8. Cartwright Journal, 25 May 1849.
9. Ibid.
10. Gray Journal, 26 May 1849.
11. Ibid., 25 May 1849.
12. *Newark Daily Advertiser*, 23 August 1849.
13. Gray Journal, 27 May 1849.
14. Ibid., 29 May 1849.
15. Ibid., 30 May 1849.
16. Ibid., 31 May 1849.
17. Ibid.
18. Cartwright Journal, 26–27 May 1849.
19. Ibid., 27 May 1849; Currier Journal, 27 May 1849.
20. Cartwright Journal, 27 May 1849.
21. Kelly, *Across the Rocky Mountains*, 126–27.
22. Cartwright Journal, 1 June 1849.
23. Gray Journal, 1 June 1849.
24. Ibid.
25. Ibid., 2–4 June 1849; *Newark Daily Advertiser*, 23 August 1849.
26. Gray Journal, 2–4 June 1849; *Newark Daily Advertiser*, 23 August 1849.
27. Gray Journal, 2–4 June 1849; *Newark Daily Advertiser*, 23 August 1849.
28. Gray Journal, 5–7 June 1849.
29. Cartwright Journal, 2 June 1849; Currier Journal, 2 June 1849; Kelly, *Across the Rocky Mountains*, 130–33.
30. Currier Journal, 4 June 1849.
31. Ibid., 8 June 1849.
32. Ibid., 10 June 1849; Cartwright Journal, front page.
33. Gray Journal, 10 June 1849.
34. Ibid.
35. Delano, *Life on the Plains*, 64.
36. Gray Journal, 10 June 1849.
37. Ibid., 11 June 1849.
38. *Newark Daily Advertiser*, 23 August 1849.
39. Gray Journal, 12–13 June 1849.
40. Ibid.

41. *Newark Daily Advertiser*, 16 October 1849.
42. Sketches of Pikes Peak, Gillespie Papers.
43. Gray Journal, 14 June 1849.
44. Ibid., 16–17 June 1849.
45. Mattes, *The Great Platte River Road*, 40–41.
46. Gray Journal, 17 June 1849.
47. *New York Herald*, 24 August 1848.
48. Gray Journal, 17 June 1849; *Newark Daily Advertiser*, 16 October 1849.
49. Gray Journal, 17 June 1849.
50. Ibid., 18 June 1849.
51. Delano, *Life on the Plains*, 90–91.
52. Gray Journal, 18 June 1849.
53. *Newark Daily Advertiser*, 16 October 1849; Potter, *Trail to California*, 111.
54. Gray Journal, 19 June 1849; *Newark Daily Advertiser*, 16 October 1849.
55. Gray Journal, 19 June 1849; *Newark Daily Advertiser*, 16 October 1849.
56. Delano, *Life on the Plains*, 90–91.
57. Gray Journal, 19 June 1849; *Newark Daily Advertiser*, 16 October 1849.
58. Gray Journal, 19 June 1849; *Newark Daily Advertiser*, 16 October 1849.
59. Gray Journal, 19 June 1849; *Newark Daily Advertiser*, 16 October 1849.
60. Gray Journal, 19 June 1849; *Newark Daily Advertiser*, 16 October 1849.
61. Madsen, *Gold Rush Sojourners*, 22–24.
62. Kelly, *Across the Rocky Mountains*, 157.

Chapter 13

1. *New York Herald*, 25 June 1849.
2. Ibid.
3. *Cleveland Herald*, 18 June 1849.
4. *Newark Daily Advertiser*, 15 June 1849.
5. Ibid., 25 June 1849.
6. Ibid., 10 November 1849.
7. Ibid., 26 June 1849.

Chapter 14

1. *Newark Daily Advertiser*, 13 December 1848.
2. Delano, *Life on the Plains*, 90–91.
3. *Newark Daily Advertiser*, 8 October 1849.
4. Ibid., 16 October 1849; Gray Journal, 20 June 1849.
5. Gray Journal, 26 June 1849.
6. Decker, *The Diaries of Peter Decker*, 105.
7. Bruff, *Gold Rush*, 53.
8. *Ohio Observer*, 24 October 1849.
9. Gray Journal, 29 June 1849.
10. Ibid., 25 June 1849.

11. Ibid., 5 July 1849.

12. Ibid., 5 July, 16 September 1849.

13. Ibid., 30 June 1849.

14. Ibid., 28 June, 1 July 1849.

15. Ibid., 1–4 July 1849.

16. Ibid.

17. Ibid.; *Newark Daily Advertiser*, 1 October 1849.

18. Gray Journal, 3 July 1849.

19. Kull, "New Brunswick Adventurers of '49," 20–21.

20. Ibid.

21. Gray Journal, 7 July 1849; Alter, *Jim Bridger*, 233–34; *Pinedale Roundup*, 11 February 1932.

22. Gray Journal, 13 July 1849; Madsen, *Gold Rush Sojourners*, 21.

23. Madsen, *Gold Rush Sojourners*, 22–24.

24. Gray Journal, 10 July 1849.

25. Ibid., 9–14 July 1849.

26. Ibid., 14 July 1849.

27. *Newark Daily Advertiser*, 8 October 1849.

28. Gray Journal, 14–15 July 1849.

29. Ibid.

30. Ibid., 14–15 July 1849.

31. *Newark Daily Advertiser*, 6, 8, 13 October 1849; Bond Diary, 15 July 1849.

32. Gray Journal, 14–17 July 1849; *Newark Daily Advertiser*, 13 October 1849.

33. *Newark Daily Advertiser*, 8 October 1849; Kelly, *Across the Rocky Mountains*, 161–62.

34. *Cleveland Herald*, 23 June 1847, 21 October 1848.

35. Young et al., "Epistle," 337–38.

36. *Newark Daily Advertiser*, 6, 13 October 1849; Gray Journal, 15 July 1849; Bond Diary, 16 July 1849.

37. *Newark Daily Advertiser*, 8 October 1849.

38. *Boston Investigator*, 24 October 1849.

39. Gray Journal, 14 July 1849.

40. Thomas Bullock, "Emigrant Rosters, 1849," MS 15494 LDS Church History Library, 27–28.

41. *Newark Daily Advertiser*, 13 October 1849.

42. Gray Journal, 15–16 July 1849.

43. *Newark Daily Advertiser*, 13 October 1849.

44. Ibid.

45. Bond Diary, 17 July 1849.

CHAPTER 15

1. *Newark Daily Advertiser*, 13 August 1849.

2. Ibid., 24 July 1849. "The Celestial Empire" refers to China.

3. Kull, "New Brunswick Adventurers of '49," 24.

4. *Newark Daily Advertiser*, 15 August, 1849.

5. Ibid., 6, 15 August, 1849.
6. Ibid., 14 September 1849.
7. Ibid., 15 August, 14 September 1849.
8. Ibid., 13 August 1849.
9. Ibid., 14 August 1849.
10. Ibid., 24 July, 13, 15 August 1849.
11. Ibid., 14 September 1849.
12. Ibid., 14 August 1849.
13. Ibid., 6 August 1849.
14. Kull, "New Brunswick Adventurers of '49," 24.
15. *Newark Daily Advertiser*, 12 December 1848, 13 March 1849; Sioli, *Historical Souvenir*, 38–39.
16. *Newark Daily Advertiser*, 15 August 1849.
17. Sioli, *Historical Souvenir*, 39.
18. *Placer Times*, 28 July, 1849.
19. Currier Journal, 11 July 1849.
20. Ibid., 12 July 1849.
21. Ibid.
22. Ibid.
23. Ibid., 13–14 July 1849.
24. Ibid.
25. Ibid., 14 July 1849.
26. Ibid., 16 July 1849.
27. Ibid., 17 July 1849.
28. Ibid., 20 July 1849.
29. *Newark Daily Advertiser*, 14 September 1849.
30. Currier Journal, 17 July 1849.
31. Ibid., 20 July 1849.
32. Ibid., 22 July 1849.
33. Ibid., 24 July 1849.
34. *Newark Daily Advertiser*, 23 October 1849.
35. *Placer Times*, 21 July 1849.
36. *Newark Daily Advertiser*, 15 January 1850.
37. Ibid.
38. Ibid.
39. Ibid., 14 September 1849.
40. Ibid.

CHAPTER 16

1. Gray Journal, 22 July 1849.
2. Ibid., 30 July 1849.
3. Ibid., 29 July–4 August 1849.
4. Gillespie Journal, 3.
5. *Newark Daily Advertiser*, 12 November 1849.
6. Gillespie Journal, 1–3.

7. Ibid., 6–7.
8. Ibid., 8–10.
9. Ibid.
10. Ibid.
11. Ibid., 10–11.
12. Ibid., 16.
13. Ibid., 17.
14. Ibid., 18.
15. Ibid., 19–20.
16. Ibid., 21.
17. Ibid.; Currier Journal, 22 July 1849.
18. Gillespie Journal, 25–26.
19. Ibid., 30.
20. Ibid., 27.
21. Ibid., 32.
22. *Newark Daily Advertiser*, 29 September 1849.
23. Potter, *Trail to California*, 201.
24. Perkins, *Gold Rush Diary*, 106.
25. Gray Journal, 14 August 1849.
26. Ibid., 11 August 1849.
27. Hannon, *The Boston-Newton Company Venture*, 185.
28. Gray Journal, 6 August 1849.
29. Kelly, *Across the Rocky Mountains*, 205; *New York Times*, 18 December 1912.
30. Gray Journal, 6 August 1849; oral history of William T. Lewis family.
31. Gray Journal, 13–16 August 1849.
32. Ibid., 19 August 1849.
33. Ibid., 19, 24 August 1849.
34. Ibid., 24 August 1849.
35. Ibid., 18 August 1849.
36. Ibid.
37. Ibid., 16–22 August 1849.

CHAPTER 17

1. *Newark Daily Advertiser*, 10 December 1849.
2. Ibid.
3. Ibid.
4. Ibid., 14 September 1849.
5. Ibid., 12 December 1849.
6. Ibid., 13 February 1850.
7. *Placer Times*, 3 November 1849.
8. *Newark Daily Advertiser*, 15 August 1849.
9. Ibid., 27 November 1849.
10. Ibid., 15 August 1849.
11. Ibid., 15 October 1849.
12. Ibid., 14 November 1849.

13. Ibid., 15 October 1849.

14. Cartwright Journal, front page.

15. Newmark and Newmark, *Sixty Years in Southern California*, 154.

16. *Newark Daily Advertiser*, 18 December 1912.

17. Ibid., 15 January 1850.

18. Bruff, *Gold Rush*, lxi.

19. *Newark Daily Advertiser*, 15 January 1850.

20. Ibid., 24 June 1850.

21. Ibid., 14 September 1849.

22. Gillespie Journal, 40.

23. Ibid., 123–24.

24. Ibid., 114.

25. Ibid.

26. Ibid., 115.

27. Ibid., 116.

28. Ibid., 116–22.

29. Sutter and Marshall, "The Discovery of Gold in California."

30. Gillespie Journal, 122.

31. *Newark Daily Advertiser*, 12 November 1849.

32. Ibid.

33. Ibid., 8 December 1849.

34. Cyrus Currier to Dear and Beloved Wife, 31 October 1849; Nancy M. Currier to My Dear Husband, 11 December 1849, Currier Papers.

35. *Newark Daily Advertiser*, 8 December 1849.

CHAPTER 18

1. *Newark Daily Advertiser*, 14 January 1850.

2. Delano, *Life on the Plains*, 173–74.

3. Ibid., 181–82.

4. Gray Journal, 22 August 1849.

5. Ibid., 24 August 1849.

6. Ibid., 24–26 August 1849.

7. Ibid.

8. Ibid.

9. Ibid.

10. Bruff, *Gold Rush*, 154.

11. Gray Journal, 27 August 1849.

12. Swartzlow, *Lassen*, 50.

13. Gray Journal, 27 August 1849.

14. Ibid., 27 August–1 September 1849.

15. Ibid., 4 September 1849.

16. Ibid., 16 September 1849.

17. Ibid., 6 September 1849.

18. Ibid., 8 September 1849.

19. Ibid., 11 September 1849.

20. Ibid., 13–14 September 1849.

21. Ibid.

22. Ibid.

23. Ibid., 19–21 September 1849.

24. Ibid., 22 September 1849.

25. Gray, *Off at Sunrise*, 99n166; *Newark Daily Advertiser*, 8 December 1849.

26. Gray Journal, 24 September 1849.

27. Ibid., 30 September 1849.

28. Ibid., 25 September–1 October 1849; *Alta California*, 12 December 1849.

29. Ibid., 3 October, 1849.

30. Ibid., 24 October 1849.

31. Ibid., 3–8 October 1849.

32. Ibid., 7–9 October 1849.

33. Ibid.

34. Ibid., 10 October 1849.

35. Ibid., 11–12, 16 October 1849.

36. Ibid., 13 October 1849.

37. Ibid., 17 October 1849.

38. Ibid.

39. Ibid., 19, 24 October 1849.

40. Ibid., 21–25 October 1849.

41. Ibid.

42. *Newark Daily Advertiser*, 10 December 1849. This is actually a combination of two phrases common in the 19th century. "Seen the Elephant" was very commonly used to express experiencing the extraordinary (good and bad). "The real Simon" is from a 1718 play, *A Bold Stroke for a Wife* by Susannah Centlivre, and alludes to a character named Simon who is impersonated by another.

CHAPTER 19

1. *Alta California*, 26 December 1849.

2. *Newark Daily Advertiser*, 8 December 1849.

3. Gray Journal, 25–31 October 1849.

4. Ibid., 1–9 November 1849; *Newark Daily Advertiser*, 23 March 1850.

5. Gray Journal, 9–19 November 1849.

6. Ibid.

7. *Placer Times*, 20 October 1849.

8. Ibid., 29 December 1849.

9. Rowe, *California's Pioneer Circus*, 9–10.

10. *Placer Times*, 3 November, 29 December 1849.

11. *Alta California*, 8 November 1849, reprinted in *Newark Daily Advertiser*, 26 December 1849.

12. *Newark Daily Advertiser*, 8 December 1849.

13. Ibid., 27 December 1849.

14. Ibid., 7 December 1849; Gray Journal, 19 November 1849.

15. Gray Journal, 13–19 November 1849.
16. Ibid.
17. Ibid.
18. Ibid.
19. Ibid.
20. Ibid.
21. Ibid.
22. *Newark Daily Advertiser*, 24 June 1850.
23. Cyrus Currier to Dear and Beloved Wife, 31 October 1849, Currier Papers.
24. Ibid.
25. Nancy M. Currier to My Dear Husband, 11 December 1849, Currier Papers.
26. Ibid.
27. *Newark Daily Advertiser*, 23 March 1850.
28. Ibid.
29. Ibid.
30. *Alta California*, 10 December 1849.
31. *Newark Daily Advertiser*, 8 February 1850.
32. *Placer Times*, 29 December 1849.
33. *Newark Daily Advertiser*, 14 January 1850.
34. *Alta California*, 28 December 1849.
35. Ibid., 26 December 1849.
36. Ibid.
37. Ibid., 31 December 1849.
38. *Placer Times*, 29 December 1849.
39. *Newark Daily Advertiser*, 11 February 1850.
40. Ibid., 23 March 1850.
41. Ibid., 7 December 1849.
42. Ibid.; Nucciarone, *Alexander Cartwright*, 50, 60.
43. *Newark Daily Advertiser*, 26 December 1849.
44. Ibid., 14 December 1849.

CHAPTER 20

1. *Scioto Gazette*, 9 January 1850.
2. *Newark Daily Advertiser*, 2 April 1850.
3. *New Orleans Picayune* story mentioned in *Alta California*, 31 January 1850.
4. *Newark Daily Advertiser*, 10 April 1850.
5. David Meeker to Dear Brother, 27 June 1845, MG 1146, Ward-Meeker Family Papers.
6. *Sacramento Transcript*, 12 April 1850.
7. *Alta California*, 27 January 1850.
8. *Newark Daily Advertiser*, 21 February 1850.
9. Cyrus Currier to Dear and Beloved Wife, 27 January 1850, Currier Papers.
10. *Newark Daily Advertiser*, 12 January 1850.
11. Currier to Wife, 27 January 1850.

12. Ibid.

13. *Alta California*, 2 March, 2 April 1850.

14. Perrin, *History of Delaware County and Ohio*, 714; *Alta California*, 9 February 1850.

15. *Newark Daily Advertiser*, 27 May 1850.

16. Oral history of William T. Lewis family, Lewis Family Papers.

17. *Newark Daily Advertiser*, 8 May 1850.

18. Ibid., 29 March 1850.

19. *Cherokee*, from Chagres, Passenger Manifest, Port of New York, 8 May 1850, *Passenger Lists of Vessels Arriving at New York, New York, 1820–1897*. Microfilm Publication M237, roll 087, line 25. Records of the U.S. Customs Service, Record Group 36. National Archives and Records Administration, Washington, DC.

20. Stuart-Wortley, *Travels in the United States*, 282–83.

21. Cartwright Journal, listed at end.

22. It would be a Cone descendant who would donate Gray's journal to the Huntington Library.

23. *Newark Daily Advertiser*, 30 July 1850.

24. Canfield, *A History of Thomas Canfield and of Matthew Camfield*, 97.

25. Kull, "New Brunswick Adventurers of '49," 25–27.

26. *Newark Daily Advertiser*, 11 April 1850.

27. *Butler Citizen*, 8 August 1907.

28. *Alta California*, 7 September 1850.

29. Ibid., 8 October 1850.

30. Ibid., 19 October 1850.

31. Ibid., 31 October 1850.

32. *Newark Daily Advertiser*, 10 July 1850.

33. *Sacramento Transcript*, 13 December 1850.

34. *Newark Daily Advertiser*, 21 January 1851.

35. Ibid.

36. Ibid., 25 January 1851.

37. "S. H. Meeker, an Original Forty-Niner, Writes about 'El Dorado.' Letter, 24 March 1851," Heritage Auctions, http://historical.ha.com/.

38. *Newark Daily Advertiser*, 19 February 1851.

39. Pierson, *Directory of the City of Newark for 1852–53*, 93.

40. *Crescent City*, from Chagres, Passenger Manifest, Port of New York, 15 March 1851, *Passenger Lists of Vessels Arriving at New York, New York, 1820–1897*. Microfilm Publication M237, roll 096, line 28. Records of the U.S. Customs Service, Record Group 36. National Archives and Records Administration, Washington, DC.

41. *Butler Citizen*, 8 August 1907; sketches from Gillespie Papers.

42. *El Dorado*, from Chagres, Passenger Manifest, Port of New York, 12 April 1851, *Passenger Lists of Vessels Arriving at New York, New York, 1820–1897*. Microfilm Publication M237, roll 097, line 6. Records of the U.S. Customs Service, Record Group 36. National Archives and Records Administration, Washington, DC.

43. Charles B. Gillespie, "Journal from 20 December 1850 to 24 April 1851," Gillespie Papers.

44. Charles B. Gillespie, "Homeward Bound," Gillespie Papers.

45. "The World's Fair in America," 237.

CHAPTER 21

1. *Sacramento Daily Union*, 17 May 1851.

2. Ibid., 21 May 1851; *Sacramento Transcript*, 14 May 1851.

3. "S. H. Meeker, an Original Forty-Niner, Writes about 'El Dorado.' Letter, 24 March 1851," Heritage Auctions, http://historical.ha.com/.

4. Ibid.

5. Ibid.

6. Ibid.

7. Phelps, *Contemporary Biographies of California's Representative Men*, 196–97. John I. Plume was erroneously identified as "John J. Plume" in this source.

8. *New York Times*, 6 October 1851.

9. *Alta California*, 31 December 1851. This article identifies "Scholl" as the Purser, likely a misspelling or printer error.

10. *Marysville Daily Herald*, 8 March 1851.

11. *Sacramento Daily Union*, 14 December 1851.

12. Ibid., 3 January 1852.

13. Ibid., 21 June 1852.

14. Ibid., 11, 12, 14 August 1852.

15. Ibid., 14 October 1852; *Alta California*, 30 September 1852.

16. *Sacramento Daily Union*, 14 October 1852.

17. *New York Herald*, 11 December 1852.

18. *Alta California*, 6 November 1852.

19. Ibid.

20. Ibid.; *New York Herald*, 11 December 1852.

21. *Sacramento Daily Union*, 20 November 1852.

22. Caroline Meeker to My Dear Sister, 30 March 1853, from Margaret Riddle, Meeker Family Papers.

23. Ibid.

24. Ibid.

25. Ibid.

26. Ibid.

27. *Alta California*, 6 February 1853.

28. Ibid.

29. Caroline Meeker to Sister, 30 March 1853.

30. *Newark Daily Advertiser*, 10 January 1853.

31. Ibid., 14 March 1853.

32. *New York Evening World*, 2 April 1890; *New York Times*, 1 April 1890.

33. Wren, *A History of the State of Nevada*, 434–35; *Acts of the Sixty-Sixth General Assembly of the State of New Jersey*, 95.

34. Wren, *A History of the State of Nevada*, 434–35.

35. Ibid.

36. LeCount and Strong, *LeCount & Strong's San Francisco City Directory for the Year 1854*, 94.

37. *Alta California*, 7 October 1853.

38. *Newark Daily Advertiser*, 29 October 1853.

39. Records in Currier family Bible, Currier Papers.

40. *Newark Daily Advertiser*, 9 October 1854.
41. Hurt, "The Rise and Fall of the 'Know Nothings' in California," 36.
42. Bragg, "Knowledge Is Power," 218–19; *Sacramento Daily Union*, 23 October 1855.
43. *California Farmer and Journal of Useful Sciences*, 23 April 1858.
44. *Alta California*, 16 March 1854.
45. Ibid., 30 January 1855.
46. Colville, *San Francisco Directory, 1856–1857*, 147.
47. *California Farmer and Journal of Useful Sciences*, 9 October 1857.
48. Ibid., 17 July 1857.
49. *New York Times*, 6 January 1855.
50. *Sacramento Daily Union*, 3 March 1856.
51. Masten, "Shake Hands?," 382–83.
52. Langley, *San Francisco Directory for the Year 1858*, 140, 216.
53. *California Farmer and Journal of Useful Sciences*, 20 May 1859.
54. *Newark Daily Advertiser*, 1 May 1849.
55. *New York Times*, 17 June 1858.
56. *Newark Daily Advertiser*, 30 November 1855.
57. Currier family Bible.
58. *Butler Citizen*, 8 August 1907.
59. *Sacramento Daily Union*, 3 September 1856.

Chapter 22

1. Miller, *San Francisco's Financial District*, 28; Mechanics' Institute, *Report of the First Industrial Exhibition*, 124–29.
2. Mechanics' Institute, *Report of the First Industrial Exhibition*, xx.
3. Ibid., iii.
4. Ibid., 131.
5. *Marysville Herald*, 23 September 1856.
6. Mechanics' Institute, *Report of the First Industrial Exhibition*, 4, 97.
7. Ibid., 124–29.
8. Ibid., 66, 97, 99; Kirk, "As Jolly as a Clam at High Water," 186–87.
9. Mechanics' Institute, *Report of the First Industrial Exhibition*, xx.
10. *Los Angeles Star*, 26 September 1857.
11. Ibid., 29 May 1858.
12. Ibid.
13. Ibid.
14. Ibid.
15. Ibid., 29 May 1858
16. Ibid., 12 June 1858.
17. *San Francisco Daily Evening Bulletin*, 9 July 1859.
18. *Newark Daily Advertiser*, 7 December 1858.
19. Kirsch, *Baseball and Cricket*, 162.
20. *Newark Daily Advertiser*, 7 December 1858.
21. Ibid., 8 December 1858.

22. Ibid., 10 December 1858.
23. *New York Evening World*, 2 April 1890; *New York Times*, 1 April 1890.
24. Mechanics' Institute, *Report of the Second Industrial Exhibition*, 28.
25. *Alta California*, 16 March 1860.
26. *New York Times*, 23 July 1860.

Chapter 23

1. *Frank Leslie's Illustrated Newspaper*, 16 November 1861.
2. *Lancaster Intelligencer*, 29 October 1861.
3. Gancas, *Dear Teres*, 12.
4. *Lancaster Intelligencer*, 29 October 1861.
5. *Frank Leslie's Illustrated Newspaper*, 16 November 1861.
6. Gibson, *History of the 78th*, 24–25; Gancas, *Dear Teres*, 13–14.
7. *Pittsburgh Gazette and Advertiser*, 18 October 1861.
8. Ibid.
9. Ibid.
10. Ibid.
11. Gancas, *Dear Teres*, 12–13.
12. Gibson, *History of the 78th*, 23–24.
13. "Dust to Dust: [Susan Brunker] Gillespie," typescript for *Freeport Journal*, 21 April 1905, Gillespie Papers.
14. Gancas, *Dear Teres*, 8; Gibson, *History of the 78th*, 24.
15. "Dust to Dust: [Charles B.] Gillespie," typescript for *Freeport Journal*, 9 August 1907, Gillespie Papers.
16. *Sacramento Daily Union*, 6 August 1861.
17. Civil War Pension file, Lewis B. Baldwin (Widow Amanda), Application No. 221963, National Archives and Records Administration, Washington, DC.
18. *Macon Telegraph*, 23 April 1861.
19. Knights of Pythias, *Official Record of Proceedings*, 10588–89.
20. Ibid., 10589.
21. *Newark Daily Advertiser*, 9 July 1862.
22. Compiled Military Service Records, Lewis B. Baldwin, National Archives and Records Administration, Washington, DC.
23. *New York Times*, 19 July 1862.
24. John R. Crockett to Brig. Gen'l L. Thomas, 29 July 1862, Letters Received by the Adjutant General's Office, 1860–70, National Archives and Records Administration, Washington, DC.
25. John R. Crockett to Sir, 3 September 1862, Letters Received by the Adjutant General's Office, 1860–70, National Archives and Records Administration, Washington, DC.
26. *Newark Daily Advertiser*, 16 August 1870.
27. Compiled Military Service Records, Lewis B. Baldwin, National Archives and Records Administration, Washington, DC.
28. Gibson, *History of the 78th*, 34.
29. Ibid., 34–37.

30. Ibid.

31. Ibid.

32. Charles B. Gillespie to H. M. Brackenridge, 21 May 1862, Gillespie Papers; Gancas, *Dear Teres*, 85, 102.

33. "Dust to Dust: [Susan Brunker] Gillespie," typescript for *Freeport Journal*, 21 April 1905, Gillespie Papers.

34. Charles B. Gillespie to My Dear Mary, 26 April 1863, Gillespie Papers.

35. Compiled Military Service Records, Charles B. Gillespie, National Archives and Records Administration, Washington, DC.

36. Charles B. Gillespie to H. M. Brackenridge, 21 May 1862, Gillespie Papers.

37. Ibid.

38. *Sacramento Daily Union*, 22 May 1862.

39. Ibid., 3 May 1861.

40. *California Farmer and Journal of Useful Sciences*, 4 July 1862; *Alta California*, 13 April 1863.

41. *Alta California*, 13 April 1863.

42. *California Farmer and Journal of Useful Sciences*, 17 April 1863.

43. *Los Angeles Star*, 2 May 1863.

44. Ibid.

45. *New York Times*, 31 May 1863.

46. *Los Angeles Star*, 2 May 1863.

47. *Alta California*, 1 May 1863.

48. *Los Angeles Star*, 2 May 1863.

49. *Alta California*, 1 May 1863.

50. *San Francisco Daily Evening Bulletin*, 1 May 1863.

51. Nancy Pratt Melton, "Lone Mountain Cemetery VII: Inscriptions Copied from Headstones," Rootsweb, http://freepages.genealogy.rootsweb.ancestry.com/~npmelton/lonecem.htm.

52. *California Farmer and Journal of Useful Sciences*, 22 May 1863; *San Francisco Daily Evening Bulletin*, 16 May 1863.

53. Staff member from Church of the Transfiguration, New York City, telephone interview with author, 22 March 2011.

54. *Alta California*, 17 May 1863.

55. Ibid., 30 July 1863.

56. *California Farmer and Journal of Useful Sciences*, 24 March 1865.

57. Compiled Military Service Records, Charles B. Gillespie, National Archives and Records Administration, Washington, DC.

58. Charles B. Gillespie to Mary Gillespie, 26 April 1863, Gillespie Papers.

59. Compiled Military Service Records, Charles B. Gillespie, National Archives and Records Administration, Washington, DC.

60. Charles B. Gillespie to F. D. Lowther, J. R. Magill, W. Bowen, W. Morehead, and J. W. McKee, 22 October 1863, Gillespie Papers.

61. *Newark Daily Advertiser*, 23 October 1863.

62. Ibid., 24 October 1863.

63. Ibid., 26 October 1863.

64. Ibid.

65. Ibid.

66. Ibid.

67. Ibid.

68. Civil War discharge record of Joseph Freeman, private family collection of great-great-grandson Jerome Marshall, copy in authors' possession.

69. Joseph Freeman, "11th New York Cavalry Letters by the Saddler Sergeant," Washington, DC, 12 March 1863, Raynors' Historical Collectible Auctions, www.hca auctions.com/lot-3772.aspx.

70. Civil War Pension file, Charles B. Gillespie, Application 870532, National Archives and Records Administration, Washington, DC.

71. Baquet, *History of the First Brigade, New Jersey Volunteers*, 184.

72. Compiled Military Service Records, Lewis B. Baldwin, National Archives and Records Administration, Washington, DC.

73. *Newark Daily Advertiser*, 14 March 1865, 16 August 1870.

74. Civil War Pension file, Daniel Birdsall (Widow Eliza A.), Application No. WC56442, National Archives and Records Administration, Washington, DC.

CHAPTER 24

1. "Henry Peters Gray, Jr. (b. 1844)," New-York Historical Society Museum and Library, www.nyhistory.org/exhibit/henry-peters-gray-jr-b-1844.

2. *New York Sun*, 9 June 1897.

3. *Alta California*, 24 December 1865.

4. *Sacramento Daily Union*, 26 December 1865.

5. *San Francisco Daily Evening Bulletin*, 13 February 1866. The article mistakenly reported three instead of two children.

6. *Alta California*, 30 July 1863, 7 May 1866.

7. *Mariposa Gazette*, 16 June 1866.

8. Ibid., 9 June 1866.

9. *San Francisco Daily Evening Bulletin*, 8 June 1866; *New York Times*, 3 July 1866.

10. *New York Herald*, 22 November 1867.

11. *New York Times*, 15 November 1868.

12. *Utica Morning Herald*, 18 July 1868.

13. Abby Tyler Oakes, US Passport Application, State of New York, 27 June 1868, National Archives and Records Administration, Washington, DC.

14. *Real Estate Record and Builders' Guide* (Brooklyn, NY), 26 March 1870.

15. *Newark Daily Advertiser*, 16 August 1870.

16. *New York Herald*, 27 October 1869.

17. Ibid., 17 January 1873.

18. *Newark Daily Advertiser*, 3 September 1866.

19. Holbrook, *Holbrook's Newark City Directory* (1878), 701; Holbrook, *Holbrook's Newark City Directory* (1880), 726; John W. Shaff, 1880 US Federal Census, Newark, Essex County, New Jersey, 11 June 1889.

20. *Pittsburgh Leader*, 23 October 1904; Marraro, "Canadian and American Zouaves," 88; *Washington Reporter*, 18 May 1870.

21. McDermott, "Fort Laramie Soldier Leo Degar Schnyder," 9.

22. Knights of Pythias, *Official Record of Proceedings*, 10587–95.

23. Ibid.

24. Middleton, *Bayonne Passages*, 14.

25. Nucciarone, *Alexander Cartwright*, 51–52.

26. *Spirit of the Times*, 11 August 1888; *New York Times*, 4 April 1890.

27. Gravestone at Evergreen Cemetery, Saint Augustine, St. John's County, Florida.

28. *New Brunswick Daily Press*, 27 December 1900.

CHAPTER 25

1. *New Jersey Journal*, 8 March 1875; Wren, *A History of the State of Nevada*, 435.

2. Wren, *A History of the State of Nevada*, 434; *Acts of the Sixty-Sixth General Assembly*, 95.

3. Wren, *A History of the State of Nevada*, 435; *Newark Daily Advertiser*, 2 March 1849.

4. Wren, *A History of the State of Nevada*, 434–35.

5. *Newark Daily Advertiser*, 22 January 1862.

6. *Alta California*, 16 June 1868.

7. *Trenton State Gazette*, 9 February 1870.

8. Wren, *A History of the State of Nevada*, 434–35.

9. Jay Clemons, 1880 US Federal Census, Gold Hill, Storey County, Nevada, 12 June 1880.

10. Isaac Overton Application Form, Society of California Pioneers, San Francisco, 5 October 1874.

11. Ratay, *Pioneers of the Ponderosa*, 25–26.

12. Shamberger, *The Story of the Water Supply*, 23.

13. Ratay, *Pioneers of the Ponderosa*, 26–29.

14. Ibid., 25–26.

15. *Nevada State Journal*, 29 January 1903.

16. *Territorial Enterprise*, 17 August 1875, quoted in Shamberger, *The Story of the Water Supply*, 23.

17. Ratay, *Pioneers of the Ponderosa*, 26.

18. Ibid., 41n22.

19. *Nevada State Journal*, 22 February 1896.

20. *San Francisco Call*, 6 September 1899.

21. Shamberger, *The Story of the Water Supply*, 29.

22. *Territorial Enterprise*, 15 August 1894.

23. Ratay, *Pioneers of the Ponderosa*, 26–29.

24. *Reno Evening Gazette*, 27 September 1909.

25. Ibid., 14 October 1909, 19, 24 August 1915.

26. "Torp v. Clemons," 1115.

27. Ibid., 1117.

28. *Nevada State Journal*, 2 July 1913.

CHAPTER 26

1. *Reno Evening Gazette*, 1 September 1916.

2. Charles Gedney Gray, Death Certificate 27127, New York City.

Bibliography

Primary sources were used in every case reasonable and possible. These include military pension and service records, city directories, ship manifests, federal and state census records, US passports, vital records, voter registers, church records, cemetery markers and files, obituaries, wills, and probate documents. With some exceptions below, these sources are cited only in notes.

Newspapers were also critically important, both for the letters and overland journal entries printed in hometown papers and for the reporting that provided facts and a contemporary editorial voice. Publications cited or deemed important to the research are listed below.

Newspapers

Alta California (San Francisco)
Arkansas State Democrat (Little Rock)
Baltimore Sun
Boston Courier
Boston Daily Atlas
Boston Investigator
Brooklyn Eagle and Kings County Democrat
Butler (PA) Citizen
Butler (PA) Times
California Farmer and Journal of Useful Sciences (San Francisco)
Californian (San Francisco)
Cleveland Herald
Daily National Intelligencer (Washington, DC)
Daily Picayune (New Orleans)
Emancipator & Republican (Boston)
Frank Leslie's Illustrated Newspaper (New York)
Freeport (PA) Journal
Georgia Weekly Telegraph (Macon)
Greenville (SC) Mountaineer
Hawaiian Gazette (Honolulu)
Lancaster (PA) Intelligencer

BIBLIOGRAPHY

Liberator (Boston)
Los Angeles Star
Macon (GA) Telegraph
Mariposa (CA) Gazette
Marysville (CA) Appeal
Marysville (CA) Herald
Milwaukee Sentinel and Gazette
Missouri Courier (Hannibal)
Nevada State Journal (Reno)
Newark (NJ) Daily Advertiser
Newark (NJ) Daily Journal
Newark (NJ) Mercury
Newark (NJ) Morning Eagle
New Brunswick (NJ) Daily Press
New Brunswick (NJ) Fredonian
New Hampshire Statesman (Concord)
New Jersey Journal (Jersey City)
New York Evening World
New York Herald
New York Spectator
New York Sun
New York Times
New York Tribune
North American and Daily Advertiser (Philadelphia)
North American and United States Gazette (Philadelphia)
Ohio Observer (Hudson)
Ohio Statesman (Columbus)
Pacific Rural Press (San Francisco)
Pittsburgh Dispatch
Pittsburgh Gazette and Advertiser
Pittsburgh Leader
Placer Times (Sacramento)
Reno Evening Gazette
Sacramento Daily Union
Sacramento Transcript
San Francisco Call
San Francisco Daily Evening Bulletin
Scioto Gazette (Chillicothe, OH)
Sentinel of Freedom (Newark, NJ)
Spirit of the Times (New York)
St. Louis Republican
Territorial Enterprise (Virginia City, NV)
Trenton (NJ) Federalist
Trenton (NJ) State Gazette
Utica (NY) Morning Herald
Vermont Chronicle (Bellows Falls)
Washington (PA) Reporter

BIBLIOGRAPHY

MANUSCRIPT COLLECTIONS

Baldwin, Augustus, Family Papers. Private collection of Marian Wilkin Fleming.

Bickford, William H., Diary, July 10, 1849–August 26, 1850. BANC78/83C, Negative Number 2773. Bancroft Library, University of California, Berkeley.

Bond, Robert, Diary, 1849. Yale Collection of Western Americana, Beinecke Rare Book and Manuscript Library, Yale University.

Bullock, Thomas, comp. "Emigrant rosters, 1849." MS 15494. Church of Jesus Christ of Latter-day Saints Church History Library, Salt Lake City, UT.

Cartwright, Alexander Joy, Jr. "Journal of a trip across the Plains from Independence to San Francisco via South Pass, Rocky Mountains, and the Sierra Nevada." MS Doc 55, Bernice Pauahi Bishop Museum Archives, Honolulu, Hawaii.

Casterline, Benjamin, Family Papers. Private collection of Margaret Casterline Bowen.

Clark, Thomas D., Papers. Special Collections. Margaret I. King Library, University of Kentucky, Lexington.

Cone, Gordon C. "Journal of Travels from Waukesha, Wisconsin, to California, by the 'South Pass' in the Summer of 1849." Vault MSS 661, Harold B. Lee Library, Brigham Young University, Provo, UT.

Currier, Cyrus. "Journal to California by the Northern Overland Route from Newark, State of New Jersey." H-77. Wyoming State Archives, Cheyenne.

————. "Cyrus Currier's Journal to California by the Northern Overland Route from Newark, State of New Jersey," MSS 1123. Transcription by Richard L. Rieck, 1999. Wyoming State Archives, Cheyenne.

Currier, Cyrus, and Nancy Currier, Letters and Bible records. Private collection of Nancy Currier Dorian and Ewen Currier McEwen.

Darcy, Timothy Johnes, Papers, 1811–1900. MC 564. Special Collections, University Archives, Alexander Library, Rutgers University, New Brunswick, NJ.

Freeman, Joseph, Family Papers. Private collection of Jerome Marshall.

Gillespie, Charles B., Journal, 4 August–25 October 1849. Copy given to authors on 25 February 2014 by great-grandson Richard M. Rogers.

Gillespie, Charles B., Papers, journals, letters, sketches and paintings. Copies given to authors on 25 February 2014 by great-grandson Richard M. Rogers.

Gray, Charles G. "Journal of an Overland Passage from Independence Missouri to San Francisco, California in 1849." HM 16520. Huntington Library, San Marino, California.

Hittle, Jonas, Diary 1849. Transcribed by Richard L. Rieck, 2000. Illinois State Historical Library, Springfield.

Jackson, Edward. "Journal of Edward Jackson on his route from Fort Independence to California in 1849." MSS 661 SC 2493, Harold B. Lee Library, Brigham Young University.

Lewis, William T., Family Papers. Private collection of Gwendolyn J. Hiles.

Meeker, David. Ward-Meeker Family Papers. MG 1146. New Jersey Historical Society, Newark.

Meeker Family Papers. Private collection of Margaret Riddle.

Minges, Abram. "A Journal of a Trip from St. Joseph's, Missouri to Sacramento City, California by A. M. & others in the Spring of 1849." Transcribed by

Richard L. Rieck, 2003. 85320 AA Vault, Bentley Historical Library, University of Michigan, Ann Arbor.

Spooner, Elijah Allen. Letters and Journal, 1849–1850. Vault MSS 662, Harold B. Lee Library, Brigham Young University.

BOOKS AND ARTICLES

Acts of the Sixty-Sixth General Assembly of the State of New Jersey. Somerville: S. L. B. Baldwin, 1842.

Alter, J. Cecil. *Jim Bridger.* Norman: University of Oklahoma Press, 1962.

Bagley, Will. *South Pass: Gateway to a Continent.* Norman: University of Oklahoma Press, 2014.

————. *With Golden Visions Bright before Them: Trails to the Mining West 1849–1852.* Norman: University of Oklahoma Press, 2012.

Baldwin, Charles Candee. *Baldwin Genealogy from 1500–1881.* Cleveland: Leader, 1881.

Bancroft, Hubert Howe. *History of California.* Vol. 7. San Francisco: History Company, 1886–90.

Banta, Theodore M. *Sayre Family: Lineage of Thomas Sayre, a Founder of Southampton.* New York: De Vinne, 1901.

Baquet, Camille. *History of the First Brigade, New Jersey Volunteers, from 1861 to 1865.* Trenton, NJ: MacCrellish & Quigley, 1910.

Bauer, K. Jack. *Zachary Taylor: Soldier, Planter, Statesman of the Old Southwest.* Baton Rouge: Louisiana State University Press, 1985.

Beasley, Delilah L. *The Negro Trail Blazers of California.* Los Angeles: D. L. Beasley, 1919.

Beers, J. H. *Armstrong County Pennsylvania: Her People, Past and Present.* 2 vols. Chicago: J. H. Beers, 1914.

Bieber, Ralph P. "California Gold Mania." *Mississippi Valley Historical Review* 35, no. 1 (June 1948): 3–28.

Bigelow, John. *Memoir of the Life of Public Services of John Charles Fremont.* New York: Derby & Jackson, 1856.

Blakeslee, B. F. *History of the Sixteenth Connecticut Volunteers.* Hartford, CT: Case, Lockwood & Brainard, 1875.

Blanchard, Charles, ed. *Progressive Men of the Commonwealth of Pennsylvania.* 2 vols. Logansport, IN: A. W. Bowen, 1900.

Bowen, Benjamin B. *A Blind Man's Offering.* Boston: B. Bowen, 1877.

Bragg, Susan. "Knowledge Is Power: Sacramento Blacks and the Public Schools 1854–1860." *California History* 75, no. 3 (Fall 1996), 214–21.

Brands, H. W. *Age of Gold: The California Gold Rush and the New American Dream.* New York: Anchor Books, 2002.

Browning, Charles Henry. *American Historical Register* Vol. 3. Philadelphia: Historical Register Publishing, 1895.

Bruff, Joseph Goldsborough. *Gold Rush: The Journals, Drawings, and Other Papers of J. Goldsborough Bruff, Captain, Washington City and California Mining Association, April 2, 1849–July 20, 1851.* Edited by Georgia Willis Read and Ruth Gaines. New York: Columbia University Press, 1949.

BIBLIOGRAPHY

Bryant, Edwin. *What I Saw in California: Being a Journal of a Tour by the Emigrant Route and South Pass of the Rocky Mountains, across the Continent of North America, the Great Desert Basin, and through California, in the Years 1846, 1847.* 3rd edition. New York: D. Appleton, 1849.

Canfield, Frederick Alexander. *A History of Thomas Canfield and of Matthew Camfield, with a Genealogy of Their Descendants in New Jersey.* New Haven: Tuttle, 1897.

Carnahan, James R. *Pythian Knighthood: Its History and Literature.* Cincinnati: Pettibone, 1888.

Carstarphen, James E. *My Trip to California in 1849.* Fairfield, WA: Ye Galleon, 1971.

Carter, Howard Williston, comp. *Carter: A Genealogy of the Descendants of Thomas Carter.* Norfolk, CT: H. W. Carter, 1909.

Chandler, Robert Joseph. *California: An Illustrated History.* New York: Hippocrene Books, 2005.

Clark, A. Howard, ed. *National Register of the Society of the Sons of the American Revolution.* New York: Louis H. Cornish, 1902.

Clark, James Henry. *The Medical Men of New Jersey.* Newark: published for author by Evening Courier Office, 1867.

Colton, Walter. *Three Years in California.* New York: A. S. Barnes, 1850.

Colville, Samuel. *Colville's San Francisco Directory, 1856–1857.* San Francisco: Monson, Valentine, 1856.

Coy, Owen H., ed. *Pictorial History of California.* Berkeley: University of California Extension Division, 1925.

Daly, Charles P. *In Memory of Henry Peters Gray.* New York: printed for the "Century," 1878.

Davenport, John C. *The U.S.-Mexico Border: The Treaty of Guadalupe Hidalgo.* Philadelphia: Chelsea House, 2005.

Decker, Peter. *The Diaries of Peter Decker: Overland to California in 1849 and Life in the Mines, 1850–1851.* Edited by Helen S. Giffen. Georgetown, CA: Talisman, 1966.

Delano, Alonzo. *Life on the Plains and among the Diggings.* New York: Miller, Orton, 1857.

Denslow, William R. *10,000 Famous Freemasons.* 4 vols. Richmond VA: Macoy Publishing & Masonic Supply, 1957.

Ellison, Robert W. *First Impressions: Trail through Carson Valley 1848–1852.* Minden, NV: Hot Springs Mountain Press, 2000.

Ellison, William Henry. "The Movement for State Division in California, 1849–1860." *Southwestern Historical Quarterly* 17, no. 2 (October 1913): 101–39.

Fariss and Smith. *Illustrated History of Plumas, Lassen & Sierra Counties, with California from 1513 to 1850.* San Francisco: Fariss & Smith, 1882.

Field, Stephen J. *Personal Reminiscences of Early Days in California and Other Sketches.* 1893.

Flint, Martha Bockee, comp. *A Peters Lineage: Five Generations of the Descendants of Dr. Charles Peters of Hempstead.* Poughkeepsie, NY: A. V. Haight, 1896.

Flint, Thomas. *Diary of Dr. Thomas Flint.* Hollister, CA: Evening Free Lance, 1924.

Flynn, Paul V. *History of St. John's Church.* Newark: Press of the New Jersey Trade Review, 1908.

"Forty-Seventh Annual Report of the American Colonization Society: Decease of Friends." *African Repository* 40, no. 2 (February 1864): 33–34.

Franzwa, Gregory M. *Maps of the California Trail.* Tucson: Patrice Press, 1999.

———. *The Oregon Trail Revisited.* Silver anniversary ed. Tucson: Patrice Press, 1997.

Frost, John. *History of the State of California.* Auburn, CA: Derby and Miller, 1853.

Galloway, John Debo. "Early Engineering Works Contributory to the Comstock." *University of Nevada Bulletin* 16, no. 5 (June 1947): 23–105.

Gancas, Ronald S. *Dear Teres: The Civil War Letters of Andrew Joseph Duff and Dennis Dugan of Company F, the Pennsylvania Seventy-Eighth Infantry.* Edited by Dan Coyle. Butler, PA: Mechling Associates, 1999.

Garnet, Porter, ed. *Papers of the San Francisco Committee of Vigilance of 1851,* vol. 2. Berkeley: University of California Press, 1911.

Gibson, J. T., ed. *History of the Seventy-Eighth Pennsylvania Volunteer Infantry.* Pittsburgh: Press of the Pittsburgh Printing Co., 1905.

Gillespie, Charles B. "Leaves from my Journal; or, A Tour on the Prairies." *Western Literary Journal and Monthly Review* 1, no. 3 (January 1845): 153–55.

———. "Leaves from my Journal; or, A Tour on the Prairies: Catching the Wild Horse." *Western Literary Journal and Monthly Review* 1, no. 5 (March 1845): 258–60.

———. "Leaves from my Journal; or, A Tour on the Prairies: Catching the Wild Horse." *Western Literary Journal and Monthly Review* 1, no. 6 (April 1845): 345–46.

———. "Prairie Sketches No. 1." *Western Literary Casket* 3, no. 11 (July 1843): 267–69.

———. "Prairie Sketches No. 2." *Western Literary Casket* 3, no. 12 (August 1843): 288–91.

———. "Prairie Sketches No. 3—An Antelope Chase." *Western Literary Magazine* 4, no. 3 (December 1843): 59–63.

Gordon, Mary McDougall, ed. *Overland to California with the Pioneer Line: The Gold Rush Diary of Bernard J. Reid.* Stanford: Stanford University Press, 1983.

Gray, Charles G. *Off at Sunrise: The Overland Journal of Charles Glass [sic] Gray.* Edited by Thomas D. Clark. San Marino, CA: Huntington Library, 1976.

Greeley, Horace. *Recollections of a Busy Life.* New York: J. B. Ford, 1868.

Guinn, J. M. *A History of California and an Extended History of Los Angeles and Environs.* Los Angeles: Historic Record Company, 1915.

Halsey, Edmund D. *History of the Washington Association of New Jersey.* Morristown, NJ: De Vinne, 1891.

Hamilton, Edward H. "The Big Bonanza Four." *Everybody's Magazine* 7, no. 4 (October 1902): 355–58.

Hannon, Jessie Gould, ed. *The Boston-Newton Company Venture: From Massachusetts to California in 1849.* Lincoln: University of Nebraska Press, 1969.

Hardesty, Donald L. *Archaeology of the Donner Party.* Reno: University of Nevada Press, 1997.

Harris, Isaac, ed. *Harris' General Business Directory of the Cities of Pittsburgh and Allegheny.* Pittsburgh: A. A. Anderson, 1841.

Haskins, Charles W. *Argonauts of California.* New York: Fords, Howard & Hurlburt, 1890.

BIBLIOGRAPHY

Helper, Hinton R. *Land of Gold: Reality versus Fiction.* Baltimore: Henry Taylor, 1855.

Heyman, Therese Thau. *Mirror of California: Daguerreotypes.* Oakland, CA: Oakland Museum, 1973.

Holbrook, A. Stephen. *Holbrook's Newark City Directory.* Newark: A. S. Holbrook, 1878.

———. *Holbrook's Newark City Directory.* Newark: A. S. Holbrook, 1880.

Holdredge, Helen. *House of the Strange Woman.* San Carlos, CA: Nourse, 1961.

Holliday, J. S. *The World Rushed In: The California Gold Rush Experience.* New York: Simon & Schuster, 1981.

Hulbert, Archer Butler. *Forty-Niners: The Chronicle of the California Trail.* Boston: Little, Brown, 1949.

Hurt, Peyton. "The Rise and Fall of the 'Know Nothings' in California." *California Historical Quarterly* 9, no. 1 (March 1930): 16–49.

Hyde, George E. *The Pawnee Indians.* Norman: University of Oklahoma Press, 1974.

"Items of News from California." *Latter Day Saints' Millennial Star* 11, no. 23 (December 1849): 364–67.

Jackson, Joseph Henry, ed. *Gold Rush Album.* New York: Charles Scribner's Sons, 1949.

Jameson, W. C. *Buried Treasures of California.* Little Rock: August House, 1995.

"John S. Darcy: Portrait, Character, and Biography." *American Phrenological Journal* 39, no. 4 (April 1864): 100–101.

Johnson, Drew Heath, and Marcia Eymann. *Silver and Gold: Cased Images of the California Gold Rush.* Iowa City: University of Iowa, 1998.

Johnson, William Jackson. *George Washington the Christian.* New York: Abington, 1919.

Jones, David E. *Women Warriors: A History.* Dulles, VA: Brassey's, 2000.

Kelly, William. *Across the Rocky Mountains, from New York to California, with a Visit to the Celebrated Mormon Colony, at the Great Salt Lake.* 2nd ed. London: Simms & McIntyre, 1852.

———. *Excursion to California over the Prairie, Rocky Mountains, and Great Sierra Nevada, with a Stroll through the Diggings and Ranchers of That Country.* 2 vols. London: Chapman & Hall, 1851.

Kemble, John Haskell. "The 'Senator': The Biography of a Pioneer Steamship." *California Historical Society Quarterly* 16, no. 1 (March 1937): 61–70.

Kirk, Anthony. "'As Jolly as a Clam at High Water': The Rise of Art in Gold Rush California." *California History* 79, no. 2 (Summer 2000): 169–203.

Kirsch, George B. *Baseball and Cricket: The Creation of American Team Sports, 1838–72.* Urbana: University of Illinois Press, 2007.

Knights of Pythias. *Official Record of Proceedings of the Twenty-Fourth Convention of the Supreme Lodge Knights of Pythias.* Nashville: Brandon, 1906.

Kowalewski, Michael, ed. *Gold Rush: A Literary Exploration.* Berkeley: Heyday Books in conjunction with California Council for the Humanities, 1997.

Kull, Irving Stoddard. "New Brunswick Adventurers of '49." *Proceedings of the New Jersey Historical Society* 10, no 1. (January 1925), 12–28.

Langley, Henry G., comp. *San Francisco Directory for the Year 1858.* San Francisco: S. D. Valentine, 1858.

BIBLIOGRAPHY

LeCount, Josiah J., and Charles L. Strong. *LeCount & Strong San Francisco City Directory for the Year 1854*. San Francisco: Herald Office, 1854.

Lee, Francis Bazley, comp. *Genealogical and Memorial History of the State New Jersey*. 4 vols. New York: Lewis Historical Publishing, 1910.

———. *New Jersey as a Colony and as a State: One of the Original Thirteen*. 5 vols. New York: Publishing Society of New Jersey, 1902.

Leeper, David Rohrer. *Argonauts of 'Forty-Nine: Some Recollections of the Plains and the Diggings*. South Bend, IN: J. B. Stoll, 1894.

Levy, JoAnn. *They Saw the Elephant: Women in the California Gold Rush*. Hamden, CT: Shoe String Press, 1990.

Lewis, Donovan. *Pioneers of California: True Stories of Early Settlers in the Golden State*. San Francisco: Scottwall Associates, 1993.

Littell, John. *Family Records; or, Genealogies of the First Settlers of the Passaic Valley*. Feltville, NJ: Stationer's Hall Press, 1851.

Madsen, Brigham D. *Gold Rush Sojourners in the Great Salt Lake City 1849 and 1850*. Salt Lake City: University of Utah Press, 1983.

Marraro, Howard Rossario. "Canadian and American Zouaves in the Papal Army, 1868–1870." *CCHA [Canadian Catholic Historical Association] Report* 12 (1944–45), 83–102.

Marshall, Phillip C. "The Newark Overland Company." *Proceedings of the New Jersey Historical Society* 70, no. 3 (July 1952): 173–87.

———. "New Jersey Expeditions to California in 1849." *Proceedings of the New Jersey Historical Society* 70, no. 1 (January 1952): 17–36.

Masten, April F. "'Shake Hands?': Lilly Martin Spencer and the Politics of Art," *American Quarterly* 56, no. 2 (June 2004), 348–94.

Mattes, Merrill J. *The Great Platte River Road: The Covered Wagon Mainline via Fort Kearny to Fort Laramie*. Lincoln: Nebraska State Historical Society, 1969.

McDermott, John, "Fort Laramie Soldier Leo Degar Schnyder." *Annals of Wyoming* 36, no. 1 (April 1854), 5–18.

Mechanics' Institute. *Report of the First Industrial Exhibition of the Mechanics' Institute of the City of San Francisco*. San Francisco: Frank Eastman, 1858.

———. *Report of the Second Industrial Exhibition of the Mechanics' Institute of the City of San Francisco*. San Francisco: Frank Eastman, 1859.

Megquier, Mary Jane. *Apron Full of Gold: The letters of Mary Jane Megquier from San Francisco 1849–1856*. 2nd ed. Edited by Polly Welts Kaufman. Albuquerque: University of New Mexico Press, 1994.

Middleton, Kathleen M. *Bayonne Passages*. Charleston, SC: Arcadia, 2000.

Miller, Christine. *San Francisco's Financial District*. Charleston, SC: Arcadia, 2005.

"Mortuary Record: Frederick Anson Carter." *Proceedings of the New Jersey Historical Society* 10, no. 3 (Second Series, 1888): 136.

Myrick, Thomas S. *The Gold Rush: Letters of Thomas S. Myrick from California to the Jackson, Michigan, American Citizen, 1849–1855*. Compiled by John Cumming. Mount Pleasant, MI: Cumming, 1971.

Negley, Felix Casper. *Storm Stead and Way-Laid: The Gold Rush Diary of Major Felix Casper Negley*. Edited by Kevin Patrick Kopper. Old Stone House Series 4. Butler, PA: Butler Historical Society, 1999.

Nestell, D. D. T. "Case of Strangulated Inguinal Hernia." *New Jersey Medical Reporter* 2, no. 3 (April 1849): 179–81.

Bibliography

Newmark, Maurice H., and Marco R. Newmark, eds. *Sixty Years in Southern California 1853–1913, Containing the Reminiscences of Harris Newmark.* New York: Knickerbocker, 1916.

"New Jersey Colonization Society." *African Repository* 32, no.5 (May 1856): 151–52.

Nucciarone, Monica. *Alexander Cartwright: The Life behind the Baseball Legend.* Lincoln: University of Nebraska Press, 2009.

Parkes, Thomas D. "Opening the Road to El Dorado: Captain Ebenezer Brown and the Carson Pass Trail, 1848." *Overland Journal* 29, no. 4 (Winter 2011–12): 139–66.

Parkman, Francis. *The Oregon Trail.* Madison: University of Wisconsin Press, 1969.

Perkins, Elisha Douglass. *Gold Rush Diary: Being the Journal of Elisha Douglass Perkins on the Overland Trail in the Spring and Summer of 1849.* Edited by Thomas D. Clark. Lexington: University of Kentucky Press, 1967.

Perrin, William Henry, ed. *History of Delaware County and Ohio.* Chicago: O. L. Baskin, 1880.

Peshine, John Henry Hobart, comp. *The Peshine Family in Europe and in America.* Santa Barbara, CA: J. H. H. Peshine, 1916.

Peterson, Nancy. "Gold Rush Records: Clues amidst the Chaos." *New England Ancestors* 10, no. 4 (Fall 2009): 20–25.

Phelps, Alonzo. *Contemporary Biographies of California's Representative Men.* San Francisco: A. L. Bancroft, 1881.

Phillips, George Morris, comp. *Historic Letters from the Collection of the West Chester State Normal School.* Philadelphia: J. B. Lippincott, 1898.

Pierson, B. T. *Directory of the City of Newark for 1848–49.* Newark: A. S. Holbrook, Steam Press, 1848.

———. *Directory of the City of Newark for 1849–50.* Newark: A. S. Holbrook, Steam Press, 1849.

———. *Directory of the City of Newark for 1852–53.* Newark: A. S. Holbrook, 1852.

Pierson, David Lawrence. *Narratives of Newark in New Jersey from the Days of Its Founding.* Newark: Pierson, 1917.

Pitney, Henry C., ed. *History of Morris County New Jersey.* 2 vols. New York: Lewis Historical Publishing, 1914.

Polk, Dora Beale. *The Island of California: A History of the Myth.* Spokane: Arthur H. Clark, 1991.

Potter, David Morris, ed. *Trail to California: The Overland Journal of Vincent Geiger and Wakeman Bryarly.* New Haven: Yale University Press, 1945.

Price, Charity Ogden. *Family Record or Genealogies of Robert Bond and the Descendants of Jacob Price.* New York: Dodd & Mead, 1872.

Quarter Century's Progress of New Jersey's Leading Manufacturing Centres. New York: International Publishing, 1887.

Quinby, Henry Cole. *Genealogical History of the Quinby Family in England and America.* Rutland, VT: Tuttle, 1915.

Ranney, H. M. *Account of Terrific and Fatal Riot at the New-York Astor Place Opera House, on the Night of May 19th, 1849.* New York: H. M. Ranney, 1849.

Rasmussen, Louis J. *California Wagon Train Lists: April 5, 1849 to October 20, 1852.* Colma: San Francisco Historic Records, 1994.

Ratay, Myra Sauer. *Pioneers of the Ponderosa: How Washoe Valley Rescued the Comstock.* Sparks, NV: Western, 1973.

Rieck, Richard L. "Salt Lake Rosters." Transcription, database, and research notes on "Emigrant rosters, 1849," compiled by Thomas Bullock. Copy in authors' possession.

Reps, John W. *Cities on Stone: Nineteenth Century Lithograph Images of the Urban West.* Fort Worth: Amon Carter Museum of Western Art, 1976.

Richards, Leonard L. *California Gold Rush and the Coming of the Civil War.* New York: Vintage Books, 2008.

Richardson, William H. "The Argonauts of Jersey City." *Proceedings of the New Jersey Historical Society,* New Series 11 (1926): 170–86.

Ricord, Frederick W., ed. *History of Union County New Jersey.* Newark: East Jersey History Company, 1897.

———. *Biographical and Genealogical History of the City of Newark and Essex County, New Jersey.* New York: Lewis Publishing, 1898.

Rowe, Joseph Andrew. *California's Pioneer Circus: Memoirs and Personal Correspondence Relative to the Circus Business through the Gold County in the 50's.* Edited by Albert Dressler. San Francisco: H. S. Crocker, 1926.

Scamehorn, Howard L., ed. *Buckeye Rovers in the Gold Rush.* Athens: Ohio University Press, 1965.

Searight, Thomas B. *The Old Pike: A History of the National Road.* Uniontown, PA: T. B. Searight, 1894.

Sedgley, Joseph. *Overland to California in 1849.* Oakland CA: Butler & Bowman, 1877.

Shamberger, Hugh A. *The Story of the Water Supply for the Comstock, Including the Towns of Virginia City, Gold Hill, and Silver City, Nevada, together with Other Water-Related Events for the Period 1859–1969.* Washington, DC: US Government Printing Office, 1972.

Shaw, William H., comp. *History of Essex and Hudson Counties, New Jersey.* 2 vols. Philadelphia: Everts & Peck, 1884.

Sherman, Andrew M. *Historic Morristown, New Jersey: The Story of Its First Century.* Morristown: Howard, 1905.

Sioli, Paolo. *Historical Souvenir of El Dorado County, California, with Illustrations and Biographical Sketches of Its Prominent Men & Pioneers.* Oakland, CA: P. Sioli, 1883.

Smith, Elbert B. *President Zachary Taylor: The Hero President.* New York: Nova Science, 2007.

Smith, Robert Walter. *History of Armstrong County, Pennsylvania.* Chicago: Waterman, Watkins, 1883.

Smith, Thomas West. *The Story of a Cavalry Regiment: "Scott's 900" Eleventh New York Cavalry, from the St. Lawrence River to the Gulf of Mexico, 1861–1865.* Chicago: Veteran Association of the Regiment, 1897.

Soule, Frank, John H. Gihon, and James Nisbet. *Annals of San Francisco.* New York: D. Appleton, 1855.

Starr, Kevin. *Americans and the California Dream 1850–1915.* New York: Oxford University Press, 1973.

———. *California: A History.* New York: Modern Library, 2005.

Stewart, George R. *Committee of Vigilance: Revolution in San Francisco 1851.* Boston: Houghton Mifflin, 1964.

Bibliography

Stillman, Jacob D. G. *Gold Rush Letters of J. D. B. Stillman.* Palo Alto, CA: Lewis Osborne, 1967.

Stryker, Paul. "A Voyage to California in 1849." *Proceedings of the New Jersey Historical Society,* New Series 8 (1923): 17–36.

Stuart-Wortley, Emmeline. *Travels in the United States, etc., during 1849 and 1850.* 3 vols. London: Richard Bentley, 1851.

Sutter, John A., and James W. Marshall. "The Discovery of Gold in California." *Hutchings' California Magazine* 2, no. 5 (November 1857): 193–203.

Swartzlow, Ruby Johnson. *Lassen: His Life and Legacy.* Mineral, CA: Loomis Museum Association, 1964.

"Torp v. Clemons." *Pacific Reporter* 142 (31 August–12 October, 1914), 1115–19.

Unruh, John D., Jr. *The Plains Across: Overland Emigrants and the Trans-Mississippi West, 1840–1860.* Champaign: University of Illinois Press, 1979.

Upham, Samuel C. *Notes of a Voyage to California via Cape Horn, together with Scenes in El Dorado in the Years 1849–'50.* Philadelphia: S. C. Upham, 1878.

Urquhart, Frank John. *History of the City of Newark, New Jersey: Embracing Practically Two and a Half Centuries, 1666–1913.* 2 vols. New York: Lewis Historical Publishing, 1913.

W——. "Rembrandt Lockwood's Painting of the Last Judgment," *Republic* 3, no. 1 (January 1852): 185–86.

Webster, Kimball. *The Gold Seekers of '49: A Personal Narrative of the Overland Trail and Adventures in California and Oregon from 1849 to 1854.* Manchester, NH: Standard Book, 1917.

Wendt, Edmund Charles. *A Treatise on Asiatic Cholera.* New York: William Wood, 1885.

Whitehead, John. *The Passaic Valley, New Jersey, in Three Centuries: Biographical and Genealogical Records of the Valley and Vicinity of the Passaic, Past and Present, Illustrated,* vol. 2. New York: New Jersey Genealogical Company, 1901.

Wickes, Stephen. *History of Medicine in New Jersey and of its Medical Men.* Newark: Martin R. Dennis, 1879.

Wilkins, James F. *An Artist on the Overland Trail: The 1849 Diary and Sketches of James F. Wilkins.* Edited by John Francis McDermott. San Marino, CA: Huntington Library, 1968.

Woodward, Arthur. "The Old Side-Wheeler Senator." *San Diego Historical Society Quarterly* 3, no. 3 (July 1957).

"The World's Fair in America." *Scientific American* 6, no. 30 (12 April 1851).

Wren, Thomas, ed. *A History of the State of Nevada: Its Resources and People.* New York: Lewis Publishing, 1904.

Young, Brigham, Heber C. Kimball, and Willard Richards. "Epistle." *Latter Day Saints' Millennial Star* 11, no. 23 (15 November 1849): 337–38.

Young, William T. *Sketch of the Life and Public Services of General Lewis Cass.* Detroit: Markam & Elwood, 1852.

Index

References to illustrations appear in italics.